Six Plays

SIX PLAYS

AN INTRODUCTORY ANTHOLOGY

EDITED BY OTTO REINERT

University of Washington, Seattle

Little, Brown and Company   Boston

Preface

This volume appears in response to wishes expressed by users of my earlier anthologies for a briefer collection of plays. Many of them feel, understandably, that twelve to fifteen plays are more than they can conveniently include in courses divided about equally among the several literary genres.

I have chosen these six plays from my earlier volumes because they represent a variety (though necessarily small) of periods and modes and because those who have been kind enough to write to my publisher have indicated a preference for them. My critical comments on the individual plays are essentially unchanged. The general introduction is a slightly shorter version of the introduction to *Classic through Modern Drama*. The bibliographies in the appendix have been updated.

I should like to take this opportunity to thank teachers and students for their favorable reception of my other anthologies of drama. I hope the present volume will meet their wish for a shorter collection.

Contents

Introduction

A Definition of Drama

Drama, like poetry and fiction, is an art of words, a genre of literature. In drama, the words are mainly dialogue: people talking is the basic dramatic action. The talk may be interrupted by wordless activity—swordplay, love-making, silence—but such activity will derive its significance from its context of dialogue. If not, we are dealing with pantomime and not with drama.

This is a distinction more meaningfully made in general theory than in dealing with individual works of dramatic art. Films, for example, generally subordinate dialogue to photography, and yet film scripts have been published to be read. At what point of verbal artistry do they cease being scenario and production notes and become drama? Conversely, to what extent is the concept of drama covered by the old definition of theater as "three boards and a passion"?

Such questions are posed by the double aspect of dramatic language. As written words, drama is literature; as spoken words in a spectacle, it is theater. A novel or a poem is read (or listened to in recital). A play can be either read or performed, but performance affects its status as literature. Dialogue can be performed intact, but stage directions, however skillfully written, do not survive the transfer from script to stage. In fact, the more literary they are, the more they lose in the transfer. Their referents in performance—speech manner, movement, costume, set, etc.— are creations of the theater rather than of literature. This is only to say that a performance of drama is much more than just an art of words. It is the joint product of many arts, of which direction, acting, and stage design are the most important. And since what the dramatist writes is a performable script, the images he works with make up, in Ronald Peacock's words, "a composite form, using different 'arts' to one end." The language of drama includes the idiom of the physical theater. The most dramatic dialogue, it could be argued, is that which Bertolt Brecht calls "gestic": speech so cadenced that bodily postures, gestures, and movements naturally accompany it and reinforce the attitudes expressed by its semantics.

The fact that successful playwrights make more money in the box office than in the bookstores is evidence that for most people the theatrical medium of drama takes precedence over the literary one and that they find *reading* a play a pallid substitute for *seeing* it. As stage spectacle a play is intensely *there*—a three-dimensional and audible progress of absorbing physical action. Whereas words are consecutive and reading is an act in the time dimension, seeing a play is an experience of both time and space. At any one moment the spectator may be simultaneously aware of weather or time of day, of rich or shabby furniture, or of one character speaking, another listening, and a third crawling noiselessly toward the speaker with a knife between his teeth. The spatial concreteness and immediacy of staged drama enlist the attention of a larger set of the spectator's sensory responses, and do so more intensely, than the purely imaginative evocations of a printed play ever can.

Still, the popular assumption that the theatrical medium of drama is primary may be challenged. Performance is no more the play than the concert is the symphony. Most plays—like symphonies—have been written to be performed, but the artistic construct exists complete in the written words, just as the melody, harmony, rhythm, tempo, and orchestration of the symphony "are" in the printed score. The only difference between a printed play and a printed musical composition in this respect is that for most of us it is easier to "see" and "hear" a play in the imagination than it is to "hear" the music in the read score. A play is a potential but never-to-be-realized performance, an "ideal" performance in the philosophical sense, inherent in the configuration of the playwright's words and independent of the artists of the theater whom it keeps challenging to produce performed drama. Items may be cut or added in the performance of a play, just as an enterprising editor may alter a text or a conductor a score, but this does not prove that the original work was not an autonomous artistic entity.

Drama is distinguished from the other forms of literature not just by performability but also by the objectivity and externality that perform-ability implies. The statement "She is a woman without hope" is, as stage direction, undramatic. It could become a speech by one of the characters, or it could inspire an actress to perform an electrifying ges-ture of fluttering futility, but as *stage direction* it is novelistic. Not only does it not denote anything actable, it also violates the objectivity that is the condition for the playwright's craft: the tacit agreement between him and us that for the duration of the make-believe he does not exist at all, that the characters can be known only by what they reveal of themselves in speech and action. The play shows and tells itself; the characters speak for themselves.

But if the objectivity of drama is inviolate, the most elementary mis-take a critic can make is to confuse character and playwright. Whatever he may be in his private life, the dramatist is, by definition, a man of multiple voice and vision. He has, in Keats's words, "as much delight in conceiving an Iago as an Imogen. What shocks the virtuous philosopher delights the chameleon poet." We can only tentatively infer his own convictions—if we can do so at all—from the values implicit in the total, integrated set of images, verbal and nonverbal, that constitutes "the world" on stage. And we are willing to accept that world as valid and relevant only if it offers itself, freely and directly, as an object for our interpretation and evaluation. Drama is suspended tension, open op-tions, a dialectic in moving equilibrium.

Plays and movies based on novels prove that there is much that is performable in the other genres of literature as well. The art of poet and novelist, however, extends beyond dialogue and description of stage-ables. The lyric poet explores his own inner world of feeling and sensa-tion, a world different in kind from the externalized world of drama. But even narrative, whether in prose or verse, is, despite an area of possible overlap, different from drama. A novelist or an epic poet can suspend action indefinitely, do without dialogue and physical setting and event altogether ("epics of the mind"), and discourse abstractly on any num-ber of subjects in slow or quick sequence. He can judge and analyze his characters in authorial comment, by godlike ubiquity and omniscience enter at will into their hearts and souls, and just as easily exit back into straight narrative of external events. And if he never makes use of any of these novelistic freedoms, he is, in effect, a playwright, whether he calls his work a play or not.

Actually, this is a stricter definition of drama than many plays allow.

Bernard Shaw, for example, often violates dramatic objectivity in stage directions that interpret his characters for us. Perhaps the most flagrant example is the ending of *Candida*. When the heroine has sent her would-be lover, a young poet, "into the night" and turns to her husband, Shaw tells us, "They embrace. But they do not know the secret in the poet's heart." The former of these two sentences is stageable, a genuine stage direction. But no theatrical ingenuity can stage the latter—except as words flashed on a screen, like the subtitles of old silent movies. The point is not that Shaw's plays occasionally include bits of novels; we are concerned here with isolating a quality that all plays have in common, the quality that makes them, distinctly, *drama*. Performability is that quality. The spectator is in the theater to watch and listen. Shaw's comments do not exist for him, except insofar as they may have been translated into the language of the theater: sights and sounds the audience can perceive through the senses. A reader of *Candida* will, of course, make Shaw's last sentence part of his experience of the play, and an important part, too. But that does not make it a sentence of drama. The distinction is, if one likes, "academic," "purely theoretical." It certainly does not turn *Candida* into something other than a play. But to abandon it is to abandon an effort to make a general distinction between drama and other forms of literature. We *want* to be "theoretical" at this point; we are trying to suggest the outlines of a theory of drama.

This is not to exclude from the genre of drama works that cannot, for technical reasons, be staged (or staged in their entirety) in any existing theater or that, if staged, would overtax the patience and subtlety of an audience. Not only are such pragmatic criteria obviously relative; there is also a sense in which dramatic poems like *Samson Agonistes, Prometheus Unbound,* and *Peer Gynt,* though not intended for the stage and in some respects unperformable (if only, perhaps, by being bad box office), are completely dramatic. That is, their form is a system of speaking parts developing a coherent action. Whatever abstracts their total meaning includes are expressed or implied in speech, and speech is performable by impersonators of the fictitious speakers.

The mode of drama is the objectivity of the performable. Movement, directness, concreteness are its characteristics. The dramatic experience, whether in the theater or over a printed page, is one of urgent immediacy, of watching and listening to human destinies in the making, here and now, which the novelist or the poet can evoke only by being, precisely, dramatic.

Drama and the Reader

From such a definition of drama it follows that in a skillful and success-ful reading of a play the mind is being filled with a sequence of vivid and relevant images, called up by speeches and stage directions. The reader translates everything performable into concretes that participate in the total, complex image of words, physical movement, and scene that makes up the drama being enacted in the infinitely resourceful and adaptable stage of his mind. Whatever is not performable, or whatever he cannot conceive of as being performable, he will also incorporate into his inclusive reading experience, though not, strictly speaking, as *drama*.

Basic to any kind of meaningful response to literature is under-standing of the author's words in context and of the underlying condi-tions for action in the imagined world. "Understanding" depends on more than conscientious use of footnotes and dictionary; it entails a total response: intellectual, emotional, sensory. And though all readers cannot respond equally well, they can all make the effort to engage more than the top of their minds and the shallows of their souls. Gener-ally, in the case of plays from ages and cultures different from our own, *some* awareness of cultural background will be imperative, and *more* desirable, but the line between some and more is hard to draw in given cases. For some readers, at least, certain plays will create their own cli-mate of understanding.

Perhaps the ideal performance of the play, the standard by which both a theatrical production and a reading of it should be judged, will be thought of as the performance the playwright himself envisioned for his play. But this is neither a practicable nor even a really reasonable formula. There are playwrights who have left no record as to how they thought their plays should be produced, or whose ideas are too vague or incomplete to be of much help, or who refuse to answer when asked. And even if we assume that the original staging realized the playwright's ideal, for most older plays we can reconstruct it only by means of more or less inferential evidence, either within the play itself or supplied by research. Nor are the playwright's views, when available, necessarily more valid than someone else's—just as composers are not necessarily the best performers of their own works or even the best critics of the performance of their works by others. Intention is not accomplishment.

There is more force to the argument that a meaningful reading of a play requires knowledge of the kind of theater for which it was written. To read Sophocles or Shakespeare, the argument goes, we must know something about Greek and Elizabethan stagecraft, see productions that try to reproduce the contemporary performance, see models or pictures or diagrams of the playhouses, or at the very least read descriptions of them.

It is certainly true that the more knowledge the reader has of the culture—including the theatrical culture—reflected in what he reads, the more significant and enjoyable his reading will be. And the impossibility of ever knowing everything about a play and the fact that knowledge alone is insufficient for recreating the sense impressions, beliefs, attitudes, and moods of a bygone audience cannot invalidate the efforts of historians of drama and theater to know as much as possible. Though each culture, each age, each reader, even the same reader at different times, reads a literary work differently, knowledge of what can be factually known about it and its times is a protection against an anarchic subjectivity of interpretation that could eventually destroy its continuum of identity. This is part of the justification of scholarship.

But though knowledge of theatrical conditions, past or present, can discipline and enrich one's experience of a play, and though such knowledge is valuable for its own sake, it is still not a precondition for the dramatic imagination itself. The images that arise in the mind during the reading of drama can be translated into stage actualities, but they are not images of such actualities. The reader does not ordinarily imagine a staged scene but its real life counterpart—not a stage castle, crypt, or kitchen, but the real thing—Hamlet, not actor A or actor B impersonating Hamlet. The exceptions are the director, designer, and actor who read with a projected performance in mind and the reader—and he is the one who concerns us—who comes to his reading of the play fresh from an impressive performance of it. His reading experience will no doubt be more vivid than it otherwise would have been, but it will also be more limited. His imagination will be channeled by his memory of the hundreds of big and little details of voice and mimicry, movement and set, costume and light, that together make up any particular actualization of the ideal abstract the play is. Any one performance, however brilliant, is bound to be different from—both more and less than—the literary work that occasioned it, forever detached as the latter is from the impermanent particulars of the real. A good production may help a reader imagine what he found unimaginable as he read the play, or it may cool and contain an imagination that catches fire too easily, but a reader to whom a play is nothing but a blueprint for an evening in the theater has abdicated his rights as reader. It is only because most people *can* stage a play in their imagination, alive with the sights and sounds of reality, that drama is literature at all—that is, capable of being experienced through reading. The theater is the home of drama, and drama may be the occasion for theater, but all theater is not drama, nor is the drama lost without the theater.

Dramatic Conventions

Understanding the underlying condition for action in the imagined world involves understanding dramatic conventions. These are the conditions which playwright and audience between them have implicitly (whether they are conscious of it or not) agreed to accept as reality in the play. In the sense that what is called for is a willingness to take the world of imagination as reality for the time being, acceptance of conventions enters into any kind of successful experience of figurative (representational, nonabstract) art. But because the theater makes tangible the forms of the make-believe, conventions operate with particular force in the experience of drama—most insistently in the theater, but also in reading. There is a widespread, though tacit and largely uninspected, assumption that drama is the most referential of the literary genres (i.e., that it corresponds most closely to some real world of sensory phenomena) and the least purely expressive (i.e., lyrical). For this the sensory immediacy of the performable is responsible. And when an audience hesitates to accept a play that flouts all pretense to mirror an objective world of things and facts or that makes use of unfamiliar conventions, some form of the referential fallacy in the public concept of drama is likely to be involved. It is willing to accept the "realistic," but rejects the "expressionistic," conventions of drama.

Chorus, soliloquy, and aside are examples of conventions, mainly of older drama. They were no more everyday realities then than they are now, but as artistic devices they were given status as reality because they satisfied needs for dramatic expression without going beyond what the contemporary public was willing to accept as make-believe. Some conventions may have been means to achieve certain kinds of communication under the technically limiting conditions of older theater. For example, such "facts" of the imagined world as location and time of day, which in the modern theater can be established by sets and electric lights, were on the Elizabethan stage communicated by the dialogue itself. Hence the rather remarkable number of Shakespearean characters who mention time and place in their speeches, particularly in the opening of scenes. To the extent that such information is for the benefit of the audience rather than for the listeners on stage, the device is conventional: a breach of reality for the sake of establishing, economically and often beautifully, "reality" within the play.

Conventions vary with time and place. Yesterday's conventions are today's absurdities and tomorrow's brilliant innovations. No play is without them. In the ceremonial tradition of drama (Greek, Elizabethan, neoclassical tragedy), ritualistic use of language in verse and imagery and of archetypal action of aristocratic agony raises life to a plane of greater dignity, significance, intensity, and eloquence than that of ordinary life lived on naturalistic terms (classical comedy). In the illusionistic tradition (some forms of older comedy, modern dramatic realism like Ibsen's and Chekhov's), convention ignores the theatrical situation and assumes the commonplace surface of stage life to be that of actuality. In the expressionistic tradition (allegorical and symbolic drama, some of Strindberg's and O'Neill's plays, the theatricalism of Brecht, Pirandello, and Weiss, aspects of contemporary absurd theater), scenic abstractionism and stylization, dream sequences of realistic or distorted fragments of reality, montage techniques, and freedom of time and place are conventional means to the end of insinuating the reality of the single, subjective consciousness.

The actor who uses the Stanislavsky "method" to create a role from within, seeking to lose his real-life, off-stage personality in that of the human being he is projecting—"to be" rather than "to act"—is engaged in an enterprise of illusionistic theater. The Brechtian actor who deliberately plays up his double function as both impersonator and professional mimic or (in Brecht's word) "demonstrator" of a fictitious personality is practicing nonillusionistic theater, what, in this book, we shall refer to as "theatricalism," i.e., the theater's frank acknowledgment of itself as a place for the production of artifact. Actually, of course, the Stanislavsky way of acting is no less artificial, no more natural, than the Brechtian. All art is, quite properly, "artificial," that is, literally, "made by art" as conscious craft. The two acting methods differ only in the kind of effect they seek to create and in the conventions by which they create that effect.

Because our popular theater of stage, film, and television is still very largely the heir of the realist tradition of the late nineteenth century, the modern reader or playgoer may at first find older drama and contemporary avant-garde experiments "odd," "unrealistic," "obscure." The distance between his own ordinary language and Elizabethan blank-verse rhetoric or the noncommunication of absurdist dialogue may frustrate and alienate him, and he is not likely to be put at ease by the proposition that the spectacle has been put on not for its reality but for its art. Taking the conventions of realism for granted, he may fail to see that they *are* conventions. Or if he is sophisticated enough to recognize them for what they are, he may still feel they are the only "natural" conventions. But if he objects to the artificiality of the neoclassical convention of the three unities (which demanded that the action of the play be confined to a single plot, a single place, and a single day), he ought also to object to the convention of today's film and television that presents human beings as disembodied heads in facial close-ups and to the three-walled rooms of most post-Renaissance theater. And there is no reason to believe that playgoers of the past would have found a modern theater, with its artificially lighted box peeked into by a supposedly nonexistent audience, any less unnatural than we presume to find the choric rituals and public unburdenings of soul in soliloquy in their plays. If the naïve or stubbornly literal-minded person is bothered by the hero's apparent deafness to the villain's stage whisper, by the scarcity of actors on stage during Shakespeare's battle scenes, or by the free and flexible treatment of time and place in a contemporary play like *The Glass Menagerie*, he simply fails to understand or accept dramatic convention.

Character, Plot, Action, Conflict

Like most serious writing, drama represents man's use of words to make sense out of the myriad perplexities that befall him. The dramatist sees the world not primarily as shapes and colors and feelings, or as an object for religious or philosophical or scientific contemplation, or as a market, or as a reluctant machine that challenges his skill and ingenuity to make it run better. He sees it rather as an arena for human action manifested in speech.

The newcomer to the reading of drama may at first find confusing the conversations of unknowns who are discovered in the embroilments of an existence about which he knows nothing. He may miss preliminary explanations, the novelist's guiding hand. And if he has had experience with performed drama, he may also miss the aid to understanding provided by the presences and the voices of actors and by the physical spectacle in which they appear. That he can be guided by stage directions and ponder the dialogue at his leisure he may feel to be poor compensation for the absence of the sights and sounds of performance.

What the characters say and do begins to make sense only as we learn more about them, but we learn more about them only by what they say and do. Gradually they become more than a list of names. They reveal their antecedents and their present situations, their motives and purposes, they assume plot identity and "character." We learn to respond to the revealing remark or gesture, to listen to the eloquence of their silence, to sense their continuous pressure on the plot. Among them, they define and develop the dramatic action.

Dramatic action is neither physical activity nor simply the sum of everything that happens on stage: conversation, eating, people running up and down staircases, laughter, doors closing, lights going on and off. These are part of the action, but in the traditional definition action itself is a more abstract and comprehensive concept.

In the *Poetics*, Aristotle (384–322 B.C.), the first and still the single most important theorist of drama, said that all poetry is an "imitation [*mimesis*] of men in action" and that drama differs from other kinds of poetry (i.e., imaginative literature) by its manner of imitation. Unlike the epic poet, the dramatist does not narrate a human action but "presents all his characters as living and moving before us." Drama for Aristotle, then, is a stageable story. Aristotle's "imitation" has always been a controversial concept, but the full context of the *Poetics* (in which it is the first term discussed) makes it clear that he used it to mean something different from just a mindless replica of actual human behavior. "Imitation" is not a mere slice of life. Rather, as applied to drama, it denotes a selection of images or representations of human actuality so arranged as to present a coherent course of events, an "action" (*praxis*) that illuminates and verifies the changeless physical, psychological, moral, and metaphysical laws—the principles of "Nature" in the inclusive sense—by which and under which men manifest their humanity, alone or in interaction with others. Drama, like other forms of literature, has a didactic function: it teaches men to orient themselves in reality. That something close to this was what Aristotle meant by dramatic "imitation" is supported by the probability that he wrote the *Poetics* in vindication of poetry against Plato's charge (mainly in *The Republic*) that its excitation of the imagination was a threat to the stability of the state and that its fictions had inferior status as images of reality.

A further set of definitions may be useful at this point. A play is a patterning of language, character, event, and spectacle, each element a function of the other three. When the elements are mutually appropriate, the play observes dramatic *decorum*. Speech should be suited to the character and circumstance of the speaker, style and tone should be proper to the level of the action ("high" in tragedy, "middle" or "low" in comedy), and manners should be made to accord with period and place and the characters' social class. The plot of the play is the particular sequence of events that gives it the coherence and movement toward a given end that could not inhere in a random aggregate of happenings. Plot is the way the playwright has chosen to tell his story, the detailed arrangement of incidents for maximum meaning or beauty or suspense. The action of the play is both the summation of the plot and the abstraction of its meaning, the distillation of the play's totality in a single phrase. "To assert the priority of man's sacral over his secular obligations" defines the action of *Antigone*, "to restore the order of love and justice to a disordered world of hate and evil" that of *Othello*, "to save the cherry orchard" that of *The Cherry Orchard*, "to exorcise the past by evoking it" that of *The Glass Menagerie*. The advantage, as Francis Fergusson has pointed out, of defining dramatic action in such infinitive phrases is that they call attention to purpose as the motor force of action. When we perceive action in this way we exercise what Fergusson calls our "histrionic sensibility": we respond to what happens on stage as to the expression of "the changing life of the psyche," the teleology of the self interacting with its environment.

The nature and function of plot differ in different plays. It may be a strong, causal story line which we find suspenseful and convincing because of constant interaction between character and event. The nature of Iago's scheme is determined by his character and by his assessment of Othello's character, but the evolving logic of the scheme once he has set it in motion keeps revealing the characters of schemer and victim alike, until both seem defined by their entanglement in the events. Successful plot manipulation makes a character's behavior seem surprising and inevitable at the same time. Hedda Gabler's burning Eilert Løvborg's manuscript seems like an extraordinary and most unlikely event in a play that purports to be a snapshot of daily life in the upper middle class. But as an act by which a neurotic woman triumphs symbolically over her rival's superior womanliness it seems in character and not implausible at all.

In other plays plot is less a matter of dramatized narrative than of conveying a vivid sense of human presence. Molière in *The Misanthrope* and Chekhov in *The Cherry Orchard* do not base their dramas on the convenient convention that life runs in plots. They seek rather to illuminate a certain kind of human response to experience by means of juxtaposed scenes that subtly modify one another by discordant or mutually ironic styles, tones, and content. Molière takes Alceste through his paces, by turns admirable, ridiculous, and ominous, in an exposure of misanthropy in its several facets. Here plot is the display of a master passion in the round. *The Cherry Orchard* poses moments of emotional stasis against a background of moving time. The apparently arbitrary intermittence of the static moments and our simultaneous awareness of the resistless flow of time—and the contrast between them—constitute Chekhov's plot, in the sense that they give shape and point to the string of individual happenings.

In traditional anatomies of drama, plot is usually divided into four parts: (1) the *exposition,* which introduces the characters, gives essential information about their pre-play background, sets the plot in motion, and informs us about important off-stage events; (2) the *complication,* usually the bulk of the play, interweaving the characters' shifting fortunes and including the *climax,* a point of tension and the critical juncture at which a decision or an event irretrievably determines the outcome; (3) the *reversal,* or peripety, the point at which the complication culminates in the resolution of the plot: the protagonist's fortune changing from good to bad (the *catastrophe* in tragedy) or from bad to good (comedy); and (4) the *denouement,* or unraveling, which presents the consequences of the reversal, ties up loose ends, and allows the audience time to regain emotional equilibrium. Exposition and complication are likely to be the longest phases of the dramatic progress, the denouement is normally shorter, and the reversal may be marked by a single speech or event that occurs, most often, quite late in the play.

The plays in which the four parts of the plot are neatly distinct and laid end to end are few and not likely to be of the highest order. There are plays in which the exposition *is* the complication; Sophocles' *Oedipus Rex* is probably the most famous example. Others are Ibsen's late plays. In *Hedda Gabler,* personal relationships grow tenser as we learn more and more about Hedda's and Løvborg's past. In fact, the traditional paradigm of formal plot analysis often seems to apply only partly, or insignificantly, or not at all, to individual plays in the heterogeneity and generic confusion of modern drama. To a contemporary, at least, the story of modern drama is to a very large extent the story of revolt and experimentation superseding a sense of formal tradition. Past and present interpenetrate in *The Glass Menagerie.* We do not conclude that the traditional terms are useless but that they cannot be used indiscriminately or with equal relevance for all plays. Our lexicon of criticism is constantly being supplemented in response to new modes of literary expression. We may illustrate the use of the traditional terms in an analysis of the plot structure of a traditional play.

The *story* of *Antigone* is the entire chronicle of the royal house of Thebes, including the fall of Oedipus and the mutual killing of his two sons during the Argive attack on the city. These events are only referred to, not shown on stage, but *because* they are referred to they bear significantly on actions and attitudes that *are* staged. The *action* is the resolution of the two related issues: to whom do the dead, and to whom do the living, belong? The *plot* is the causally connected sequence of events that follow from Antigone's defiance of her uncle's edict. The *exposition* is over and the *complication* begins when the Sentry enters in Scene I with the news that Polyneices has been surreptitiously buried. Everything preceding his entry has been in preparation of joining the Creon–Antigone issue. The complication comprises all the encounters involved in the opposition of Creon's and Antigone's wills, including the scenes with the Sentry, with Ismene, with Haimon, with Teiresias, and with the Choragos–Chorus. The *climax* is Creon's ordering Antigone's entombment, for from it follows directly, like falling dominoes, her, Haimon's, and Eurydice's suicides. The *reversal* occurs when Creon, disturbed by Teiresias' words and urged by the Choragos, decides to set Antigone free. The plot *resolution* is the three deaths, as related by the Messenger. Creon's last, humble exchanges with the Messenger and the Choragos mark the *denouement.*

Plot generates and releases suspense, the feeling in the audience that keeps it wondering what happens next. One characteristic of great drama is that suspense survives knowledge of "how things come out," because our absorbed wait for what is going to happen concerns the outcome less than it concerns the happenings themselves and the patterns we see them forming. We may know exactly what happens in Sophocles' Theban plays and still attend, fascinated and moved, to every small step in Oedipus's movement toward tragic recognition in *Oedipus Rex* and toward apotheosis in *Oedipus at Colonus* and to the two diverging movements in *Antigone:* Antigone's to the triumph of deliberate martyrdom, and Creon's to humiliation, loss, and acceptance of guilt. In fact, superior plays have a way of seeming better in later readings. That is the reason we may rather want to see still another stage or screen production of *Othello* than a brand new play. What we lose in mere thrill we gain in understanding and enjoyment through our intimacy with the characters and our knowledge of events to come. Familiarity also increases our appreciation and enjoyment of dramaturgy: the exercise of the playwright's craft, the dexterous manipulation of plot and character in the integrated structure of successful dramatic action. As the football fan goes to the game not just to learn who wins and by what score but to enjoy the game being played and the skill of coach and players, so the lover of drama seeks vicarious experience of significant action in artistic form, and not just information about a result. The ideal spectator attends both kinds of play in a mood of disinterested fascination.

Conflict is the element in plot that creates suspense. It is what the plot is about. In *Antigone* the conflict may be variously defined. Most simply and obviously it is one between Antigone's commitment to supernatural values and Creon's to political ones. In a larger sense, we may define it as god against man. Or we may chiefly be aware of dramatic irony: the discrepancy between, on the one hand, Creon's assumption that his fatherly concern for law and order represents the will of the gods and that Antigone's refusal to distinguish between the loyal and the disloyal dead represents rebellious impiety, and, on the other, the truth of the bitter lesson he learns at the end.

Conflict may be multiple, a collection of variants of a many-sided subject, each presenting it in a new view, and all covered by a wider definition of the play's conflict. In Shakespeare's *King Lear* the main plot about Lear and his daughters and the subplot of Gloucester and his sons allow Shakespeare a fuller treatment of the theme of filial ingratitude than either plot alone would have allowed him, and the doubleness of the plot suggests the pervasiveness of the evil. In Chekhov, the situations of the several characters who fail in different ways to fulfill themselves, to achieve happiness, to establish human contact, and to take decisive action cohere in a single image of frustration, the clash of hope with reality. Plot unity is obviously not the same kind of thing in all plays. Contrasting the rambling diffuseness of small events in *The Cherry Orchard* with the closely woven plots of *Antigone, Othello,* and *Hedda Gabler* suggests the range in kinds and patterns of conflict.

Conflict is opposition of forces, one of which is likely to be a human will that is heroically uncompromising and therefore doomed in tragedy and abortive or reformable in comedy. Man against god, man against nature (a mountain, the sea, hunger), man against society, man against man, and man against himself represent (in rough terms) the five main kinds of conflict. Conflict may be as simple as it is in a fairy tale (bad queen against good princess, bad guy against good sheriff). It may be morally unequivocal as in *Othello* or ambiguous as in *The Cherry Orchard.* It may be religious as in *Antigone,* or psychological as in *Hedda Gabler.* It may be realistic as in *The Cherry Orchard* or expressionistic as in *The Glass Menagerie.* Drama without conflict is unthinkable. For the essence of the dramatic experience is the fascination with the progress of clashing forces toward resolution: the hero's death or enlightenment, the villain's defeat; the reintegration of a threatened social order in a wedding, a reconciliation, a verdict; the revelation of the transcendent nature that shapes our lives as order and meaning or as silence and darkness.

The spoken word is the medium of drama, the objectivity of the performable its mode or manner of being, the surrender of our imaginations to that of the playwright the condition for its existence for us, but the drama itself is the action of man in conflict. This action we witness partly as safe and superior deities, enjoying the pleasure of dramatic irony at the expense of people who do not know what is happening to them; partly as sympathetic observers, commiserating with the good, relishing the downfall of the bad; and partly as fellow fools and sufferers: there, but for the grace of God, *we* strut and fret.

Tragedy and Comedy

Defining tragedies as plays that end unhappily and comedies as plays that end happily sounds like a more simpleminded distinction than it actually is. There are, of course, perspectives in which the two coalesce in a vision of human life as simultaneously terrible and joyous, but the mixed view does not invalidate the original distinction. There are those who argue that tragicomedy prevails in modern drama because skepticism has placed the awe that is at the heart of older tragedy beyond our reach and because the enormity of modern experience has killed the spirit of older comedy. But if this were altogether so, we would hardly continue to respond as we do to the great tragedies and comedies of the past.

Our age is not the first to have felt the irreducible ambivalence in the human condition. Both tragedy and comedy are thought to have originated in rites propitiating the powers controlling the natural cycles of night and day, growth and decay, life and death. In communal enactments of myths of redemptive sacrifice and orgiastic abandon man paid tribute to the gods, but the fixed forms of his mimetic art were also symbols of the control he desired but did not have of the patterns imposed upon his life. The Dionysiac theater in ancient Athens staged tragic suffering and obscene ribaldry as parts of the same production. Homer and Dante and Cervantes and Dr. Johnson knew as well as do Beckett and Ionesco today that the tragic and the comic worlds cannot be kept apart. There are clowns in Shakespeare's tragedies and tragic implications in some of his comedies. Molière's *The Misanthrope* is as much a tragicomedy as Ibsen's *The Wild Duck* and Chekhov's *The Three Sisters* and *The Cherry Orchard*. Our sensibility is not unique. We may see ourselves as exiles from the conceptual universe in which the writing of pure tragedy and pure comedy was possible, but the distinction between them still gives shape to our sense of both drama and life. It is a division which man in all ages reaches for when he tries to purify his human essence, to isolate the components of his psyche, to find clarity and order in the murky mess of his actual experience. The old dichotomies of tragedy and comedy, suffering and joy, tears and laughter, the sublime and the ludicrous, still name the deepest perceptions he derives from contemplating his strange and various lot.

Tragedy and comedy, then, are terms that do more than classify plays. They stand for ways, not so much contrasting as complementary, of perceiving life. In tragedy, man is a paradox in a paradoxical existence. Fallible and vulnerable in his mortal finity, he is yet capable of transcendent greatness. Freely exercising his will (a passive hero is pathetic rather than tragic), he is yet the plaything of destiny. Acting on his virtue, he incurs guilt. Divided within by impulses and imperatives in conflict and beset without by other willful selves and by his physical environment, he pits his naked strength against forces that inhibit him and enrage him and that he can neither control nor understand. Flawed by his human nature, he is incapable of compromise. He demands that an imperfect world conform to his notions of right and good, and he is defeated because discord, injustice, pain, and moral evil are the world's warp and woof. The final paradox is man in his tragic vision saying, "I do not believe in the invincibility of evil but in the inevitability of defeat."

Why this is so is the question all tragedy asks and no tragedy answers. Plays that do answer, in vindication of the universe against man's ceaseless questioning, are moving away from tragedy proper toward religious drama. Aeschylus's *Agamemnon* is more tragic than his *Eumenides,* and *Hamlet* is more tragic than *Everyman.* Milton's *Samson Agonistes* is in form a perfect Greek tragedy, but as a "Christian tragedy" it is, perhaps, a contradiction in terms.

But in the absoluteness of his commitment, the tragic hero triumphs in the very inevitability of his defeat. Foolishly, pitifully, magnificently pressing his human potential beyond its limits, he asserts man's significance and dignity in the face of the unanswering unknown; tragic man matters. The hero's high social rank in traditional tragedy is not a sign of aristocratic prejudice but both a symbol of his superior human quality and a way of signifying that what happens to him affects others than himself. The metaphor of rank points up the grim irony that the very best specimens of mankind suffer most from the irremediableness of the human condition. Aristotle had both the moral and the social sense in mind when he distinguished tragedy from comedy by saying that "Comedy aims at representing men as worse, Tragedy as better, than in actual life." There is painful irony in this, too: in the implication that "goodness" meets disaster and "badness" survives and succeeds.

In the abstract (making allowance for intermediary and mixed types), tragedies are of two main kinds. One kind affirms the meaning and justice of the world order and gives compensation for the final calamity by the Aeschylean formula of "wisdom through suffering." In a scene of *anagnorisis* (recognition), the hero (and the spectator) understands what is happening to him and that he is responsible for it, and he and we accept his fate. In the worldly catastrophe there is an enlightenment of the spirit. If the ways of the gods are inscrutable and severe, their manifestations in human life testify to the existence of eternal laws and to man's capacity to suffer greatly and to learn from his suffering. We leave the play solemn but not depressed. This is tragedy of *catharsis:* purged of rebelliousness, fear, and self-pity, we submit to things as they mysteriously and immutably are. *Antigone* is an example.

In the other kind of tragedy, the dramatization of human suffering poses questions that challenge the order and justice of things. Why is there evil in the world? Why do the innocent suffer? Why does fineness of human qualities bring disaster? Why should we have to submit to laws that are capricious, indifferent, blindly mechanical, or malicious? We may call this kind existential or Promethean tragedy (from the demigod Prometheus in ancient myth, man's benefactor and champion who stole fire from the gods and gave it to man, thereby incurring Jove's wrath and punishment). It is tragedy that recognizes man's helplessness but asserts his dignity by protesting against it. Aeschylus's *Libation Bearers,* Euripides' *Bacchae* and *Medea,* Shakespeare's *Hamlet, Othello,* and *King Lear,* and Racine's *Phaedra* and *Berenice* are in some respects tragedies of this type. For more clear-cut examples of existential discontent in drama, we go—significantly, perhaps—to modern plays: Camus's *Caligula,* Sartre's *The Flies,* Beckett's *Waiting for Godot* and *Endgame,* Weiss's *Marat/Sade,* and Stoppard's *Rosencrantz and Guildenstern Are Dead.* In all of these, either the single tragic hero or the dialectic thrust of the whole play defies the arbitrary order in which evil and pain are undeserved or inflicted in excess of man's transgressions. The writer of Promethean tragedy withholds, on behalf of embattled mankind, resignation to the cruel discrepancy between intrinsic virtue and extrinsic evil. That he knows his refusal is absurd in its futility only stiffens his stance.

The domain of tragedy is metaphysics: solitary, unaccommodated, questing man confronting the contradictoriness and the ultimate mysteries of his being and circumstance. The domain of comedy is the physical and the social: man's triumphs and tribulations as gregarious animal. "The world," said Horace Walpole in the eighteenth century, "is a comedy to those that think, a tragedy to those that feel." He did not mean that tragedy is mindless and that comedy has no emotional appeal. He meant that the issues raised by tragedy cannot be resolved by rational analysis but relate to our awareness of our precarious position in a dark existence of uncertain meaning and purpose, in which selves may shatter in the division between passion and reason. And he meant that comedy addresses itself to our critical faculties, sharpening our perception of the ludicrous discrepancy between what man is and what he tries or pretends to be. The eccentric character, who foolishly and stubbornly deviates from sane and viable values—good nature, flexibility, moderation, social intelligence, love of others—and thereby opposes himself to the flow of life in all its varied fecundity, is a common figure in all comedy, not just in comedy of humors, where he is central. Comic laughter, said Henri Bergson, the French philosopher, follows our perception of "something mechanical encrusted upon the living": the incongruous spectacle of a human being reducing himself to a rigid automaton.

The spirit of comedy is the spirit that will tolerate everything except intolerance. The killjoy Malvolio in Shakespeare's *Twelfth Night* and Alceste, the man of uncompromising honesty, in Molière's *The Misanthrope* are its enemies. At the end, both alienate themselves from the social group. Comedy shows us the ridiculous posturings of the silly and the selfish, the vicious and the vain. It laughs folly and vice out of countenance. Its laughter is reflective but good-natured. It is capacious enough to welcome and absorb into its world the fool made wise and the sinner reformed. Where its laughter becomes shrill or bitter or sardonic, the comedy is about to turn into satire, for satire is inspired by righteous indignation rather than by tolerant amusement. Satire ridicules and contemns in order to expose and reform. Comedy, too, recognizes imperfection but accepts it and exhibits it for our thoughtful amusement, reminding us of the vices and follies which we all share. Comedy, above everything, asserts the richness of human life, valuing food, drink, and sex no less than virtue and sentiment, courage and kindness, wit and fancy.

If satire marks one end of the comic spectrum, the festive marks the other. Satiric comedy tends toward "problem" comedy or tragicomedy in its vision of human depravity. Shakespeare's *Measure for Measure* and *Troilus and Cressida*, Ben Jonson's *The Alchemist* and *Volpone* and Molière's *Tartuffe* and *The Misanthrope* are on the very edge of comedy in this sense. Pure festive comedy, such as Shakespeare's *As You Like It*, tends toward romance in its vision of a redeemed world of love, innocence, and justice. In comedy, vice and folly are psychological and social rather than metaphysical realities, and the adaptive social structure survives the threat they have posed to the ongoing joy of human life. Like tragedy, comedy says that man endures.

Six Plays

Sophocles

Antigone

An English Version by Dudley Fitts and Robert Fitzgerald

Persons Represented

ANTIGONE	HAIMON	CHORUS
ISMENE	TEIRESIAS	
EURYDICE	A SENTRY	
CREON	A MESSENGER	

Scene: *Before the palace of* CREON, *King of Thebes. A central double door, and two lateral doors. A platform extends the length of the façade, and from this platform three steps lead down into the "orchestra," or chorus-ground.*
Time: *Dawn of the day after the repulse of the Argive army from the assault on Thebes.*

PROLOGUE

(ANTIGONE *and* ISMENE *enter from the central door of the Palace.*)

ANTIGONE: Ismene, dear sister,
   You would think that we had already suffered enough
   For the curse on Oedipus:
   I cannot imagine any grief
   That you and I have not gone through. And now—
   Have they told you of the new decree of our King Creon?
ISMENE: I have heard nothing: I know

That two sisters lost two brothers, a double death
In a single hour; and I know that the Argive army
Fled in the night; but beyond this, nothing.
ANTIGONE: I thought so. And that is why I wanted you
To come out here with me. There is something we must do.
ISMENE: Why do you speak so strangely?
ANTIGONE: Listen, Ismene:
Creon buried our brother Eteocles
With military honors, gave him a soldier's funeral,
And it was right that he should; but Polyneices,
Who fought as bravely and died as miserably,—
They say that Creon has sworn
No one shall bury him, no one mourn for him,
But his body must lie in the fields, a sweet treasure
For carrion birds to find as they search for food.
That is what they say, and our good Creon is coming here
To announce it publicly; and the penalty—
Stoning to death in the public square!

                            There it is,
And now you can prove what you are:
A true sister, or a traitor to your family.
ISMENE: Antigone, you are mad! What could I possibly do?
ANTIGONE: You must decide whether you will help me or not.
ISMENE: I do not understand you. Help you in what?
ANTIGONE: Ismene, I am going to bury him. Will you come?
ISMENE: Bury him! You have just said the new law forbids it.
ANTIGONE: He is my brother. And he is your brother, too.
ISMENE: But think of the danger! Think what Creon will do!
ANTIGONE: Creon is not strong enough to stand in my way.
ISMENE: Ah sister!
Oedipus died, everyone hating him
For what his own search brought to light, his eyes
Ripped out by his own hand; and Iocaste died,
His mother and wife at once: she twisted the cords
That strangled her life; and our two brothers died,
Each killed by the other's sword. And we are left:
But oh, Antigone,
Think how much more terrible than these
Our own death would be if we should go against Creon
And do what he has forbidden! We are only women,
We cannot fight with men, Antigone!
The law is strong, we must give in to the law
In this thing, and in worse. I beg the Dead

To forgive me, but I am helpless. I must yield
To those in authority. And I think it is dangerous business
To be always meddling.
ANTIGONE: If that is what you think,
  I should not want you, even if you asked to come.
  You have made your choice, you can be what you want to be.
  But I will bury him; and if I must die,
  I say that this crime is holy: I shall lie down
  With him in death, and I shall be as dear
  To him as he is to me.
                         It is the dead,
  Not the living, who make the longest demands:
  We die for ever . . .
                         You may do as you like,
  Since apparently the laws of the gods mean nothing to you.
ISMENE: They mean a great deal to me; but I have no strength
  To break laws that were made for the public good.
ANTIGONE: That must be your excuse, I suppose. But as for me,
  I will bury the brother I love.
ISMENE: Antigone,
  I am so afraid for you!
ANTIGONE: You need not be:
  You have yourself to consider, after all.
ISMENE: But no one must hear of this, you must tell no one!
  I will keep it a secret, I promise!
ANTIGONE: Oh tell it! Tell everyone!
  Think how they'll hate you when it all comes out
  If they learn that you knew about it all the time!
ISMENE: So fiery! You should be cold with fear.
ANTIGONE: Perhaps. But I am doing only what I must.
ISMENE: But can you do it? I say that you cannot.
ANTIGONE: Very well: when my strength gives out, I shall do no more.
ISMENE: Impossible things should not be tried at all.
ANTIGONE: Go away, Ismene:
  I shall be hating you soon, and the dead will too,
  For your words are hateful. Leave me my foolish plan:
  I am not afraid of the danger; if it means death,
  It will not be the worst of deaths—death without honor.
ISMENE: Go then, if you feel that you must.
  You are unwise,
  But a loyal friend indeed to those who love you.

(*Exit into the Palace.* ANTIGONE *goes off, L. Enter the* CHORUS.)

PARODOS

CHORUS: Now the long blade of the sun, lying   [STROPHE 1
   Level east to west, touches with glory
   Thebes of the Seven Gates. Open, unlidded
   Eye of golden day! O marching light
   Across the eddy and rush of Dirce's stream,
   Striking the white shields of the enemy
   Thrown headlong backward from the blaze of morning!
CHORAGOS: Polyneices their commander
   Roused them with windy phrases,
   He the wild eagle screaming
   Insults above our land,
   His wings their shields of snow,
   His crest their marshalled helms.

CHORUS: Against our seven gates in a yawning ring   [ANTISTROPHE 1
   The famished spears came onward in the night;
   But before his jaws were sated with our blood,
   Or pinefire took the garland of our towers.
   He was thrown back; and as he turned, great Thebes—
   No tender victim for his noisy power—
   Rose like a dragon behind him, shouting war.
CHORAGOS: For God hates utterly
   The bray of bragging tongues;
   And when he beheld their smiling,
   Their swagger of golden helms,
   The frown of his thunder blasted
   Their first man from our walls.

CHORUS: We heard his shout of triumph high in the air   [STROPHE 2
   Turn to a scream; far out in a flaming arc
   He fell with his windy torch, and the earth struck him.
   And others storming in fury no less than his
   Found shock of death in the dusty joy of battle.
CHORAGOS: Seven captains at seven gates
   Yielded their clanging arms to the god
   That bends the battle-line and breaks it.
   These two only, brothers in blood,
   Face to face in matchless rage,
   Mirroring each the other's death,
   Clashed in long combat.

CHORUS: But now in the beautiful morning of victory [ANTISTROPHE 2
    Let Thebes of the many chariots sing for joy!
    With hearts for dancing we'll take leave of war:
    Our temples shall be sweet with hymns of praise,
    And the long night shall echo with our chorus.

SCENE I

CHORAGOS: But now at last our new King is coming:
    Creon of Thebes, Menoikeus' son.
    In this auspicious dawn of his reign
    What are the new complexities
    That shifting Fate has woven for him?
    What is his counsel? Why has he summoned
    The old men to hear him?

(*Enter* CREON *from the Palace, C. He addresses the* CHORUS *from the top step.*)

CREON: Gentlemen: I have the honor to inform you that our Ship of State, which recent storms have threatened to destroy, has come safely to harbor at last, guided by the merciful wisdom of Heaven. I have summoned you here this morning because I know that I can depend upon you: your devotion to King Laïos was absolute; you never hesitated in your duty to our late ruler Oedipus; and when Oedipus died, your loyalty was transferred to his children. Unfortunately, as you know, his two sons, the princes Eteocles and Polyneices, have killed each other in battle; and I, as the next in blood, have succeeded to the full power of the throne.

I am aware, of course, that no Ruler can expect complete loyalty from his subjects until he has been tested in office. Nevertheless, I say to you at the very outset that I have nothing but contempt for the kind of Governor who is afraid, for whatever reason, to follow the course that he knows is best for the State; and as for the man who sets private friendship above the public welfare—I have no use for him, either. I call God to witness that if I saw my country headed for ruin, I should not be afraid to speak out plainly; and I need hardly remind you that I would never have any dealings with an enemy of the people. No one values friendship more highly than I; but we must remember that friends made at the risk of wrecking our Ship are not real friends at all.

These are my principles, at any rate, and that is why I have made the following decision concerning the sons of Oedipus: Eteocles, who died as a man should die, fighting for his country, is to be buried with full military honors, with all the ceremony that is usual when the greatest heroes die; but his brother Polyneices, who broke his exile to come back with fire and sword against his native city and the shrines of his fathers' gods, whose one idea was to spill the blood of his blood and sell his own people into slavery—Polyneices, I say, is to have no burial: no man is to touch him or say the least prayer for him; he shall lie on the plain, unburied; and the birds and the scavenging dogs can do with him whatever they like.

This is my command, and you can see the wisdom behind it. As long as I am King, no traitor is going to be honored with the loyal man. But whoever shows by word and deed that he is on the side of the State—he shall have my respect while he is living, and my reverence when he is dead.

CHORAGOS: If that is your will, Creon son of Menoikeus,
You have the right to enforce it: we are yours.

CREON: That is my will. Take care that you do your part.

CHORAGOS: We are old men: let the younger ones carry it out.

CREON: I do not mean that: the sentries have been appointed.

CHORAGOS: Then what is it that you would have us do?

CREON: You will give no support to whoever breaks this law.

CHORAGOS: Only a crazy man is in love with death!

CREON: And death it is; yet money talks, and the wisest
Have sometimes been known to count a few coins too many.

(*Enter* SENTRY *from L.*)

SENTRY: I'll not say that I'm out of breath from running, King, because every time I stopped to think about what I have to tell you, I felt like going back. And all the time a voice kept saying, "You fool, don't you know you're walking straight into trouble?"; and then another voice: "Yes, but if you let somebody else get the news to Creon first, it will be even worse than that for you!" But good sense won out, at least I hope it was good sense, and here I am with a story that makes no sense at all; but I'll tell it anyhow, because, as they say, what's going to happen's going to happen, and—

CREON: Come to the point. What have you to say?

SENTRY: I did not do it. I did not see who did it. You must not punish me for what someone else has done.

CREON: A comprehensive defense! More effective, perhaps,
If I knew its purpose. Come: what is it?

SENTRY: A dreadful thing . . . I don't know how to put it—

CREON: Out with it!

SENTRY: Well, then;

The dead man—
                    Polyneices—

(*Pause. The* SENTRY *is overcome, fumbles for words.* CREON *waits impassively.*)

                    out there—
                              someone,—

New dust on the slimy flesh!

(*Pause. No sign from* CREON.)

Someone has given it burial that way, and
Gone . . .

(*Long pause.* CREON *finally speaks with deadly control.*)

CREON: And the man who dared do this?
SENTRY: I swear I
    Do not know! You must believe me!
                              Listen:
    The ground was dry, not a sign of digging, no,
    Not a wheeltrack in the dust, no trace of anyone.
    It was when they relieved us this morning: and one of them,
    The corporal, pointed to it.
                              There it was,
    The strangest—
              Look:
    The body, just mounded over with light dust: you see?
    Not buried really, but as if they'd covered it
    Just enough for the ghost's peace. And no sign
    Of dogs or any wild animal that had been there.

    And then what a scene there was! Every man of us
    Accusing the other: we all proved the other man did it,
    We all had proof that we could not have done it.
    We were ready to take hot iron in our hands,
    Walk through fire, swear by all the gods,
    It was not I!
    I do not know who it was, but it was not I!

(CREON'S *rage has been mounting steadily, but the* SENTRY *is too intent upon his story to notice it.*)

    And then, when this came to nothing, someone said
    A thing that silenced us and made us stare
    Down at the ground: you had to be told the news,

And one of us had to do it! We threw the dice,
And the bad luck fell to me. So here I am,
No happier to be here than you are to have me:
Nobody likes the man who brings bad news.

CHORAGOS: I have been wondering, King: can it be that the gods have
done this?

CREON (*furiously*): Stop!
Must you doddering wrecks
Go out of your heads entirely? "The gods!"
Intolerable!
The gods favor this corpse? Why? How had he served them?
Tried to loot their temples, burn their images,
Yes, and the whole State, and its laws with it!
Is it your senile opinion that the gods love to honor bad men?
A pious thought!—

                No, from the very beginning
There have been those who have whispered together,
Stiff-necked anarchists, putting their heads together,
Scheming against me in alleys. These are the men,
And they have bribed my own guard to do this thing.

(*Sententiously.*)

Money!
There's nothing in the world so demoralizing as money.
Down go your cities,
Homes gone, men gone, honest hearts corrupted,
Crookedness of all kinds, and all for money!
(*To* SENTRY.)   But you—!
I swear by God and by the throne of God,
The man who has done this thing shall pay for it!
Find the man, bring him here to me, or your death
Will be the least of your problems: I'll string you up
Alive, and there will be certain ways to make you
Discover your employer before you die;
And the process may teach you a lesson you seem to have missed:
The dearest profit is sometimes all too dear:
That depends on the source. Do you understand me?
A fortune won is often misfortune.

SENTRY: King, may I speak?

CREON: Your very voice distresses me.

SENTRY: Are you sure that it is my voice, and not your conscience?

CREON· By God, he wants to analyze me now!

SENTRY: It is not what I say, but what has been done, that hurts you.

CREON: You talk too much.
SENTRY: Maybe, but I've done nothing.
CREON: Sold your soul for some silver: that's all you've done.
SENTRY: How dreadful it is when the right judge judges wrong!
CREON: Your figures of speech
   May entertain you now; but unless you bring me the man,
   You will get little profit from them in the end.

   (*Exit* CREON *into the Palace.*)

SENTRY: "Bring me the man"—!
   I'd like nothing better than bringing him the man!
   But bring him or not, you have seen the last of me here.
   At any rate, I am safe!

   (*Exit* SENTRY.)

ODE I

CHORUS: Numberless are the world's wonders, but none   [STROPHE 1
   More wonderful than man; the stormgray sea
   Yields to his prows, the huge crests bear him high;
   Earth, holy and inexhaustible, is graven
   With shining furrows where his plows have gone
   Year after year, the timeless labor of stallions.
                                                         [ANTISTROPHE 1

   The lightboned birds and beasts that cling to cover,
   The lithe fish lighting their reaches of dim water,
   All are taken, tamed in the net of his mind;
   The lion on the hill, the wild horse windy-maned,
   Resign to him; and his blunt yoke has broken
   The sultry shoulders of the mountain bull.

   Words also, and thought as rapid as air,   [STROPHE 2
   He fashions to his good use; statecraft is his,
   And his the skill that deflects the arrows of snow,
   The spears of winter rain: from every wind
   He has made himself secure—from all but one:
   In the late wind of death he cannot stand.

   O clear intelligence, force beyond all measure!   [ANTISTROPHE 2
   O fate of man, working both good and evil!
   When the laws are kept, how proudly his city stands!

When the laws are broken, what of his city then?
Never may the anarchic man find rest at my hearth,
Never be it said that my thoughts are his thoughts.

SCENE II

(*Re-enter* SENTRY *leading* ANTIGONE.)

CHORAGOS: What does this mean? Surely this captive woman
Is the Princess, Antigone. Why should she be taken?
SENTRY: Here is the one who did it! We caught her
In the very act of burying him.—Where is Creon?
CHORAGOS: Just coming from the house.

(*Enter* CREON, C.)

CREON: What has happened?
Why have you come back so soon?
SENTRY (*expansively*):   O King,
A man should never be too sure of anything: I would have sworn
That you'd not see me here again: your anger
Frightened me so, and the things you threatened me with;
But how could I tell then
That I'd be able to solve the case so soon?

No dice-throwing this time: I was only too glad to come!

Here is this woman, She is the guilty one:
We found her trying to bury him.
Take her, then; question her; judge her as you will.
I am through with the whole thing now, and glad of it.
CREON: But this is Antigone! Why have you brought her here?
SENTRY: She was burying him, I tell you!
CREON (*severely*):   Is this the truth?
SENTRY: I saw her with my own eyes. Can I say more?
CREON: The details: come, tell me quickly!
SENTRY: It was like this:
After those terrible threats of yours, King,
We went back and brushed the dust away from the body.
The flesh was soft by now, and stinking,
So we sat on a hill to windward and kept guard.
No napping this time! We kept each other awake.

But nothing happened until the white round sun
Whirled in the center of the round sky over us:
Then, suddenly,
A storm of dust roared up from the earth, and the sky
Went out, the plain vanished with all its trees
In the stinging dark. We closed our eyes and endured it.
The whirlwind lasted a long time, but it passed;
And then we looked, and there was Antigone!
I have seen
A mother bird come back to a stripped nest, heard
Her crying bitterly a broken note or two
For the young ones stolen. Just so, when this girl
Found the bare corpse, and all her love's work wasted,
She wept, and cried on heaven to damn the hands
That had done this thing.
                    And then she brought more dust
And sprinkled wine three times for her brother's ghost.

We ran and took her at once. She was not afraid,
Not even when we charged her with what she had done.
She denied nothing.
              And this was a comfort to me,
And some uneasiness: for it is a good thing
To escape from death, but it is no great pleasure
To bring death to a friend.
                  Yet I always say
There is nothing so comfortable as your own safe skin!

CREON (*slowly, dangerously*): And you, Antigone,
    You with your head hanging,—do you confess this thing?

ANTIGONE: I do. I deny nothing.

CREON (*to* SENTRY):   You may go.   (*Exit* SENTRY.)
    (*To* ANTIGONE.) Tell me, tell me briefly:
    Had you heard my proclamation touching this matter?

ANTIGONE: It was public. Could I help hearing it?

CREON: And yet you dared defy the law.

ANTIGONE: I dared.
    It was not God's proclamation. That final Justice
    That rules the world below makes no such laws.
    Your edict, King, was strong,
    But all your strength is weakness itself against
    The immortal unrecorded laws of God.
    They are not merely now: they were, and shall be,
    Operative for ever, beyond man utterly.

I knew I must die, even without your decree:
I am only mortal. And if I must die
Now, before it is my time to die,
Surely this is no hardship: can anyone
Living, as I live, with evil all about me,
Think Death less than a friend? This death of mine
Is of no importance; but if I had left my brother
Lying in death unburied, I should have suffered.
Now I do not.
     You smile at me. Ah Creon,
Think me a fool, if you like; but it may well be
That a fool convicts me of folly.

CHORAGOS: Like father, like daughter: both headstrong, deaf to reason!
 She has never learned to yield.

CREON: She has much to learn.
 The inflexible heart breaks first, the toughest iron
 Cracks first, and the wildest horses bend their necks
 At the pull of the smallest curb.
         Pride? In a slave?
 This girl is guilty of a double insolence,
 Breaking the given laws and boasting of it.
 Who is the man here,
 She or I, if this crime goes unpunished?
 Sister's child, or more than sister's child,
 Or closer yet in blood—she and her sister
 Win bitter death for this!
 (*To* SERVANTS.)   Go, some of you,
 Arrest Ismene. I accuse her equally.
 Bring her: you will find her sniffling in the house there.

 Her mind's a traitor: crimes kept in the dark
 Cry for light, and the guardian brain shudders;
 But how much worse than this
 Is brazen boasting of barefaced anarchy!

ANTIGONE: Creon, what more do you want than my death?

CREON: Nothing.
 That gives me everything.

ANTIGONE: Then I beg you: kill me.
 This talking is a great weariness: your words
 Are distasteful to me, and I am sure that mine
 Seem so to you. And yet they should not seem so:
 I should have praise and honor for what I have done.

All these men here would praise me
Were their lips not frozen shut with fear of you.

(*Bitterly.*)

Ah the good fortune of kings,
Licensed to say and do whatever they please!

CREON: You are alone here in that opinion.

ANTIGONE: No, they are with me. But they keep their tongues in leash.

CREON: Maybe. But you are guilty, and they are not.

ANTIGONE: There is no guilt in reverence for the dead.

CREON: But Eteocles—was he not your brother too?

ANTIGONE: My brother too.

CREON: And you insult his memory?

ANTIGONE (*softly*): The dead man would not say that I insult it.

CREON: He would: for you honor a traitor as much as him.

ANTIGONE: His own brother, traitor or not, and equal in blood.

CREON: He made war on his country. Eteocles defended it.

ANTIGONE: Nevertheless, there are honors due all the dead.

CREON: But not the same for the wicked as for the just.

ANTIGONE: Ah Creon, Creon,
Which of us can say what the gods hold wicked?

CREON: An enemy is an enemy, even dead.

ANTIGONE: It is my nature to join in love, not hate.

CREON (*finally losing patience*): Go join them, then; if you must have
your love,
Find it in hell!

CHORAGOS: But see, Ismene comes:

(*Enter* ISMENE, *guarded.*)

Those tears are sisterly, the cloud
That shadows her eyes rains down gentle sorrow.

CREON: You too, Ismene,
Snake in my ordered house, sucking my blood
Stealthily—and all the time I never knew
That these two sisters were aiming at my throne!
Ismene,
Do you confess your share in this crime, or deny it?
Answer me.

ISMENE: Yes, if she will let me say so. I am guilty.

ANTIGONE (*coldly*): No, Ismene, You have no right to say so.
You would not help me, and I will not have you help me.

ISMENE: But now I know what you meant; and I am here

To join you, to take my share of punishment.
ANTIGONE: The dead man and the gods who rule the dead
  Know whose act this was. Words are not friends.
ISMENE: Do you refuse me, Antigone? I want to die with you:
  I too have a duty that I must discharge to the dead.
ANTIGONE: You shall not lessen my death by sharing it.
ISMENE: What do I care for life when you are dead?
ANTIGONE: Ask Creon. You're always hanging on his opinions.
ISMENE: You are laughing at me. Why, Antigone?
ANTIGONE: It's a joyless laughter, Ismene.
ISMENE: But can I do nothing?
ANTIGONE: Yes. Save yourself. I shall not envy you.
  There are those who will praise you; I shall have honor, too.
ISMENE: But we are equally guilty!
ANTIGONE: No more, Ismene.
  You are alive, but I belong to Death.
CREON (*to the* CHORUS): Gentlemen, I beg you to observe these girls:
  One has just now lost her mind; the other,
  It seems, has never had a mind at all.
ISMENE: Grief teaches the steadiest minds to waver, King.
CREON: Yours certainly did, when you assumed guilt with the guilty!
ISMENE: But how could I go on living without her?
CREON: You are.
  She is already dead.
ISMENE: But your own son's bride!
CREON: There are places enough for him to push his plow.
  I want no wicked women for my sons!
ISMENE: O dearest Haimon, how your father wrongs you!
CREON: I've had enough of your childish talk of marriage!
CHORAGOS: Do you really intend to steal this girl from your son?
CREON: No; Death will do that for me.
CHORAGOS: Then she must die?
CREON (*ironically*): You dazzle me.
                          —But enough of this talk!

(*To* GUARDS.)

You, there, take them away and guard them well:
For they are but women, and even brave men run
When they see Death coming.

(*Exeunt* ISMENE, ANTIGONE, *and* GUARDS.)

ODE II

CHORUS: Fortunate is the man who has never tasted God's vengeance!
   Where once the anger of heaven has struck, that house is shaken
   For ever: damnation rises behind each child
   Like a wave cresting out of the black northeast,
   When the long darkness under sea roars up
   And bursts drumming death upon the windwhipped sand.

[ANTISTROPHE 1

   I have seen this gathering sorrow from time long past
   Loom upon Oedipus' children: generation from generation
   Takes the compulsive rage of the enemy god.
   So lately this last flower of Oedipus' line
   Drank the sunlight! but now a passionate word
   And a handful of dust have closed up all its beauty.

       What mortal arrogance   [STROPHE 2
       Transcends the wrath of Zeus?
   Sleep cannot lull him, nor the effortless long months
   Of the timeless gods: but he is young for ever,
   And his house is the shining day of high Olympus.
         All that is and shall be,
         And all the past, is his.
   No pride on earth is free of the curse of heaven.

       The straying dreams of men   [ANTISTROPHE 2
       May bring them ghosts of joy:
   But as they drowse, the waking embers burn them;
   Or they walk with fixed eyes, as blind men walk.
   But the ancient wisdom speaks for our own time:
         Fate works most for woe
         With Folly's fairest show.
   Man's little pleasure is the spring of sorrow.

SCENE III

CHORAGOS: But here is Haimon, King, the last of all your sons.
   Is it grief for Antigone that brings him here,
   And bitterness at being robbed of his bride?

(*Enter* HAIMON.)

CREON: We shall soon see, and no need of diviners.

—Son,
You have heard my final judgment on that girl:
Have you come here hating me, or have you come
With deference and with love, whatever I do?
HAIMON: I am your son, father. You are my guide.
You make things clear for me, and I obey you.
No marriage means more to me than your continuing wisdom.
CREON: Good. That is the way to behave: subordinate
Everything else, my son, to your father's will.
This is what a man prays for, that he may get
Sons attentive and dutiful in his house,
Each one hating his father's enemies,
Honoring his father's friends. But if his sons
Fail him, if they turn out unprofitably,
What has he fathered but trouble for himself
And amusement for the malicious?

So you are right
Not to lose your head over this woman.
Your pleasure with her would soon grow cold, Haimon,
And then you'd have a hellcat in bed and elsewhere.
Let her find her husband in Hell!
Of all the people in this city, only she
Has had contempt for my law and broken it.
Do you want me to show myself weak before the people?
Or to break my sworn word? No, and I will not.
The woman dies.
I suppose she'll plead "family ties." Well, let her.
If I permit my own family to rebel,
How shall I earn the world's obedience?
Show me the man who keeps his house in hand,
He's fit for public authority.

I'll have no dealings
With law-breakers, critics of the government:
Whoever is chosen to govern should be obeyed—
Must be obeyed, in all things, great and small,
Just and unjust! O Haimon,
The man who knows how to obey, and that man only,
Knows how to give commands when the time comes.
You can depend on him, no matter how fast
The spears come: he's a good soldier, he'll stick it out.

Anarchy, anarchy! Show me a greater evil!
This is why cities tumble and the great houses rain down,
This is what scatters armies!

No, no: good lives are made so by discipline.
We keep the laws then, and the lawmakers,
And no woman shall seduce us. If we must lose,
Let's lose to a man, at least! Is a woman stronger than we?
CHORAGOS: Unless time has rusted my wits,
What you say, King, is said with point and dignity.
HAIMON (*boyishly earnest*): Father:
Reason is God's crowning gift to man, and you are right
To warn me against losing mine. I cannot say—
I hope that I shall never want to say!—that you
Have reasoned badly. Yet there are other men
Who can reason, too; and their opinions might be helpful.
You are not in a position to know everything
That people say or do, or what they feel:
Your temper terrifies them—everyone
Will tell you only what you like to hear.
But I, at any rate, can listen; and I have heard them
Muttering and whispering in the dark about this girl.
They say no woman has ever, so unreasonably,
Died so shameful a death for a generous act:
"She covered her brother's body. Is this indecent?
She kept him from dogs and vultures. Is this a crime?
Death?—She should have all the honor that we can give her!"

This is the way they talk out there in the city.

You must believe me:
Nothing is closer to me than your happiness.
What could be closer? Must not any son
Value his father's fortune as his father does his?
I beg you, do not be unchangeable:
Do not believe that you alone can be right.
The man who thinks that,
The man who maintains that only he has the power
To reason correctly, the gift to speak, the soul—
A man like that, when you know him, turns out empty.

It is not reason never to yield to reason!

In flood time you can see how some trees bend,
And because they bend, even their twigs are safe,
While stubborn trees are torn up, roots and all.
And the same thing happens in sailing:
Make your sheet fast, never slacken,—and over you go,
Head over heels and under: and there's your voyage.
Forget you are angry! Let yourself be moved!
I know I am young; but please let me say this:
The ideal condition
Would be, I admit, that men should be right by instinct;
But since we are all too likely to go astray,
The reasonable thing is to learn from those who can teach.

CHORAGOS: You will do well to listen to him, King,
If what he says is sensible. And you, Haimon,
Must listen to your father.—Both speak well.

CREON: You consider it right for a man of my years and experience
To go to school to a boy?

HAIMON: It is not right
If I am wrong. But if I am young, and right,
What does my age matter?

CREON: You think it right to stand up for an anarchist?

HAIMON: Not at all. I pay no respect to criminals.

CREON: Then she is not a criminal?

HAIMON: The City would deny it, to a man.

CREON: And the City proposes to teach me how to rule?

HAIMON: Ah. Who is it that's talking like a boy now?

CREON: My voice is the one voice giving orders in this City!

HAIMON: It is no City if it takes orders from one voice.

CREON: The State is the King!

HAIMON: Yes, if the State is a desert.

(*Pause.*)

CREON: This boy, it seems has sold out to a woman.

HAIMON: If you are a woman: my concern is only for you.

CREON: So? Your "concern"! In a public brawl with your father!

HAIMON: How about you, in a public brawl with justice?

CREON: With justice, when all that I do is within my rights?

HAIMON: You have no right to trample on God's right.

CREON (*completely out of control*): Fool, adolescent fool! Taken in by a
woman!

HAIMON: You'll never see me taken in by anything vile.

CREON: Every word you say is for her!

HAIMON (*quietly, darkly*):   And for you.

And for me. And for the gods under the earth.

CREON: You'll never marry her while she lives.

HAIMON: Then she must die.—But her death will cause another.

CREON: Another?

Have you lost your senses? Is this an open threat?

HAIMON: There is no threat in speaking to emptiness.

CREON: I swear you'll regret this superior tone of yours!

You are the empty one!

HAIMON: If you were not my father,

I'd say you were perverse.

CREON: You girlstruck fool, don't play at words with me!

HAIMON: I am sorry. You prefer silence.

CREON: Now, by God—!

I swear, by all the gods in heaven above us,

You'll watch it, I swear you shall!

(*To the* SERVANTS.)   Bring her out!

Bring the woman out! Let her die before his eyes!

Here, this instant, with her bridegroom beside her!

HAIMON: Not here, no; she will not die here, King.

And you will never see my face again.

Go on raving as long as you've a friend to endure you.

(*Exit* HAIMON.)

CHORAGOS: Gone, gone.

Creon, a young man in a rage is dangerous!

CREON: Let him do, or dream to do, more than a man can.

He shall not save these girls from death.

CHORAGOS: These girls?

You have sentenced them both?

CREON: No, you are right.

I will not kill the one whose hands are clean.

CHORAGOS: But Antigone?

CREON (*somberly*):   I will carry her far away

Out there in the wilderness, and lock her

Living in a vault of stone. She shall have food,

As the custom is, to absolve the State of her death.

And there let her pray to the gods of hell:

They are her only gods:

Perhaps they will show her an escape from death,

Or she may learn,

          though late,

That piety shown the dead is pity in vain.

(*Exit* CREON.)

ODE III

CHORUS: Love, unconquerable   [STROPHE
    Waster of rich men, keeper
    Of warm lights and all-night vigil
    In the soft face of a girl:
    Sea-wanderer, forest-visitor!
    Even the pure Immortals cannot escape you,
    And mortal man, in his one day's dusk,
    Trembles before your glory.

    Surely you swerve upon ruin   [ANTISTROPHE
    The just man's consenting heart,
    As here you have made bright anger
    Strike between father and son—
    And none has conquered but Love!
    A girl's glance working the will of heaven:
    Pleasure to her alone who mocks us,
    Merciless Aphrodite.

SCENE IV

(As ANTIGONE enters guarded.)

CHORAGOS: But I can no longer stand in awe of this,
    Nor, seeing what I see, keep back my tears.
    Here is Antigone, passing to that chamber
    Where all find sleep at last.

ANTIGONE: Look upon me, friends, and pity me   [STROPHE 1
    Turning back at the night's edge to say
    Good-by to the sun that shines for me no longer;
    Now sleepy Death
    Summons me down to Acheron, that cold shore:
    There is no bridesong there, nor any music.
CHORUS: Yet not unpraised, not without a kind of honor,
    You walk at last into the underworld;
    Untouched by sickness, broken by no sword.
    What woman has ever found your way to death?

ANTIGONE: How often I have heard the story of Niobe,   [ANTISTROPHE 1

Tantalos' wretched daughter, how the stone
Clung fast about her, ivy-close: and they say
The rain falls endlessly
And sifting soft snow; her tears are never done.
I feel the loneliness of her death in mine.
CHORUS: But she was born of heaven, and you
Are woman, woman-born. If her death is yours,
A mortal woman's, is this not for you
Glory in our world and in the world beyond?

ANTIGONE: You laugh at me. Ah, friends, friends,   [STROPHE 2
Can you not wait until I am dead? O Thebes,
O men many-charioted, in love with Fortune,
Dear springs of Dirce, sacred Theban grove,
Be witnesses for me, denied all pity,
Unjustly judged! and think a word of love
For her whose path turns
Under dark earth, where there are no more tears.
CHORUS: You have passed beyond human daring and come at last
Into a place of stone where Justice sits.
I cannot tell
What shape of your father's guilt appears in this.

                                       [ANTISTROPHE 2
ANTIGONE: You have touched it at last: that bridal bed
Unspeakable, horror of son and mother mingling:
Their crime, infection of all our family!
O Oedipus, father and brother!
Your marriage strikes from the grave to murder mine.
I have been a stranger here in my own land:
All my life
The blasphemy of my birth has followed me.
CHORUS: Reverence is a virtue, but strength
Lives in established law: that must prevail.
You have made your choice,
Your death is the doing of your conscious hand.

ANTIGONE: Then let me go, since all your words are bitter,   [EPODE
And the very light of the sun is cold to me.
Lead me to my vigil, where I must have
Neither love nor lamentation; no song, but silence.

(CREON *interrupts impatiently.*)

CREON: If dirges and planned lamentations could put off death,
Men would be singing for ever.
(*To the* SERVANTS.)   Take her, go!
You know your orders: take her to the vault
And leave her alone there. And if she lives or dies,
That's her affair, not ours: our hands are clean.

ANTIGONE: O tomb, vaulted bride-bed in eternal rock,
Soon I shall be with my own again
Where Persephone welcomes the thin ghosts underground:
And I shall see my father again, and you, mother,
And dearest Polyneices—
                dearest indeed
To me, since it was my hand
That washed him clean and poured the ritual wine:
And my reward is death before my time!

And yet, as men's hearts know, I have done no wrong,
I have not sinned before God. Or if I have,
I shall know the truth in death. But if the guilt
Lies upon Creon who judged me, then, I pray,
May his punishment equal my own.

CHORAGOS: O passionate heart,
Unyielding, tormented still by the same winds!

CREON: Her guards shall have good cause to regret their delaying.

ANTIGONE: Ah! That voice is like the voice of death!

CREON: I can give you no reason to think you are mistaken.

ANTIGONE: Thebes, and you my fathers' gods,
And rulers of Thebes, you see me now, the last
Unhappy daughter of a line of kings,
Your kings, led away to death. You will remember
What things I suffer, and at what men's hands,
Because I would not transgress the laws of heaven.

(*To the* GUARDS, *simply.*)

Come: let us wait no longer.

(*Exit* ANTIGONE, *L., guarded.*)

ODE IV

CHORUS: All Danae's beauty was locked away   [STROPHE 1
In a brazen cell where the sunlight could not come:

A small room, still as any grave, enclosed her.
Yet she was a princess too,
And Zeus in a rain of gold poured love upon her.
O child, child,
No power in wealth or war
Or tough sea-blackened ships
Can prevail against untiring Destiny!

And Dryas' son also, that furious king,   [ANTISTROPHE 1
Bore the god's prisoning anger for his pride:
Sealed up by Dionysus in deaf stone,
His madness died among echoes.
So at the last he learned what dreadful power
His tongue had mocked:
For he had profaned the revels,
And fired the wrath of the nine
Implacable Sisters that love the sound of the flute.

And old men tell a half-remembered tale   [STROPHE 2
Of horror done where a dark ledge splits the sea
And a double surf beats on the gray shores:
How a king's new woman, sick
With hatred for the queen he had imprisoned,
Ripped out his two sons' eyes with her bloody hands
While grinning Ares watched the shuttle plunge
Four times: four blind wounds crying for revenge,

Crying, tears and blood mingled.—Piteously born,   [ANTISTROPHE 2
Those sons whose mother was of heavenly birth!
Her father was the god of the North Wind
And she was cradled by gales,
She raced with young colts on the glittering hills
And walked untrammeled in the open light:
But in her marriage deathless Fate found means
To build a tomb like yours for all her joy.

SCENE V

(Enter blind TEIRESIAS, *led by a* BOY. *The opening speeches of* TEIRESIAS *should be in singsong contrast to the realistic lines of* CREON.*)*

TEIRESIAS: This is the way the blind man comes, Princes, Princes,
    Lock-step, two heads lit by the eyes of one.
CREON: What new thing have you to tell us, old Teiresias?
TEIRESIAS: I have much to tell you: listen to the prophet, Creon.
CREON: I am not aware that I have ever failed to listen.
TEIRESIAS: Then you have done wisely, King, and ruled well.
CREON: I admit my debt to you. But what have you to say?
TEIRESIAS: This, Creon: you stand once more on the edge of fate.
CREON: What do you mean? Your words are a kind of dread.
TEIRESIAS: Listen, Creon:
    I was sitting in my chair of augury, at the place
    Where the birds gather about me. They were all a-chatter,
    As is their habit, when suddenly I heard
    A strange note in their jangling, a scream, a
    Whirring fury; I knew that they were fighting,
    Tearing each other, dying
    In a whirlwind of wings clashing. And I was afraid.
    I began the rites of burnt-offering at the altar,
    But Hephaistos failed me: instead of bright flame,
    There was only the sputtering slime of the fat thigh-flesh
    Melting: the entrails dissolved in gray smoke,
    The bare bone burst from the welter. And no blaze!

    This was a sign from heaven. My boy described it,
    Seeing for me as I see for others.

    I tell you, Creon, you yourself have brought
    This new calamity upon us. Our hearths and altars
    Are stained with the corruption of dogs and carrion birds
    That glut themselves on the corpse of Oedipus' son.
    The gods are deaf when we pray to them, their fire
    Recoils from our offering, their birds of omen
    Have no cry of comfort, for they are gorged
    With the thick blood of the dead.
                         O my son,
    These are no trifles! Think: all men make mistakes,

But a good man yields when he knows his course is wrong,
And repairs the evil. The only crime is pride.

Give in to the dead man, then: do not fight with a corpse—
What glory is it to kill a man who is dead?
Think, I beg you:
It is for your own good that I speak as I do.
You should be able to yield for your own good.

CREON: It seems that prophets have made me their especial province.
  All my life long
  I have been a kind of butt for the dull arrows
  Of doddering fortune-tellers!
                  No, Teiresias:
  If your birds—if the great eagles of God himself
  Should carry him stinking bit by bit to heaven,
  I would not yield. I am not afraid of pollution:
  No man can defile the gods.
               Do what you will,
  Go into business, make money, speculate
  In India gold or that synthetic gold from Sardis,
  Get rich otherwise than by my consent to bury him.
  Teiresias, it is a sorry thing when a wise man
  Sells his wisdom, lets out his words for hire!
TEIRESIAS: Ah Creon! Is there no man left in the world—
CREON: To do what?—come, let's have the aphorism!
TEIRESIAS: No man who knows that wisdom outweighs any wealth?
CREON: As surely as bribes are baser than any baseness.
TEIRESIAS: You are sick, Creon! You are deathly sick!
CREON: As you say: it is not my place to challenge a prophet.
TEIRESIAS: Yet you have said my prophecy is for sale.
CREON: The generation of prophets has always loved gold.
TEIRESIAS: The generation of kings has always loved brass.
CREON: You forget yourself! You are speaking to your King.
TEIRESIAS: I know it. You are a king because of me.
CREON: You have a certain skill; but you have sold out.
TEIRESIAS: King, you will drive me to words that—
CREON: Say them, say them!
  Only remember: I will not pay you for them.
TEIRESIAS: No, you will find them too costly.
CREON: No doubt. Speak:
  Whatever you say, you will not change my will.
TEIRESIAS: Then take this, and take it to heart!

The time is not far off when you shall pay back
Corpse for corpse, flesh of your own flesh.
You have thrust the child of this world into living night,
You have kept from the gods below the child that is theirs:
The one in a grave before her death, the other,
Dead, denied the grave. This is your crime:
And the Furies and the dark gods of Hell
Are swift with terrible punishment for you.

Do you want to buy me now, Creon?

                              Not many days,
And your house will be full of men and women weeping,
And curses will be hurled at you from far
Cities grieving for sons unburied, left to rot
Before the walls of Thebes.

These are my arrows, Creon: they are all for you.

(*To* BOY.)

But come, child: lead me home.
Let him waste his fine anger upon younger men.
Maybe he will learn at last
To control a wiser tongue in a better head.

(*Exit* TEIRESIAS.)

CHORAGOS: The old man has gone, King, but his words
    Remain to plague us. I am old, too,
    But I cannot remember that he was ever false.
CREON: That is true. . . . It troubles me.
    Oh it is hard to give in! but it is worse
    To risk everything for stubborn pride.
CHORAGOS: Creon: take my advice.
CREON: What shall I do?
CHORAGOS: Go quickly: free Antigone from her vault
    And build a tomb for the body of Polyneices.
CREON: You would have me do this?
CHORAGOS: Creon, yes!
    And it must be done at once: God moves
    Swiftly to cancel the folly of stubborn men.
CREON: It is hard to deny the heart! But I
    Will do it: I will not fight with destiny.
CHORAGOS: You must go yourself, you cannot leave it to others.

CREON: I will go.
                    —Bring axes, servants:
Come with me to the tomb. I buried her, I
Will set her free.
                    Oh quickly!
My mind misgives—
The laws of the gods are mighty, and a man must serve them
To the last day of his life!

(*Exit* CREON.)

PAEAN

CHORAGOS: God of many names   [STROPHE 1
CHORUS: O Iacchos
                                   son
    of Kadmeian Sémele
                    O born of the Thunder!
    Guardian of the West
                    Regent
    of Eleusis' plain
                    O Prince of maenad Thebes
    and the Dragon Field by rippling Ismenos:

CHORAGOS: God of many names   [ANTISTROPHE 1
CHORUS: the flame of torches
    flares on our hills
                    the nymphs of Iacchos
    dance at the spring of Castalia:

    from the vine-close mountain
                    come ah come in ivy:
    Evohé evohé! sings through the streets of Thebes

CHORAGOS: God of many names   [STROPHE 2
CHORUS: Iacchos of Thebes
    heavenly Child
                    of Sémele bride of the Thunderer!
    The shadow of plague is upon us:
                                   come
    with clement feet
                    oh come from Parnassus

down the long slopes
> across the lamenting water

CHORAGOS: Io Fire! Chorister of the throbbing stars!   [ANTISTROPHE 2
O purest among the voices of the night!
Thou son of God, blaze for us!
CHORUS: Come with choric rapture of circling Maenads
Who cry Io Iacche!
> *God of many names!*

EXODOS

(*Enter* MESSENGER, *L.*)

MESSENGER: Men of the line of Kadmos, you who live
Near Amphion's citadel:
> I cannot say
Of any condition of human life, "This is fixed,
This is clearly good, or bad." Fate raises up,
And Fate casts down the happy and unhappy alike:
No man can foretell his Fate.
> Take the case of Creon:
Creon was happy once, as I count happiness:
Victorious in battle, sole governor of the land,
Fortunate father of children nobly born.
And now it has all gone from him! Who can say
That a man is still alive when his life's joy fails?
He is a walking dead man. Grant him rich,
Let him live like a king in his great house:
If his pleasure is gone, I would not give
So much as the shadow of smoke for all he owns.
CHORAGOS: Your words hint at sorrow: what is your news for us?
MESSENGER: They are dead. The living are guilty of their death.
CHORAGOS: Who is guilty? Who is dead? Speak!
MESSENGER:
> Haimon.
Haimon is dead; and the hand that killed him
Is his own hand.
CHORAGOS: His father's? or his own?
MESSENGER: His own, driven mad by the murder his father had done.
CHORAGOS: Teiresias, Teiresias, how clearly you saw it all!
MESSENGER: This is my news: you must draw what conclusions you can
from it.

CHORAGOS: But look: Eurydice, our Queen:
　Has she overheard us?

(*Enter* EURYDICE *from the Palace, C.*)

EURYDICE: I have heard something, friends:
　As I was unlocking the gate of Pallas' shrine,
　For I needed her help today, I heard a voice
　Telling of some new sorrow. And I fainted
　There at the temple with all my maidens about me.
　But speak again: whatever it is, I can bear it:
　Grief and I are no strangers.

MESSENGER: 　　　　　　　Dearest Lady,
　I will tell you plainly all that I have seen.
　I shall not try to comfort you: what is the use,
　Since comfort could lie only in what is not true?
　The truth is always best.

　　　　　　　　　I went with Creon
　To the outer plain where Polyneices was lying,
　No friend to pity him, his body shredded by dogs.
　We made our prayers in that place to Hecate
　And Pluto, that they would be merciful. And we bathed
　The corpse with holy water, and we brought
　Fresh-broken branches to burn what was left of it,
　And upon the urn we heaped up a towering barrow
　Of the earth of his own land.
　　　　　　　　　When we were done, we ran
　To the vault where Antigone lay on her couch of stone.
　One of the servants had gone ahead,
　And while he was yet far off he heard a voice
　Grieving within the chamber, and he came back
　And told Creon. And as the King went closer,
　The air was full of wailing, the words lost,
　And he begged us to make all haste. "Am I a prophet?"
　He said, weeping, "And must I walk this road,
　The saddest of all that I have gone before?
　My son's voice calls me on. Oh quickly, quickly!
　Look through the crevice there, and tell me
　If it is Haimon, or some deception of the gods!"
　We obeyed; and in the cavern's farthest corner
　We saw her lying:
　She had made a noose of her fine linen veil
　And hanged herself. Haimon lay beside her,
　His arms about her waist, lamenting her,

His love lost under ground, crying out
That his father had stolen her away from him.
When Creon saw him the tears rushed to his eyes
And he called to him: "What have you done, child? Speak to me.
What are you thinking that makes your eyes so strange?
O my son. my son, I come to you on my knees!"
But Haimon spat in his face. He said not a word,
Staring—
        And suddenly drew his sword
And lunged. Creon shrank back, the blade missed; and the boy,
Desperate against himself, drove it half its length
Into his own side, and fell. And as he died
He gathered Antigone close in his arms again,
Choking, his blood bright red on her white cheek.
And now he lies dead with the dead, and she is his
At last, his bride in the houses of the dead.

(*Exit* EURYDICE *into the Palace.*)

CHORAGOS: She has left us without a word. What can this mean?
MESSENGER: It troubles me, too; yet she knows what is best,
  Her grief is too great for public lamentation,
  And doubtless she has gone to her chamber to weep
  For her dead son, leading her maidens in his dirge.
CHORAGOS: It may be so: but I fear this deep silence.

(*Pause.*)

MESSENGER: I will see what she is doing. I will go in.

(*Exit* MESSENGER *into the Palace. Enter* CREON *with attendants, bearing* HAIMON'S *body.*)

CHORAGOS: But here is the King himself: oh look at him,
  Bearing his own damnation in his arms.
CREON: Nothing you say can touch me any more.
  My own blind heart has brought me
  From darkness to final darkness. Here you see
  The father murdering, the murdered son—
  And all my civic wisdom!

  Haimon my son, so young, so young to die,
  I was the fool, not you; and you died for me.
CHORAGOS: That is the truth; but you were late in learning it.
CREON: This truth is hard to bear. Surely a god
  Has crushed me beneath the hugest weight of heaven.

And driven me headlong a barbaric way
To trample out the thing I held most dear.

The pains that men will take to come to pain!

(*Enter* MESSENGER *from the Palace.*)

MESSENGER: The burden you carry in your hands is heavy,
But it is not all: you will find more in your house.
CREON: What burden worse than this shall I find there?
MESSENGER: The Queen is dead.
CREON: O port of death, deaf world,
Is there no pity for me? And you, Angel of evil,
I was dead, and your words are death again.
Is it true, boy? Can it be true?
Is my wife dead? Has death bred death?
MESSENGER: You can see for yourself.

(*The doors are opened, and the body of* EURYDICE *is disclosed within.*)

CREON: Oh pity!
All true, all true, and more than I can bear!
O my wife, my son!
MESSENGER: She stood before the altar, and her heart
Welcomed the knife her own hand guided,
And a great cry burst from her lips for Megareus dead,
And for Haimon dead, her sons; and her last breath
Was a curse for their father, the murderer of her sons.
And she fell, and the dark flowed in through her closing eyes.
CREON: O God, I am sick with fear.
Are there no swords here? Has no one a blow for me?
MESSENGER: Her curse is upon you for the deaths of both.
CREON: It is right that it should be. I alone am guilty.
I know it, and I say it. Lead me in,
Quickly, friends.
I have neither life nor substance. Lead me in.
CHORAGOS: You are right, if there can be right in so much wrong.
The briefest way is best in a world of sorrow.
CREON: Let it come,
Let death come quickly, and be kind to me.
I would not ever see the sun again.
CHORAGOS: All that will come when it will; but we, meanwhile,
Have much to do. Leave the future to itself.
CREON: All my heart was in that prayer!

CHORAGOS: Then do not pray any more: the sky is deaf.
CREON: Lead me away. I have been rash and foolish.
  I have killed my son and my wife.
  I look for comfort; my comfort lies here dead.
  Whatever my hands have touched has come to nothing.
  Fate has brought all my pride to a thought of dust.

(As CREON *is being led into the house, the* CHORAGOS *advances and speaks directly to the audience.*)

CHORAGOS: There is no happiness where there is no wisdom;
  No wisdom but in submission to the gods.
  Big words are always punished,
  And proud men in old age learn to be wise.

Iacchos of Thebes . . .
  The shadow of plague is upon us:

                                       come
   with clement feet
                    oh come from Parnassus
  down the long slopes
                across the lamenting water

So chants the Chorus in dark apprehension of further doom as the shaken Creon goes off to save his victim Antigone. The invocation of Dionysus, the many-named god of fertility and rebirth, is only incidental to the plot proper, but it is very much to the purpose of the tragic feeling in the play, and it is everything to an understanding of the position of tragedy in the communal life of fifth-century Athens.* In the spring of every year three tetralogies (three tragedies and a satyr play, all acted in one day) were selected for performance in a competition that was part of the larger rites of the Greater (or Urban) Dionysia. Although we do not know the origin of tragedy, nothing in the plays themselves nor in what we know of the manner of their performance

---

*By tragic drama in this connection is meant serious drama on metaphysically important themes but not necessarily of catastrophic outcome. The word "tragedy" means literally "goat-song," perhaps with reference to the early satyr plays in which the choric performers of the dithyrambic dance-song were dressed in goat skins. The origin of Greek drama in the cult of Dionysus has been disputed by some scholars, but there is general agreement that the Dionysiac festival was the exclusive setting for theatrical performance.

prevents our believing that tragic drama arose from the desire in the celebrants of nature's seasonal revival to express, in music, movement, chant, and spectacle, their sense of divine power over human life. Staging and acting in Dionysiac plays was a religious and civic obligation on free citizens and victory in the contest one of the supreme communal honors. For us drama is primarily entertainment, or, at most, stimulus to reflection and debate. To a fifth-century Athenian it was a ceremony that was meaningful in more than one area of his being. Only with this in mind will we understand the partly extra-dramatic function of the chorus as a kind of audience representative on the periphery of the action, worried and ignorant, affected by what happens but not participant in it.

Our knowledge of the specific physical features of the Dionysiac theater of Athens is uncertain. The audience—perhaps as many as 15,000—was seated on benches in rising concentric tiers on the southeastern slope of the Acropolis. The plays were enacted before a long, low, wooden building (*skene*), that served both as dressing room and as the palace front of conventional dramatic setting. The main action took place immediately before it. Nearer the audience and probably on a somewhat lower level was a circular area (*orchestra*), with an altar for Dionysus in the center. Here the chorus—in Sophoclean tragedy a group of fifteen men—led by the *coryphaeus* and accompanied by flute playing, moved in slow and stately measures while chanting lyrical odes dealing with the inscrutable ways of gods with men and usually having some particular reference to the immediate dramatic situation. Thus, when Haimon, desperate and angry, leaves at the end of Scene III after pleading in vain with his father for Antigone's life, the Chorus praises the power of Aphrodite, the goddess of love. The odes were divided into stanzas, called *strophes* and *antistrophes,* delivered, respectively, as the chorus moved first in one and then in the opposite direction. In the absence of a curtain one function of the odes was to mark the divisions between the different episodes (the first of which was the *prologos,* the last the *exodos*). Both actors and chorus wore masks, not, as was once thought, for reasons of acoustics (each mask serving as a kind of megaphone), but rather, perhaps, in order to create an impression of depersonalized and universal myth and to permit doubling of roles. They were dressed in colored robes. Women's parts were played by men. Performance of a tetralogy took most of the daylight hours.

Antigone was written about 440 B.C., when Sophocles was already in his mid-fifties. It is among his earliest plays. We do not know its fortune in the annual competition, but together with *Oedipus Rex* (not part of the same tetralogy; we don't have *Antigone's* companion pieces), *Antigone* is traditionally considered one of the purest specimens of Greek tragedy.

The two plays have more in common than a high reputation. In both Sophocles imparts a tragic lesson about man's powerlessness before the gods, and in both he does so by means of the old legend of the divine curse on the Theban royal family, the house of Labdacus.* Dramatic irony is important in both, as it almost inevitably must be in any literary expression of man's tragic–absurd awareness of the perils of his position. Dramatic irony is what we are aware of when, in something said or in some circumstance of the plot, we sense a meaning beyond or at odds with the overt meaning. Below the surface truth there is a larger truth, usually inimical to the speaker and unsuspected by him. When Oedipus in *Oedipus Rex* swears to avenge the murdered King Laïos "as if he were my own father," it is by dramatic irony that we sense the nature of his approaching doom. We are dealing here not just with an artistic device or a trick of playmaking but with a mode of language by which parts of a complex truth are perceived and held in suspension. The irony points up the discrepancy between what the speaker is and what he thinks he is—between what is and what appears to be. It gives expression, situational or verbal, to the inadequacy of man's defenses and the folly of his feeling of safety and power (*hubris*) in an existence he can actually neither comprehend nor control. It is the literary equivalent of the paradox that we both master and are mastered by our circumstances, that our entrapment in time gives to each of our free acts a terrible and final significance. It is existential tension encapsuled and made available for disinterested contemplation. Creon's telling the

---

*Labdacus's son was Laïos. Despite Laïos's and his wife Jocasta's efforts to circumvent the prophecy of the Delphic oracle, he was killed by his son Oedipus, who next, in further unwitting fulfillment of his destiny, married Jocasta. Their children were Eteocles, Polyneices, Ismene, and Antigone. Later Oedipus discovered his true parentage and realized that his terrible fate had come to pass.

There is nothing extraordinary in the fact that the story of *Oedipus Rex* is referred to in *Antigone*, though the latter is the earlier of the two plays. The history of the royal house of Thebes was part of traditional legend and as well known to Sophocles' audience as to Sophocles himself. For a playwright there is limitation in this but also strength. He is tied to the known facts, but by the same token he can dispense with the laborious exposition that clutters many an "original" play of more modern times. With the tragic myth given, he can proceed at once to essentials: not the telling of a story but dramatizing its meaning.

Chorus that the defiant Antigone "has much to learn" and his words to the girl herself that "your death will give me everything" convey, in context, a sense that pride and complacency are forms of ignorance.

The tragic place is bare and bleak and its climate violent. Tragic life runs to extremes, stripped of the softening and sheltering loose ends and compromises, half-tones and compensations, of ordinary life. In Aeschylean and Sophoclean tragedy dramatic movement is so spare and single and so momentous that the busy fuss of illusionism would be an impertinence. Larger issues are involved than making the world look and sound like everyday reality. Tragic realism confronts man with the supernatural dimension. When Aristotle said (in the *Poetics*) that the end of tragedy is imitation of action, he did not lay down a law. He was being inductive; he stated what seemed to him a fact about existing plays. They were imitations of action not by being faithful copies of appearances (as is representational art), but by dramatizing archetypes.

The function of tragedy, Aristotle says, is to effect *katharsis,* i.e., the purgation of the emotions of pity and fear in the audience. The exact meaning of the concept has been debated, but the medical denotation suggests that Aristotle had in mind some kind of soul therapy: witnessing the tragic action the spectator harmlessly expends his subrational passions on vicarious suffering. Because the effect presupposes a degree of audience identification, the protagonist can be neither vicious nor perfect. Suffering vice commands no sympathy, and suffering perfection would seem merely preposterous.

Art is moral to the extent that it furthers the percipient's grasp of reality, principally the reality of himself. But the nature of that for which a moral function is predicated is, precisely, artistic, and all criticism is in a sense criticism of form. First, because form and moral content are inseparable (though not indistinguishable), just as the "meaning" of any work of art inheres in the configuration our senses perceive rather than, abstractly, in any detachable dictum. Thus, in the middle part of *Antigone,* the changes in Creon's emotions from the sententiousness of his opening address to the Chorus, through his anger and contempt and impatience in the scenes with the two sisters and with Haimon, to his fear of Teiresias, constitute a scenic image of instability that defines a condition in which and by which man suffers. Second, the achievement of meaningful form is itself meaningful. In tragedy the containment of metaphysics in coherent speech–action is a demiurgic gesture shaping order out of debris, beauty out of pain. In the imagined world his art makes, man, the maker, triumphs over agony and anger by transfixing them in art's frozen moment. Form illumines his fate and allows him to see that it matters. This is why elation and dignity, not depression, attend the tragic vision and *katharsis* becomes one with enlightenment.

The action of both *Oedipus Rex* and *Antigone* illustrates the tragic formula of "the evil that good men do." Creon is unaware, till it is too late, of what he is doing to his life. But if good intentions exculpate, does he deserve his punishment? "The sky is deaf." Tragedy cannot answer; it only shows punishment taking place. If the spectacle offends our sense of justice, so be it. Existence is not answerable before our puny tribunals. What the play *does* do is describe a dramatic movement that exactly covers its larger "truth." When the play begins, Antigone is alone against all the others: Ismene, Creon, the Chorus, the Sentry. At the end it is Creon who is isolated. First Ismene, then Haimon, take Antigone's side. Then Teiresias appears with his warning, the Chorus wavers in fear and uncertainty, Creon himself goes off to submit to his enemy, and finally the eloquent Messenger takes the boorish Sentry's place as spokesman for the common soldier's judgment on the issue between king and girl. The shift in public support from one to the other is as simple and striking as theater as it is subtle in meaning. Take the Sentry. Too often dismissed as mere "comic relief," actually his two appearances (apart from their obvious plot function) foreshadow in a lower key Creon's equally sudden and unexpected change of attitude near the end. First timid and trembling, then all smug swagger, the Sentry undergoes a psychological movement that is reversely analogous to Creon's from imperious bluster to broken pathos. He serves to make Sophocles' religious point that clown and king alike are pawns in the hands of higher powers that mock man's firmest resolutions.

That Creon rather than Antigone might be the tragic protagonist may seem contradicted by the title, and the issue of whose play *Antigone* is is less simple than the discussion above has suggested. Without Antigone, no challenge, no conflict, no play. The tragedy is double: first hers, then Creon's. But the title does not imply her tragic precedence—if it did the play would be imbalanced, as she disappears about two thirds of the way through—and her almost perfect integrity of character and singleness of purpose suggest a saint rather than an erring and embattled hero. The tragic status of the sainted martyr is problematic, for eschatology annuls the tragic premise that human existence is finite. The saint's tragedy is less the saint's own than the world's, which in ignorance deprives itself of its savior. Of the two tragic destinies in the play, only Creon's completes the tragic arc into self-recognition: "I have been rash and foolish." By the time the play ends, Antigone's and Ismene's opening scene appears as the first phase in Creon's tragedy, a prologue introducing the issue on which he is going to be wrecked.

Antigone is simple where Creon is complex, strong where he is weak. Her mind is made up from the beginning, and hardly anything happens to her that she has not foreseen. Her strength marks her "right" against her uncle's "wrong," but it also comes close to making her a character without inner conflict. She is dramatically the less interesting of the two. Her humanity is first evident in the scene (II) in which Ismene appears a second time and pleads with her sister to let her share her punishment. Its point is not the superfluous one of strengthening the justice of Antigone's cause but the rescue of Creon's antagonist from the thin, chill air of homiletic parable. In Antigone's cruelty to Ismene the professional martyr vanishes and the anguished young woman takes her place, jealous of the lonely glory of her death.*

For Antigone's character is compact with uncompromising religious idealism, which the play consistently presents as an absolute right (in both senses of the word), and her martyrdom is victory and not defeat. But for Creon both the inner and the outer universe go to pieces. When Antigone departs for her cave death at the end of Scene IV, the conflict is no longer that of two equally stubborn convictions. It, too, turns inward, as Creon's *hubris* begins to disintegrate under the successive blows of religious fear and family deaths. Perhaps the grimmest irony of all in the play is the fact that he who would force his sister's child and his son's bride to repudiate a family bond pays for his tyranny with the loss of niece, son, and wife. Eurydice's late entry into the action only to die is therefore not gratuitous melodrama. It illustrates the rationale of tragic nemesis, the power of retribution.

To Creon, newly called to power and as yet untried in authority, anarchy is the greatest evil. In the light of the immediate Theban past he can hardly be held to be wrong. And his fierce stubbornness in up-

---

* Read in this light, the scene serves to support Professor Kitto's contention (in *Greek Tragedy*) that there is added tragic feeling and psychological penetration in Antigone's pitifully sophistical defense of her action on the grounds that only a brother is worthy of the sacrifice she makes, because, both her parents being dead, a brother, unlike a husband and a son, is irreplaceable. Fitts and Fitzgerald omit the passage from their translation as "dismal stuff," which "the best critics" have thought spurious. It consists of sixteen lines at the very end of Scene IV, just before Antigone asks to be led away.

holding his edict does not so much bespeak a tyrant's temper as the defense mechanism of a troubled and conscientious man in a responsible position in which he has yet to prove himself. He cannot afford to see more than one side of the issue. Political circumstance joins his own character in limiting his vision to the immediate business of governing a war-torn state. A more fatal limitation in his psyche, one of imagination, is suggested by his repeated assertion that money must be the motive behind the unlawful burial of Polyneices.

Up to a point Creon's attitude is of course right. Within the sphere of good government and social order anarchy is indeed a very great evil. But there is a sphere, the play says, beyond law and order which Creon, the anxious king, has lost sight of. On one level the conflict between Antigone and him is a conflict between individual liberty—freedom of faith, if one likes—and a totalitarian tyranny that presumes to dictate to the individual conscience in all areas of life. It was as exponent of this topical theme that the play was performed on several of Europe's liberated stages right after World War II. But on another level the dramatic allegory is not political at all or even ethical, but religious, and the conflict is one between eternal and temporal schemes of value, or, more exactly, between a sacramental and a civic–pragmatic view of life. Not that Creon's tragic flaw (*hamartia*) is that he is irreligious. He, too, is sure that he executes the will of the gods. But it does not occur to him that the gods rule by higher considerations than those of police-state expediency. As the purely symbolic nature of Antigone's burial of Polyneices suggests, disposal of a body is not the issue but which of two allegiances is to have priority, that to the state or that to the gods. By pursuing punishment of the traitor (and note that Antigone never denies the justice of Creon's label for her brother) beyond the limits of life Creon seeks to extend his rule into eschatological regions. In retaliation, the angry gods strike the trespasser down. Again truth is communicated in dramatic irony: Theban events prove that he who is nothing but a good citizen fails to be even that, for Antigone's course of action would have saved the city from further supernatural visitation. By the laws of a larger realm than the city state it is Creon himself, the usurper of divine power, who stands convicted of anarchy. And the difference in the nature of the two realms is pointed up in the paradox—from the world's point of view—that a young girl, a subject, triumphs over a mature man, a king.

The Messenger who reports Creon's punishment expresses a wisdom

of humble resignation to the fact of human finitude that keeps man
from challenging fate.

> I cannot say
> Of any condition of human life, "This is fixed,
> This is clearly good, or bad." Fate raises up,
> And Fate casts down the happy and unhappy alike:
> No man can foretell his Fate.
>   Take the case of Creon:
>
>   .   .   .
>   I would not give
> So much as the shadow of smoke for all he owns.

The Messenger is the individual spokesman for this view—the classical
view—of human existence. The Chorus is the communal voice. With
Sophocles the chorus is not, as with Aeschylus, one of the two main
actors in the tragic dialogue, but neither is it the merely traditional and
rather cumbersome appendage that it tended to be with Euripides. At
times, its comments here are amusingly naïve, as when it remains anxiously neutral in the quarrel between father and son:

> You will do well to listen to him, King,
> If what he says is sensible. And you, Haimon,
> Must listen to your father.—Both speak well.

The choric odes are above such comical inanity. Often they extend the
relevance of the archetypal action by mythical allusion (as in Ode IV),
or they contribute to the pervasive ironic pattern by expressing the fears
and ignorance of the common man. A particularly striking example is
the first ode, which praises ingenious man's many achievements. Its
second strophe ends in what we later perceive to have been an ominous
warning:

> . . . from every wind
> He [man] has made himself secure—from all but one:
> In the late wind of death he cannot stand.

This is what the play is about: the fact that with death the survivor's
control must cease, lest he transcend the limits set to mortality, and the
fact of death itself—here Antigone's, Haimon's, and Eurydice's—which
smashes all Creon's arrogance.

Literally, the Chorus is a group of old Thebans—councillors, according to traditional interpretation. As such, they speak in character when they chant the triumphant end of the war with Argos and when the Choragos sums up the meaning of Creon's fate:

> There is no happiness where there is no wisdom;
> No wisdom but in submission to the gods.

The Chorus's continuous stage presence relates Creon's tragedy to the weal of the community he meant to govern so well. Creon's tragic dilemma of reconciling allegiance to the world with allegiance to the world's supernatural rulers is everyman's dilemma.

But his royal position implies that his failure to resolve the dilemma matters more than everyman's. The calamity that follows upon his sacrilegious refusal to bury the dead Polyneices is, as Teiresias knows, not just Creon's but all Thebes'. Creon's suffering is public expiation for an act of suprapersonal consequence, for in the traditional view the king incarnates his people. His fall from fortune followed from his kingly rank, and his redemptive suffering is therefore properly witnessed by representatives of the people whose scapegoat the stricken king of the myth, innocent of intent if not of act, in the end becomes. In the tragic spectacle of the "rash and foolish" Creon the Athenian spectator sensed his own ambiguous position in the cosmic drama and his own dark destiny—both as man and as citizen.

William Shakespeare

Othello

Characters

DUKE OF VENICE
BRABANTIO a *Senator*
SENATORS
GRATIANO *Brother to Brabantio*
LODOVICO *Kinsman to Brabantio*
OTHELLO a *noble Moor; in the service of the Venetian State*
CASSIO *his Lieutenant*
IAGO *his Ancient*
RODERIGO a *Venetian Gentleman*
MONTANO *Othello's predecessor in the Government of Cyprus*
CLOWN *Servant to Othello*
DESDEMONA *Daughter to Brabantio, and Wife to Othello*
EMILIA *Wife to Iago*
BIANCA *Mistress to Cassio*
SAILOR, OFFICERS, GENTLEMEN, MESSENGERS, MUSICIANS, HERALDS,
   ATTENDANTS

Scene: *For the first Act, in Venice; during the rest of the Play, at a Sea-port in Cyprus.*

ACT I

Scene 1 [Venice. A Street.]

(*Enter* RODERIGO *and* IAGO.)

RODERIGO: Tush! Never tell me; I take it much unkindly
   That thou, Iago, who hast had my purse

As if the strings were thine, shouldst know of this.[1]

IAGO: 'Sblood,[2] but you will not hear me:
  If ever I did dream of such a matter,
  Abhor me.

RODERIGO: Thou told'st me thou didst hold him[3] in thy hate.

IAGO: Despise me if I do not. Three great ones of the city,
  In personal suit to make me his lieutenant,
  Off-capp'd[4] to him; and, by the faith of man,
  I know my price, I am worth no worse a place;
  But he, as loving his own pride and purposes,
  Evades them, with a bombast circumstance[5]
  Horribly stuff'd with epithets of war;
  And, in conclusion,
  Nonsuits[6] my mediators;[7] for, 'Certes,'[8] says he,
  'I have already chose my officer.'
  And what was he?
  Forsooth, a great arithmetician,
  One Michael Cassio, a Florentine,
  A fellow almost damn'd in a fair wife;[9]
  That never set a squadron in the field,
  Nor the division of a battle knows
  More than a spinster; unless[10] the bookish theoric,[11]
  Wherein the toged consuls can propose
  As masterly as he: mere prattle, without practice,
  Is all his soldiership. But he, sir, had the election;
  And I—of whom his eyes had seen the proof
  At Rhodes, at Cyprus, and on other grounds
  Christian and heathen—must be be-lee'd[12] and calm'd
  By debitor and creditor; this counter-caster,[13]
  He, in good time, must his lieutenant be,
  And I—God bless the mark!—his Moorship's ancient.[14]

RODERIGO: By heaven, I rather would have been his hangman.

IAGO: Why, there's no remedy: 'tis the curse of the service,
  Preferment goes by letter and affection,

---

[1] i.e., Othello's successful courtship of Desdemona [2] by God's blood [3] i.e., Othello [4] took off their caps [5] pompous wordiness, circumlocution [6] turns down [7] spokesmen [8] in truth [9] A much debated phrase. In the Italian source the Captain (i.e., Cassio) was married, and it may be that Shakespeare originally intended Bianca to be Cassio's wife but later changed his mind and failed to alter the phrase here accordingly. Or perhaps Iago simply sneers at Cassio as a notorious ladies' man. [10] except [11] theory [12] left without wind for my sails [13] bookkeeper (cf. "arithmetician" above) [14] ensign (but Iago's position in the play seems to be that of Othello's aide-de-camp)

Not by the old gradation,[15] where each second
Stood heir to the first. Now, sir, be judge yourself,
Whe'r[16] I in any just term am affin'd[17]
To love the Moor.

RODERIGO: I would not follow him then.

IAGO: O! sir, content you;
I follow him to serve my turn upon him;
We cannot all be masters, nor all masters
Cannot be truly follow'd. You shall mark
Many a duteous and knee-crooking knave,
That, doting on his own obsequious bondage,
Wears out his time, much like his master's ass,
For nought but provender, and when he's old, cashier'd;
Whip me such honest knaves. Others there are
Who, trimm'd in forms and visages of duty,
Keep yet their hearts attending on themselves,
And, throwing but shows of service on their lords,
Do well thrive by them, and when they have lin'd their coats
Do themselves homage: these fellows have some soul;
And such a one do I profess myself. For, sir,
It is as sure as you are Roderigo,
Were I the Moor, I would not be Iago:
In following him, I follow but myself;
Heaven is my judge, not I for love and duty,
But seeming so, for my peculiar end:
For when my outward action doth demonstrate
The native act and figure of my heart
In compliment extern,[18] 'tis not long after
But I will wear my heart upon my sleeve
For daws to peck at: I am not what I am.

RODERIGO: What a full fortune does the thick-lips owe,[19]
If he can carry 't thus!

IAGO: Call up her father;
Rouse him, make after him, poison his delight,
Proclaim him in the streets, incense her kinsmen,
And, though he in a fertile climate dwell,[20]
Plague him with flies; though that his joy be joy,
Yet throw such changes of vexation on 't
As it may lose some colour.

RODERIGO: Here is her father's house; I'll call aloud.

IAGO: Do; with like timorous[21] accent and dire yell

---

[15]seniority [16]whether [17]obliged [18]external show [19]own [20]i.e., is fortunate [21]frightening

As when, by night and negligence, the fire
Is spied in populous cities.

RODERIGO: What, ho! Brabantio! Signior Brabantio, ho!

IAGO: Awake! what, ho! Brabantio! thieves! thieves! thieves!
Look to your house, your daughter, and your bags!
Thieves! thieves!

(*Enter* BRABANTIO, *above, at a window.*)

BRABANTIO: What is the reason of this terrible summons?
What is the matter there?

RODERIGO: Signior, is all your family within?

IAGO: Are your doors lock'd?

BRABANTIO: Why? wherefore ask you this?

IAGO: 'Zounds![22] sir, you're robb'd; for shame, put on your gown;
Your heart is burst, you have lost half your soul;
Even now, now, very now, an old black ram
Is tupping[23] your white ewe. Arise, arise!
Awake the snorting[24] citizens with the bell,
Or else the devil will make a grandsire of you.
Arise, I say?

BRABANTIO: What! have you lost your wits?

RODERIGO: Most reverend signior, do you know my voice?

BRABANTIO: Not I, what are you?

RODERIGO: My name is Roderigo.

BRABANTIO: The worser welcome:
I have charg'd thee not to haunt about my doors:
In honest plainness thou hast heard me say
My daughter is not for thee; and now, in madness,
Being full of supper and distempering draughts,
Upon malicious knavery dost thou come
To start my quiet.

RODERIGO: Sir, sir, sir!

BRABANTIO: But thou must needs be sure
My spirit and my place[25] have in them power
To make this bitter to thee.

RODERIGO: Patience, good sir.

BRABANTIO: What tell'st thou me of robbing? this is Venice;
My house is not a grange.[26]

RODERIGO: Most grave Brabantio,
In simple and pure soul I come to you.

IAGO: 'Zounds! sir, you are one of those that will not serve God if the

---

[22] by God's wounds [23] copulating [24] snoring [25] position [26] isolated farm house

devil bid you. Because we come to do you service and you think we
are ruffians, you 'll have your daughter covered with a Barbary horse;
you 'll have your nephews neigh to you; you 'll have coursers for
cousins and gennets[27] for germans.[28]

BRABANTIO: What profane wretch art thou?

IAGO: I am one, sir, that comes to tell you, your daughter and the
    Moor are now making the beast with two backs.

BRABANTIO: Thou art a villain.

IAGO: You are—a senator.

BRABANTIO: This thou shalt answer; I know thee, Roderigo.

RODERIGO: Sir, I will answer any thing. But, I beseech you,
   If 't be your pleasure and most wise consent,—
   As partly, I find, it is,—that your fair daughter,
   At this odd-even[29] and dull watch o' the night,
   Transported with no worse nor better guard
   But with a knave of common hire, a gondolier,
   To the gross clasps of a lascivious Moor,—
   If this be known to you, and your allowance,[30]
   We then have done you bold and saucy wrongs;
   But if you know not this, my manners tell me
   We have your wrong rebuke. Do not believe
   That, from[31] the sense of all civility,
   I thus would play and trifle with your reverence:
   Your daughter, if you have not given her leave,
   I say again, hath made a gross revolt;
   Tying her duty, beauty, wit and fortunes
   In[32] an extravagant[33] and wheeling stranger
   Of here and every where. Straight satisfy yourself:
   If she be in her chamber or your house,
   Let loose on me the justice of the state
   For thus deluding you.

BRABANTIO: Strike on the tinder, ho!
   Give me a taper! call up all my people!
   This accident[34] is not unlike my dream;
   Belief of it oppresses me already.
   Light, I say! light!   *(Exit, from above.)*

IAGO: Farewell, for I must leave you:
   It seems not meet nor wholesome to my place
   To be produc'd,[35] as, if I stay, I shall,
   Against the Moor; for I do know the state,

---

[27] Spanish horses   [28] blood relations   [29] between night and morning   [30] by your approval
[31] away from   [32] to   [33] expatriate   [34] happening   [35] i.e., as a witness

However this may gall him with some check,[36]
Cannot with safety cast him; for he 's embark'd
With such loud reason to the Cyprus wars,—
Which even now stand in act,—that, for their souls,
Another of his fathom[37] they have none,
To lead their business; in which regard,
Though I do hate him as I do hell-pains,
Yet, for necessity of present life,
I must show out a flag and sign of love,
Which is indeed but sign. That you shall surely find him,
Lead to the Sagittary[38] the raised search;
And there will I be with him. So, farewell.   (*Exit.*)

(*Enter below,* BRABANTIO, *and* SERVANTS *with torches.*)

BRABANTIO: It is too true an evil: gone she is,
    And what 's to come of my despised time
    Is nought but bitterness. Now, Roderigo,
    Where didst thou see her? O, unhappy girl!
    With the Moor, sayst thou? Who would be a father!
    How didst thou know 'twas she? O, she deceives me
    Past thought. What said she to you? Get more tapers!
    Raise all my kindred! Are they married, think you?
RODERIGO: Truly, I think they are.
BRABANTIO: O heaven! How got she out? O treason of the blood:
    Fathers, from hence trust not your daughters' minds
    By what you see them act. Are there not charms
    By which the property of youth and maidhood
    May be abus'd? Have you not read, Roderigo,
    Of some such thing?
RODERIGO: Yes, sir, I have indeed.
BRABANTIO: Call up my brother. O! that you had had her.
    Some one way, some another! Do you know
    Where we may apprehend her and the Moor?
RODERIGO: I think I can discover him, if you please
    To get good guard and go along with me.
BRABANTIO: Pray you, lead on. At every house I 'll call;
    I may command at most. Get weapons, ho!
    And raise some special officers of night.
    On, good Roderigo; I 'll deserve[39] your pains.   (*Exeunt.*)

---

[36] restraining adversity   [37] caliber, ability   [38] the name of an inn(?)   [39] i.e., reward

Scene 2 [Another Street.]

(*Enter* OTHELLO, IAGO, *and* ATTENDANTS, *with torches.*)

IAGO: Though in the trade of war I have slain men,
    Yet do I hold it very stuff o' the conscience
    To do no contriv'd murder: I lack iniquity
    Sometimes to do me service. Nine or ten times
    I had thought to have yerk'd[40] him here under the ribs.
OTHELLO: 'Tis better as it is.
IAGO: Nay, but he prated,
    And spoke such scurvy and provoking terms
    Against your honour
    That, with the little godliness I have,
    I did full hard forbear him. But, I pray, sir,
    Are you fast married? Be assur'd of this,
    That the magnifico[41] is much belov'd,
    And hath in his effect a voice potential
    As double[42] as the duke's; he will divorce you,
    Or put upon you what restraint and grievance
    The law—with all his might to enforce it on—
    Will give him cable.[43]
OTHELLO: Let him do his spite:
    My services which I have done the signiory[44]
    Shall out-tongue his complaints. 'Tis yet to know,[45]
    Which when I know that boasting is an honour
    I shall promulgate, I fetch my life and being
    From men of royal siege, and my demerits[46]
    May speak unbonneted[47] to as proud a fortune
    As this[48] that I have reach'd; for know, Iago,
    But that I love the gentle Desdemona,
    I would not my unhoused[49] free condition
    Put into circumscription and confine
    For the sea's worth. But, look! what lights come yond?
IAGO: Those are the raised[50] father and his friends:
    You were best[51] go in.
OTHELLO: Not I; I must be found:

---

[40] stabbed   [41] one of the grandees, or rulers, of Venice; here, Brabantio   [42] Iago means that Brabantio's influence equals that of the Doge's, with his double vote.   [43] i.e., scope   [44] the Venetian government   [45] i.e., the signiory does not as yet know   [46] merits   [47] i.e., as equals   [48] i.e., that of Desdemona's family   [49] unconfined   [50] aroused   [51] had better

My parts, my title, and my perfect[52] soul
  Shall manifest me rightly. Is it they?
IAGO: By Janus,[53] I think no.

(*Enter* CASSIO *and certain* OFFICERS, *with torches.*)

OTHELLO: The servants of the duke, and my lieutenant.
  The goodness of the night upon you, friends!
  What is the news?
CASSIO: The duke does greet you, general,
  And he requires your haste-post-haste appearance,
  Even on the instant.
OTHELLO: What is the matter, think you?
CASSIO: Something from Cyprus, as I may divine.
  It is a business of some heat;[54] the galleys
  Have sent a dozen sequent[55] messengers
  This very night at one another's heels,
  And many of the consuls,[56] rais'd and met,
  Are at the duke's already. You have been hotly call'd for;
  When, being not at your lodging to be found,
  The senate hath sent about three several[57] quests
  To search you out.
OTHELLO: 'Tis well I am found by you.
  I will but spend a word here in the house,
  And go with you.   (*Exit.*)
CASSIO: Ancient, what makes he here?
IAGO: Faith, he to-night hath boarded a land carrack;[58]
  If it prove lawful prize, he's made for ever.
CASSIO: I do not understand.
IAGO: He 's married.
CASSIO: To who?

(*Re-enter* OTHELLO.)

IAGO: Marry,[59] to—Come, captain, will you go?
OTHELLO: Have with you.
CASSIO: Here comes another troop to seek for you.
IAGO: It is Brabantio. General, be advis'd;
  He comes to bad intent.

(*Enter* BRABANTIO, RODERIGO, *and* OFFICERS, *with torches and weapons.*)

[52]untroubled by a bad conscience [53]the two-faced Roman god of portals and doors and (hence) of beginnings and ends [54]urgency [55]following one another [56]i.e., senators [57]separate [58]treasure ship [59]by the Virgin Mary

OTHELLO: Holla! stand there!
RODERIGO: Signior, it is the Moor.
BRABANTIO: Down with him, thief!

(*They draw on both sides.*)

IAGO: You, Roderigo! come, sir, I am for you.[60]
OTHELLO: Keep up your bright swords, for the dew will rust them.
    Good signior, you shall more command with years
    Than with your weapons.
BRABANTIO: O thou foul thief! where hast thou stow'd my daughter?
    Damn'd as thou art, thou hast enchanted her;
    For I 'll refer me to all things of sense,
    If she in chains of magic were not bound,
    Whether a maid so tender, fair, and happy,
    So opposite to marriage that she shunn'd
    The wealthy curled darlings of our nation,
    Would ever have, to incur a general mock,
    Run from her guardage to the sooty bosom
    Of such a thing as thou; to fear, not to delight.
    Judge me the world, if 'tis not gross in sense[61]
    That thou hast practis'd on her with foul charms,
    Abus'd her delicate youth with drugs or minerals
    That weaken motion:[62] I 'll have 't disputed on;
    'Tis probable, and palpable to thinking.
    I therefore apprehend and do attach[63] thee
    For an abuser of the world, a practiser
    Of arts inhibited and out of warrant.[64]
    Lay hold upon him: if he do resist,
    Subdue him at his peril.
OTHELLO: Hold your hands,
    Both you of my inclining,[65] and the rest:
    Were it my cue to fight, I should have known it
    Without a prompter. Where will you that I go
    To answer this your charge?
BRABANTIO: To prison; till fit time
    Of law and course of direct session[66]
    Call thee to answer.
OTHELLO: What if I do obey?
    How may the duke be therewith satisfied,
    Whose messengers are here about my side,

[60] let you and me fight   [61] obvious   [62] normal reactions   [63] arrest   [64] prohibited and illegal
[65] party   [66] normal process of law

Upon some present[67] business of the state
To bring me to him?

OFFICER: 'Tis true, most worthy signior;
The duke 's in council, and your noble self,
I am sure, is sent for.

BRABANTIO: How! the duke in council!
In this time of the night! Bring him away.
Mine 's not an idle cause: the duke himself,
Or any of my brothers of the state,[68]
Cannot but feel this wrong as 'twere their own;
For if such actions may have passage free,
Bond-slaves and pagans shall our statesmen be.   (*Exeunt.*)

Scene 3 [A Council Chamber.]

(*The* DUKE *and* SENATORS *sitting at a table.* OFFICERS *attending.*)

DUKE: There is no composition[69] in these news
That gives them credit.

FIRST SENATOR: Indeed, they are disproportion'd;
My letters say a hundred and seven galleys.

DUKE: And mine, a hundred and forty.

SECOND SENATOR: And mine, two hundred:
But though they jump[70] not on a just[71] account,—
As in these cases, where the aim[72] reports,
'Tis oft with difference,—yet do they all confirm
A Turkish fleet, and bearing up to Cyprus.

DUKE: Nay, it is possible enough to judgment:
I do not so secure me in[73] the error,
But the main article[74] I do approve[75]
In fearful sense.

SAILOR (*within*): What, ho! what, ho! what, ho!

OFFICER: A messenger from the galleys.

(*Enter a* SAILOR.)

DUKE: Now, what 's the business?

SAILOR: The Turkish preparation makes for Rhodes;
So was I bid report here to the state
By Signior Angelo.

---

[67] immediate, pressing   [68] fellow senators   [69] consistency, agreement   [70] coincide   [71] exact
[72] conjecture   [73] draw comfort from   [74] substance   [75] believe

DUKE: How say you by this change?

FIRST SENATOR: This cannot be
By no[76] assay[77] of reason; 'tis a pageant[78]
To keep us in false gaze.[79] When we consider
The importancy of Cyprus to the Turk,
And let ourselves again but understand,
That as it more concerns the Turk than Rhodes,
So may he with more facile question bear[80] it,
For that it stands not in such warlike brace,[81]
But altogether lacks the abilities
That Rhodes is dress'd in: if we make thought of this,
We must not think the Turk is so unskilful
To leave that latest which concerns him first,
Neglecting an attempt of ease and gain,
To wake and wage a danger profitless.

DUKE: Nay, in all confidence, he 's not for Rhodes.

OFFICER: Here is more news.

(*Enter a* MESSENGER.)

MESSENGER: The Ottomites,[82] reverend and gracious
Steering with due course toward the isle of Rhodes,
Have there injointed[83] them with an after fleet.[84]

FIRST SENATOR: Ay, so I thought. How many, as you guess?

MESSENGER: Of thirty sail; and now they do re-stem[85]
Their backward course, bearing with frank appearance
Their purposes toward Cyprus. Signior Montano,
Your trusty and most valiant servitor,
With his free duty[86] recommends[87] you thus,
And prays you to believe him.

DUKE: 'Tis certain then, for Cyprus.
Marcus Luccicos, is not he in town?

FIRST SENATOR: He 's now in Florence.

DUKE: Write from us to him; post-post-haste dispatch.

FIRST SENATOR: Here comes Brabantio and the valiant Moor.

(*Enter* BRABANTIO, OTHELLO, IAGO, RODERIGO, *and* OFFICERS.)

DUKE: Valiant Othello, we must straight employ you
Against the general enemy Ottoman.
(*To* BRABANTIO) I did not see you; welcome, gentle signior;

---

[76] any [77] test [78] (deceptive) show [79] looking in the wrong direction [80] more easily capture
[81] state of defense [82] Turks [83] joined [84] fleet that followed after [85] steer again [86] unqualified
expressions of respect [87] informs

We lack'd your counsel and your help to-night.

BRABANTIO: So did I yours. Good your Grace, pardon me;
Neither my place nor aught I heard of business
Hath rais'd me from my bed, nor doth the general care
Take hold of me, for my particular grief
Is of so flood-gate[88] and o'erbearing nature
That it engluts and swallows other sorrows
And it is still itself.

DUKE: Why, what 's the matter?

BRABANTIO: My daughter! O! my daughter.

DUKE: ⎫
SENATORS: ⎭   Dead?

BRABANTIO: Ay, to me;
She is abus'd, stol'n from me, and corrupted
By spells and medicines bought of mountebanks;
For nature so preposterously to err,
Being not deficient, blind, or lame of sense,
Sans[89] witchcraft could not.

DUKE: Whoe'er he be that in this foul proceeding
Hath thus beguil'd your daughter of herself
And you of her, the bloody book of law
You shall yourself read in the bitter letter
After your own sense; yea, though our proper[90] son
Stood[91] in your action.[92]

BRABANTIO: Humbly I thank your Grace.
Here is the man, this Moor; whom, now, it seems,
Your special mandate for the state affairs
Hath hither brought.

DUKE: ⎫
SENATORS: ⎭   We are very sorry for it.

DUKE (to OTHELLO): What, in your own part, can you say to this?

BRABANTIO: Nothing, but this is so.

OTHELLO: Most potent, grave, and reverend signiors,
My very noble and approv'd[93] good masters,
That I have ta'en away this old man's daughter,
It is most true; true, I have married her:
The very head and front of my offending
Hath this extent, no more. Rude am I in my speech,
And little bless'd with the soft phrase of peace;
For since these arms of mine had seven years' pith,[94]
Till now some nine moons wasted,[95] they have us'd

---

[88] torrential   [89] without   [90] own   [91] were accused   [92] suit   [93] tested (by past experience)
[94] strength   [95] past

Their dearest action in the tented field;
And little of this great world can I speak,
More than pertains to feats of broil and battle;
And therefore little shall I grace my cause
In speaking for myself. Yet, by your gracious patience,
I will a round[96] unvarnish'd tale deliver
Of my whole course of love; what drugs, what charms,
What conjuration, and what mighty magic,
For such proceeding I am charg'd withal,
I won his daughter.

BRABANTIO: A maiden never bold;
Of spirit so still and quiet, that her motion
Blush'd at herself;[97] and she, in spite of nature,
Of years, of country, credit, every thing,
To fall in love with what she fear'd to look on!
It is a judgment maim'd and most imperfect
That will confess[98] perfection so could err
Against all rules of nature, and must be driven
To find out practices of cunning hell,
Why this should be. I therefore vouch again
That with some mixtures powerful o'er the blood,
Or with some dram conjur'd to this effect,
He wrought upon her.

DUKE: To vouch this, is no proof,
Without more certain and more overt test
Than these thin habits[99] and poor likelihoods
Of modern[100] seeming do prefer against him.

FIRST SENATOR: But, Othello, speak:
Did you by indirect and forced courses
Subdue and poison this young maid's affections;
Or came it by request and such fair question[101]
As soul to soul affordeth?

OTHELLO: I do beseech you;
Send for the lady to the Sagittary,
And let her speak of me before her father:
If you do find me foul in her report,
The trust, the office I do hold of you,
Not only take away, but let your sentence
Even fall upon my life.

DUKE: Fetch Desdemona hither.

---

[96] blunt   [97] i.e., (her modesty was such that) she blushed at her own emotions; or: could not move without blushing   [98] assert   [99] weak appearances   [100] commonplace   [101] conversation

OTHELLO: Ancient, conduct them; you best know the place.

(*Exeunt* IAGO *and* ATTENDANTS.)

And, till she come, as truly as to heaven
I do confess the vices of my blood,
So justly to your grave ears I 'll present
How I did thrive in this fair lady's love,
And she in mine.

DUKE: Say it, Othello.

OTHELLO: Her father lov'd me; oft invited me;
Still[102] question'd me the story of my life
From year to year, the battles, sieges, fortunes
That I have pass'd.
I ran it through, even from my boyish days
To the very moment that he bade me tell it;
Wherein I spake of most disastrous chances,
Of moving accidents by flood and field,
Of hair-breadth 'scapes i' the imminent deadly breach,
Of being taken by the insolent foe
And sold to slavery, of my redemption thence
And portance[103] in my travel's history;
Wherein of antres[104] vast and deserts idle,[105]
Rough quarries, rocks, and hills whose heads touch heaven,
It was my hint[106] to speak, such was the process;
And of the Cannibals that each other eat,
The Anthropophagi,[107] and men whose heads
Do grow beneath their shoulders. This to hear
Would Desdemona seriously incline;
But still the house-affairs would draw her thence;
Which ever as she could with haste dispatch,
She'd come again, and with a greedy ear
Devour up my discourse. Which I observing,
Took once a pliant[108] hour, and found good means
To draw from her a prayer of earnest heart
That I would all my pilgrimage dilate,[109]
Whereof by parcels[110] she had something heard,
But not intentively:[111] I did consent;
And often did beguile her of her tears,
When I did speak of some distressful stroke
That my youth suffer'd. My story being done,
She gave me for my pains a world of sighs:

---

[102] always, regularly [103] behavior [104] caves [105] empty, sterile [106] opportunity [107] man-eaters
[108] suitable [109] relate in full [110] piecemeal [111] in sequence

She swore, in faith, 'twas strange, 'twas passing¹¹² strange;
'Twas pitiful, 'twas wondrous pitiful:
She wish'd she had not heard it, yet she wish'd
That heaven had made her¹¹³ such a man; she thank'd me,
And bade me, if I had a friend that lov'd her,
I should but teach him how to tell my story,
And that would woo her. Upon this hint I spake.
She lov'd me for the dangers I had pass'd,
And I lov'd her that she did pity them.
This only is the witchcraft I have us'd:
Here comes the lady; let her witness it.

(*Enter* DESDEMONA, IAGO, *and* ATTENDANTS.)

DUKE: I think this tale would win my daughter too.
　Good Brabantio,
　Take up this mangled matter at the best;
　Men do their broken weapons rather use
　Than their bare hands.

BRABANTIO:　　　　　　　I pray you, hear her speak:
　If she confess that she was half the wooer,
　Destruction on my head, if my bad blame
　Light on the man! Come hither, gentle mistress:
　Do you perceive in all this noble company
　Where most you owe obedience?

DESDEMONA:　　　　　　My noble father,
　I do perceive here a divided duty:
　To you I am bound for life and education;
　My life and education both do learn¹¹⁴ me
　How to respect you; you are the lord of duty,
　I am hitherto your daughter: but here 's my husband;
　And so much duty as my mother show'd
　To you, preferring you before her father,
　So much I challenge¹¹⁵ that I may profess
　Due to the Moor my lord.

BRABANTIO:　　　　　　God be with you! I have done.
　Please it your Grace, on to the state affairs:
　I had rather to adopt a child than get it.
　Come hither, Moor:
　I here do give thee that with all my heart
　Which, but thou hast¹¹⁶ already, with all my heart
　I would keep from thee. For your sake,¹¹⁷ jewel,

---

¹¹²surpassing　¹¹³direct object; not "for her"　¹¹⁴teach　¹¹⁵claim as right　¹¹⁶didn't you have it　¹¹⁷because of you

I am glad at soul I have no other child;
For thy escape would teach me tyranny,
To hang clogs on them. I have done, my lord.

DUKE: Let me speak like yourself and lay a sentence,[118]
Which as a grize[119] or step, may help these lovers
Into your favour.
When remedies are past, the griefs are ended
By seeing the worst, which[120] late on hopes depended.
To mourn a mischief that is past and gone
Is the next way to draw new mischief on.
What cannot be preserv'd when Fortune takes,
Patience her injury a mockery makes.[121]
The robb'd that smiles steals something from the thief;
He robs himself that spends a bootless grief.

BRABANTIO: So let the Turk of Cyprus us beguile;
We lose it not so long as we can smile.
He bears the sentence[122] well that nothing bears
But the free comfort which from thence he hears;
But he bears both the sentence and the sorrow
That, to pay grief, must of poor patience borrow.
These sentences, to sugar, or to gall,
Being strong on both sides, are equivocal:[123]
But words are words; I never yet did hear
That the bruis'd heart was pierced[124] through the ear.
I humbly beseech you, proceed to the affairs of state.

DUKE: The Turk with a most mighty preparation makes for Cyprus.
Othello, the fortitude[125] of the place is best known to you; and though
we have there a substitute of most allowed sufficiency,[126] yet opinion,
a sovereign mistress of effects, throws a more safer voice on you:[127]
you must therefore be content to slubber[128] the gloss of your new fortunes with this more stubborn[129] and boisterous expedition.

OTHELLO: The tyrant custom, most grave senators,
Hath made the flinty and steel couch of war
My thrice-driven[130] bed of down: I do agnize[131]
A natural and prompt alacrity
I find in hardness, and do undertake

---

[118]provide a maxim [119]step [120]the antecedent is "griefs" [121]to suffer an irreparable loss
patiently is to make light of injury (i.e., to triumph over adversity) [122](1) verdict, (2)
maxim [123]sententious comfort (like the Duke's trite maxims) can hurt as well as soothe
[124](1) lanced (i.e., cured), (2) wounded [125]strength [126]admitted competence [127]general
opinion, which mainly determines action, thinks Cyprus safer with you in command
[128]besmear [129]rough [130]made as soft as possible [131]recognize

These present wars against the Ottomites.
Most humbly therefore bending to your state,[132]
I crave fit disposition[133] for my wife,
Due reference of place and exhibition,[134]
With such accommodation and besort[135]
As levels with[136] her breeding.

DUKE: If you please,
Be 't at her father's.

BRABANTIO: I 'll not have it so.

OTHELLO: Nor I.

DESDEMONA: Nor I; I would not there reside,
To put my father in impatient thoughts
By being in his eye. Most gracious duke,
To my unfolding[137] lend your gracious ear;
And let me find a charter[138] in your voice
To assist my simpleness.

DUKE: What would you, Desdemona?

DESDEMONA: That I did love the Moor to live with him,
My downright violence and storm of fortunes
May trumpet to the world; my heart 's subdu'd
Even to the very quality of my lord;[139]
I saw Othello's visage in his mind,
And to his honours and his valiant parts
Did I my soul and fortunes consecrate.
So that, dear lords, if I be left behind,
A moth of peace, and he go to the war,
The rites[140] for which I love him are bereft me,
And I a heavy interim shall support[141]
By his dear[142] absence: Let me go with him.

OTHELLO: Let her have your voices.
Vouch with me, heaven, I therefore beg it not
To please the palate of my appetite,
Nor to comply with heat,—the young affects[143]
In me defunct,—and proper satisfaction,
But to be free and bounteous to her mind;
And heaven defend[144] your good souls that you think
I will your serious and great business scant

---

[132] submitting to your authority [133] disposal [134] provision [135] fitness [136] is proper to
[137] explanation [138] permission [139] i.e., I have become a soldier, like Othello [140] i.e., of
marriage, or of war, or of both [141] endure [142] closely concerning (me, i.e., Desdemona)
[143] the passions of youth (hence, here *immoderate* sexual passion) [144] forbid

For[145] she is with me. No, when light-wing'd toys
Of feather'd Cupid seel[146] with wanton dulness
My speculative and offic'd instruments,[147]
That[148] my disports corrupt and taint my business,
Let housewives make a skillet of my helm,
And all indign[149] and base adversities
Make head against my estimation![150]

DUKE: Be it as you shall privately determine,
Either for her stay or going. The affair cries haste,
And speed must answer it.

FIRST SENATOR: You must away to-night.

OTHELLO: With all my heart.

DUKE: At nine i' the morning here we'll meet again.
Othello, leave some officer behind,
And he shall our commission bring to you;
With such things else of quality and respect
As doth import you.[151]

OTHELLO: So please your Grace, my ancient;
A man he is of honesty and trust:
To his conveyance I assign my wife,
With what else needful your good grace shall think
To be sent after me.

DUKE: Let it be so.
Good-night to every one. (*To* BRABANTIO) And, noble signior,
If virtue no delighted[152] beauty lack,
Your son-in-law is far more fair than black.

FIRST SENATOR: Adieu, brave Moor! use Desdemona well.

BRABANTIO: Look to her, Moor, if thou hast eyes to see:
She has deceiv'd her father, and may thee.

                        (*Exeunt* DUKE, SENATORS, OFFICERS, & C.)

OTHELLO: My life upon her faith! Honest Iago,
My Desdemona must I leave to thee:
I prithee, let thy wife attend on her;
And bring them after in the best advantage.[153]
Come, Desdemona; I have but an hour
Of love, of wordly matters and direction,
To spend with thee: we must obey the time.

                        (*Exeunt* OTHELLO *and* DESDEMONA.)

RODERIGO: Iago!

IAGO: What sayst thou, noble heart?

---

[145] because [146] blind (v.) by sewing up the eyelids (a term from falconry) [147] reflective and
executive faculties and organs [148] so that [149] shameful [150] reputation [151] concern
[152] delightful [153] opportunity

RODERIGO: What will I do, think'st thou?

IAGO: Why, go to bed, and sleep.

RODERIGO: I will incontinently[154] drown myself.

IAGO: Well, if thou dost, I shall never love thee after.
Why, thou silly gentleman!

RODERIGO: It is silliness to live when to live is torment; and then have
we a prescription to die when death is our physician.

IAGO: O! villanous; I have looked upon the world for four times seven
years, and since I could distinguish betwixt a benefit and an injury, I
never found man that knew how to love himself. Ere I would say, I
would drown myself for the love of a guinea-hen, I would change my
humanity with a baboon.

RODERIGO: What should I do? I confess it is my shame to be so fond;[155]
but it is not in my virtue[156] to amend it.

IAGO: Virtue! a fig! 'tis in ourselves that we are thus, or thus. Our bodies
are our gardens, to the which our wills are gardeners; so that if we will
plant nettles or sow lettuce, set hyssop and weed up thyme, supply
it with one gender[157] of herbs or distract it with many, either to have
it sterile with idleness or manured with industry, why, the power and
corrigible[158] authority of this lies in our wills. If the balance of our lives
had not one scale of reason to poise another of sensuality, the blood
and baseness of our natures would conduct us to most preposterous
conclusions; but we have reason to cool our raging motions, our car-
nal stings, our unbitted[159] lusts, whereof I take this that you call love
to be a sect or scion.[160]

RODERIGO: It cannot be.

IAGO: It is merely a lust of the blood and a permission of the will. Come,
be a man. Drown thyself! drown cats and blind puppies. I have pro-
fessed me thy friend, and I confess me knit to thy deserving with
cables of perdurable toughness; I could never better stead thee than
now. Put money in thy purse; follow these wars; defeat thy favour[161]
with a usurped[162] beard; I say, put money in thy purse. It cannot be
that Desdemona should long continue her love to the Moor,—put
money in thy purse,—nor he his to her. It was a violent commence-
ment in her, and thou shalt see an answerable sequestration;[163] put
but money in thy purse. These Moors are changeable in their wills;—
fill thy purse with money:—the food that to him now is as luscious as
locusts,[164] shall be to him shortly as bitter as coloquintida.[165] She must

---

[154] forthwith [155] infatuated [156] strength [157] kind [158] corrective [159] i.e., uncontrolled
[160] offshoot [161] change thy appearance (for the worse?) [162] assumed [163] estrangement
[164] sweet-tasting fruits (perhaps the carob, the edible seed-pod of an evergreen tree in the
Mediterranean area) [165] purgative derived from a bitter apple

change for youth: when she is sated with his body, she will find the error of her choice. She must have change, she must: therefore put money in thy purse. If thou wilt needs damn thyself, do it a more delicate way than drowning. Make all the money thou canst. If sanctimony and a frail vow betwixt an erring[166] barbarian and a super-subtle[167] Venetian be not too hard for my wits and all the tribe of hell, thou shalt enjoy her; therefore make money. A pox of drowning thyself! it is clean out of the way: seek thou rather to be hanged in compassing thy joy than to be drowned and go without her.

RODERIGO: Wilt thou be fast to my hopes, if I depend on the issue?[168]

IAGO: Thou art sure of me: go, make money. I have told thee often, and I re-tell thee again and again, I hate the Moor; my cause is hearted; thine hath no less reason. Let us be conjunctive[169] in our revenge against him; if thou canst cuckold him, thou dost thyself a pleasure, me a sport. There are many events in the womb of time which will be delivered. Traverse;[170] go: provide thy money. We will have more of this to-morrow. Adieu.

RODERIGO: Where shall we meet i' the morning?

IAGO: At my lodging.

RODERIGO: I 'll be with thee betimes.

IAGO: Go to: farewell. Do you hear, Roderigo?

RODERIGO: What say you?

IAGO: No more of drowning, do you hear?

RODERIGO: I am changed. I 'll sell all my land.

IAGO: Go to; farewell! put money enough in your purse.

(*Exit* RODERIGO.)

Thus do I ever make my fool my purse;
For I mine own gain'd knowledge should profane,
If I would time expend with such a snipe[171]
But for my sport and profit. I hate the Moor,
And it is thought abroad[172] that 'twixt my sheets
He has done my office: I know not if 't be true,
But I, for mere suspicion in that kind,
Will do as if for surety.[173] He holds me well;[174]
The better shall my purpose work on him.
Cassio's a proper[175] man; let me see now:
To get his place; and to plume up[176] my will
In double knavery; how, how? Let's see:
After some time to abuse Othello's ear

---

[166]vagabond   [167]exceedingly refined   [168]rely on the outcome   [169]allied   [170]march   [171]dupe   [172]people think   [173]as if it were certain   [174]in high regard   [175]handsome   [176]make ready

That he[177] is too familiar with his wife:
He hath a person and a smooth dispose[178]
To be suspected; framed[179] to make women false,
The Moor is of a free and open nature,
That thinks men honest that but seem to be so,
And will as tenderly be led by the nose
As asses are.
I have 't; it is engender'd: hell and night
Must bring this monstrous birth to the world's light.   (*Exit.*)

ACT II

Scene 1 [A Sea-port Town in Cyprus. An Open Place
near the Quay.]

(*Enter* MONTANO *and two* GENTLEMEN.)

MONTANO: What from the cape can you discern at sea?
FIRST GENTLEMAN: Nothing at all: it is a high wrought flood;
    I cannot 'twixt the heaven and the main[180]
    Descry a sail.
MONTANO: Methinks the wind hath spoke aloud at land;
    A fuller blast ne'er shook our battlements;
    If it hath ruffian'd so upon the sea,
    What ribs of oak, when mountains melt on them,
    Can hold the mortise?[181] What shall we hear of this?
SECOND GENTLEMAN: A segregation[182] of the Turkish fleet;
    For do but stand upon the foaming shore,
    The chidden billow seems to pelt the clouds;
    The wind-shak'd surge, with high and monstrous mane,
    Seems to cast water on the burning bear[183]
    And quench the guards of the ever-fixed pole:[184]
    I never did like[185] molestation view
    On the enchafed[186] flood.
MONTANO: If that[187] the Turkish fleet
    Be not enshelter'd and embay'd, they are drown'd;
    It is impossible they bear it out.
    (*Enter a* THIRD GENTLEMAN.)

---

[177] i.e., Cassio   [178] bearing   [179] designed, apt   [180] ocean   [181] hold the joints together
[182] scattering   [183] Ursa Minor (the Little Dipper)   [184] Polaris, the North Star, almost directly
above the Earth's axis, is part of the constellation of the Little Bear, or Dipper.   [185] similar
[186] agitated   [187] if

THIRD GENTLEMAN: News, lad! our wars are done.
    The desperate tempest hath so bang'd the Turks
    That their designment halts;[188] a noble ship of Venice
    Hath seen a grievous wrack and suffrance[189]
    On most part of their fleet.
MONTANO: How! is this true?
THIRD GENTLEMAN: The ship is here put in,
    A Veronesa;[190] Michael Cassio,
    Lieutenant to the warlike Moor Othello,
    Is come on shore: the Moor himself 's at sea,
    And is in full commission here for Cyprus.
MONTANO: I am glad on 't; 'tis a worthy governor.
THIRD GENTLEMAN: But this same Cassio, though he speak of comfort
    Touching the Turkish loss, yet he looks sadly
    And prays the Moor be safe; for they were parted
    With foul and violent tempest.
MONTANO: Pray heaven he be;
    For I have serv'd him, and the man commands
    Like a full soldier. Let's to the sea-side, ho!
    As well to see the vessel that 's come in
    As to throw out our eyes for brave Othello,
    Even till we make the main and the aerial blue
    An indistinct regard.[191]
THIRD GENTLEMAN: Come, let's do so;
    For every minute is expectancy
    Of more arrivance.

    (*Enter* CASSIO.)

CASSIO: Thanks, you the valiant of this warlike isle,
    That so approve the Moor. O! let the heavens
    Give him defence against the elements,
    For I have lost him on a dangerous sea.
MONTANO: Is he well shipp'd?
CASSIO: His bark is stoutly timber'd, and his pilot
    Of very expert and approv'd allowance;[192]
    Therefore my hopes, not surfeited to death,[193]
    Stand in bold cure.[194]

    (*Within,* 'A sail!—a sail!—a sail!' *Enter a* MESSENGER.)

[188] plan is stopped   [189] damage   [190] probably a *type* of ship, rather than a ship from Verona—not only because Verona is an inland city but also because of "a noble ship of Venice" above   [191] till our (straining) eyes can no longer distinguish sea and sky   [192] admitted and proven to be expert   [193] overindulged   [194] with good chance of being fulfilled

CASSIO: What noise?

MESSENGER: The town is empty; on the brow o' the sea
  Stand ranks of people, and they cry 'A sail!'

CASSIO: My hopes do shape him for the governor.

  (*Guns heard.*)

SECOND GENTLEMAN: They do discharge their shot of courtesy;
  Our friends at least.

CASSIO: I pray you, sir, go forth.
  And give us truth who 'tis that is arriv'd.

SECOND GENTLEMAN: I shall   (*Exit.*)

MONTANO: But, good lieutenant, is your general wiv'd?

CASSIO: Most fortunately: he hath achiev'd a maid
  That paragons[195] description and wild fame;
  One that excels the quirks[196] of blazoning pens,
  And in th' essential vesture of creation[197]
  Does tire the ingener.[198]

  (*Re-enter* SECOND GENTLEMAN.)

                          How now! who has put in?

SECOND GENTLEMAN: 'Tis one Iago, ancient to the general.

CASSIO: He has had most favourable and happy speed:
  Tempests themselves, high seas, and howling winds,
  The gutter'd[199] rocks, and congregated sands,
  Traitors ensteep'd[200] to clog the guiltless keel,
  As having sense of beauty, do omit
  Their mortal[201] natures, letting go safely by
  The divine Desdemona.

MONTANO: What is she?

CASSIO: She that I spake of, our great captain's captain,
  Left in the conduct of the bold Iago,
  Whose footing[202] here anticipates our thoughts
  A se'nnight's[203] speed. Great Jove, Othello guard,
  And swell his sail with thine own powerful breath,
  That he may bless this bay with his tall[204] ship,
  Make love's quick pants in Desdemona's arms,
  Give renew'd fire to our extinct spirits,
  And bring all Cyprus comfort!

  (*Enter* DESDEMONA, EMILIA, IAGO, RODERIGO, *and* ATTENDANTS.)

---

[195] exceeds, surpasses [196] ingenuities [197] i.e., just as God made her; or: (even in) the (mere) essence of human nature [198] inventor (i.e., of her praises?) [199] jagged; or: submerged [200] submerged [201] deadly [202] landing [203] week's [204] brave

O! behold,
The riches of the ship is come on shore.
Ye men of Cyprus, let her have your knees.
Hail to thee, lady! and the grace of heaven,
Before, behind thee, and on every hand,
Enwheel thee round!

DESDEMONA: I thank you, valiant Cassio.
What tidings can you tell me of my lord?

CASSIO: He is not yet arriv'd; nor know I aught
But that he's well, and will be shortly here.

DESDEMONA: O! but I fear—How lost you company?

CASSIO: The great contention of the sea and skies
Parted our fellowship. But hark! a sail.

(*Cry within*, 'A sail—a sail!' *Guns heard.*)

SECOND GENTLEMAN: They give their greeting to the citadel:
This likewise is a friend.

CASSIO: See for the news!   (*Exit* GENTLEMAN.)
Good ancient, you are welcome:—(*To* EMILIA) welcome, mistress.
Let it not gall your patience, good Iago,
That I extend my manners; 'tis my breeding
That gives me this bold show of courtesy.   (*Kissing her.*)

IAGO: Sir, would she give you so much of her lips
As of her tongue she oft bestows on me,
You'd have enough.

DESDEMONA: Alas! she has no speech.

IAGO: In faith, too much;
I find it still when I have list[205] to sleep:
Marry, before your ladyship, I grant,
She puts her tongue a little in her heart,
And chides with thinking.[206]

EMILIA: You have little cause to say so.

IAGO: Come on, come on; you are pictures[207] out of doors,
Bells[208] in your parlours, wild cats in your kitchens,
Saints in your injuries, devils being offended,
Players[209] in your housewifery,[210] and housewives[211] in your beds.

DESDEMONA: O! fie upon thee, slanderer.

IAGO: Nay, it is true, or else I am a Turk:
You rise to play and go to bed to work.

EMILIA: You shall not write my praise.

---

[205] wish   [206] i.e., without words   [207] i.e., made up, "painted"   [208] i.e., jangly   [209] triflers, wastrels
[210] housekeeping   [211] (1) hussies, (2) (unduly) frugal with their sexual favors, (3) businesslike, serious

IAGO: No, let me not.

DESDEMONA: What wouldst thou write of me, if thou shouldst praise me?

IAGO: O gentle lady, do not put me to 't,
    For I am nothing if not critical.

DESDEMONA: Come on; assay. There 's one gone to the harbour?

IAGO: Ay, madam.

DESDEMONA: I am not merry, but I do beguile
    The thing I am by seeming otherwise.
    Come, how wouldst thou praise me?

IAGO: I am about it; but indeed my invention
    Comes from my pate[212] as birdlime does from frize;[213]
    It plucks out brains and all: but my muse labours
    And thus she is deliver'd.
    If she be fair and wise, fairness and wit,
    The one's for use, the other useth it.

DESDEMONA: Well prais'd! How if she be black and witty?

IAGO: If she be black,[214] and thereto have a wit,
    She'll find a white that shall her blackness fit.

DESDEMONA: Worse and worse.

EMILIA: How if fair and foolish?

IAGO: She never yet was foolish that was fair,
    For even her folly[215] help'd her to an heir.

DESDEMONA: These are old fond[216] paradoxes to make fools laugh i' the
    alehouse. What miserable praise hast thou for her that 's foul and
    foolish?

IAGO: There's none so foul and foolish thereunto,
    But does foul pranks which fair and wise ones do.

DESDEMONA: O heavy ignorance! thou praisest the worst best. But what
    praise couldst thou bestow on a deserving woman indeed, one that,
    in the authority of her merit, did justly put on the vouch[217] of very
    malice itself?

IAGO: She that was ever fair and never proud,
    Had tongue at will and yet was never loud,
    Never lack'd gold and yet went never gay,
    Fled from her wish and yet said 'Now I may,'
    She that being anger'd, her revenge being nigh,
    Bade her wrong stay and her displeasure fly,
    She that in wisdom never was so frail
    To change the cod's head for the salmon's tail,[218]

---

[212]head [213]coarse cloth [214]brunette, dark-haired [215]here also, wantonness [216]foolish
[217]compel the approval [218]to make a foolish exchange (a bawdy secondary meaning is
probable)

She that could think and ne'er disclose her mind,
See suitors following and not look behind,
She was a wight, if ever such wight were,—

DESDEMONA: To do what?

IAGO: To suckle fools and chronicle small beer.[219]

DESDEMONA: O most lame and impotent conclusion! Do not learn of him, Emilia, though he be thy husband. How say you, Cassio? Is he not a most profane and liberal[220] counsellor?

CASSIO: He speaks home,[221] madam; you may relish him more in the soldier than in[222] the scholar.

IAGO (aside): He takes her by the palm: ay, well said, whisper; with as little a web as this will I ensnare as great a fly as Cassio. Ay, smile upon her, do; I will gyve[223] thee in thine own courtship. You say true, 'tis so, indeed. If such tricks as these strip you out of your lieutenantry, it had been better you had not kissed your three fingers so oft, which now again you are most apt to play the sir[224] in. Very good; well kissed! an excellent courtesy! 'tis so, indeed. Yet again your fingers to your lips? would they were clyster-pipes[225] for your sake! (A trumpet heard.) The Moor! I know his trumpet.[226]

CASSIO: 'Tis truly so.

DESDEMONA: Let 's meet him and receive him.

CASSIO: Lo! where he comes.

(Enter OTHELLO and ATTENDANTS.)

OTHELLO: O my fair warrior!

DESDEMONA: My dear Othello!

OTHELLO: It gives me wonder great as my content
    To see you here before me. O my soul's joy!
    If after every tempest come such calms,
    May the winds blow till they have waken'd death!
    And let the labouring bark climb hills of seas
    Olympus-high, and duck again as low
    All hell 's from heaven! If it were now to die,
    'Twere now to be most happy, for I fear
    My soul hath her content so absolute
    That not another comfort like to this
    Succeeds in unknown fate.

DESDEMONA: The heavens forbid
    But that our loves and comforts should increase
    Even as our days do grow!

[219] i.e., keep petty household accounts [220] free-spoken, licentious [221] to the mark, aptly [222] as . . . as [223] entangle [224] gentleman [225] syringes, enema pipes [226] i.e., Othello's distinctive trumpet call

OTHELLO: Amen to that, sweet powers!
  I cannot speak enough of this content;
  It stops me here; it is too much of joy:
  And this, and this, the greatest discords be   (*Kissing her.*)
  That e'er our hearts shall make!
IAGO (*aside*):   O! you are well tun'd now,
  But I 'll set down[227] the pegs that make this music,
  As honest as I am.
OTHELLO: Come, let us to the castle.
  News, friends; our wars are done, the Turks are drown'd.
  How does my old acquaintance of this isle?
  Honey, you shall be well desir'd[228] in Cyprus;
  I have found great love amongst them. O my sweet,
  I prattle out of fashion, and I dote
  In mine own comforts. I prithee, good Iago,
  Go to the bay and disembark my coffers.
  Bring thou the master to the citadel;
  He is a good one, and his worthiness
  Does challenge much respect. Come, Desdemona,
  Once more well met at Cyprus.

                              (*Exeunt all except* IAGO *and* RODERIGO.)

IAGO: Do thou meet me presently at the harbour. Come hither. If thou
  be'st valiant, as they say base men being in love have then a nobility
  in their natures more than is native to them, list[229] to me. The lieutenant to-night watches on the court of guard:[230] first, I must tell thee this,
  Desdemona is directly in love with him.
RODERIGO: With him! Why, 'tis not possible.
IAGO: Lay thy finger thus, and let thy soul be instructed. Mark me with
  what violence she first loved the Moor but for bragging and telling her
  fantastical lies; and will she love him still for prating? let not thy discreet heart think it. Her eye must be fed; and what delight shall she
  have to look on the devil? When the blood is made dull with the act
  of sport, there should be, again to inflame it, and to give satiety a fresh
  appetite, loveliness in favour, sympathy in years, manners, and beauties; all which the Moor is defective in. Now, for want of these required conveniences, her delicate tenderness will find itself abused,
  begin to heave the gorge,[231] disrelish and abhor the Moor; very nature
  will instruct her in it, and compel her to some second choice. Now,
  sir, this granted, as it is a most pregnant[232] and unforced position, who
  stands so eminently in the degree of this fortune as Cassio does? a
  knave very voluble, no further conscionable[233] than in putting on the

---

[227]loosen [228]welcomed [229]listen to [230]guardhouse [231]vomit [232]obvious [233]conscientious

mere form of civil and humane seeming, for the better compassing of his salt[234] and most hidden loose affection? why, none; why, none; a slipper[235] and subtle knave, a finder-out of occasions, that has an eye can stamp and counterfeit advantages, though true advantage never present itself; a devilish knave! Besides, the knave is handsome, young, and hath all those requisites in him that folly and green minds look after; a pestilent complete knave! and the woman hath found him already.

RODERIGO: I cannot believe that in her; she is full of most blessed condition.

IAGO: Blessed fig's end! the wine she drinks is made of grapes;[236] if she had been blessed she would never have loved the Moor; blessed pudding! Didst thou not see her paddle with the palm of his hand? didst not mark that?

RODERIGO: Yes, that I did; but that was but courtesy.

IAGO: Lechery, by this hand! an index[237] and obscure prologue to the history of lust and foul thoughts. They met so near with their lips, that their breaths embraced together. Villanous thoughts, Roderigo! when these mutualities so marshal the way, hard at hand comes the master and main exercise, the incorporate[238] conclusion. Pish![239] But, sir, be you ruled by me: I have brought you from Venice. Watch you to-night; for the command, I 'll lay 't upon you: Cassio knows you not. I 'll not be far from you: do you find some occasion to anger Cassio, either by speaking too loud, or tainting[240] his discipline; or from what other course you please, which the time shall more favourably minister.

RODERIGO: Well.

IAGO: Sir, he is rash and very sudden in choler, and haply may strike at you: provoke him, that he may; for even out of that will I cause these of Cyprus to mutiny, whose qualification[241] shall come into no true taste again but by the displanting of Cassio. So shall you have a shorter journey to your desires by the means I shall then have to prefer[242] them; and the impediment most profitably removed, without the which there were no expectation of our prosperity.

RODERIGO: I will do this, if I can bring it to any opportunity.

IAGO: I warrant thee. Meet me by and by at the citadel: I must fetch his necessaries ashore. Farewell.

RODERIGO: Adieu.   (*Exit.*)

IAGO: That Cassio loves her, I do well believe it;
    That she loves him, 'tis apt,[243] and of great credit:[244]

---

[234]lecherous [235]slippery [236]i.e., she is only flesh and blood [237]pointer [238]carnal [239]exclamation of disgust [240]disparaging [241]appeasement [242]advance [243]natural, probable [244]easily believable

The Moor, howbeit that I endure him not,
Is of a constant, loving, noble nature;
And I dare think he 'll prove to Desdemona
A most dear[245] husband. Now, I do love her too;
Not out of absolute lust,—though peradventure[246]
I stand accountant[247] for as great a sin,—
But partly led to diet my revenge,
For that I do suspect the lusty Moor
Hath leap'd into my seat; the thought whereof
Doth like a poisonous mineral gnaw my inwards;
And nothing can or shall content my soul
Till I am even'd with him, wife for wife;
Or failing so, yet that I put the Moor
At least into a jealousy so strong
That judgment cannot cure. Which thing to do,
If this poor trash[248] of Venice, whom I trash[249]
For his quick hunting, stand the putting-on,[250]
I 'll have our Michael Cassio on the hip;
Abuse him to the Moor in the rank garb,[251]
For I fear Cassio with my night-cap too,
Make the Moor thank me, love me, and reward me
For making him egregiously an ass
And practising upon his peace and quiet
Even to madness. 'Tis here, but yet confus'd:
Knavery's plain face is never seen till us'd.   (*Exit.*)

Scene 2 [A Street.]

(*Enter a* HERALD *with a proclamation; people following.*)

HERALD: It is Othello's pleasure, our noble and valiant general, that,
upon certain tidings now arrived, importing the mere[252] perdition of
the Turkish fleet, every man put himself into triumph; some to dance,
some to make bonfires, each man to what sport and revels his addic-
tion leads him; for, besides these beneficial news, it is the celebration
of his nuptial. So much was his pleasure should be proclaimed. All
offices[253] are open, and there is full liberty of feasting from this present
hour of five till the bell have told eleven. Heaven bless the isle of
Cyprus and our noble general Othello!   (*Exeunt.*)

[245] a pun on the word in the sense of: expensive [246] perchance, perhaps [247] accountable
[248] i.e., Roderigo [249] check, control [250] inciting [251] gross manner [252] utter [253] kitchens and
storehouses

Scene 3 [A Hall in the Castle.]

(*Enter* OTHELLO, DESDEMONA, CASSIO, *and* ATTENDANTS.)

OTHELLO: Good Michael, look you to the guard to-night:
  Let 's teach ourselves that honourable stop,[254]
  Not to outsport discretion.
CASSIO: Iago hath direction what to do:
  But, notwithstanding, with my personal[255] eye
  Will I look to 't.
OTHELLO: Iago is most honest.
  Michael, good-night; to-morrow with your earliest
  Let me have speech with you. (*To* DESDEMONA.) Come, my dear love,
  The purchase made, the fruits are to ensue;
  That profit 's yet to come 'twixt me and you.
  Good-night.

                    (*Exeunt* OTHELLO, DESDEMONA, *and* ATTENDANTS.)

(*Enter* IAGO.)

CASSIO: Welcome, Iago; we must to the watch.
IAGO: Not this hour, lieutenant; 'tis not yet ten o' the clock. Our general
  casts us thus early for the love of his Desdemona, who let us not
  therefore blame; he hath not yet made wanton the night with her, and
  she is sport for Jove.
CASSIO: She's a most exquisite lady.
IAGO: And, I 'll warrant her, full of game.
CASSIO: Indeed, she is a most fresh and delicate creature.
IAGO: What an eye she has! methinks it sounds a parley[256] of provoca-
  tion.
CASSIO: An inviting eye: and yet methinks right modest.
IAGO: And when she speaks, is it not an alarum[257] to love?
CASSIO: She is indeed perfection.
IAGO: Well, happiness to their sheets! Come, lieutenant, I have a stoup
  of wine, and here without are a brace[258] of Cyprus gallants that would
  fain have a measure to the health of black Othello.
CASSIO: Not to-night, good Iago: I have very poor and unhappy brains
  for drinking: I could well wish courtesy would invent some other cus-
  tom of entertainment.
IAGO: O! they are our friends; but one cup: I 'll drink for you.
CASSIO: I have drunk but one cup to-night, and that was craftily quali-

---

[254]discipline [255]own [256]conference [257]call-to-arms [258]pair

fied[259] too, and, behold, what innovation[260] it makes here: I am unfortunate in the infirmity, and dare not task my weakness with any more.

IAGO: What, man! 'tis a night of revels; the gallants desire it.

CASSIO: Where are they?

IAGO: Here at the door; I pray you, call them in.

CASSIO: I 'll do 't; but it dislikes me.   (*Exit.*)

IAGO: If I can fasten but one cup upon him,
  With that which he hath drunk to-night already,
  He 'll be as full of quarrel and offence
  As my young mistress' dog. Now, my sick fool Roderigo,
  Whom love has turn'd almost the wrong side out,
  To Desdemona hath to-night carous'd
  Potations pottle-deep;[261] and he 's to watch.
  Three lads of Cyprus, noble swelling spirits,
  That hold their honours in a wary distance,[262]
  The very elements[263] of this warlike isle,
  Have I to-night fluster'd with flowing cups,
  And they watch too. Now, 'mongst this flock of drunkards,
  Am I to put our Cassio in some action
  That may offend the isle. But here they come.
  If consequence[264] do but approve my dream,
  My boat sails freely, both with wind and stream.

(*Re-enter* CASSIO, *with him* MONTANO, *and* GENTLEMEN. SERVANT *following with wine.*)

CASSIO: 'Fore God, they have given me a rouse[265] already.

MONTANO: Good faith, a little one; not past a pint, as I am a soldier.

IAGO: Some wine, ho!

  (*Sings*)   And let me the canakin[266] clink, clink;
              And let me the canakin clink:
              A soldier's a man;
              A life's but a span;
              Why then let a soldier drink.

  Some wine, boys!

CASSIO: 'Fore God, an excellent song.

IAGO: I learned it in England, where indeed they are most potent in potting; your Dane, your German, and your swag-bellied[267] Hollander,—drink, ho!—are nothing to your English.

CASSIO: Is your Englishman so expert in his drinking?

---

[259]diluted [260]change, revolution [261]bottoms-up [262]take offense easily [263]types
[264]succeeding events [265]drink [266]small cup [267]with a pendulous belly

IAGO: Why, he drinks you[268] with facility your Dane dead drunk; he sweats not to overthrow your Almain;[269] he gives your Hollander a vomit ere the next pottle can be filled.

CASSIO: To the health of our general!

MONTANO: I am for it, lieutenant; and I 'll do you justice.

IAGO: O sweet England!

(*Sings*) King Stephen was a worthy peer,
   His breeches cost him but a crown;
He held them sixpence all too dear,
   With that he call'd the tailor lown.[270]
He was a wight of high renown,
   And thou art but of low degree:
'Tis pride that pulls the country down,
   Then take thine auld cloak about thee.

Some wine, ho!

CASSIO: Why, this is a more exquisite song than the other.

IAGO: Will you hear 't again?

CASSIO: No; for I hold him to be unworthy of his place that does those things. Well, God 's above all; and there be souls must be saved, and there be souls must not be saved.

IAGO: It 's true, good lieutenant.

CASSIO: For mine own part,—no offence to the general, nor any man of quality,—I hope to be saved.

IAGO: And so do I too, lieutenant.

CASSIO: Ay; but, by your leave, not before me; the lieutenant is to be saved before the ancient. Let 's have no more of this; let 's to our affairs. God forgive us our sins! Gentlemen, let 's look to our business. Do not think, gentlemen, I am drunk: this is my ancient; this is my right hand, and this is my left hand. I am not drunk now; I can stand well enough, and speak well enough.

ALL: Excellent well.

CASSIO: Why, very well, then; you must not think then that I am drunk.
                                                                    (*Exit.*)

MONTANO: To the platform, masters; come, let 's set the watch.

IAGO: You see this fellow that is gone before;
He is a soldier fit to stand by Caesar
And give direction; and do but see his vice;
'Tis to his virtue a just equinox,[271]
The one as long as the other; 'tis pity of him.
I fear the trust Othello puts him in,
On some odd time of his infirmity,

---

[268]the "ethical" dative, i.e., you'll see that he drinks [269]German [270]lout, rascal
[271]equivalent

Will shake this island.
MONTANO: But is he often thus?
IAGO: 'Tis evermore the prologue to his sleep;
    He 'll watch the horologe a double set,[272]
    If drink rock not his cradle.
MONTANO: It were well
    The general were put in mind of it.
    Perhaps he sees it not; or his good nature
    Prizes the virtue that appears in Cassio,
    And looks not on his evils. Is not this true?

(*Enter* RODERIGO.)

IAGO (*aside to him*): How now, Roderigo!
    I pray you, after the lieutenant; go.   (*Exit* RODERIGO.)
MONTANO: And 'tis great pity that the noble Moor
    Should hazard such a place as his own second
    With one of an ingraft[273] infirmity;
    It were an honest action to say
    So to the Moor.
IAGO: Not I, for this fair island:
    I do love Cassio well, and would do much
    To cure him of this evil. But hark! what noise?

(*Cry within,* 'Help! Help!' *Re-enter* CASSIO, *driving in* RODERIGO.)

CASSIO: You rogue! you rascal!
MONTANO: What 's the matter, lieutenant?
CASSIO: A knave teach me my duty!
    I 'll beat the knave into a twiggen[274] bottle.
RODERIGO: Beat me!
CASSIO: Dost thou prate, rogue?

(*Striking* RODERIGO.)

MONTANO (*staying him*): Nay, good lieutenant;
    I pray you, sir, hold your hand.
CASSIO: Let me go, sir,
    Or I 'll knock you o'er the mazzard.[275]
MONTANO: Come, come; you're drunk.
CASSIO: Drunk!

(*They fight.*)

IAGO (*aside to* RODERIGO): Away, I say! go out, and cry a mutiny.
                        (*Exit* RODERIGO.)

[272] stand watch twice twelve hours   [273] ingrained   [274] wicker   [275] head

Nay, good lieutenant! God's will, gentlemen!
Help, ho! Lieutenant! sir! Montano! sir!
Help, masters! Here 's a goodly watch indeed!

(*Bell rings.*)

Who's that that rings the bell? Diablo, ho!
The town will rise: God's will! lieutenant, hold!
You will be sham'd for ever.

(*Re-enter* OTHELLO *and* ATTENDANTS.)

OTHELLO: What is the matter here?
MONTANO: 'Zounds! I bleed still; I am hurt to the death.

(*He faints.*)

OTHELLO: Hold, for your lives!
IAGO: Hold, ho, lieutenant! Sir! Montano! gentlemen!
    Have you forgot all sense of place and duty?
    Hold! the general speaks to you; hold for shame!
OTHELLO: Why, how now, ho! from whence ariseth this?
    Are we turn'd Turks, and to ourselves do that
    Which heaven hath forbid the Ottomites?
    For Christian shame put by this barbarous brawl;
    He that stirs next to carve for his own rage
    Holds his soul light; he dies upon his motion.
    Silence that dreadful bell! it frights the isle
    From her propriety. What is the matter, masters?
    Honest Iago, that look'st dead with grieving,
    Speak, who began this? on thy love, I charge thee.
IAGO: I do not know; friends all but now, even now,
    In quarter[276] and in terms like bride and groom
    Devesting[277] them for bed; and then, but now,—
    As if some planet had unwitted men,—
    Swords out, and tilting one at other's breast,
    In opposition bloody. I cannot speak
    Any beginning to this peevish odds,[278]
    And would in action glorious I had lost
    Those legs that brought me to a part of it!
OTHELLO: How comes it, Michael, you are thus forgot?
CASSIO: I pray you, pardon me; I cannot speak.
OTHELLO: Worthy Montano, you were wont be civil;
    The gravity and stillness of your youth

---

[276] on duty   [277] undressing   [278] silly quarrel

The world hath noted, and your name is great
In mouths of wisest censure:[279] what 's the matter,
That you unlace[280] your reputation thus
And spend your rich opinion[281] for the name
Of a night-brawler? give me answer to it.
MONTANO: Worthy Othello, I am hurt to danger;
    Your officer, Iago, can inform you,
    While I spare speech, which something now offends[282] me,
    Of all that I do know; nor know I aught
    By me that 's said or done amiss this night,
    Unless self-charity be sometimes a vice,
    And to defend ourselves it be a sin
    When violence assails us.
OTHELLO: Now, by heaven,
    My blood begins my safer guides to rule,
    And passion, having my best judgment collied,[283]
    Assays to lead the way. If I once stir,
    Or do but lift this arm, the best of you
    Shall sink in my rebuke. Give me to know
    How this foul rout began, who set it on;
    And he that is approv'd[284] in this offence,
    Though he had twinn'd with me—both at a birth—
    Shall lose me. What! in a town of war,
    Yet wild, the people's hearts brimful of fear,
    To manage private and domestic quarrel,
    In night, and on the court and guard of safety!
    'Tis monstrous, Iago, who began 't?
MONTANO: If partially affin'd,[285] or leau'd in office,
    Thou dost deliver more or less than truth,
    Thou art no soldier.
IAGO: Touch me not so near;
    I had rather[286] have this tongue cut from my mouth
    Than it should do offence to Michael Cassio;
    Yet, I persuade myself, to speak the truth
    Shall nothing wrong him. Thus it is, general.
    Montano and myself being in speech,
    There comes a fellow crying out for help,
    And Cassio following with determin'd sword
    To execute upon him. Sir, this gentleman
    Steps in to Cassio, and entreats his pause;

[279]judgment [280]undo [281]high reputation [282]pains, harms [283]clouded [284]proved (i.e., guilty) [285]favorably biased (by ties of friendship, or as Cassio's fellow officer) [286]more quickly

Myself the crying fellow did pursue,
Lest by his clamour, as it so fell out,
The town might fall in fright; he, swift of foot,
Outran my purpose, and I return'd the rather
For that I heard the clink and fall of swords,
And Cassio high in oath, which till to-night
I ne'er might say before. When I came back,—
For this was brief,—I found them close together,
At blow and thrust, even as again they were
When you yourself did part them.
More of this matter can I not report:
But men are men; the best sometimes forget:
Though Cassio did some little wrong to him,
As men in rage strike those that wish them best,
Yet, surely Cassio, I believe, receiv'd
From him that fled some strange indignity,
Which patience could not pass.

OTHELLO: I know, Iago,
Thy honesty and love doth mince[287] this matter,
Making it light to Cassio. Cassio, I love thee;
But never more be officer of mine.

(*Enter* DESDEMONA, *attended.*)

Look! if my gentle love be not rais'd up;
(*To* CASSIO.) I'll make thee an example.
DESDEMONA: What's the matter?
OTHELLO: All 's well now, sweeting; come away to bed.
Sir, for your hurts, myself will be your surgeon.
Lead him off.   (MONTANO *is led off.*)
Iago, look with care about the town,
And silence those whom this vile brawl distracted.
Come, Desdemona; 'tis the soldier's life,
To have their balmy slumbers wak'd with strife.
                              (*Exeunt all but* IAGO *and* CASSIO.)
IAGO: What! are you hurt, lieutenant?
CASSIO: Ay; past all surgery.
IAGO: Marry, heaven forbid!
CASSIO: Reputation, reputation, reputation! O! I have lost my reputation.
I have lost the immortal part of myself, and what remains is bestial.
My reputation, Iago, my reputation!
IAGO: As I am an honest man, I thought you had received some bodily

---

[287] tone down

wound; there is more offence in that than in reputation. Reputation is an idle and most false imposition;[288] oft got without merit, and lost without deserving: you have lost no reputation at all, unless you repute yourself such a loser. What! man; there are ways to recover the general again; you are but now cast in his mood,[289] a punishment more in policy[290] than in malice; even so as one would beat his offenceless dog to affright an imperious lion. Sue to him again, and he is yours.

CASSIO: I will rather sue to be despised than to deceive so good a commander with so slight, so drunken and so indiscreet an officer. Drunk! and speak parrot![291] and squabble, swagger, swear, and discourse fustian[292] with one's own shadow! O thou invisible spirit of wine! if thou hast no name to be known by, let us call thee devil!

IAGO: What was he that you followed with your sword? What hath he done to you?

CASSIO: I know not.

IAGO: Is 't possible?

CASSIO: I remember a mass of things, but nothing distinctly; a quarrel, but nothing wherefore. O God! that men should put an enemy in their mouths to steal away their brains; that we should, with joy, pleasance,[293] revel, and applause, transform ourselves into beasts.

IAGO: Why, but you are now well enough; how came you thus recovered?

CASSIO: It hath pleased the devil drunkenness to give place to the devil wrath; one unperfectness shows me another, to make me frankly despise myself.

IAGO: Come, you are too severe a moraler. As the time, the place, and the condition of this country stands, I could heartily wish this had not befallen, but since it is as it is, mend it for your own good.

CASSIO: I will ask him for my place again; he shall tell me I am a drunkard! Had I as many mouths as Hydra,[294] such an answer would stop them all. To be now a sensible man, by and by a fool, and presently a beast! O strange! Every inordinate cup is unblessed and the ingredient[295] is a devil.

IAGO: Come, come; good wine is a good familiar creature if it be well used; exclaim no more against it. And, good lieutenant, I think you think I love you.

CASSIO: I have well approved it, sir. I drunk!

IAGO: You or any man living may be drunk at some time, man. I 'll tell

---

[288] something external [289] dismissed because he is angry [290] i.e., more for the sake of the example, or to show his fairness [291] i.e., without thinking [292] i.e., nonsense [293] pleasure [294] many-headed snake in Greek mythology [295] contents

you what you shall do. Our general's wife is now the general: I may say so in this respect, for that he hath devoted and given up himself to the contemplation, mark, and denotement of her parts and graces: confess yourself freely to her; importune her; she 'll help to put you in your place again. She is of so free, so kind, so apt, so blessed a disposition, that she holds it a vice in her goodness not to do more than she is requested. This broken joint between you and her husband entreat her to splinter;[296] and, my fortunes against any lay[297] worth naming, this crack of your love shall grow stronger than it was before.

CASSIO: You advise me well.

IAGO: I protest, in the sincerity of love and honest kindness.

CASSIO: I think it freely; and betimes in the morning I will beseech the virtuous Desdemona to undertake for me. I am desperate of my fortunes if they check me here.

IAGO: You are in the right. Good-night, lieutenant; I must to the watch.

CASSIO: Good-night, honest Iago!   (*Exit.*)

IAGO: And what's he then that says I play the villain?
When this advice is free I give and honest,
Probal[298] to thinking and indeed the course
To win the Moor again? For 'tis most easy
The inclining Desdemona to subdue
In any honest suit; she 's fram'd as fruitful[299]
As the free elements. And then for her
To win the Moor, were 't to renounce his baptism,
All seals and symbols of redeemed sin,
His soul is so enfetter'd to her love,
That she may make, unmake, do what she list,
Even as her appetite shall play the god
With his weak function.[300] How am I then a villain
To counsel Cassio to this parallel[301] course,
Directly to his good? Divinity of hell!
When devils will the blackest sins put on,
They do suggest at first with heavenly shows,
As I do now; for while this honest fool
Plies Desdemona to repair his fortunes,
And she for him pleads strongly to the Moor,
I 'll pour this pestilence into his ear
That she repeals[302] him for her body's lust;
And, by how much she strives to do him good,
She shall undo her credit with the Moor.

---

[296] bind up with splints   [297] wager   [298] provable   [299] generous   [300] faculties   [301] purposeful
[302] i.e., seeks to recall

So will I turn her virtue into pitch,
And out of her own goodness make the net
That shall enmesh them all.

(*Re-enter* RODERIGO.)

How now, Roderigo!

RODERIGO: I do follow here in the chase, not like a hound that hunts, but one that fills up the cry.[303] My money is almost spent; I have been to-night exceedingly well cudgelled; and I think the issue will be, I shall have so much experience for my pains; and so, with no money at all and a little more wit, return again to Venice.

IAGO: How poor are they that have not patience!
What wound did ever heal but by degrees?
Thou know'st we work by wit and not by witchcraft,
And wit depends on dilatory time.
Does 't not go well? Cassio hath beaten thee,
And thou by that small hurt hast cashiered Cassio.
Though other things grow fair against the sun,
Yet fruits that blossom first will first be ripe:
Content thyself awhile. By the mass, 'tis morning;
Pleasure and action make the hours seem short.
Retire thee; go where thou art billeted:
Away, I say; thou shalt know more hereafter:
Nay, get thee gone. (*Exit* RODERIGO.) Two things are to be done,
My wife must move for Cassio to her mistress;
I 'll set her on;
Myself the while to draw the Moor apart,
And bring him jump[304] when he may Cassio find
Soliciting his wife: ay, that 's the way:
Dull not device by coldness and delay.   (*Exit.*)

ACT III

Scene 1 [Cyprus. Before the Castle.]

(*Enter* CASSIO, *and some* MUSICIANS.)

CASSIO: Masters, play here, I will content your pains;[305]
Something that 's brief; and bid 'Good-morrow, general.' (*Music.*)

(*Enter* CLOWN.)

---

[303] pack (hunting term) [304] at the exact moment [305] reward your efforts

CLOWN: Why, masters, have your instruments been in Naples, that they speak i' the nose[306] thus?

FIRST MUSICIAN: How, sir, how?

CLOWN: Are these, I pray you, wind-instruments?

FIRST MUSICIAN: Ay, marry, are they, sir.

CLOWN: O! thereby hangs a tail.

FIRST MUSICIAN: Whereby hangs a tale, sir?

CLOWN: Marry, sir, by many a wind-instrument that I know. But, masters, here 's money for you; and the general so likes your music, that he desires you, for love's sake, to make no more noise with it.

FIRST MUSICIAN: Well, sir, we will not.

CLOWN: If you have any music that may not be heard, to 't again; but, as they say, to hear music the general does not greatly care.

FIRST MUSICIAN: We have none such, sir.

CLOWN: Then put up your pipes in your bag, for I 'll away.
Go; vanish into air; away! (*Exeunt* MUSICIANS.)

CASSIO: Dost thou hear, mine honest friend?

CLOWN: No, I hear not your honest friend; I hear you.

CASSIO: Prithee, keep up thy quillets.[307] There 's a poor piece of gold for thee. If the gentlewoman that attends the general's wife be stirring, tell her there 's one Cassio entreats her a little favour of speech: wilt thou do this?

CLOWN: She is stirring, sir: if she will stir hither, I shall seem to notify unto her.

CASSIO: Do, good my friend. (*Exit* CLOWN.)

(*Enter* IAGO.)

In happy time, Iago.

IAGO: You have not been a-bed, then?

CASSIO: Why, no; the day had broke
Before we parted. I have made bold, Iago,
To send in to your wife; my suit to her
Is, that she will to virtuous Desdemona
Procure me some access.

IAGO: I 'll send her to you presently;
And I 'll devise a mean to draw the Moor
Out of the way, that your converse and business
May be more free.

CASSIO: I humbly thank you for 't. (*Exit* IAGO.)
I never knew

---

[306] Naples was notorious for venereal disease, and syphilis was believed to affect the nose.
[307] quibbles

A Florentine more kind and honest.[308]

(*Enter* EMILIA.)

EMILIA: Good-morrow, good lieutenant: I am sorry
For your displeasure;[309] but all will soon be well.
The general and his wife are talking of it,
And she speaks for you stoutly: the Moor replies
That he you hurt is of great fame in Cyprus
And great affinity,[310] and that in wholesome wisdom
He might not but refuse you; but he protests he loves you,
And needs no other suitor but his likings
To take the safest occasion by the front[311]
To bring you in again.[312]
CASSIO: Yet, I beseech you,
If you think fit, or that it may be done,
Give me advantage of some brief discourse
With Desdemona alone.
EMILIA: Pray you, come in:
I will bestow you where you shall have time
To speak your bosom[313] freely.
CASSIO: I am much bound to you.

(*Exeunt.*)

Scene 2 [A Room in the Castle.]

(*Enter* OTHELLO, IAGO, *and* GENTLEMEN.)

OTHELLO: These letters give, Iago, to the pilot,
And by him do my duties to the senate;
That done, I will be walking on the works;
Repair there to me.
IAGO: Well, my good lord, I 'll do 't.
OTHELLO: This fortification, gentlemen, shall we see 't?
GENTLEMEN: We 'll wait upon your lordship.   (*Exeunt.*)

Scene 3 [Before the Castle.]

(*Enter* DESDEMONA, CASSIO, *and* EMILIA.)

DESDEMONA: Be thou assur'd, good Cassio, I will do
All my abilities in thy behalf.

---

[308] Cassio means that not even a fellow Florentine could behave to him in a friendlier fashion than does Iago. [309] disgrace [310] family connection [311] forelock [312] restore you (to Othello's favor) [313] heart, inmost thoughts

EMILIA: Good madam, do: I warrant it grieves my husband,
  As if the case were his.
DESDEMONA: O! that's an honest fellow. Do not doubt, Cassio,
  But I will have my lord and you again
  As friendly as you were.
CASSIO: Bounteous madam,
  Whatever shall become of Michael Cassio,
  He 's never any thing but your true servant.
DESDEMONA: I know 't; I thank you. You do love my lord;
  You have known him long; and be you well assur'd
  He shall in strangeness[314] stand no further off
  Than in a politic[315] distance.
CASSIO: Ay, but, lady,
  That policy may either last so long,
  Or feed upon such nice[316] and waterish diet,
  Or breed itself so out of circumstance,
  That, I being absent and my place supplied,
  My general will forget my love and service.
DESDEMONA: Do not doubt[317] that; before Emilia here
  I give thee warrant of thy place. Assure thee,
  If I do vow a friendship, I 'll perform it
  To the last article; my lord shall never rest;
  I 'll watch him tame,[318] and talk him out of patience;
  His bed shall seem a school, his board a shrift;[319]
  I 'll intermingle every thing he does
  With Cassio's suit. Therefore be merry, Cassio;
  For thy solicitor shall rather die
  Than give thy cause away.[320]

(*Enter* OTHELLO, *and* IAGO *at a distance.*)

EMILIA: Madam, here comes my lord.
CASSIO: Madam, I 'll take my leave.
DESDEMONA: Why, stay, and hear me speak.
CASSIO: Madam, not now; I am very ill at ease,
  Unfit for mine own purposes.
DESDEMONA: Well, do your discretion.   (*Exit* CASSIO.)
IAGO: Ha! I like not that.
OTHELLO: What dost thou say?
IAGO: Nothing, my lord: or if—I know not what.
OTHELLO: Was not that Cassio parted from my wife?

---

[314] aloofness [315] i.e., dictated by policy [316] slight, trivial [317] fear [318] outwatch him (i.e., keep him awake) till he submits [319] confessional [320] abandon your cause

IAGO: Cassio, my lord? No, sure, I cannot think it,
　　That he would steal away so guilty-like,
　　Seeing you coming.
OTHELLO:　　　　　　　I do believe 'twas he.
DESDEMONA: How now, my lord!
　　I have been talking with a suitor here,
　　A man that languishes in your displeasure.
OTHELLO: Who is 't you mean?
DESDEMONA: Why, your lieutenant, Cassio. Good my lord,
　　If I have any grace or power to move you,
　　His present[321] reconciliation take;
　　For if he be not one that truly loves you,
　　That errs in ignorance and not in cunning,
　　I have no judgment in an honest face.
　　I prithee[322] call him back.
OTHELLO:　　　　　　　Went he hence now?
DESDEMONA: Ay, sooth; so humbled,
　　That he hath left part of his grief with me,
　　To suffer with him. Good love, call him back.
OTHELLO: Not now, sweet Desdemona; some other time.
DESDEMONA: But shall 't be shortly?
OTHELLO:　　　　　　　The sooner, sweet, for you.
DESDEMONA: Shall 't be to-night at supper?
OTHELLO:　　　　　　　No, not to-night.
DESDEMONA: To-morrow dinner, then?
OTHELLO:　　　　　　　I shall not dine at home;
　　I meet the captains at the citadel.
DESDEMONA: Why, then, to-morrow night; or Tuesday morn;
　　Or Tuesday noon, or night; or Wednesday morn:
　　I prithee name the time, but let it not
　　Exceed three days: in faith, he 's penitent;
　　And yet his trespass, in our common reason,—
　　Save that they say, the wars must make examples
　　Out of their best,—is not almost[323] a fault
　　To incur a private check.[324] When shall he come?
　　Tell me, Othello: I wonder in my soul,
　　What you could ask me, that I should deny,
　　Or stand so mammering[325] on. What! Michael Cassio,
　　That came a wooing with you, and so many a time,
　　When I have spoke of you dispraisingly,
　　Hath ta'en your part; to have so much to do

---

[321]immediate　[322]pray thee　[323]hardly　[324](even) a private reprimand　[325]shilly-shallying

To bring him in! Trust me, I could do much—
OTHELLO: Prithee, no more; let him come when he will;
I will deny thee nothing.
DESDEMONA: Why, this is not a boon;
'Tis as I should entreat you wear your gloves,
Or feed on nourishing dishes, or keep you warm,
Or sue to you to do a peculiar profit
To your own person: nay, when I have a suit
Wherein I mean to touch your love indeed,
It shall be full of poise[326] and difficult weight,
And fearful to be granted.
OTHELLO: I will deny thee nothing:
Whereon, I do beseech thee, grant me this,
To leave me but a little to myself.
DESDEMONA: Shall I deny you? no: farewell, my lord.
OTHELLO: Farewell, my Desdemona: I'll come to thee straight.
DESDEMONA: Emilia, come. Be as your fancies teach you;
Whate'er you be, I am obedient.   (*Exit, with* EMILIA.)
OTHELLO: Excellent wretch![327] Perdition catch my soul,
But I do love thee! and when I love thee not,
Chaos is[328] come again.
IAGO: My noble lord,—
OTHELLO: What dost thou say, Iago?
IAGO: Did Michael Cassio, when you woo'd my lady,
Know of your love?
OTHELLO: He did, from first to last: why dost thou ask?
IAGO: But for a satisfaction of my thought;
No further harm.
OTHELLO: Why of thy thought, Iago?
IAGO: I did not think he had been acquainted with her.
OTHELLO: O! yes; and went between us very oft.
IAGO: Indeed!
OTHELLO: Indeed! ay, indeed; discern'st thou aught in that?
Is he not honest?
IAGO: Honest, my lord?
OTHELLO: Honest! ay, honest.
IAGO: My lord, for aught I know.
OTHELLO: What dost thou think?
IAGO: Think, my lord!
OTHELLO: Think, my lord!
By heaven, he echoes me,

---

[326] weight   [327] here, a term of endearment   [328] will have

As if there were some monster in his thought
Too hideous to be shown. Thou dost mean something:
I heard thee say but now, thou lik'dst not that,
When Cassio left my wife; what didst not like?
And when I told thee he was of my counsel
In my whole course of wooing, thou criedst, 'Indeed!'
And didst contract and purse thy brow together,
As if thou then hadst shut up in thy brain
Some horrible conceit.[329] If thou dost love me,
Show me thy thought.

IAGO: My lord, you know I love you.

OTHELLO: I think thou dost;
And, for[330] I know thou art full of love and honesty,
And weigh'st thy words before thou givest them breath,
Therefore these stops[331] of thine fright me the more;
For such things in a false disloyal knave
Are tricks of custom, but in a man that 's just
They are close delations,[332] working from the heart
That passion cannot rule.

IAGO: For Michael Cassio,
I dare be sworn I think that he is honest.

OTHELLO: I think so too.

IAGO: Men should be what they seem;
Or those that be not, would they might seem none!

OTHELLO: Certain, men should be what they seem.

IAGO: Why then, I think Cassio 's an honest man.

OTHELLO: Nay, yet there's more in this.
I pray thee, speak to me as to thy thinkings,
As thou dost ruminate, and give thy worst of thoughts
The worst of words.

IAGO: Good my lord, pardon me;
Though I am bound to every act of duty,
I am not bound to[333] that all slaves are free to.
Utter my thoughts? Why, say they are vile and false;
As where 's that palace whereinto foul things
Sometimes intrude not? who has a breast so pure
But some uncleanly apprehensions[334]
Keep leets and law-days,[335] and in session sit
With meditations lawful?

OTHELLO: Thou dost conspire against thy friend, Iago,

---

[329] fancy [330] because [331] interruptions, hesitations [332] secret (i.e., involuntary, unconscious)
revelations [333] bound with regard to [334] conceptions [335] sittings of the local courts

If thou but think'st him wrong'd, and mak'st his ear
A stranger to thy thoughts.

IAGO: I do beseech you,
Though I perchance am vicious in my guess,—
As, I confess, it is my nature's plague
To spy into abuses, and oft my jealousy[336]
Shapes faults that are not,—that your wisdom yet,
From one that so imperfectly conceits,
Would take no notice, nor build yourself a trouble
Out of his scattering and unsure observance.
It were not for your quiet nor your good,
Nor for my manhood, honesty, or wisdom,
To let you know my thoughts.

OTHELLO: What dost thou mean?

IAGO: Good name in man and woman, dear my lord,
Is the immediate jewel of[337] their souls:
Who steals my purse steals trash; 'tis something, nothing;
'Twas mine, 'tis his, and has been slave to thousands;
But he that filches from me my good name
Robs me of that which not enriches him,
And makes me poor indeed.

OTHELLO: By heaven, I 'll know thy thoughts.

IAGO: You cannot, if my heart were in your hand;
Nor shall not, whilst 'tis in my custody.

OTHELLO: Ha!

IAGO: O! beware, my lord, of jealousy;
It is the green-ey'd monster which doth mock
The meat it feeds on; that cuckold[338] lives in bliss
Who, certain of his fate, loves not his wronger;
But, O! what damned minutes tells[339] he o'er
Who dotes, yet doubts; suspects, yet soundly loves!

OTHELLO: O misery!

IAGO: Poor and content is rich, and rich enough,
But riches fineless[340] is as poor as winter
To him that ever fears he shall be poor.
Good heaven, the souls of all my tribe defend
From jealousy!

OTHELLO: Why, why is this?
Think'st thou I'd make a life of jealousy,
To follow still the changes of the moon
With fresh suspicions? No, to be once in doubt

---

[336] suspicion   [337] jewel closest to   [338] husband of an adulterous woman   [339] counts
[340] boundless

Is once to be resolved. Exchange me for a goat
When I shall turn the business of my soul
To such exsufflicate[341] and blown[342] surmises,
Matching thy inference. 'Tis not to make me jealous
To say my wife is fair, feeds well, loves company,
Is free of speech, sings, plays, and dances well;
Where virtue is, these are more virtuous:
Nor from mine own weak merits will I draw
The smallest fear, or doubt of her revolt;
For she had eyes, and chose me. No, Iago;
I 'll see before I doubt; when I doubt, prove;
And, on the proof, there is no more but this,
Away at once with love or jealousy!

IAGO: I am glad of it; for now I shall have reason
To show the love and duty that I bear you
With franker spirit; therefore, as I am bound,
Receive it from me; I speak not yet of proof.
Look to your wife; observe her well with Cassio;
Wear your eye thus, not jealous nor secure:
I would not have your free and noble nature
Out of self-bounty[343] be abus'd; look to 't:
I know our country disposition[344] well;
In Venice they do let heaven see the pranks
They dare not show their husbands; their best conscience
Is not to leave 't undone, but keep 't unknown.

OTHELLO: Dost thou say so?

IAGO: She did deceive her father, marrying you;
And when she seem'd to shake and fear your looks,
She lov'd them most.

OTHELLO: And so she did.

IAGO: Why, go to,[345] then;
She that so young could give out such a seeming,
To seel her father's eyes up close as oak,
He thought 'twas witchcraft; but I am much to blame;
I humbly do beseech you of your pardon
For too much loving you.

OTHELLO: I am bound to thee for ever.

IAGO: I see, this hath a little dash'd your spirits.

OTHELLO: Not a jot, not a jot.

IAGO: I' faith, I fear it has.
I hope you will consider what is spoke

---

[341] spat out (?) [342] fly-blown [343] innate generosity [344] i.e., that of Venice [345] colloquialism;
here, something like "all right"

Comes from my love. But I do see you're mov'd;
I am to pray you not to strain my speech
To grosser issues nor to larger reach
Than to suspicion.

OTHELLO: I will not.

IAGO: Should you do so, my lord,
My speech should fall into such vile success
As my thoughts aim not at. Cassio 's my worthy friend—
My lord, I see you're mov'd.

OTHELLO: No, not much mov'd:
I do not think but Desdemona's honest.[346]

IAGO: Long live she so! and long live you to think so!

OTHELLO: And yet, how nature erring from itself,—

IAGO: Ay, there's the point: as, to be bold with you,
Not to affect many proposed matches
Of her own clime,[347] complexion, and degree,[348]
Whereto, we see, in all things nature tends;
Foh! one may smell in such, a will most rank,
Foul disproportion, thoughts unnatural.
But pardon me; I do not in position[349]
Distinctly[350] speak of her, though I may fear
Her will, recoiling[351] to her better judgment,
May fall to match you with her country forms
And happily[352] repent.

OTHELLO: Farewell, farewell:
If more thou dost perceive, let me know more;
Set on thy wife to observe. Leave me, Iago.

IAGO: My lord, I take my leave.   (*Going.*)

OTHELLO: Why did I marry? This honest creature, doubtless,
Sees and knows more, much more, than he unfolds.

IAGO (*returning*): My lord, I would I might entreat your honour
To scan this thing no further; leave it to time.
Although 'tis fit that Cassio have his place,
For, sure he fills it up with great ability,
Yet, if you please to hold him off awhile,
You shall by that perceive him and his means:
Note if your lady strain his entertainment[353]
With any strong or vehement importunity;
Much will be seen in that. In the mean time,
Let me be thought too busy[354] in my fears,

---

[346]chaste   [347]country   [348]social rank   [349]in definite assertion   [350]specifically   [351]reverting
[352]perhaps   [353]urge his re-welcome (i.e., to Othello's trust and favor)   [354]meddlesome

As worthy cause I have to fear I am,
And hold he free, I do beseech your honour.
OTHELLO: Fear not my government.
IAGO: I once more take my leave.   (*Exit.*)
OTHELLO: This fellow 's of exceeding honesty,
And knows all qualities, with a learned spirit,
Of human dealings; if I do prove her haggard,[355]
Though that her jesses[356] were my dear heart-strings,
I 'd whistle her off and let her down the wind,[357]
To prey at fortune. Haply, for I am black,
And have not those soft parts of conversation
That chamberers[358] have, or, for I am declin'd
Into the vale of years—yet that 's not much—
She 's gone, I am abus'd;[359] and my relief
Must be to loathe her. O curse of marriage!
That we can call these delicate creatures ours,
And not their appetites. I had rather be a toad,
And live upon the vapour of a dungeon,
Than keep a corner in the thing I love
For others' uses. Yet, 'tis the plague of great ones;
Prerogativ'd[360] are they less than the base;
'Tis destiny unshunnable, like death:
Even then this forked plague[361] is fated to us
When we do quicken.[362]
                              Look! where she comes.
If she be false, O! then heaven mocks itself.
I 'll not believe it.

(*Re-enter* DESDEMONA *and* EMILIA.)

DESDEMONA: How now, my dear Othello!
Your dinner and the generous[363] islanders
By you invited, do attend your presence.
OTHELLO: I am to blame.
DESDEMONA: Why do you speak so faintly?
Are you not well?
OTHELLO: I have a pain upon my forehead here.[364]
DESDEMONA: Faith, that 's with watching; 'twill away again:
Let me but bind it hard, within this hour

---

[355] wild hawk [356] leather thongs by which the hawk's legs were strapped to the trainer's wrist [357] I'd let her go and take care of herself [358] courtiers; or (more specifically): gallants, frequenters of bed chambers [359] deceived [360] privileged [361] i.e., the cuckold's proverbial horns [362] are conceived, come alive [363] noble [364] Othello again refers to his cuckoldom.

It will be well.

OTHELLO: Your napkin[365] is too little:

(*She drops her handkerchief.*)

Let it alone. Come, I 'll go in with you.

DESDEMONA: I am very sorry that you are not well.

(*Exeunt* OTHELLO *and* DESDEMONA.)

EMILIA: I am glad I have found this napkin;
This was her first remembrance from the Moor;
My wayward husband hath a hundred times
Woo'd me to steal it, but she so loves the token,
For he conjur'd her she should ever keep it,
That she reserves it evermore about her
To kiss and talk to. I 'll have the work ta'en out,[366]
And give 't Iago:
What he will do with it heaven knows, not I;
I nothing but[367] to please his fantasy.[368]

(*Enter* IAGO.)

IAGO: How now! what do you here alone?

EMILIA: Do not you chide; I have a thing for you.

IAGO: A thing for me? It is a common thing—

EMILIA: Ha!

IAGO: To have a foolish wife.

EMILIA: O! is that all? What will you give me now
For that same handkerchief?

IAGO: What handkerchief?

EMILIA: What handkerchief!
Why, that the Moor first gave to Desdemona:
That which so often you did bid me steal.

IAGO: Hath stol'n it from her?

EMILIA: No, faith; she let it drop by negligence,
And, to the advantage, I, being there, took 't up.
Look, here it is.

IAGO: A good wench; give it me.

EMILIA: What will you do with 't, that you have been so earnest
To have me filch it?

IAGO: Why, what 's that to you? (*Snatches it.*)

EMILIA: If it be not for some purpose of import
Give 't me again; poor lady! she 'll run mad
When she shall lack it.

---

[365]handkerchief [366]pattern copied [367]i.e., only want [368]whim

IAGO: Be not acknown on 't;[369] I have use for it.
  Go, leave me.   (*Exit* EMILIA.)
  I will in Cassio's lodging lose this napkin,
  And let him find it; trifles light as air
  Are to the jealous confirmations strong
  As proofs of holy writ; this may do something.
  The Moor already changes with my poison:
  Dangerous conceits are in their natures poisons,
  Which at the first are scarce found to distaste,[370]
  But with a little act upon the blood,
  Burn like the mines of sulphur. I did say so:
  Look! where he comes!

(*Enter* OTHELLO.)

                     Not poppy,[371] nor mandragora,[372]
  Nor all the drowsy syrups[373] of the world,
  Shall ever medicine thee to that sweet sleep
  Which thou owedst yesterday.
OTHELLO: Ha! ha! false to me?
IAGO: Why, how now, general! no more of that.
OTHELLO: Avaunt! be gone! thou hast set me on the rack;
  I swear 'tis better to be much abus'd
  Than but to know 't a little.
IAGO: How now, my lord!
OTHELLO: What sense had I of her stol'n hours of lust?
  I saw 't not, thought it not, it harm'd not me;
  I slept the next night well, was free and merry;
  I found not Cassio's kisses on her lips;
  He that is robb'd, not wanting what is stol'n,
  Let him not know 't, and he 's not robb'd at all.
IAGO: I am sorry to hear this.
OTHELLO: I had been happy, if the general camp,[374]
  Pioners[375] and all, had tasted her sweet body,
  So[376] I had nothing known. O! now, for ever
  Farewell the tranquil mind; farewell content!
  Farewell the plumed troop and the big wars
  That make ambition virtue! O, farewell!
  Farewell the neighing steed, and the shrill trump,
  The spirit-stirring drum, the ear-piercing fife,
  The royal banner, and all quality,

[369] you know nothing about it   [370] scarce can be tasted   [371] opium   [372] a soporific   [373] i.e., soporifics   [374] whole army   [375] lowest rank of manual laborers in the army   [376] as long as

Pride, pomp, and circumstance[377] of glorious war!
And, O you mortal engines,[378] whose rude throats
The immortal Jove's dread clamours counterfeit,
Farewell! Othello's occupation 's gone!

IAGO: Is it possible, my lord?

OTHELLO: Villain, be sure thou prove my love a whore,
Be sure of it; give me the ocular proof;
Or, by the worth of mine eternal soul,
Thou hadst been better have been born a dog
Than answer my wak'd wrath.

IAGO: Is 't come to this?

OTHELLO: Make me to see 't; or, at the least, so prove it,
That the probation[379] bear no hinge nor loop
To hang a doubt on; or woe upon thy life!

IAGO: My noble lord,—

OTHELLO: If thou dost slander her and torture me,
Never pray more; abandon all remorse;
On horror's head horrors accumulate;
Do deeds to make heaven weep, all earth amaz'd;
For nothing canst thou to damnation add
Greater than that.

IAGO: O grace! O heaven forgive me!
Are you a man! have you a soul or sense?
God be wi' you; take mine office. O wretched fool!
That liv'st to make thine honesty a vice.
O monstrous world! Take note, take note, O world!
To be direct and honest is not safe.
I thank you for this profit,[380] and, from hence
I 'll love no friend, sith[381] love breeds such offence.

OTHELLO: Nay, stay; thou shouldst be honest.

IAGO: I should be wise; for honesty 's a fool,
And loses that it works for.

OTHELLO: By the world,
I think my wife be honest and think she is not;
I think that thou art just and think thou art not.
I 'll have some proof. Her name, that was as fresh
As Dian's[382] visage, is now begrim'd and black
As mine own face. If there be cords or knives,
Poison or fire or suffocating streams,
I 'll not endure it. Would I were satisfied!

IAGO: I see, sir, you are eaten up with passion.

---

[377]pageantry   [378]deadly artillery   [379]proof   [380]lesson   [381]since   [382]Diana's, the goddess of the moon

I do repent me that I put it to you.
You would be satisfied?
OTHELLO: Would! nay, I will.
IAGO: And may; but how? how satisfied, my lord?
   Would you, the supervisor,[383] grossly gape on;
   Behold her tupp'd?
OTHELLO: Death and damnation! O!
IAGO: It were a tedious[384] difficulty, I think,
   To bring them to that prospect; damn them then,
   If ever mortal eyes do see them bolster[385]
   More[386] than their own! What then? how then?
   What shall I say? Where 's satisfaction?
   It is impossible you should see this,
   Were they as prime[387] as goats, as hot as monkeys,
   As salt as wolves in pride,[388] and fools as gross
   As ignorance made drunk; but yet, I say,
   If imputation, and strong circumstances,
   Which lead directly to the door of truth,
   Will give you satisfaction, you may have it.
OTHELLO: Give me a living reason she 's disloyal.
IAGO: I do not like the office;
   But, sith I am enter'd in this cause so far,
   Prick'd to 't by foolish honesty and love,
   I will go on. I lay with Cassio lately;
   And, being troubled with a raging tooth,
   I could not sleep.
   There are a kind of men so loose of soul
   That in their sleeps will mutter their affairs;
   One of this kind is Cassio.
   In sleep I heard him say. 'Sweet Desdemona,
   Let us be wary, let us hide our loves!'
   And then, sir, would he gripe[389] and wring my hand,
   Cry, 'O, sweet creature!' and then kiss me hard,
   As if he pluck'd up kisses by the roots,
   That grew upon my lips; then laid his leg
   Over my thigh, and sigh'd, and kiss'd; and then
   Cried, 'Cursed fate, that gave thee to the Moor!'
OTHELLO: O monstrous! monstrous!
IAGO: Nay, this was but his dream.
OTHELLO: But this denoted a foregone conclusion:[390]

---

[383] observer   [384] laborious   [385] lie together   [386] other   [387] lustful   [388] heat   [389] seize   [390] previous consummation

'Tis a shrewd doubt,[391] though it be but a dream.

IAGO: And this may help to thicken other proofs
　That do demonstrate thinly.

OTHELLO:　　　　　　　　　　　　I 'll tear her all to pieces.

IAGO: Nay, but be wise; yet we see nothing done;
　She may be honest yet. Tell me but this:
　Have you not sometimes seen a handkerchief
　Spotted with strawberries in your wife's hand?

OTHELLO: I gave her such a one; 'twas my first gift.

IAGO: I know not that; but such a handkerchief—
　I am sure it was your wife's—did I to-day
　See Cassio wipe his beard with.

OTHELLO:　　　　　　　　　　　　If it be that,—

IAGO: If it be that, or any that was hers,
　It speaks against her with the other proofs.

OTHELLO: O! that the slave had forty thousand lives;
　One is too poor, too weak for my revenge.
　Now do I see 'tis true. Look here, Iago;
　All my fond love thus do I blow to heaven:
　'Tis gone.
　Arise, black vengeance, from the hollow hell!
　Yield up, O love! thy crown and hearted throne
　To tyrannous hate. Swell, bosom, with thy fraught,[392]
　For 'tis of aspics'[393] tongues!

IAGO:　　　　　　　　　　　　Yet be content.[394]

OTHELLO: O! blood, blood, blood!

IAGO: Patience, I say; your mind, perhaps, may change.

OTHELLO: Never, Iago. Like to the Pontic sea,[395]
　Whose icy current and compulsive course
　Ne'er feels retiring ebb, but keeps due on
　To the Propontic and the Hellespont,[396]
　Even so my bloody thoughts, with violent pace,
　Shall ne'er look back, ne'er ebb to humble love,
　Till that a capable[397] and wide revenge
　Swallow them up.　　　　　　　　　　　　(Kneels.)
　　　　　　　　Now, by yond marble heaven,
　In the due reverence of a sacred vow
　I here engage my words.

IAGO:　　　　　　　　　　　　Do not rise yet.　　(Kneels.)
　Witness, you ever-burning lights above!

---

[391](1) cursed, (2) acute, suspicion　[392]burden　[393]poisonous snakes　[394]patient　[395]the Black Sea　[396]the Sea of Marmara, the Dardanelles　[397]comprehensive

You elements that clip[398] us round about!
Witness, that here Iago doth give up
The execution of his wit, hands, heart,
To wrong'd Othello's service! Let him command,
And to obey shall be in me remorse,[399]
What bloody business ever.[400]   *(They rise.)*

OTHELLO: I greet thy love,
  Not with vain thanks, but with acceptance bounteous,
  And will upon the instant put thee to 't:
  Within these three days let me hear thee say
  That Cassio 's not alive.

IAGO: My friend is dead; 'tis done at your request:
  But let her live.

OTHELLO: Damn her, lewd minx! O, damn her!
  Come, go with me apart; I will withdraw.
  To furnish me with some swift means of death
  For the fair devil. Now art thou my lieutenant.

IAGO: I am your own for ever.   *(Exeunt.)*

Scene 4 [Before the Castle.]

(Enter DESDEMONA, EMILIA, *and* CLOWN.)

DESDEMONA: Do you know, sirrah,[401] where Lieutenant Cassio lies?[402]

CLOWN: I dare not say he lies any where.

DESDEMONA: Why, man?

CLOWN: He is a soldier; and for one to say a soldier lies, is stabbing.[403]

DESDEMONA: Go to;[404] where lodges he?

CLOWN: To tell you where he lodges is to tell you where I lie.

DESDEMONA: Can anything be made of this?

CLOWN: I know not where he lodges, and for me to devise[405] a lodging,
  and say he lies here or he lies there, were to lie in mine own throat.

DESDEMONA: Can you inquire him out, and be edified by report?

CLOWN: I will catechize the world for him; that is, make questions, and
  by them answer.

DESDEMONA: Seek him, bid him come hither; tell him I have moved my
  lord in his behalf, and hope all will be well.

CLOWN: To do this is within the compass of man's wit, and therefore I
  will attempt the doing it.   *(Exit.)*

[398] encompass [399] probably a corrupt line; the meaning appears to be; "to obey shall be my solemn obligation" [400] soever [401] common form of address to inferiors [402] lives [403] i.e., is cause for stabbing [404] here apparently: "Come on!" [405] invent

DESDEMONA: Where should I lose that handkerchief, Emilia?

EMILIA: I know not, madam.

DESDEMONA: Believe me, I had rather have lost my purse
Full of cruzadoes;[406] and, but my noble Moor
Is true of mind, and made of no such baseness
As jealous creatures are, it were enough
To put him to ill thinking.

EMILIA: Is he not jealous?

DESDEMONA: Who! he? I think the sun where he was born
Drew all such humours from him.

EMILIA: Look! where he comes.

DESDEMONA: I will not leave him now till Cassio
Be call'd to him.

(*Enter* OTHELLO.)

                              How is 't with you, my lord?

OTHELLO: Well, my good lady. (*Aside*) O! hardness to dissemble.
How do you, Desdemona?

DESDEMONA: Well, my good lord.

OTHELLO: Give me your hand. This hand is moist,[407] my lady.

DESDEMONA: It yet has felt no age nor known no sorrow.

OTHELLO: This argues fruitfulness and liberal[408] heart;
Hot, hot, and moist; this hand of yours requires
A sequester[409] from liberty, fasting and prayer,
Much castigation, exercise devout;
For here 's a young and sweating devil here,
That commonly rebels. 'Tis a good hand,
A frank one.

DESDEMONA: You may, indeed, say so;
For 'twas that hand that gave away my heart.

OTHELLO: A liberal hand; the hearts of old gave hands,
But our new heraldry[410] is hands not hearts.

DESDEMONA: I cannot speak of this. Come now, your promise.

OTHELLO: What promise, chuck?[411]

DESDEMONA: I have sent to bid Cassio come speak with you.

OTHELLO: I have a salt and sorry rheum offends me.
Lend me thy handkerchief.

DESDEMONA: Here, my lord.

OTHELLO: That which I gave you.

---

[406] Portuguese gold coins   [407] a supposed symptom of a lustful nature   [408] with overtones of: too free, loose   [409] separation   [410] i.e., new heraldic symbolism (Othello means that the new way is not to give the heart together with the hand.)   [411] common term of endearment

DESMEDONA: I have it not about me.

OTHELLO: Not?

DESDEMONA: No, indeed, my lord.

OTHEILO: That is a fault.

  That handkerchief
  Did an Egyptian[412] to my mother give;
  She was a charmer,[413] and could almost read
  The thoughts of people; she told her, while she kept it,
  'Twould make her amiable[414] and subdue my father
  Entirely to her love, but if she lost it
  Or made a gift of it, my father's eye
  Should hold her loathed, and his spirits should hunt
  After new fancies.[415] She dying gave it me;
  And bid me, when my fate would have me wive,
  To give it her. I did so: and take heed on 't;
  Make it a darling like your precious eye;
  To love 't or give 't away, were such perdition
  As nothing else could match.

DESDEMONA: Is 't possible?

OTHELLO: 'Tis true; there 's magic in the web of it;
  A sibyl,[416] that had number'd in the world
  The sun to course two hundred compasses,
  In her prophetic fury sew'd the work;
  The worms were hallow'd that did breed the silk,
  And it was dy'd in mummy[417] which the skilful
  Conserv'd of maidens' hearts.

DESDEMONA: Indeed! is 't true?

OTHELLO: Most veritable; therefore look to 't well.

DESDEMONA: Then would to heaven that I had never seen it!

OTHELLO: Ha! wherefore?

DESDEMONA: Why do you speak so startingly and rash?

OTHELLO: Is 't lost? is 't gone? Speak, is it out o' the way?

DESDEMONA: Heaven bless us!

OTHELLO: Say you?

DESDEMONA: It is not lost: but what an if[418] it were?

OTHELLO: How!

DESDEMONA: I say, it is not lost.

OTHELLO: Fetch 't, let me see 't!

DESDEMONA: Why, so I can, sir, but I will not now.
  This is a trick to put me from my suit:
  Pray you let Cassio be receiv'd again.

---

[412]Gypsy [413]sorceress [414]lovable, desirable [415]loves [416]prophetess [417]drug (medicinal or magic) derived from embalmed bodies [418]if

OTHELLO: Fetch me the handkerchief; my mind misgives.

DESDEMONA: Come, come;
You'll never meet a more sufficient[419] man.

OTHELLO: The handkerchief!

DESDEMONA: I pray, talk[420] me of Cassio.

OTHELLO: The handkerchief!

DESDEMONA: A man that all his time
Hath founded his good fortunes on your love,
Shar'd dangers with you,—

OTHELLO: The handkerchief!

DESDEMONA: In sooth, you are to blame.

OTHELLO: Away!   (*Exit.*)

EMILIA: Is not this man jealous?

DESDEMONA: I ne'er saw this before.
Sure, there 's some wonder in this handkerchief;
I am most unhappy in the loss of it.

EMILIA: 'Tis not a year or two shows us a man;
They are all but[421] stomachs, and we all but[421] food;
They eat us hungerly, and when they are full
They belch us. Look you! Cassio and my husband.

(*Enter* IAGO *and* CASSIO.)

IAGO: There is no other way; 'tis she must do 't:
And, lo! the happiness:[422] go and importune her.

DESDEMONA: How now, good Cassio! what 's the news with you?

CASSIO: Madam, my former suit: I do beseech you
That by your virtuous means I may again
Exist, and be a member of his love
Whom I with all the office[423] of my heart
Entirely honour; I would not be delay'd.
If my offence be of such mortal kind
That nor my service past, nor present sorrows,
Nor purpos'd merit in futurity,
Can ransom me into his love again,
But to know so must be my benefit;
So shall I clothe me in a forc'd content,
And shut myself up in some other course
To fortune's alms.

DESDEMONA: Alas! thrice-gentle Cassio!
My advocation is not now in tune;
My lord is not my lord; nor should I know him,

---

[419]adequate [420]talk to [421]only . . . only [422]"what luck!" [423]duty

Were he in favour[424] as in humour alter'd.
So help me every spirit sanctified,
As I have spoken for you all my best
And stood within the blank of[425] his displeasure
For my free speech. You must awhile be patient;
What I can do I will, and more I will
Than for myself I dare: let that suffice you.

IAGO: Is my lord angry?

EMILIA: He went hence but now,
And certainly in strange unquietness.

IAGO: Can he be angry? I have seen the cannon,
When it hath blown his ranks[426] into the air,
And, like the devil, from his very arm
Puff'd his own brother; and can he be angry?
Something of moment[427] then; I will go meet him;
There 's matter in 't indeed, if he be angry.

DESDEMONA: I prithee, do so. (*Exit* IAGO.) Something, sure, of state,[428]
Either from Venice, or some unhatch'd[429] practice
Made demonstrable here in Cyprus to him,
Hath puddled[430] his clear spirit; and, in such cases
Men's natures wrangle with inferior things,
Though great ones are their object. 'Tis even so;
For let our finger ache, and it indues[431]
Our other healthful members even to that sense
Of pain. Nay, we must think men are not gods,
Nor of them look for such observancy[432]
As fits the bridal.[433] Beshrew me much, Emilia,
I was—unhandsome warrior as I am—
Arraigning his unkindness with[434] my soul;
But now I find I had suborn'd the witness,[435]
And he's indicted falsely.

EMILIA: Pray heaven it be state matters, as you think,
And no conception,[436] nor no jealous toy[437]
Concerning you.

DESDEMONA: Alas the day! I never gave him cause.

EMILIA: But jealous souls will not be answer'd so;
They are not ever jealous for the cause,
But jealous for they are jealous; 'tis a monster
Begot upon itself, born on itself.

---

[424] appearance   [425] as the target for   [426] i.e., his soldiers   [427] important   [428] public affairs
[429] abortive or budding plot   [430] muddied   [431] brings, leads   [432] attention   [433] wedding   [434] to
[435] i.e., caused my soul to bring in wrong charges   [436] fancy, supposition   [437] fancy

DESDEMONA: Heaven keep that monster from Othello's mind!
EMILIA: Lady, amen.
DESDEMONA: I will go seek him. Cassio, walk hereabout;
  If I do find him fit, I 'll move your suit
  And seek to effect it to my uttermost.
CASSIO: I humbly thank your ladyship.

(Exeunt DESDEMONA and EMILIA.)

(Enter BIANCA.)

BIANCA: Save you, friend Cassio!
CASSIO: What make you from home?
  How is it with you, my most fair Bianca?
  I' faith, sweet love, I was coming to your house.
BIANCA: And I was going to your lodging, Cassio.
  What! keep a week away? seven days and nights?
  Eight score eight hours? and lovers' absent hours.
  More tedious than the dial eight score times?
  O weary reckoning!
CASSIO: Pardon me, Bianca,
  I have this while with leaden thoughts been press'd;
  But I shall, in a more continuate[438] time,
  Strike off[439] this score of absence. Sweet Bianca,

(Giving her DESDEMONA'S handkerchief.)

  Take me this work out.
BIANCA: O Cassio! whence came this?
  This is some token from a newer friend;
  To the felt absence now I feel a cause;
  Is 't come to this? Well, well.
CASSIO: Go to, woman!
  Throw your vile guesses in the devil's teeth,
  From whence you have them. You are jealous now
  That this is from some mistress, some remembrance:
  No, in good troth, Bianca.
BIANCA: Why, whose is it?
CASSIO: I know not, sweet; I found it in my chamber.
  I like the work well; ere it be demanded,—[440]
  As like enough it will,—I'd have it copied;
  Take it and do 't; and leave me for this time.
BIANCA: Leave you! wherefore?
CASSIO: I do attend here on[441] the general,

---

[438] uninterrupted [439] cancel (i.e., make up for) [440] asked for [441] wait for

And think it no addition,[442] nor my wish,
To have him see me woman'd.
BIANCA: Why, I pray you?
CASSIO: Not that I love you not.
BIANCA: But that you do not love me.
  I pray you, bring me on the way a little
  And say if I shall see you soon at night.
CASSIO: 'Tis but a little way that I can bring you,
  For I attend here; but I 'll see you soon.
BIANCA: 'Tis very good; I must be circumstanc'd.[443]   (*Exeunt.*)

ACT IV

Scene 1 [Cyprus. Before the Castle.]

(*Enter* OTHELLO *and* IAGO.)

IAGO: Will you think so?
OTHELLO: Think so, Iago!
IAGO: What!
  To kiss in private?
OTHELLO: An unauthoriz'd kiss.
IAGO: Or to be naked with her friend a-bed
  An hour or more, not meaning any harm?
OTHELLO: Naked a-bed, Iago, and not mean harm?
  It is hypocrisy against the devil:[444]
  They that mean virtuously, and yet do so,
  The devil their virtue tempts, and they tempt heaven.
IAGO: If they do nothing, 'tis a venial slip;
  But if I give my wife a handkerchief,—
OTHELLO: What then?
IAGO: Why, then, 'tis hers, my lord; and, being hers,
  She may, I think, bestow 't on any man.
OTHELLO: She is protectress of her honour too;
  May she give that?
IAGO: Her honour is an essence that 's not seen;
  They have it very oft that have it not:[445]
  But for the handkerchief,—

---

[442] advantage, credit [443] governed by circumstances [444] i.e., by not committing the sin which the situation invites [445] i.e., some unchaste women are thought chaste

OTHELLO: By heaven, I would most gladly have forgot it:—
    Thou said'st,—O! it comes o'er my memory,
    As doth the raven[446] o'er the infected house,
    Boding to all,—he had my handkerchief.
IAGO: Ay, what of that?
OTHELLO: That's not so good now.
IAGO: What,
    If I had said I had seen him do you wrong?
    Or heard him say, as knaves be such abroad,[447]
    Who having, by their own importunate suit,
    Or voluntary dotage[448] of some mistress,
    Convinced or supplied them,[449] cannot choose
    But they must blab.
OTHELLO: Hath he said any thing?
IAGO: He hath, my lord; but be you well assur'd,
    No more than he 'll unswear.
OTHELLO: What hath he said?
IAGO: Faith, that he did—I know not what he did.
OTHELLO: What? what?
IAGO: Lie—
OTHELLO: With her?
IAGO: With her, on her; what you will.
OTHELLO: Lie with her; lie on her! We say, lie on her, when they belie her. Lie with her! that's fulsome. Handkerchief,—confessions,—handkerchief! To confess, and be hanged for his labour. First, to be hanged, and then to confess: I tremble at it. Nature would not invest herself in such shadowing passion without some instruction.[450] It is not words that shake me thus. Pish! Noses, ears, and lips. Is it possible?—Confess!—Handkerchief!—O devil!

(*Falls in a trance.*)

IAGO: Work on,
    My medicine, work! Thus credulous fools are caught;
    And many worthy and chaste dames even thus,
    All guiltless, meet reproach. What ho! my lord!
    My lord, I say! Othello!

(*Enter* CASSIO.)

                  How now, Cassio!

---

[446] (1) a bad omen, (2) a carrier of the plague   [447] as there are some such in the world
[448] foolish affection   [449] overcome (their reluctance) or satisfied (their desires)   [450] I would not fall into such passion unless there were some real grounds for it.

CASSIO: What's the matter?

IAGO: My lord is fallen into an epilepsy;[451]
 This is his second fit; he had one yesterday.

CASSIO: Rub him about the temples.

IAGO: No, forbear;
 The lethargy[452] must have his quiet course,
 If not, he foams at mouth, and by and by
 Breaks out to savage madness. Look! he stirs;
 Do you withdraw yourself a little while,
 He will recover straight; when he is gone,
 I would on great occasion[453] speak with you.   (*Exit* CASSIO.)
 How is it, general? have you not hurt your head?

OTHELLO: Dost thou mock me?[454]

IAGO: I mock you! no, by heaven.
 Would you would bear your fortune like a man!

OTHELLO: A horned man's a monster and a beast.

IAGO: There's many a beast then, in a populous city,
 And many a civil[455] monster.

OTHELLO: Did he confess it?

IAGO: Good sir, be a man;
 Think every bearded fellow that 's but yok'd
 May draw[456] with you; there 's millions now alive
 That nightly lie in those unproper[457] beds
 Which they dare swear peculiar;[458] your case is better.
 O! 'tis the spite of hell, the fiend's arch-mock,
 To lip[459] a wanton in a secure[460] couch,
 And to suppose her chaste. No, let me know;
 And knowing what I am, I know what she shall be.

OTHELLO: O! thou art wise; 'tis certain.

IAGO: Stand you awhile apart;
 Confine yourself but in a patient list.[461]
 Whilst you were here o'erwhelmed with your grief,—
 A passion most unsuiting such a man,—
 Cassio came hither; I shifted him away,
 And laid good 'scuse upon your ecstasy;[462]
 Bade him anon return and here speak with me;
 The which he promis'd. Do but encave yourself,
 And mark the fleers, the gibes, and notable scorns,

---

[451] seizure, fit   [452] coma   [453] important matter   [454] another allusion to the cuckold's horns
[455] citizen   [456] i.e., pull the burden of cuckoldom   [457] not exclusively their own
[458] exclusively their own   [459] kiss   [460] i.e., without suspicion of having a rival   [461] bounds of
patience   [462] derangement, trance

That dwell in every region of his face;
For I will make him tell the tale anew,
Where, how, how oft, how long ago, and when
He hath, and is again to cope[463] your wife:
I say, but mark his gesture. Marry, patience;
Or I shall say you are all in all in spleen,[464]
And nothing of a man.

OTHELLO: Dost thou hear, Iago?
I will be found most cunning in my patience;
But—dost thou hear?—most bloody.

IAGO: That's not amiss;
But yet keep time[465] in all. Will you withdraw?

                                    (OTHELLO *goes apart.*)

Now will I question Cassio of Bianca,
A housewife[466] that by selling her desires
Buys herself bread and clothes; it is a creature
That dotes on Cassio; as 'tis the strumpet's plague
To beguile many and be beguil'd by one.
He, when he hears of her, cannot refrain
From the excess of laughter. Here he comes:

(*Re-enter* CASSIO.)

As he shall smile, Othello shall go mad;
And his unbookish[467] jealousy must construe
Poor Cassio's smiles, gestures, and light behaviour
Quite in the wrong. How do you now, lieutenant?

CASSIO: The worser that you give me the addition[468]
Whose want[469] even kills me.

IAGO: Ply Desdemona well, and you are sure on 't.
(*Speaking lower.*) Now, if this suit lay in Bianca's power,
How quickly should you speed!

CASSIO: Alas! poor caitiff![470]

OTHELLO: Look! how he laughs already!

IAGO: I never knew woman love man so.

CASSIO: Alas! poor rogue, I think, i' faith, she loves me.

OTHELLO: Now he denies it faintly, and laughs it out.

IAGO: Do you hear, Cassio?

OTHELLO: Now he importunes him
To tell it o'er: go to; well said, well said.

---

[463] close with [464] completely overcome by passion [465] maintain control [466] hussy
[467] unpracticed, naïve [468] title [469] the want of which [470] wretch

IAGO: She gives it out that you shall marry her;
　Do you intend it?

CASSIO: Ha, ha, ha!

OTHELLO: Do you triumph, Roman?[471] do you triumph?

CASSIO: I marry her! what? a customer?[472] I prithee, bear some charity to my wit;[473] do not think it so unwholesome. Ha, ha, ha!

OTHELLO: So, so, so, so. They laugh that win.[474]

IAGO: Faith, the cry goes that you shall marry her.

CASSIO: Prithee, say true.

IAGO: I am a very villain else.

OTHELLO: Have you scored me?[475] Well.

CASSIO: This is the monkey's own giving out: she is persuaded I will marry her, out of her own love and flattery, not out of my promise.

OTHELLO: Iago beckons me;[476] now he begins the story.

CASSIO: She was here even now; she haunts me in every place. I was the other day talking on the sea-bank with certain Venetians, and thither comes this bauble,[477] and, by this hand, she falls me thus about my neck;—

OTHELLO: Crying, 'O dear Cassio!' as it were; his gesture imports it.

CASSIO: So hangs and lolls and weeps upon me; so hales[478] and pulls me; ha, ha, ha!

OTHELLO: Now he tells how she plucked him to my chamber. O! I see that nose of yours, but not the dog I shall throw it to.

CASSIO: Well, I must leave her company.

IAGO: Before me![479] look, where she comes.

CASSIO: 'Tis such another fitchew![480] marry, a perfumed one.

(*Enter* BIANCA.)

What do you mean by this haunting of me?

BIANCA: Let the devil and his dam haunt you! What did you mean by that same handkerchief you gave me even now? I was a fine fool to take it. I must take out the work! A likely piece of work, that you should find it in your chamber, and not know who left it there! This is some minx's token, and I must take out the work! There, give it your hobby-horse;[481] wheresoever you had it I'll take out no work on 't.

CASSIO: How now, my sweet Bianca! how now, how now!

OTHELLO: By heaven, that should be[482] my handkerchief!

---

[471] i.e., one who triumphs (?) [472] courtesan, prostitute [473] give me credit for some sense [474] "he who laughs last laughs longest" (?) [475] wounded, defaced (?); or: settled my account (?) [476] signals [477] plaything [478] hauls [479] an exclamation of surprise [480] polecat, noted both for its strong smell and for its lechery [481] harlot [482] i.e., I think that is

BIANCA: An you 'll come to supper to-night, you may; an you will not, come when you are next prepared[483] for. (*Exit.*)

IAGO: After her, after her.

CASSIO: Faith, I must; she 'll rail in the street else.

IAGO: Will you sup there?

CASSIO: Faith, I intend so.

IAGO: Well, I may chance to see you, for I would very fain[484] speak with you.

CASSIO: Prithee come; will you?

IAGO: Go to; say no more. (*Exit* CASSIO.)

OTHELLO (*advancing*): How shall I murder him, Iago?

IAGO: Did you perceive how he laughed at his vice?

OTHELLO: O! Iago!

IAGO: And did you see the handkerchief?

OTHELLO: Was that mine?

IAGO: Yours, by this hand; and to see how he prizes the foolish woman your wife! she gave it him, and he hath given it his whore.

OTHELLO: I would have him nine years a-killing. A fine woman! a fair woman! a sweet woman!

IAGO: Nay, you must forget that.

OTHELLO: Ay, let her rot, and perish, and be damned to-night; for she shall not live. No, my heart is turned to stone; I strike it, and it hurts my hand. O! the world hath not a sweeter creature; she might lie by an emperor's side and command him tasks.

IAGO: Nay, that's not your way.[485]

OTHELLO: Hang her! I do but say what she is. So delicate with her needle! An admirable musician! O, she will sing the savageness out of a bear. Of so high and plenteous wit and invention!

IAGO: She 's the worse for all this.

OTHELLO: O! a thousand, a thousand times. And then, of so gentle a condition![486]

IAGO: Ay, too gentle.[487]

OTHELLO: Nay, that 's certain;—but yet the pity of it, Iago!
O! Iago, the pity of it, Iago!

IAGO: If you are so fond over her iniquity, give her patent to offend; for, if it touch not you, it comes near nobody.

OTHELLO: I will chop her into messes.[488] Cuckold me!

IAGO: O! 'tis foul in her.

OTHELLO: With mine officer!

IAGO: That 's fouler.

---

[483] expected (Bianca means that if he does not come that night, she will never want to see him again.) [484] gladly [485] proper course [486] so much the high-born lady [487] i.e., yielding [488] bits

OTHELLO: Get me some poison, Iago; this night: I 'll not expostulate with her, lest her body and beauty unprovide my mind again.[489] This night, Iago.

IAGO: Do it not with poison, strangle her in her bed, even the bed she hath contaminated.

OTHELLO: Good, good; the justice of it pleases; very good.

IAGO: And for Cassio, let me be his undertaker;[490] you shall hear more by midnight.

OTHELLO: Excellent good. (*A trumpet within.*) What trumpet is that same?

IAGO: Something from Venice, sure. 'Tis Lodovico,
Come from the duke; and see, your wife is with him.

(*Enter* LODOVICO, DESDEMONA, *and* ATTENDANTS.)

LODOVICO: God save you, worthy general!

OTHELLO: With all my heart, sir.

LODOVICO: The duke and senators of Venice greet you.

(*Gives him a packet.*)

OTHELLO: I kiss the instrument of their pleasures.

(*Opens the packet, and reads.*)

DESDEMONA: And what's the news, good cousin Lodovico?

IAGO: I am very glad to see you, signior;
Welcome to Cyprus.

LODOVICO: I thank you. How does Lieutenant Cassio?

IAGO: Lives, sir.

DESDEMONA: Cousin, there 's fall'n between him and my lord
An unkind[491] breach; but you shall make all well.

OTHELLO: Are you sure of that?

DESDEMONA: My lord?

OTHELLO (*reads*): 'This fail you not to do, as you will'—

LODOVICO: He did not call; he 's busy in the paper.
Is there division[492] 'twixt my lord and Cassio?

DESDEMONA: A most unhappy one; I would do much
To atone[493] them, for the love I bear to Cassio.

OTHELLO: Fire and brimstone!

DESDEMONA: My lord?

OTHELLO: Are you wise?

DESDEMONA: What! is he angry?

LODOVICO: May be the letter mov'd him;
For, as I think, they do command him home,

---

[489] unsettle my intention [490] dispatcher [491] unnatural [492] estrangement [493] reconcile

Deputing Cassio in his government.

DESDEMONA: Trust me, I am glad on 't.

OTHELLO: Indeed!

DESDEMONA: My lord?

OTHELLO: I am glad to see you mad.

DESDEMONA: Why, sweet Othello?

OTHELLO: Devil!   (*Strikes her.*)

DESDEMONA: I have not deserved this.

LODOVICO: My lord, this would not be believ'd in Venice,
     Though I should swear I saw 't; 'tis very much;
     Make her amends, she weeps.

OTHELLO: O devil, devil!
     If that the earth could teem with woman's tears,
     Each drop she falls[494] would prove a crocodile.[495]
     Out of my sight!

DESDEMONA: I will not stay to offend you.   (*Going.*)

LODOVICO: Truly, an obedient lady;
     I do beseech your lordship, call her back.

OTHELLO: Mistress!

DESDEMONA: My lord?

OTHELLO: What would you with her, sir?

LODOVICO: Who, I, my lord?

OTHELLO: Ay; you did wish that I would make her turn:
     Sir, she can turn, and turn, and yet go on,
     And turn again; and she can weep, sir, weep;
     And she 's obedient, as you say, obedient,
     Very obedient. Proceed you in your tears.
     Concerning this, sir,—O well-painted passion!—
     I am commanded home. Get you away;
     I 'll send for you anon. Sir, I obey the mandate,
     And will return to Venice. Hence! avaunt![496]   (*Exit* DESDEMONA.)
     Cassio shall have my place. And, sir, to-night,
     I do entreat that we may sup together;
     You are welcome, sir, to Cyprus. Goats and monkeys!   (*Exit.*)

LODOVICO: Is this the noble Moor whom our full senate
     Call all-in-all sufficient; is this the noble nature
     Whom passion could not shake? whose solid virtue
     The shot of accident nor dart of chance
     Could neither graze nor pierce?

IAGO: He is much chang'd.

LODOVICO: Are his wits safe? is he not light of brain?

---

[494] lets fall   [495] the crocodile's tears were supposed to be hypocritical   [496] begone!

IAGO: He 's that he is; I may not breathe my censure.
   What he might be, if, what he might, he is not,
   I would to heaven he were![497]
LODOVICO: What! strike his wife!
IAGO: Faith, that was not so well; yet would I knew
   That stroke would prove the worst!
LODOVICO: Is it his use?
   Or did the letters work upon his blood,
   And new-create this fault?
IAGO: Alas, alas!
   It is not honesty in me to speak
   What I have seen and known. You shall observe him,
   And his own courses[498] will denote him so
   That I may save my speech. Do but go after
   And mark how he continues.
LODOVICO: I am sorry that I am deceiv'd in him.   (*Exeunt.*)

Scene 2 [A Room in the Castle.]

(*Enter* OTHELLO *and* EMILIA.)

OTHELLO: You have seen nothing, then?
EMILIA: Nor ever heard, nor ever did suspect.
OTHELLO: Yes, you have seen Cassio and her together.
EMILIA: But then I saw no harm, and then I heard
   Each syllable that breath made up between them.
OTHELLO: What! did they never whisper?
EMILIA: Never, my lord.
OTHELLO: Nor send you out o' the way?
EMILIA: Never.
OTHELLO: To fetch her fan, her gloves, her mask, nor nothing?[499]
EMILIA: Never, my lord.
OTHELLO: That 's strange.
EMILIA: I durst, my lord, to wager she is honest,
   Lay down my soul at stake: if you think other,
   Remove your thought; it doth abuse your bosom.
   If any wretch have put this in your head,
   Let heaven requite it with the serpent's curse!
   For, if she be not honest, chaste, and true,
   There 's no man happy; the purest of their wives
   Is foul as slander.

---

[497] another of Iago's gnomic speeches; perhaps approximately: "If now he is not himself, I wish he would be what he could be!"   [498] actions   [499] anything

OTHELLO: Bid her come hither; go. (*Exit* EMILIA.)
She says enough; yet she 's a simple[500] bawd
That cannot say as much. This is a subtle whore,
A closet lock and key of villanous secrets;
And yet she 'll kneel and pray; I have seen her do 't.

(*Re-enter* EMILIA *with* DESDEMONA.)

DESDEMONA: My lord, what is your will?
OTHELLO: Pray, chuck, come hither.
DESDEMONA: What is your pleasure?
OTHELLO: Let me see your eyes;
Look in my face.
DESDEMONA: What horrible fancy 's this?
OTHELLO (*to* EMILIA): Some of your function,[501] mistress;
Leave procreants alone and shut the door;
Cough or cry 'hem' if any body come;
Your mystery,[502] your mystery; nay, dispatch. (*Exit* EMILIA.)
DESDEMONA: Upon my knees, what doth your speech import?
I understand a fury in your words.
But not the words.
OTHELLO: Why, what art thou?
DESDEMONA: Your wife, my lord; your true
And loyal wife.
OTHELLO: Come, swear it, damn thyself;
Lest, being like one of heaven, the devils themselves
Should fear to seize thee; therefore be double-damn'd;
Swear thou art honest.
DESDEMONA: Heaven doth truly know it.
OTHELLO: Heaven truly knows that thou art false as hell.
DESDEMONA: To whom, my lord? with whom? how am I false?
OTHELLO: Ah! Desdemona; away, away, away!
DESDEMONA: Alas, the heavy day!—Why do you weep?
Am I the motive of these tears, my lord?
If haply you my father do suspect
An instrument of this your calling back,
Lay not your blame on me; if you have lost him,
Why, I have lost him too.
OTHELLO: Had it pleas'd heaven
To try me with affliction, had he rain'd
All kinds of sores and shames on my bare head,
Steep'd me in poverty to the very lips,

---

[500] simpleminded [501] duty, business [502] trade

Given to captivity me and my utmost hopes,
I should have found in some part of my soul
A drop of patience; but, alas! to make me
The fixed figure for the time of scorn[503]
To point his slow and moving finger at;
Yet could I bear that too; well, very well:
But there, where I have garner'd[504] up my heart,
Where either I must live or bear no life,
The fountain from the which my current runs
Or else dries up; to be discarded thence!
Or keep it as a cistern for foul toads
To knot and gender in![505] Turn thy complexion there,[506]
Patience, thou young and rose-lipp'd cherubin;
Ay, there, look grim as hell!

DESDEMONA: I hope my noble lord esteems me honest.

OTHELLO: O! ay; as summer flies are in the shambles,[507]
That quicken even with blowing. O thou weed!
Who art so lovely fair and smell'st so sweet
That the sense aches at thee, would thou hadst ne'er been born.

DESDEMONA: Alas! what ignorant sin have I committed?

OTHELLO: Was this fair paper, this most goodly book,
Made to write 'whore' upon? What committed!
Committed! O thou public commoner![508]
I should make very forges of my cheeks,
That would to cinders burn up modesty,
Did I but speak thy deeds. What committed!
Heaven stops the nose at it and the moon winks,[509]
The bawdy wind that kisses all it meets
Is hush'd within the hollow mine of earth,
And will not hear it. What committed!
Impudent strumpet!

DESDEMONA: By heaven, you do me wrong.

OTHELLO: Are not you a strumpet?

DESDEMONA: No, as I am a Christian.
If to preserve this vessel for my lord
From any other foul unlawful touch
Be not to be a strumpet, I am none.

OTHELLO: What! not a whore?

DESDEMONA: No, as I shall be sav'd.

OTHELLO: Is it possible?

---

[503] i.e., the scornful world   [504] stored   [505] bunch up and procreate   [506] i.e., change your color to suit the "cistern for foul toads"   [507] slaughterhouse   [508] harlot   [509] closes her eyes

DESDEMONA: O! heaven forgive us.

OTHELLO: I cry you mercy,[510] then;
   I took you for that cunning whore of Venice
   That married with Othello. You, mistress,
   That have the office opposite to Saint Peter,
   And keep the gate of hell!

(*Re-enter* EMILIA.)

                      You, you, ay, you!
   We have done our course; there 's money for your pains.
   I pray you, turn the key and keep our counsel.   (*Exit.*)

EMILIA: Alas! what does this gentleman conceive?[511]
   How do you, madam? how do you, my good lady?

DESDEMONA: Faith, half asleep.

EMILIA: Good madam, what 's the matter with my lord?

DESDEMONA: With who?

EMILIA: Why, with my lord, madam.

DESDEMONA: Who is thy lord?

EMILIA: He that is yours, sweet lady.

DESDEMONA: I have none; do not talk to me, Emilia;
   I cannot weep, nor answer have I none,
   But what should go by water.[512] Prithee, to-night
   Lay on my bed my wedding sheets: remember:
   And call thy husband hither.

EMILIA: Here is a change indeed!   (*Exit.*)

DESDEMONA: 'Tis meet I should be us'd so, very meet.
   How have I been behav'd, that he might stick
   The small'st opinion on my least misuse?[513]

(*Re-enter* EMILIA, *with* IAGO.)

IAGO: What is your pleasure, madam? How is it with you?

DESDEMONA: I cannot tell. Those that do teach young babes
   Do it with gentle means and easy tasks;
   He might have chid me so; for, in good faith,
   I am a child to chiding.

IAGO: What 's the matter, lady?

EMILIA: Alas; Iago, my lord hath so bewhor'd her,
   Thrown such despite[514] and heavy terms upon her,
   As true hearts cannot bear.

DESDEMONA: Am I that name, Iago?

---

[510]beg your pardon   [511]imagine   [512]be conveyed by means of tears   [513]the least suspicion on my slightest misconduct   [514]abuse

IAGO: What name, fair lady?

DESDEMONA: Such as she says my lord did say I was.

EMILIA: He call'd her whore; a beggar in his drink
   Could not have laid such terms upon his callat.[515]

IAGO: Why did he so?

DESDEMONA: I do not know; I am sure I am none such.

IAGO: Do not weep, do not weep. Alas the day!

EMILIA: Has she forsook so many noble matches,
   Her father and her country and her friends,
   To be call'd whore? would it not make one weep?

DESDEMONA: It is my wretched fortune.

IAGO: Beshrew[516] him for it!
   How comes this trick upon him?

DESDEMONA: Nay, heaven doth know.

EMILIA: I will be hang'd, if some eternal villain,
   Some busy and insinuating rogue,
   Some cogging[517] cozening slave, to get some office,
   Have not devis'd this slander; I 'll be hang'd else.

IAGO: Fie! there is no such man; it is impossible.

DESDEMONA: If any such there be, heaven pardon him!

EMILIA: A halter pardon him, and hell gnaw his bones!
   Why should he call her whore? who keeps her company?
   What place? what time? what form? what likelihood?
   The Moor 's abus'd by some most villanous knave,
   Some base notorious knave, some scurvy fellow.
   O heaven! that such companions[518] thou'dst unfold,
   And put in every honest hand a whip
   To lash the rascals naked through the world,
   Even from the east to the west!

IAGO: Speak within door.

EMILIA: O! fie upon them. Some such squire he was
   That turn'd your wit the seamy side without,[519]
   And made you to suspect me with the Moor.

IAGO: You are a fool; go to.

DESDEMONA: O good Iago,
   What shall I do to win my lord again?
   Good friend, go to him; for, by this light of heaven,
   I know not how I lost him. Here I kneel:
   If e'er my will did trespass 'gainst his love,
   Either in discourse of thought or actual deed,
   Or that mine eyes, mine ears, or any sense,

[515] slut   [516] curse   [517] cheating   [518] fellows (derogatory)   [519] outward

Delighted them[520] in any other form;
Or that I do not yet,[521] and ever did,
And ever will, though he do shake me off
To beggarly divorcement, love him dearly,
Comfort forswear me! Unkindness may do much;
And his unkindness may defeat[522] my life,
But never taint my love. I cannot say 'whore':
It does abhor me now I speak the word;
To do the act that might the addition earn
Not the world's mass of vanity could make me.

IAGO: I pray you be content, 'tis but his humour;
The business of the state does him offence,
And he does chide with you.

DESDEMONA: If 'twere no other,—

IAGO: 'Tis but so, I warrant.   (*Trumpets.*)
Hark! how these instruments summon to supper;
The messengers of Venice stay the meat:
Go in, and weep not; all things shall be well.

(*Exeunt* DESDEMONA *and* EMILIA.)

(*Enter* RODERIGO.)

How now, Roderigo!

RODERIGO: I do not find that thou dealest justly with me.

IAGO: What in the contrary?[523]

RODERIGO: Every day thou daffest me[524] with some device, Iago; and rather, as it seems to me now, keepest from me all conveniency,[525] than suppliest me with the least advantage of hope. I will indeed no longer endure it, nor am I yet persuaded to put up[526] in peace what already I have foolishly suffered.

IAGO: Will you hear me, Roderigo?

RODERIGO: Faith, I have heard too much, for your words and performances are no kin together.

IAGO: You charge me most unjustly.

RODERIGO: With nought but truth. I have wasted myself out of my means. The jewels you have had from me to deliver to Desdemona would half have corrupted a votarist;[527] you have told me she has received them, and returned me expectations and comforts of sudden respect[528] and acquaintance, but I find none.

IAGO: Well; go to; very well:

---

[520]found delight   [521]still   [522]destroy   [523]i.e., what reason do you have for saying that   [524]you put me off   [525]favorable circumstances   [526]put up with   [527]nun   [528]immediate consideration

RODERIGO: Very well! go to! I cannot go to, man; 'tis not very well: by this hand, I say, it is very scurvy, and begin to find myself fobbed[529] in it.

IAGO: Very well.

RODERIGO: I tell you 'tis not very well. I will make myself known to Desdemona; if she will return me my jewels, I will give over my suit and repent my unlawful solicitation; if not, assure yourself I will seek satisfaction of you.

IAGO: You have said now.[530]

RODERIGO: Ay, and said nothing, but what I protest intendment of doing.

IAGO: Why, now I see there's mettle in thee, and even from this instant do build on thee a better opinion than ever before. Give me thy hand, Roderigo; thou hast taken against me a most just exception; but yet, I protest, I have dealt most directly in thy affair.

RODERIGO: It hath not appeared.

IAGO: I grant indeed it hath not appeared, and your suspicion is not without wit and judgment. But, Roderigo, if thou hast that in thee indeed, which I have greater reason to believe now than ever, I mean purpose, courage, and valour, this night show it: if thou the next night following enjoy not Desdemona, take me from this world with treachery and devise engines for[531] my life.

RODERIGO: Well, what is it? is it within reason and compass?

IAGO: Sir, there is especial commission come from Venice to depute Cassio in Othello's place.

RODERIGO: Is that true? why, then Othello and Desdemona return again to Venice.

IAGO: O, no! he goes into Mauritania, and takes away with him the fair Desdemona, unless his abode be lingered here by some accident; wherein none can be so determinate[532] as the removing of Cassio.

RODERIGO: How do you mean, removing of him?

IAGO: Why, by making him uncapable of Othello's place; knocking out his brains.

RODERIGO: And that you would have me do?

IAGO: Ay; if you dare do yourself a profit and a right. He sups to-night with a harlotry,[533] and thither will I go to him; he knows not yet of his honourable fortune. If you will watch his going thence,—which I will fashion to fall out between twelve and one,—you may take him at your pleasure; I will be near to second your attempt, and he shall fall between us. Come, stand not amazed at it, but go along with me; I will show you such a necessity in his death that you shall think yourself

---

[529]cheated   [530]i.e., "I suppose you're through?" (?); or: "Now you're talking" (?)   [531]devices against   [532]effective   [533]harlot

bound to put it on him. It is now high supper-time, and the night grows to waste; about it.

RODERIGO: I will hear further reason for this.

IAGO: And you shall be satisfied.   (*Exeunt.*)

Scene 3 [Another Room in the Castle.]

(*Enter* OTHELLO, LODOVICO, DESDEMONA, EMILIA, *and* ATTENDANTS.)

LODOVICO: I do beseech you, sir, trouble yourself no further.

OTHELLO: O! pardon me; 'twill do me good to walk.

LODOVICO: Madam, good-night; I humbly thank your ladyship.

DESDEMONA: Your honour is most welcome.

OTHELLO: Will you walk, sir?
   O! Desdemona,—

DESDEMONA: My lord?

OTHELLO: Get you to bed on the instant; I will be returned forthwith; dismiss your attendant there; look it be done.

DESDEMONA: I will, my lord.

                         (*Exeunt* OTHELLO, LODOVICO, *and* ATTENDANTS.)

EMILIA: How goes it now? He looks gentler than he did.

DESDEMONA: He says he will return incontinent;[534]
   He hath commanded me to go to bed,
   And bade me to dismiss you.

EMILIA: Dismiss me!

DESDEMONA: It was his bidding; therefore, good Emilia,
   Give me my nightly wearing, and adieu:
   We must not now displease him.

EMILIA: I would you had never seen him.

DESDEMONA: So would not I; my love doth so approve him,
   That even his stubbornness,[535] his checks[536] and frowns,—
   Prithee, unpin me,—have grace and favour in them.

EMILIA: I have laid those sheets you bade me on the bed.

DESDEMONA: All 's one.[537] Good faith! how foolish are our minds!
   If I do die before thee, prithee, shroud me
   In one of those same sheets.

EMILIA: Come, come, you talk.

DESDEMONA: My mother had a maid call'd Barbara;
   She was in love, and he she lov'd prov'd mad[538]
   And did forsake her; she had a song of 'willow';
   An old thing 'twas, but it express'd her fortune,

---

[534] at once   [535] roughness   [536] rebukes   [537] i.e., it doesn't matter   [538] wild

And she died singing it; that song to-night
Will not go from my mind; I have much to do
But to go hang my head all at one side,
And sing it like poor Barbara. Prithee, dispatch.

EMILIA: Shall I go fetch your night-gown?

DESDEMONA: No, unpin me here.
   This Lodovico is a proper man.

EMILIA: A very handsome man.

DESDEMONA: He speaks well.

EMILIA: I know a lady in Venice would have walked barefoot to Palestine
   for a touch of his nether lip.

DESDEMONA (*sings*):
   The poor soul sat sighing by a sycamore tree,
      Sing all a green willow;
   Her hand on her bosom, her head on her knee,
      Sing willow, willow, willow:
   The fresh streams ran by her, and murmur'd her moans;
      Sing willow, willow, willow:
   Her salt tears fell from her, and soften'd the stones;—

Lay by these:—
   Sing willow, willow, willow:

Prithee, hie thee;[539] he 'll come anon.—

   Sing all a green willow must be my garland.
   Let nobody blame him, his scorn I approve,—

Nay, that 's not next. Hark! who is it that knocks?

EMILIA: It is the wind.

DESDEMONA:
   I call'd my love false love; but what said he then?
      Sing willow, willow, willow:
   If I court moe[540] women, you 'll couch with moe men.

So, get thee gone; good-night. Mine eyes do itch;
   Doth that bode weeping?

EMILIA: 'Tis neither here nor there.

DESDEMONA: I have heard it said so. O! these men, these men!
   Dost thou in conscience think, tell me, Emilia,
   That there be women do abuse their husbands
   In such gross kind?

EMILIA: There be some such, no question.

[539] hurry   [540] more

DESDEMONA: Wouldst thou do such a deed for all the world?

EMILIA: Why, would not you?

DESDEMONA: No, by this heavenly light!

EMILIA: Nor I neither by this heavenly light;
   I might do 't as well i' the dark.

DESDEMONA: Wouldst thou do such a deed for all the world?

EMILIA: The world is a huge thing; 'tis a great price
   For a small vice.

DESDEMONA: In troth, I think thou wouldst not.

EMILIA: In troth, I think I should, and undo 't when I had done. Marry,
   I would not do such a thing for a joint-ring,[541] nor measures of lawn,[542]
   nor for gowns, petticoats, nor caps, nor any petty exhibition;[543] but for
   the whole world, who would not make her husband a cuckold to
   make him a monarch? I should venture purgatory for 't.

DESDEMONA: Beshrew me, if I would do such a wrong
   For the whole world.

EMILIA: Why, the wrong is but a wrong i' the world; and having the world
   for your labour, 'tis a wrong in your own world, and you might quickly
   make it right.

DESDEMONA: I do not think there is any such woman.

EMILIA: Yes, a dozen; and as many to the vantage,[544] as
   Would store[545] the world they played for.
   But I do think it is their husbands' faults
   If wives do fall. Say that they slack their duties,
   And pour our treasures into foreign laps,
   Or else break out in peevish jealousies,
   Throwing restraint upon us; or say they strike us,
   Or scant[546] our former having[547] in despite;
   Why, we have galls,[548] and though we have some grace,
   Yet have we some revenge. Let husbands know
   Their wives have sense like them; they see and smell,
   And have their palates both for sweet and sour,
   As husbands have. What is it that they do
   When they change us for others? Is it sport?[549]
   I think it is; and doth affection breed it?
   I think it doth; is 't frailty that thus errs?
   It is so too; and have not we affections,
   Desires for sport, and frailty, as men have?
   Then, let them use us well; else let them know,
   The ills we do, their ills instruct us so.

---

[541] ring made in separable halves [542] fine linen [543] offer, gift [544] over and above [545] populate
[546] reduce [547] allowance [548] spirits, temper [549] lust, sexual enjoyment

DESDEMONA: Good-night, good-night; heaven me such usage[550] send,
    Not to pick bad from bad, but by bad mend!   (*Exeunt.*)

ACT V

Scene 1 [Cyprus. A Street.]

(*Enter* IAGO *and* RODERIGO.)

IAGO: Here, stand behind this bulk;[551] straight will he come:
    Wear thy good rapier bare, and put it home.
    Quick, quick; fear nothing; I 'll be at thy elbow.
    It makes us, or it mars us; think on that,
    And fix most firm thy resolution.
RODERIGO: Be near at hand; I may miscarry in 't.
IAGO: Here, at thy hand: be bold, and take thy stand.   (*Retires.*)
RODERIGO: I have no great devotion to the deed;
    And yet he has given me satisfying reasons:
    'Tis but a man gone: forth, my sword; he dies.
IAGO: I have rubb'd this young quat[552] almost to the sense,[553]
    And he grows angry. Now, whether he kill Cassio,
    Or Cassio him, or each do kill the other,
    Every way makes my gain: live Roderigo,
    He calls me to a restitution large
    Of gold and jewels that I bobb'd[554] from him,
    As gifts to Desdemona;
    It must not be: if Cassio do remain,
    He hath a daily beauty in his life
    That makes me ugly: and, besides, the Moor
    May unfold me to him; there stand I in much peril.
    No, he must die. But so;[555] I hear him coming.

(*Enter* CASSIO.)

RODERIGO: I know his gait; 'tis he. Villain, thou diest!

(*Makes a pass at* CASSIO.)

CASSIO: That thrust had been mine enemy indeed
    But that my coat is better than thou know'st;
    I will make proof of thine.

(*Draws, and wounds* RODERIGO.)

---

[550] habits (?), treatment (?)   [551] jutting part of a wall   [552] pimple   [553] to the quick   [554] swindled
[555] i.e., that's the only way

RODERIGO: O! I am slain.

(IAGO *from behind wounds* CASSIO *in the leg, and exit.*)

CASSIO: I am maim'd for ever. Help, ho! murder! murder! (*Falls.*)

(*Enter* OTHELLO, *at a distance.*)

OTHELLO: The voice of Cassio: Iago keeps his word.
RODERIGO: O! villain that I am!
OTHELLO: It is e'en so.
CASSIO: O, help, ho! light! a surgeon!
OTHELLO: 'Tis he: O brave Iago, honest and just!
   That hast such noble sense of thy friend's wrong;
   Thou teachest me. Minion,[556] your dear lies dead,
   And your unblest fate hies; strumpet, I come!
   Forth of my heart those charms, thine eyes, are blotted;
   Thy bed lust-stain'd shall with lust's blood be spotted.   (*Exit.*)

(*Enter* LODOVICO *and* GRATIANO, *at a distance.*)

CASSIO: What ho! no watch? no passage?[557] murder! murder!
GRATIANO: 'Tis some mischance; the cry is very direful.
CASSIO: O, help!
LODOVICO: Hark!
RODERIGO: O wretched villain!
LODOVICO: Two or three groans: it is a heavy[558] night;
   These may be counterfeits; let 's think 't unsafe
   To come in to the cry[559] without more help.
RODERIGO: Nobody come? then shall I bleed to death.
LODOVICO: Hark!

(*Re-enter* IAGO, *with a light.*)

GRATIANO: Here 's one comes in his shirt, with light and weapons.
IAGO: Who 's there? whose noise is this that cries on murder?
LODOVICO: We do not know.
IAGO: Did not you hear a cry?
CASSIO: Here, here! for heaven's sake, help me.
IAGO: What 's the matter?
GRATIANO: This is Othello's ancient, as I take it.
LODOVICO: The same indeed; a very valiant fellow.
IAGO: What are you here that cry so grievously?
CASSIO: Iago? O! I am spoil'd, undone by villains!
   Give me some help.

---

[556](Cassio's) darling, i.e., Desdemona   [557]passer-by   [558]dark   [559]where the cry comes from

IAGO: O me, lieutenant! what villains have done this?

CASSIO: I think that one of them is hereabout,
And cannot make away.

IAGO: O treacherous villains!
(*To* LODOVICO *and* GRATIANO.) What are you there? come in, and give
some help.

RODERIGO: O! help me here.

CASSIO: That 's one of them.

IAGO: O murderous slave! O villain!

(*Stabs* RODERIGO.)

RODERIGO: O damn'd Iago! O inhuman dog!

IAGO: Kill men i' the dark! Where be these bloody thieves?
How silent is this town! Ho! murder! murder!
What may you be? are you of good or evil?

LODOVICO: As you shall prove us, praise us.

IAGO: Signior Lodovico?

LODOVICO: He, sir.

IAGO: I cry you mercy. Here 's Cassio hurt by villains.

GRATIANO: Cassio!

IAGO: How is it, brother?

CASSIO: My leg is cut in two.

IAGO: Marry, heaven forbid.
Light, gentlemen; I 'll bind it with my shirt.

(*Enter* BIANCA.)

BIANCA: What is the matter, ho? who is 't that cried?

IAGO: Who is 't that cried!

BIANCA: O my dear Cassio! my sweet Cassio!
O Cassio, Cassio, Cassio!

IAGO: O notable strumpet! Cassio, may you suspect
Who they should be that have thus mangled you?

CASSIO: No.

GRATIANO: I am sorry to find you thus; I have been to seek you.

IAGO: Lend me a garter. So. O! for a chair,
To bear him easily hence!

BIANCA: Alas; he faints! O Cassio, Cassio, Cassio!

IAGO: Gentlemen all, I do suspect this trash[560]
To be a party in this injury.
Patience awhile, good Cassio, Come, come.
Lend me a light. Know we this face, or no?

---

[560] i.e., Bianca

Alas! my friend and my dear countryman,
Roderigo? no: yes, sure, O heaven! Roderigo.
GRATIANO: What! of Venice?
IAGO: Even he, sir: did you know him?
GRATIANO: Know him! ay.
IAGO: Signior Gratiano? I cry you gentle pardon;
These bloody accidents must excuse my manners,
That so neglected you.
GRATIANO: I am glad to see you.
IAGO: How do you, Cassio? O! a chair, a chair!
GRATIANO: Roderigo!

(*A chair brought in.*)

IAGO: He, he, 'tis he,—O! that 's well said; the chair:
Some good men bear him carefully from hence;
I 'll fetch the general's surgeon. (*To* BIANCA.) For you, mistress,
Save you your labour. He that lies slain here; Cassio,
Was my dear friend. What malice was between you?
CASSIO: None in the world; nor do I know that man.
IAGO (*to* BIANCA): What! look you pale? O! bear him out o' the air—

(CASSIO *and* RODERIGO *are borne off.*)

Stay you, good gentlemen. Look you pale, mistress?—
Do you perceive the gastness[561] of her eye?
Nay, if you stare, we shall hear more anon.
Behold her well; I pray you, look upon her.
Do you see, gentlemen? nay, guiltiness will speak
Though tongues were out of use.

(*Enter* EMILIA.)

EMILIA: 'Las! what 's the matter? what 's the matter, husband?
IAGO: Cassio hath here been set on in the dark
By Roderigo and fellows that are 'scaped:
He 's almost slain, and Roderigo dead.
EMILIA: Alas! good gentleman; alas! good Cassio!
IAGO: This is the fruit of whoring. Prithee, Emilia,
Go know of Cassio where he supp'd to-night.
(*To* BIANCA.) What! do you shake at that?
BIANCA: He supp'd at my house; but I therefore shake not.
IAGO: O! did he so? I charge you, go with me.
EMILIA: Fie, fie upon thee, strumpet!

[561] terror

BIANCA: I am no strumpet, but of life as honest
    As you that thus abuse me.
EMILIA: As I! foh! fie upon thee!
IAGO: Kind gentlemen, let 's go see poor Cassio dress'd.[562]
    Come, mistress, you must tell 's another tale.
    Emilia, run you to the citadel,
    And tell my lord and lady what hath happ'd.
    Will you go on afore? (*Aside.*) This is the night
    That either makes me or fordoes[563] me quite.   (*Exeunt.*)

Scene 2 [A Bedchamber in the Castle. DESDEMONA in bed asleep. A light burning.]

(*Enter* OTHELLO.)

OTHELLO: It is the cause,[564] it is the cause, my soul;
    Let me not name it to you, you chaste stars!
    It is the cause. Yet I 'll not shed her blood,
    Nor scar that whiter skin of hers than snow,
    And smooth as monumental alabaster.
    Yet she must die, else she 'll betray more men.
    Put out the light, and then put out the light:
    If I quench thee, thou flaming minister,[565]
    I can again thy former light restore,
    Should I repent me; but once put out thy light,
    Thou cunning'st[566] pattern of excelling nature,
    I know not where is that Promethean[567] heat
    That can thy light relume.[568] When I have pluck'd the rose,
    I cannot give it vital growth again,
    It needs must wither: I 'll smell it on the tree. (*Kisses her.*)
    O balmy breath, that dost almost persuade
    Justice to break her sword! One more, one more.
    Be thus when thou art dead, and I will kill thee,
    And love thee after. One more, and this the last:
    So sweet was ne'er so fatal. I must weep,
    But they are cruel tears; this sorrow 's heavenly,
    It strikes where it doth love. She wakes.
DESDEMONA: Who 's there? Othello?

---

[562]bandaged [563]ruins [564]i.e., Desdemona's unchastity (Othello means that the severity of the punishment is required by the nature of her sin.) [565]i.e., the candle [566]most intricately wrought [567]in Greek mythology the demi-god Prometheus stole fire from the gods and gave it to man [568]relight

OTHELLO: Ay, Desdemona.

DESDEMONA: Will you come to bed, my lord?

OTHELLO: Have you pray'd to-night, Desdemona?

DESDEMONA: Ay, my lord.

OTHELLO: If you bethink yourself of any crime
   Unreconcil'd as yet to heaven and grace,
   Solicit for it straight.

DESDEMONA: Alas! my lord, what may you mean by that?

OTHELLO: Well, do it, and be brief; I will walk by:[569]
   I would not kill thy unprepared spirit;
   No; heaven forfend![570] I would not kill thy soul.

DESDEMONA: Talk you of killing?

OTHELLO: Ay, I do.

DESDEMONA: Then heaven
   Have mercy on me!

OTHELLO: Amen! with all my heart.

DESDEMONA: If you say so, I hope you will not kill me.

OTHELLO: Hum!

DESDEMONA: And yet I fear you; for you are fatal then
   When your eyes roll so. Why I should fear I know not,
   Since guiltiness I know not; but yet I feel I fear.

OTHELLO: Think on thy sins.

DESDEMONA: They are loves I bear to you.

OTHELLO: Ay, and for that thou diest.

DESDEMONA: That death 's unnatural that kills for loving.
   Alas! why gnaw you so your nether lip?
   Some bloody passion shakes your very frame;
   These are portents,[571] but yet, I hope, I hope
   They do not point on me.

OTHELLO: Peace, and be still!

DESDEMONA: I will so. What 's the matter?

OTHELLO: That handkerchief which I so lov'd and gave thee
   Thou gav'st to Cassio.

DESDEMONA: No, by my life and soul!
   Send for the man and ask him.

OTHELLO: Sweet soul, take heed,
   Take heed of perjury; thou 'rt on thy death-bed.

DESDEMONA: Ay, but not yet to die.

OTHELLO: Yes, presently;[572]
   Therefore confess thee freely of thy sin;
   For to deny each article with oath

---

[569]nearby   [570]forbid   [571]omens   [572]at once

Cannot remove nor choke the strong conception[573]
That I do groan withal. Thou art to die.
DESDEMONA: Then Lord have mercy on me!
OTHELLO: I say, amen.
DESDEMONA: And have you mercy too! I never did
Offend you in my life; never lov'd Cassio
But with such general warranty[574] of heaven
As I might love; I never gave him token.
OTHELLO: By heaven, I saw my handkerchief in 's hand.
O perjur'd woman! thou dost stone[575] my heart,
And mak'st me call what I intend to do
A murder, which I thought a sacrifice:
I saw the handkerchief.
DESDEMONA: He found it then;
I never gave it him. Send for him hither;
Let him confess a truth.
OTHELLO: He hath confessed.
DESDEMONA: What, my lord?
OTHELLO: That he hath us'd thee.
DESDEMONA: How? Unlawfully?
OTHELLO: Ay.
DESDEMONA: He will not say so.
OTHELLO: No; his mouth is stopp'd:
Honest Iago hath ta'en order for 't.[576]
DESDEMONA: O! my fear interprets. What! is he dead?
OTHELLO: Had all his hairs been lives, my great revenge
Had stomach[577] for them all.
DESDEMONA: Alas! he is betray'd and I undone.
OTHELLO: Out, strumpet! Weep'st thou for him to my face?
DESDEMONA: O! banish me, my lord, but kill me not!
OTHELLO: Down, strumpet!
DESDEMONA: Kill me to-morrow; let me live to-night!
OTHELLO: Nay, if you strive,—
DESDEMONA: But half an hour!
OTHELLO: Being done, there is no pause.
DESDEMONA: But while I say one prayer!
OTHELLO: It is too late.
                          (*He smothers her.*)

EMILIA (*within*): My lord, my lord! what, ho! my lord, my lord!
OTHELLO: What noise is this? Not dead? not yet quite dead?
I that am cruel am yet merciful;

---

[573]belief [574]permission [575]turn to stone [576]taken steps [577]appetite

I would not have thee linger in thy pain.
So, so.

EMILIA (*within*): What, ho! my lord, my lord!

OTHELLO: Who's there?

EMILIA (*within*): O! good my lord, I would speak a word with you!

OTHELLO: Yes; 'tis Emilia: by and by.[578] She 's dead.
'Tis like[579] she comes to speak of Cassio's death;
The noise was high. Ha! no more moving?
Still as the grave. Shall she come in? Were 't good?[580]
I think she stirs again: no. What 's best to do?
If she come in she 'll sure speak to my wife:
My wife! my wife! what wife? I have no wife:
O, insupportable! O heavy hour!
Methinks it should be now a huge eclipse
Of sun and moon, and that the affrighted globe
Should yawn[581] at alteration.

EMILIA (*within*):   I do beseech you
That I may speak with you, O! good my lord.

OTHELLO: I had forgot thee: O! come in. Emilia:
Soft, by and by: let me the curtains draw.
Where art thou?   (*Unlocks the door.*)

(*Enter* EMILIA.)

                        What 's the matter with thee now?

EMILIA: O! my good lord, yonder 's foul murder done.

OTHELLO: What! now?

EMILIA: But now, my lord.

OTHELLO: It is the very error[582] of the moon;
She comes more near the earth than she was wont,
And makes men mad.

EMILIA: Cassio, my lord, has kill'd a young Venetian
Call'd Roderigo.

OTHELLO: Roderigo kill'd!
And Cassio kill'd?

EMILIA: No, Cassio is not kill'd.

OTHELLO: Not Cassio kill'd! then murder 's out of tune,
And sweet revenge grows harsh.

DESDEMONA: O! falsely, falsely murder'd.

EMILIA: Alas! what cry is that?

OTHELLO: That! what?

EMILIA: Out, and alas! that was my lady's voice:

---

[578]i.e., "just a moment"   [579]likely   [580]would that be wise   [581]open up (as in an earthquake)
[582]straying

Help! Help, ho! help! O lady, speak again!
Sweet Desdemona! O! sweet mistress, speak.
DESDEMONA: A guiltless death I die.
EMILIA: O! who hath done this deed?
DESDEMONA: Nobody; I myself; farewell:
Commend me to my kind lord. O! farewell!   (*Dies.*)
OTHELLO: Why, how should she be murder'd?
EMILIA: Alas! who knows?
OTHELLO: You heard her say herself it was not I.
EMILIA: She said so; I must needs report the truth.
OTHELLO: She 's like a liar gone to burning hell;
'Twas I that kill'd her.
EMILIA: O! the more angel she,
And you the blacker devil.
OTHELLO: She turn'd to folly, and she was a whore.
EMILIA: Thou dost belie her, and thou art a devil.
OTHELLO: She was false as water.
EMILIA: Thou art rash as fire to say
That she was false: O! she was heavenly true.
OTHELLO: Cassio did tup her; ask thy husband else.
O! I were damn'd beneath all depth in hell
But that I did proceed[583] upon just grounds
To this extremity. Thy husband knew it all.
EMILIA: My husband!
OTHELLO: Thy husband.
EMILIA: That she was false to wedlock?
OTHELLO: Ay, with Cassio. Nay, had she been true,
If heaven would make me such another world
Of one entire and perfect chrysolite,[584]
I 'd not have sold her for it.
EMILIA: My husband!
OTHELLO: Ay, 'twas he that told me first:
An honest man he is, and hates the slime
That sticks on filthy deeds.
EMILIA: My husband!
OTHELLO: What needs this iterance,[585] woman? I say thy husband.
EMILIA: O mistress! villainy hath made mocks with love.
My husband say that she was false!
OTHELLO: He, woman;
I say, thy husband: dost understand the word?
My friend, thy husband, honest, honest Iago.

---

[583] had I not proceeded   [584] topaz   [585] repetition

EMILIA: If he say so, may his pernicious soul
　　Rot half a grain a day! he lies to the heart:
　　She was too fond of her most filthy bargain.[586]
OTHELLO: Ha!
EMILIA: Do thy worst:
　　This deed of thine is no more worthy heaven
　　Than thou wast worthy her.
OTHELLO: 　　　　　　　　　　　Peace! you were best.[587]
EMILIA: Thou hast not half the power to do me harm
　　As I have to be hurt. O gull! O dolt!
　　As ignorant as dirt! thou hast done a deed,—
　　I care not for thy sword; I 'll make thee known,
　　Though I lost twenty lives. Help! help, ho! help!
　　The Moor has kill'd my mistress! murder! murder!

　　(*Enter* MONTANO, GRATIANO, IAGO, *and others.*)

MONTANO: What is the matter? How now, general!
EMILIA: O! are you come, Iago? you have done well.
　　That men must lay their murders on your neck.
GRATIANO: What is the matter?
EMILIA: Disprove this villain if thou be'st a man:
　　He says thou told'st him that his wife was false.
　　I know thou didst not, thou 'rt not such a villain.
　　Speak, for my heart is full.
IAGO: I told him what I thought, and told no more
　　Than what he found himself was apt and true.
EMILIA: But did you ever tell him she was false?
IAGO: I did.
EMILIA: You told a lie, an odious damned lie;
　　Upon my soul, a lie, a wicked lie;
　　She false with Cassio! Did you say with Cassio?
IAGO: With Cassio, mistress. Go to, charm[588] your tongue.
EMILIA: I will not charm my tongue; I am bound to speak.
　　My mistress here lies murder'd in her bed.
ALL: O heavens forfend!
EMILIA: And your reports have set the murder on.
OTHELLO: Nay, stare not, masters; it is true, indeed.
GRATIANO: 'Tis a strange truth.
MONTANO: O monstrous act!
EMILIA: 　　　　　　　　　Villainy! villainy! villainy!
　　I think upon 't, I think, I smell 't; O villainy!

---

[586] i.e., Othello　[587] you'd better be quiet　[588] i.e., into silence

I thought so then;[589] I 'll kill myself for grief.
O! villainy, villainy!

IAGO: What! are you mad? I charge you, get you home.

EMILIA: Good gentlemen, let me have leave to speak:
'Tis proper I obey him, but not now.
Perchance, Iago, I will ne'er go home.

OTHELLO: O! O! O!   (*Falls on the bed.*)

EMILIA: Nay, lay thee down and roar,
For thou hast kill'd the sweetest innocent
That e'er did lift up eye.

OTHELLO: O! she was foul.   (*Rises.*)
I scarce did know you, uncle. There lies your niece,
Whose breath, indeed, these hands have newly stopp'd:
I know this act shows terrible and grim.

GRATIANO: Poor Desdemona! I am glad thy father 's dead.
Thy match was mortal to him, and pure grief
Shore[590] his old thread in twain: did he live now,
This sight would make him do a desperate turn,
Yea, curse his better angel from his side,
And fall to reprobation.[591]

OTHELLO: 'Tis pitiful; but yet Iago knows
That she with Cassio hath the act of shame
A thousand times committed; Cassio confess'd it:
And she did gratify[592] his amorous works
With that recognizance and pledge of love
Which I first gave her. I saw it in his hand:
It was a handkerchief, an antique token
My father gave my mother.

EMILIA: O heaven! O heavenly powers!

IAGO: Come, hold your peace.

EMILIA: 'Twill out, 'twill out: I hold my peace, sir? no;
No, I will speak as liberal as the north;[593]
Let heaven and men and devils, let them all,
All, all, cry shame against me, yet I 'll speak.

IAGO: Be wise, and get you home.

EMILIA: I will not.

(IAGO *threatens to stab* EMILIA.)

---

[589] cf. "I will be hang'd, if some eternal villain, / Some busy and insinuating rogue, / Some cogging cozening slave, to get some office, / Have not devis'd this slander; . . ." (IV, 2, p. 113). Emilia means, not that she guessed Iago's guilt, but that she rightly guessed the slanderer's motive.   [590] cut   [591] damnation   [592] reward   [593] i.e., the north wind (?), the supposedly free-spoken people of north England (?)

GRATIANO: Fie!
  Your sword upon a woman!
EMILIA: O thou dull Moor! that handkerchief thou speak'st of
  I found by fortune and did give my husband;
  For often, with a solemn earnestness,
  More than, indeed, belong'd to such a trifle,
  He begg'd of me to steal it.
IAGO: Villainous whore!
EMILIA: She give it Cassio! no, alas! I found it,
  And I did give 't my husband.
IAGO: Filth, thou liest!
EMILIA: By heaven, I do not, I do not, gentlemen.
  O murderous coxcomb![594] what should such a fool
  Do with so good a wife?
OTHELLO: Are there no stones[595] in heaven
  But what serve for the thunder? Precious villain!

  (*He runs at* IAGO. IAGO *stabs* EMILIA.)

GRATIANO: The woman falls: sure, he has kill'd his wife.   (*Exit* IAGO.)
EMILIA: Ay, ay; O! lay me by my mistress' side.
GRATIANO: He 's gone; but his wife 's kill'd.
MONTANO: 'Tis a notorious[596] villain. Take you this weapon,
  Which I have here recover'd from the Moor.
  Come, guard the door without; let him not pass,
  But kill him rather. I 'll after that same villain,
  For 'tis a damned slave.   (*Exeunt* MONTANO *and* GRATIANO.)
OTHELLO: I am not valiant neither,
  But every puny whipster[597] gets my sword.
  But why should honour outlive honesty?
  Let it go all.
EMILIA: What did thy song bode, lady?
  Hark, canst thou hear me? I will play the swan,
  And die in music:—
  (*Sings*.)   Willow, willow, willow.
  Moor, she was chaste; she lov'd thee, cruel Moor;
  So come my soul to bliss as I speak true;
  So speaking as I think, I die, I die.   (*Dies*.)
OTHELLO: I have another weapon in this chamber;
  It is a sword of Spain, the ice-brook's temper.[598]

---

[594]idiot [595]i.e., thunderbolts (to strike Iago down) [596]notable [597]i.e., a small boy whipping a top [598]tempered in icy water (or the reference may be to Innsbruck, famed for the quality of its steel, but this hardly fits "a sword of Spain")

O! here it is. Uncle, I must come forth.

GRATIANO(*within*): If thou attempt it, it will cost thee dear:
Thou hast no weapon, and perforce must suffer.

OTHELLO: Look in upon me then, and speak with me,
Or, naked[599] as I am, I will assault thee.

(*Re-enter* GRATIANO.)

GRATIANO: What is the matter?

OTHELLO: Behold! I have a weapon;
A better never did itself sustain
Upon a soldier's thigh: I have seen the day,
That with this little arm, and this good sword,
I have made my way through more impediments
Than twenty times your stop: but, O vain boast!
Who can control his fate? 'tis not so now.
Be not afraid, though you do see me weapon'd;
Here is my journey's end, here is my butt,[600]
And very sea-mark of my utmost sail.[601]
Do you go back dismay'd? 'tis a lost fear;
Man but a rush[602] against Othello's breast,
And he retires. Where should Othello go?
Now how dost thou look now? O ill-starr'd wench!
Pale as thy smock! when we shall meet at compt,[603]
This look of thine will hurl my soul from heaven,
And fiends will snatch at it. Cold, cold, my girl!
Even like thy chastity.
O! cursed, cursed slave. Whip me, ye devils,
From the possession of this heavenly sight!
Blow me about in winds! roast me in sulphur!
Wash me in steep-down gulfs of liquid fire!
O Desdemona! Desdemona! dead!
Oh! Oh! Oh!

(*Enter* LODOVICO, MONTANO, CASSIO *carried in a chair, and* OFFI-
CERS *with* IAGO, *prisoner.*)

LODOVICO: Where is this rash and most unfortunate man?

OTHELLO: That 's he that was Othello; here I am.

LODOVICO: Where is that viper? bring the villain forth.

OTHELLO: I look down towards his feet;[604] but that 's a fable.
If that thou be'st a devil, I cannot kill thee.   (*Wounds* IAGO.)

---

[599]unarmed   [600]goal, end, limit   [601]destination of my farthest journey   [602]wield but a reed
[603]on the day of judgment   [604]i.e., for the Devil's cloven hoof

LODOVICO: Wrench his sword from him.   (OTHELLO *is disarmed.*)
IAGO: I bleed, sir; but not kill'd.
OTHELLO: I am not sorry neither; I 'd have thee live;
    For, in my sense,[605] 'tis happiness to die.
LODOVICO: O thou Othello! that wert once so good,
    Fall'n in the practice[606] of a damned slave,[607]
    What shall be said to thee?
OTHELLO: Why, any thing:
    An honourable murderer, if you will;
    For nought did I in hate, but all in honour.
LODOVICO: This wretch hath part confess'd his villainy:
    Did you and he consent in Cassio's death?
OTHELLO: Ay.
CASSIO: Dear general, I never gave you cause.
OTHELLO: I do believe it, and I ask your pardon.
    Will you, I pray, demand that demi-devil
    Why he hath thus ensnar'd my soul and body?
IAGO: Demand me nothing: what you know, you know:
    From this time forth I never will speak word.
LODOVICO: What! not to pray?
GRATIANO: Torments will ope[608] your lips.
OTHELLO: Well, thou dost best.
LODOVICO: Sir, you shall understand what hath befall'n,
    Which, as I think, you know not. Here is a letter
    Found in the pocket of the slain Roderigo,
    And here another; the one of them imports
    The death of Cassio to be undertook
    By Roderigo.
OTHELLO: O villain!
CASSIO: Most heathenish and most gross!
LODOVICO: Now here's another discontented paper,
    Found in his pocket too; and this, it seems,
    Roderigo meant to have sent this damned villain,
    But that, belike,[609] Iago in the interim[610]
    Came in and satisfied him.
OTHELLO: O the pernicious caitiff!
    How came you, Cassio, by that handkerchief
    That was my wife's?
CASSIO: I found it in my chamber;
    And he himself confess'd but even now
    That there he dropp'd it for a special purpose

---

[605]the way I feel [606]plot, machination [607]i.e., Iago [608]open [609]most likely [610]in the meantime

Which wrought to his desire.

OTHELLO: O fool! fool! fool!

CASSIO: There is besides in Roderigo's letter
  How he upbraids Iago that he made him
  Brave me upon the watch; whereon it came
  That I was cast:[611] and even but now he spake,
  After long seeming dead, Iago hurt him,
  Iago set him on.

LODOVICO: You must forsake this room and go with us;
  Your power and your command is taken off,
  And Cassio rules in Cyprus. For this slave,
  If there be any cunning cruelty
  That can torment him much and hold him long,
  It shall be his. You shall close prisoner rest,
  Till that the nature of your fault be known
  To the Venetian state. Come, bring him away.

OTHELLO: Soft you; a word or two before you go.
  I have done the state some service, and they know 't;
  No more of that. I pray you, in your letters,
  When you shall these unlucky deeds relate,
  Speak of me as I am; nothing extenuate,
  Nor set down aught[612] in malice: then, must you speak
  Of one that lov'd not wisely but too well;
  Of one not easily jealous, but, being wrought,
  Perplex'd[613] in the extreme; of one whose hand
  Like the base Indian,[614] threw a pearl away
  Richer than all his tribe; of one whose subdu'd[615] eyes
  Albeit unused to the melting mood,
  Drop tears as fast as the Arabian trees
  Their med'cinable gum. Set you down this;
  And say besides, that in Aleppo once,
  Where a malignant and a turban'd Turk
  Beat a Venetian and traduc'd the state,
  I took by the throat the circumcised dog,
  And smote him, thus.   *(Stabs himself.)*

LODOVICO: O bloody period![616]

GRATIANO: All that's spoke is marr'd.

OTHELLO: I kiss'd thee ere I killed thee; no way but this,
                    (Falling upon DESDEMONA.*)*

---

[611] dismissed   [612] anything   [613] distracted   [614] The Folio reads "Iudean." Both readings denote the foolish infidel who fails to appreciate the treasure he possesses.   [615] overcome (by grief)   [616] ending

Killing myself to die upon a kiss.   (*Dies.*)
CASSIO: This did I fear, but thought he had no weapon;
  For he was great of heart.
LODOVICO (*to* IAGO):   O Spartan dog!
  More fell[617] than anguish, hunger, or the sea.
  Look on the tragic loading of this bed;
  This is thy work; the object poisons sight;
  Let it be hid. Gratiano, keep the house,
  And seize upon the fortunes of the Moor,
  For they succeed on you. To you, lord governor,
  Remains the censure of this hellish villain,
  The time, the place, the torture; O! enforce it.
  Myself will straight aboard, and to the state
  This heavy act with heavy heart relate.   (*Exeunt.*)

[617] grim, cruel

Court records show that *Othello* was performed before King James I on November 1, 1604. We do not know the date of composition; most likely it did not much precede the performance. The metre and the dramatic rather than merely decorative use of imagery are internal evidence that *Othello* belongs to Shakespeare's maturity as playwright, and the theme of nobility corrupted and innocence destroyed suggests that it belongs to the period of the other great tragedies of evil rampant and of the "dark" comedies of cynical disgust. It was a time when the Elizabethan exuberance of the 1590's was turning into the restless ennui and tortured introspection of the Jacobean age.

Othello was included in the first collected edition of Shakespeare's plays, the famous First Folio* of 1623, compiled by John Heminges and Henry Condell, two of Shakespeare's actor friends and partners in the King's Men company. The year before, *Othello* had appeared in a quarto* edition, whose text at some points differs from that of the Folio. Most modern editions, including the present, give a compromise reading, with the Folio as base.

Although first given at court, subsequent performances of *Othello*

---

*"Folio" and "quarto" are printer's terms and refer to page format. Folio is the size of a printer's sheet folded once. Thus folded, a sheet makes two leaves (four pages). Quarto is the size of a sheet folded twice (four leaves, eight pages).

took place at the Globe Theater on the south side of the Thames, in the suburb of Bankside. The Globe had been built by the King's Men in 1599. It was, probably, an octagonal building of three levels of galleries surrounding a center space, perhaps some 55 by 55 feet, more than half of which was occupied by the stage, "the apron," that jutted out from the dressing room, or tiring-house, in the building itself. Two doors, one on each side, led from the tiring-house to the stage. Between them may have been a recess that could be curtained off, or "inner" scenes (like that in Desdemona's bedroom in V, 2) may have been staged in a tent-like structure on the apron itself, with walls that could be pulled to reveal the interior to the view of the audience. The apron itself was a low, wooden platform, partly covered by a roof, "the shadow" or "the heavens" supported by posts and with a trap door in the floor for the appearance of ghosts and devils from below ("the hell"). Above the recess was a balcony for physically high action. Here Brabantio would appear in I, 1, and the gentleman lookout for the Venetian ships in II, 1. The open area surrounding the apron on three sides was called the "pit." Here stood the poorer spectators, or "groundlings." Their social betters were seated in the galleries. Fully occupied, the theater may have held upward of 2,000 spectators. Costumes were elaborate but historically unauthentic. Props were used (lanterns, swords, a chair of state, a bed), but hardly any effort was made to create verisimilitude. The stage picture was of a symbolic rather than an actual world. Performance took place in the daytime. It was an intimate theater, of convention rather than of illusion, and one in which actor and audience were both physically and psychologically closer than in a modern, picture-frame theater of artificial lighting. And the absence of elaborate sets or stage machinery invited an imaginative, fluid, and fast-paced dramatic form.

Shakespeare's source for *Othello* was a tale in a collection entitled *Hecatommithi* by Giraldi Cinthio, which appeared in Venice in 1566. There is no record of an English translation, but Shakespeare may have read the story in French or even in the original Italian (we do not know what foreign languages, if any, Shakespeare knew). He altered Cinthio's tale on several points. Lust for Desdemona rather than resentment at a failed promotion is Iago's motive for revenge in the original. There is no Roderigo and instead of Brabantio only a brief reference to Desdemona's parents opposing the marriage. Bianca is Cassio's wife, not his mistress as in Shakespeare, and neither she nor Emilia is connected with the handkerchief plot. The Turkish wars, Othello's and Desdemona's separate sea voyages, the tempest, and Cassio's drunkenness are all original with Shakespeare. In Cinthio, Desdemona is beaten to death with a stocking filled with sand, the Moor goes mad after the murder, is tortured, and long afterward killed by his wife's relatives. In Cinthio only Desdemona is given a proper name.

What Shakespeare saw in Cinthio's sprawling tale was the story of the monstrous conception, growth, and murderous issue of sexual jealousy. Unlike Lear, Othello does not arraign the very order of the universe at the bar of human justice. Compared with Hamlet's exquisitely labyrinthine mind his seems like a child's. And his fall does not, like Macbeth's, shake the whole structure of society. The play is a domestic tragedy. But the smaller scope makes for a swiftness of compacted drama and a degree of poignancy lacking in the larger tragedies. *Othello* is the most tidily constructed of all Shakespeare's plays, in effect if not in literal fact faithful to "the rules." Every character, every incident, every speech, contributes to the single, accelerating assault on our emotions.

The formative pressure of imaginative intelligence is exerted in every area of the drama. In consequence, the shaped substance of the whole play is not caught in plot synopsis. Images of scene and speech register psychological movement and moral values, fleshing the narrative skeleton with interlocking meanings of symbolic hyperbole and contrast and with enriched immediacy of scene, figure, gesture, and voice. The result is the kind of realism that gives an audience not a replica of its own reality, but an overwhelming sense of tragic life. The double time scheme in *Othello* is an example of the freedom and economy of means Shakespeare employed to achieve a certain end.* The foreground of swift and the background of slow events reconcile the conflicting demands for a

---

*The action begins on the night of Othello's and Desdemona's wedding. That same night Othello, Cassio, and Iago all set sail for Cyprus, aboard different ships. Desdemona travels with Iago. The day of the landing is declared a public holiday. During the celebration that night Cassio forfeits his lieutenancy. The next morning Desdemona promises to plead for his reinstatement, and Iago is able to set his plot in motion.

Clearly, this time scheme allows no opportunity for an affair between Cassio and Desdemona. To conceal the absurdity Shakespeare introduces passages that imply a background of events of longer duration than the thirty-some hours that actually pass between the arrival in Cyprus and the murder of Desdemona (that is, if the action is assumed to be continuous between Acts III and IV, as dramatic "feeling" certainly suggests that it is). Examples of such passages are Emilia's finding the handkerchief which Iago "a hundred times" had asked her to steal (III, 3), Iago's "I lay with Cassio lately" (III, 3), Bianca's complaint of Cassio's long neglect (III, 4), Lodovico's arrival with the senate's new directives after the destruction of the Turkish fleet (IV, 1), and Othello's questioning Emilia about his wife (IV, 2). See M. R. Ridley's Introduction to his edition of *Othello* in the New Arden Shakespeare (London, 1958), pp. lxvii–lxx.

rush of tragic fate and for gradual psychological change in the protagonist. The inconsistency also suggests the irrationality of the jealous mind that fails to arrest the manifest untruth of Iago's lies with the obvious question which it remains for Emilia to ask in IV, 2:

> Who keeps her company?
> What place? what time? what form? what likelihood?

And in the gathering fear and suspense we cease to be aware of any discrepancy between chronological and psychological time, feeling instead the action to take place in some timeless void in which the hero-victim is suspended with his agony between absolute evil and absolute innocence.

The device of the double time scheme is characteristic of Shakespeare's dramatic method. Facts and circumstance assume symbolic power without losing their primary status. In *Othello* they build a world, mysterious, capricious, dangerous, in which an Iago is allowed to exercise his evil intelligence on corruptible and incorruptible innocence alike, and in which the question of *why* he is allowed to is as irrepressible as it is unanswerable. "Demand me nothing," says Iago at the end. "What you know you know." But what the tragic hero knows is only the fact of suffering and his own responsibility for it, not its ultimate reason.

The move from Venice to Cyprus between Acts I and II is both a plausible narrative event and a structural device that separates the prologue from the main phase of the action: Iago's unsuccessful from his successful raid on Othello's happiness. But it also represents a move from an ordered polity to

> a town of war
> Yet wild, the people's hearts brimful of fear,

less a fortified island in the Mediterranean than a place for the exhibition of tragic passion. In Act I Iago's obscene cries in the night are silenced by Othello's calm and beautiful rhetoric and by the fair and disciplined deliberations of the Venetian senate, including Brabantio's submission to its judgment in favor of Othello. In contrast, Cyprus is a place of drunken revelry and riot, of assassination in the dark, governed by a general who can rule neither himself nor his men, who cashiers his most devoted officer, trusts his worst enemy, and murders his innocent wife.

Whether Shakespeare and his audience thought of Othello as a Negro or as an Arab or whether they made the distinction at all is less important than the fact that he is the one dark-skinned person in the play. Not that race in the modern sense is at issue, but the contrast keeps attention fastened on the hero and emphasizes his position as an alien. Almost literally, he is seen to represent an ethos darker, more inscrutable, perhaps wilder and more barbaric, than that of his plausible Venetian environment. His blackness suggests the magic and witchcraft which Brabantio charges him with having used to win Desdemona and gives insinuating power to Iago's hint that Desdemona's feelings have only been a young girl's short-lived infatuation with an exotic stranger.

As Othello's blackness bears upon theme and feeling so does his speech. Iago's poison disintegrates his eloquence. In Act I Othello vindicates his courtship of Desdemona in dignified narrative of rich and sonorous imagery. In Acts III and IV he talks in spasmodic ejaculations of broken syntax and images of animal sexuality. There is no more striking evidence of Iago's skill than his success in befouling Othello's imagination. It accounts for the peculiar power of the scene (IV, 2) in which Othello treats Desdemona as an inmate of a brothel of which Emilia is the madam. But while such images in Othello come out in half-crazed expletives, hideous symptoms of beclouding passion, in Iago they are a facile, casual jargon, as in his conversations with Roderigo. And from V, 2, till the end Othello is again in full possession of his eloquence. Desdemona's killer is not a raging cuckold but an impartial judge–executor.

> It is the cause, it is the cause, my soul;
> Let me not name it to you, you chaste stars!
> It is the cause. Yet I'll not shed her blood,
> Nor scar that whiter skin of hers than snow,
> And smooth as monumental alabaster.
> Yet she must die, else she 'll betray more men.

Power of discourse is proof of man's grasp of his experience, and when in his final soliloquy Othello sees himself as the "malignant Turk" who "Beat a Venetian and traduced the state," he recognizes the nature of his destiny. The catastrophe is past and unalterable, but his language makes of the sufferer's suicide a ceremony in which suffering is absorbed and which restores him to his prelapsarian state. Iago ends by deserting the language that for a while served him so well: "From this time forth I never will speak word." Language in the end does not desert Othello.

Part of the heartbreaking quality of *Othello* is the disparity between the injury Iago thinks he has received and the nature of the revenge he seeks. ". . . when I love thee not, Chaos is come again," says Othello as his eyes follow the departing Desdemona in III, 3. Ths cosmos that Iago immediately proceeds to undermine is built of Othello's pride of profession and his trust in Desdemona's virtue and love. Iago's revenge may be defined as cynicism assaulting faith. He abnegates all values but the rational exercise of the selfish will. Even the perfection of womanhood, he says in a moment of almost pleasant banter (II, 1), is good for nothing but

> To suckle fools and chronicle small beer.

His evil spreads like a contamination. He violates civic peace, military order, property, justice, friendship, marriage, life itself. "If thou be'st a devil, I cannot kill thee," says Othello, lunging at his tormentor. "I bleed, sir, but not killed," is Iago's terrifying reply. Recurrent imagery of devils, monsters, conjurers, thieves, and animals establish the Satanic nature of Iago's world. It is a world of impish irony. Othello escapes the storm at sea only to be ravaged by jealousy ashore. He denies having won Desdemona's heart by witchcraft but relies on the handkerchief of the magic web as sole proof of her fidelity. It is, like *Hamlet's,* a world of seeming. Othello seems proof against jealousy but is, if not easily, then terribly, jealous. His character and behavior belie his savage looks—until passion reduces him to Desdemona's "most filthy bargain." In deceptiveness there is actually little to choose between him and honest Iago. Cassio seems a reliable officer but isn't, Desdemona seems bewitched but isn't, does not seem chaste but is, and, for all her innocence, *does* deceive her father, *does* "beguile The thing I am by seeming otherwise," and *does* lie about the handkerchief (saying it is not lost when she knows it is). Emilia speaks coarsely but acts nobly, seems a most loyal wife but isn't. Even external events participate: Rhodes seems threatened but isn't, the rescue from the tempest seems a blessing but isn't. That *Othello* is the only one of Shakespeare's tragedies that could have turned to comedy (in the sense of having a happy outcome) as late as the middle of the fifth act is further evidence that its setting is a world ruled by whim.

Whim ultimately controls even Iago. His success, certainly, is to an extent the triumph of reason over instinct and passion. He skillfully acts the part of the bluff soldier, the rough diamond, whose integrity compels him to speak the truth even when it hurts his friends. He knows how to exploit Othello's "free and open nature That thinks men honest that but seem to be so." He plays upon his victim's half-suppressed awareness that his race, his age, and his profession all argue against the depth and durability of Desdemona's love and that he is ignorant of the silken ways of Venetian ladies. He knows how to make use of Desdemona's passivity in suffering, a defect inherent in the very virtue of her love, obedience, and forgivingness.

But at any time after Act III any one of a number of chance meetings and chance remarks would have exposed Iago's plot. That no such meeting or remark occurs is a matter of luck, and so is the fact that, instead, the handkerchief comes to his hand just when Othello demands proof and that first Cassio and then Bianca arrive at the scene at exactly the right moment to further his scheme (IV, 1). All along he brilliantly improvises each new step in his plot, but in Act V his improvisations suddenly stop working, and events begin to get away from him. He is pressed for time. He realizes that murder breeds murder. Roderigo, blundering gull to the last, does *not* kill Cassio. Dead himself, his letters incriminate Iago. And Emilia will not obey her husband's command to be silent. The master manipulator manipulates himself into shackles and torture and sees all his machinations end in as bitter an irony for himself as any he ever ensnared Othello in: the promotion of Cassio to the governorship.

Coleridge found in Iago a "motiveless malignity," but his character may rather be thought a critical problem because his revenge is too amply motivated: by professional frustration and jealousy, suspicion of an affair between Othello and Emilia, hatred of Cassio's winning ways, and lust for Desdemona. As his own soliloquies are the authority for all these motives and as soliloquies are always, by dramatic convention, sincere, this cool and cynical egotist, this penetrating judge of others, comes to seem confused as to the reasons for his own actions. There is a paradox that diminishes his stature as a force of evil in the fact that he is driven to destroy virtues he professes not to believe exist. That the combination of Othello's soldierliness and Desdemona's innocence should amount to a tragic flaw seems due to such a special and unlikely set of circumstances that Iago's strategy appears gratuitous. At the end he looms in our mind less as a consummate deceiver-intriguer than as a horrible accident in Othello's life. Here again, as in so many other of his plays, Shakespeare has used and transcended a convention of Elizabethan drama. Machiavellian stage villainy, a commonplace by

1604, has been made subservient to a tragic metaphysic. In 1692 the neoclassical critic Thomas Rymer dismissed *Othello* with a sneer as a "bloody farce," good only for teaching housewives to "look well to their linen."* But in responding to the trivial and accidental nature of the pivotal plot event Rymer responded to something crucial to the tragic effect. The world of *Othello* is one in which a dropped handkerchief *will* lead to catastrophe. Its controlling force remains a dark riddle, but the final events of the play make it clear that the riddler, whoever he is, is not Iago. Scheming malice does not conquer. And not his cynicism and silence but the dying Desdemona's words of love and Othello's self-recognition and dying kiss mark the human gesture.

*A Short View of Tragedy (dated 1693).

Molière

The Misanthrope

English Version by Richard Wilbur

Characters

ALCESTE *in love with Célimène*
PHILINTE *Alceste's friend*
ORONTE *in love with Célimène*
CÉLIMÈNE *Alceste's beloved*
ÉLIANTE *Célimène's cousin*
ARSINOÉ *a friend of Célimène's*
ACASTE ⎱ *Marquesses*
CLITANDRE ⎰
BASQUE *Célimène's servant*
A GUARD *of the Marshalsea*
DUBOIS *Alceste's valet*

The Scene throughout is in Célimène's house at Paris.

ACT I

Scene 1 [PHILINTE, ALCESTE]

PHILINTE: Now, what's got into you?

ALCESTE (*seated*):   Kindly leave me alone.

PHILINTE: Come, come, what is it? This lugubrious tone . . .

ALCESTE: Leave me, I said; you spoil my solitude.

PHILINTE: Oh, listen to me, now, and don't be rude.

ALCESTE: I choose to be rude, Sir, and to be hard of hearing.

PHILINTE: These ugly moods of yours are not endearing;
  Friends though we are, I really must insist . . .

ALCESTE (*abruptly rising*): Friends? Friends, you say? Well, cross me off
      your list.
  I've been your friend till now, as you well know;
  But after what I saw a moment ago
  I tell you flatly that our ways must part.
  I wish no place in a dishonest heart.

PHILINTE: Why, what have I done, Alceste? Is this quite just?

ALCESTE: My God, you ought to die of self-disgust.
  I call your conduct inexcusable, Sir,
  And every man of honor will concur.
  I see you almost hug a man to death,
  Exclaim for joy until you're out of breath,
  And supplement these loving demonstrations
  With endless offers, vows, and protestations;
  Then when I ask you "Who was that?" I find
  That you can barely bring his name to mind!
  Once the man's back is turned, you cease to love him,
  And speak with absolute indifference of him!
  By God, I say it's base and scandalous
  To falsify the heart's affections thus;
  If I caught myself behaving in such a way,
  I'd hang myself for shame, without delay.

PHILINTE: It hardly seems a hanging matter to me;
  I hope that you will take it graciously
  If I extend myself a slight reprieve,
  And live a little longer, by your leave.

ALCESTE: How dare you joke about a crime so grave?

PHILINTE: What crime? How else are people to behave?

ALCESTE: I'd have them be sincere, and never part
  With any word that isn't from the heart.

PHILINTE: When someone greets us with a show of pleasure,

It's but polite to give him equal measure,
  Return his love the best that we know how,
  And trade him offer for offer, vow for vow.
ALCESTE: No, no, this formula you'd have me follow,
  However fashionable, is false and hollow,
  And I despise the frenzied operations
  Of all these barterers of protestations,
  These lavishers of meaningless embraces,
  These utterers of obliging commonplaces,
  Who court and flatter everyone on earth
  And praise the fool no less than the man of worth.
  Should you rejoice that someone fondles you,
  Offers his love and service, swears to be true,
  And fills your ears with praises of your name,
  When to the first damned fop he'll say the same?
  No, no: no self-respecting heart would dream
  Of prizing so promiscuous an esteem;
  However high the praise, there's nothing worse
  Than sharing honors with the universe.
  Esteem is founded on comparison:
  To honor all men is to honor none.
  Since you embrace this indiscriminate vice,
  Your friendship comes at far too cheap a price;
  I spurn the easy tribute of a heart
  Which will not set the worthy man apart:
  I choose, Sir, to be chosen; and in fine,
  The friend of mankind is no friend of mine.
PHILINTE: But in polite society, custom decrees
  That we show certain outward courtesies. . . .
ALCESTE: Ah, no! we should condemn with all our force
  Such false and artificial intercourse
  Let men behave like men; let them display
  Their inmost hearts in everything they say;
  Let the heart speak, and let our sentiments
  Not mask themselves in silly compliments.
PHILINTE: In certain cases it would be uncouth
  And most absurd to speak the naked truth;
  With all respect for your exalted notions,
  It's often best to veil one's true emotions.
  Wouldn't the social fabric come undone
  If we were wholly frank with everyone?
  Suppose you met with someone you couldn't bear;
  Would you inform him of it then and there?
ALCESTE: Yes.

PHILINTE: Then you'd tell old Emilie it's pathetic
  The way she daubs her features with cosmetic
  And plays the gay coquette at sixty-four?
ALCESTE: I would.
PHILINTE: And you'd call Dorilas a bore,
  And tell him every ear at court is lame
  From hearing him brag about his noble name?
ALCESTE: Precisely.
PHILINTE: Ah, you're joking.
ALCESTE: *Au contraire:*
  In this regard there's none I'd choose to spare.
  All are corrupt; there's nothing to be seen
  In court or town but aggravates my spleen.
  I fall into deep gloom and melancholy
  When I survey the scene of human folly,
  Finding on every hand base flattery,
  Injustice, fraud, self-interest, treachery. . . .
  Ah, it's too much; mankind has grown so base,
  I mean to break with the whole human race.
PHILINTE: This philosophic rage is a bit extreme;
  You've no idea how comical you seem;
  Indeed, we're like those brothers in the play
  Called *School for Husbands,* one of whom was prey . . .
ALCESTE: Enough, now! None of your stupid similes.
PHILINTE: Then let's have no more tirades, if you please.
  The world won't change, whatever you say or do;
  And since plain speaking means so much to you,
  I'll tell you plainly that by being frank
  You've earned the reputation of a crank,
  And that you're thought ridiculous when you rage
  And rant against the manners of the age.
ALCESTE: So much the better; just what I wish to hear.
  No news could be more grateful to my ear.
  All men are so detestable in my eyes,
  I should be sorry if they thought me wise.
PHILINTE: Your hatred's very sweeping, is it not?
ALCESTE: Quite right: I hate the whole degraded lot.
PHILINTE: Must all poor human creatures be embraced,
  Without distinction, by your vast distaste?
  Even in these bad times, there are surely a few . . .
ALCESTE: No, I include all men in one dim view:
  Some men I hate for being rogues; the others
  I hate because they treat the rogues like brothers,
  And, lacking a virtuous scorn for what is vile,

villain with a complaisant smile.
tolerant people choose to be
bold rascal who's at law with me.
lish can't conceal his nature;
once that he's a treacherous creature;
d possibly be taken in
By those soft speeches and that sugary grin.
The whole world knows the shady means by which
The low-brow's grown so powerful and rich,
And risen to a rank so bright and high
That virtue can but blush, and merit sigh.
Whenever his name comes up in conversation,
None will defend his wretched reputation;
Call him knave, liar, scoundrel, and all the rest,
Each head will nod, and no one will protest.
And yet his smirk is seen in every house,
He's greeted everywhere with smiles and bows,
And when there's any honor that can be got
By pulling strings, he'll get it, like as not.
My God! It chills my heart to see the ways
Men come to terms with evil nowadays;
Sometimes, I swear, I'm moved to flee and find
Some desert land unfouled by humankind.

PHILINTE: Come, let's forget the follies of the times
And pardon mankind for its petty crimes;
Let's have an end of rantings and of railings,
And show some leniency toward human failings.
This world requires a pliant rectitude;
Too stern a virtue makes one stiff and rude;
Good sense views all extremes with detestation,
And bids us to be noble in moderation.
The rigid virtues of the ancient days
Are not for us; they jar with all our ways
And ask of us too lofty a perfection.
Wise men accept their times without objection,
And there's no greater folly, if you ask me,
Than trying to reform society.
Like you, I see each day a hundred and one
Unhandsome deeds that might be better done,
But still, for all the faults that meet my view,
I'm never known to storm and rave like you.
I take men as they are, or let them be,
And teach my soul to bear their frailty;
And whether in court or town, whatever the scene,

My phlegm's as philosophic as your spleen.

ALCESTE: This phlegm which you so eloquently commend,
    Does nothing ever rile it up, my friend?
    Suppose some man you trust should treacherously
    Conspire to rob you of your property,
    And do his best to wreck your reputation?
    Wouldn't you feel a certain indignation?

PHILINTE: Why, no. These faults of which you so complain
    Are part of human nature, I maintain,
    And it's no more a matter for disgust
    That men are knavish, selfish and unjust,
    Than that the vulture dines upon the dead,
    And wolves are furious, and apes ill-bred.

ALCESTE: Shall I see myself betrayed, robbed, torn to bits,
    And not . . . Oh, let's be still and rest our wits.
    Enough of reasoning, now. I've had my fill.

PHILINTE: Indeed, you would do well, Sir, to be still.
    Rage less at your opponent, and give some thought
    To how you'll win this lawsuit that he's brought.

ALCESTE: I assure you I'll do nothing of the sort.

PHILINTE: Then who will plead your case before the court?

ALCESTE: Reason and right and justice will plead for me.

PHILINTE: Oh, Lord. What judges do you plan to see?

ALCESTE: Why, none. The justice of my cause is clear.

PHILINTE: Of course, man; but there's politics to fear. . . .

ALCESTE: No, I refuse to lift a hand. That's flat.
    I'm either right, or wrong.

PHILINTE: Don't count on that.

ALCESTE: No, I'll do nothing.

PHILINTE: Your enemy's influence
    Is great, you know . . .

ALCESTE: That makes no difference.

PHILINTE: It will; you'll see.

ALCESTE: Must honor bow to guile?
    If so, I shall be proud to lose the trial.

PHILINTE: Oh, really . . .

ALCESTE: I'll discover by this case
    Whether or not men are sufficiently base
    And impudent and villainous and perverse
    To do me wrong before the universe.

PHILINTE: What a man!

ALCESTE: Oh, I could wish, whatever the cost,
    Just for the beauty of it, that my trial were lost.

PHILINTE: If people heard you talking so, Alceste,

They'd split their sides. Your name would be a jest.
ALCESTE: So much the worse for jesters.
PHILINTE: May I enquire
  Whether this rectitude you so admire,
  And these hard virtues you're enamored of
  Are qualities of the lady whom you love?
  It much surprises me that you, who seem
  To view mankind with furious disesteem,
  Have yet found something to enchant your eyes
  Amidst a species which you so despise.
  And what is more amazing, I'm afraid,
  Is the most curious choice your heart has made.
  The honest Éliante is fond of you,
  Arsinoé, the prude, admires you too;
  And yet your spirit's been perversely led
  To choose the flighty Célimène instead,
  Whose brittle malice and coquettish ways
  So typify the manners of our days.
  How is it that the traits you most abhor
  Are bearable in this lady you adore?
  Are you so blind with love that you can't find them?
  Or do you contrive, in her case, not to mind them?
ALCESTE: My love for that young widow's not the kind
  That can't perceive defects; no, I'm not blind.
  I see her faults, despite my ardent love,
  And all I see I fervently reprove.
  And yet I'm weak; for all her falsity,
  That woman knows the art of pleasing me,
  And though I never cease complaining of her,
  I swear I cannot manage not to love her.
  Her charm outweighs her faults; I can but aim
  To cleanse her spirit in my love's pure flame.
PHILINTE: That's no small task; I wish you all success.
  You think then that she loves you?
ALCESTE: Heavens, yes!
  I wouldn't love her did she not love me.
PHILINTE: Well, if her taste for you is plain to see,
  Why do these rivals cause you such despair?
ALCESTE: True love, Sir, is possessive, and cannot bear
  To share with all the world. I'm here today
  To tell her she must send that mob away.
PHILINTE: If I were you, and had your choice to make,
  Éliante, her cousin, would be the one I'd take;
  That honest heart, which cares for you alone,

Would harmonize far better with your own.
ALCESTE: True, true: each day my reason tells me so;
  But reason doesn't rule in love, you know.
PHILINTE: I fear some bitter sorrow is in store;
  This love . . .

Scene 2 [ORONTE, ALCESTE, PHILINTE]

ORONTE (*to* ALCESTE): The servants told me at the door
  That Éliante and Célimène were out,
  But when I heard, dear Sir, that you were about,
  I came to say, without exaggeration,
  That I hold you in the vastest admiration,
  And that it's always been my dearest desire
  To be the friend of one I so admire.
  I hope to see my love of merit requited,
  And you and I in friendship's bond united.
  I'm sure you won't refuse—if I may be frank—
  A friend of my devotedness—and rank.

(*During this speech of* ORONTE'S, ALCESTE *is abstracted, and seems unaware that he is being spoken to. He only breaks off his reverie when*
ORONTE *says:*)

It was for you, if you please, that my words were intended.
ALCESTE: For me, Sir?
ORONTE: Yes, for you. You're not offended?
ALCESTE: By no means. But this much surprises me. . . .
  The honor comes most unexpectedly. . . .
ORONTE: My high regard should not astonish you;
  The whole world feels the same. It is your due.
ALCESTE: Sir . . .
ORONTE: Why, in all the State there isn't one
  Can match your merits; they shine, Sir, like the sun.
ALCESTE: Sir . . .
ORONTE: You are higher in my estimation
  Than all that's most illustrious in the nation.
ALCESTE: Sir . . .
ORONTE: If I lie, may heaven strike me dead!
  To show you that I mean what I have said,
  Permit me, Sir, to embrace you most sincerely,
  And swear that I will prize our friendship dearly.
  Give me your hand. And now, Sir, if you choose,
  We'll make our vows.

ALCESTE: Sir . . . .

ORONTE: What! You refuse?

ALCESTE: Sir, it's a very great honor you extend:
   But friendship is a sacred thing, my friend;
   It would be profanation to bestow
   The name of friend on one you hardly know.
   All parts are better played when well-rehearsed;
   Let's put off friendship, and get acquainted first.
   We may discover it would be unwise
   To try to make our natures harmonize.

ORONTE: By heaven! You're sagacious to the core;
   This speech has made me admire you even more.
   Let time, then, bring us closer day by day;
   Meanwhile, I shall be yours in every way.
   If, for example, there should be anything
   You wish at court, I'll mention it to the King.
   I have his ear, of course; it's quite well known
   That I am much in favor with the throne.
   In short, I am your servant. And now, dear friend,
   Since you have such fine judgment, I intend
   To please you, if I can, with a small sonnet
   I wrote not long ago. Please comment on it,
   And tell me whether I ought to publish it.

ALCESTE: You must excuse me, Sir; I'm hardly fit
   To judge such matters.

ORONTE: Why not?

ALCESTE: I am, I fear,
   Inclined to be unfashionably sincere.

ORONTE: Just what I ask; I'd take no satisfaction
   In anything but your sincere reaction.
   I beg you not to dream of being kind.

ALCESTE: Since you desire it, Sir, I'll speak my mind.

ORONTE: *Sonnet.* It's a sonnet. . . . *Hope* . . . The poem's addressed
   To a lady who wakened hopes within my breast.
   Hope . . . this is not the pompous sort of thing,
   Just modest little verses, with a tender ring.

ALCESTE: Well, we shall see.

ORONTE: *Hope* . . . I'm anxious to hear
   Whether the style seems properly smooth and clear,
   And whether the choice of words is good or bad.

ALCESTE: We'll see, we'll see.

ORONTE: Perhaps I ought to add
   That it took me only a quarter-hour to write it.

ALCESTE: The time's irrelevant, Sir: kindly recite it.

ORONTE (*reading*):
> Hope comforts us awhile, 'tis true,
> Lulling our cares with careless laughter,
> And yet such joy is full of rue,
> My Phyllis, if nothing follows after.

PHILINTE: I'm charmed by this already; the style's delightful.

ALCESTE (*sotto voce, to* PHILINTE): How can you say that? Why, the thing is frightful.

ORONTE:
> Your fair face smiled on me awhile,
> But was it kindness so to enchant me?
> 'Twould have been fairer not to smile,
> If hope was all you meant to grant me.

PHILINTE: What a clever thought! How handsomely you phrase it!

ALCESTE (*sotto voce, to* PHILINTE): You know the thing is trash. How dare you praise it?

ORONTE:
> If it's to be my passion's fate
> Thus everlastingly to wait,
> Then death will come to set me free:
> For death is fairer than the fair;
> Phyllis, to hope is to despair
> When one must hope eternally.

PHILINTE: The close is exquisite—full of feeling and grace.

ALCESTE (*sotto voce, aside*): Oh, blast the close; you'd better close your face
Before you send your lying soul to hell.

PHILINTE: I can't remember a poem I've liked so well.

ALCESTE (*sotto voce, aside*): Good Lord!

ORONTE (*to* PHILINTE): I fear you're flattering me a bit.

PHILINTE: Oh, no!

ALCESTE (*sotto voce, aside*): What else d'you call it, you hypocrite?

ORONTE (*to* ALCESTE): But you, Sir, keep your promise now: don't shrink
From telling me sincerely what you think.

ALCESTE: Sir, these are delicate matters; we all desire
To be told that we've the true poetic fire.
But once, to one whose name I shall not mention,
I said, regarding some verse of his invention,
That gentlemen should rigorously control
That itch to write which often afflicts the soul;
That one should curb the heady inclination
To publicize one's little avocation;
And that in showing off one's works of art
One often plays a very clownish part.

ORONTE: Are you suggesting in a devious way
   That I ought not . . .
ALCESTE: Oh, that I do not say.
   Further, I told him that no fault is worse
   Than that of writing frigid, lifeless verse,
   And that the merest whisper of such a shame
   Suffices to destroy a man's good name.
ORONTE: D'you mean to say my sonnet's dull and trite?
ALCESTE: I don't say that. But I went on to cite
   Numerous cases of once-respected men
   Who came to grief by taking up the pen.
ORONTE: And am I like them? Do I write so poorly?
ALCESTE: I don't say that. But I told this person, "Surely
   You're under no necessity to compose;
   Why you should wish to publish, heaven knows.
   There's no excuse for printing tedious rot
   Unless one writes for bread, as you do not.
   Resist temptation, then, I beg of you;
   Conceal your pastimes from public view;
   And don't give up, on any provocation,
   Your present high and courtly reputation,
   To purchase at a greedy printer's shop
   The name of silly author and scribbling fop."
   These were the points I tried to make him see.
ORONTE: I sense that they are also aimed at me;
   But now—about my sonnet—I'd like to be told . . .
ALCESTE: Frankly, that sonnet should be pigeonholed.
   You've chosen the worst models to imitate.
   The style's unnatural. Let me illustrate:
              For example, *Your fair face smiled on me awhile,*
              Followed by, *'Twould have been fairer not to smile!*
              Or this: *such joy is full of rue;*
              Or this: *For death is fairer than the fair;*
              Or, *Phyllis, to hope is to despair*
                 When one must hope eternally!
   This artificial style, that's all the fashion,
   Has neither taste, nor honesty, nor passion;
   It's nothing but a sort of wordy play,
   And nature never spoke in such a way.
   What, in this shallow age, is not debased?
   Our fathers, though less refined, had better taste;
   I'd barter all that men admire today
   For one old love song I shall try to say:
              If the King had given me for my own

>*Paris, his citadel,*
>*And I for that must leave alone*
>*Her whom I love so well,*
>*I'd say then to the Crown,*
>*Take back your glittering town;*
>*My darling is more fair, I swear,*
>*My darling is more fair.*

The rhyme's not rich, the style is rough and old,
But don't you see that it's the purest gold
Beside the tinsel nonsense now preferred,
And that there's passion in its every word?

>*If the King had given me for my own*
>*Paris, his citadel,*
>*And I for that must leave alone*
>*Her whom I love so well,*
>*I'd say then to the Crown,*
>*Take back your glittering town;*
>*My darling is more fair, I swear,*
>*My darling is more fair.*

There speaks a loving heart. (*To* PHILINTE.) You're laughing, eh?
Laugh on, my precious wit. Whatever you say,
I hold that song's worth all the bibelots
That people hail today with ah's and oh's.

ORONTE: And I maintain my sonnet's very good.
ALCESTE: It's not at all surprising that you should.
   You have your reasons; permit me to have mine
   For thinking that you cannot write a line.
ORONTE: Others have praised my sonnet to the skies.
ALCESTE: I lack their art of telling pleasant lies.
ORONTE: You seem to think you've got no end of wit.
ALCESTE: To praise your verse, I'd need still more of it.
ORONTE: I'm not in need of your approval, Sir.
ALCESTE: That's good; you couldn't have it if you were.
ORONTE: Come now, I'll lend you the subject of my sonnet;
   I'd like to see you try to improve upon it.
ALCESTE: I might, by chance, write something just as shoddy;
   But then I wouldn't show it to everybody.
ORONTE: You're most opinionated and conceited
ALCESTE: Go find your flatterers, and be better treated.
ORONTE: Look here, my little fellow, pray watch your tone.
ALCESTE: My great big fellow, you'd better watch your own.
PHILINTE (*stepping between them*): Oh, please, please, gentlemen!
   This will never do.
ORONTE: The fault is mine, and I leave the field to you.

I am your servant, Sir, in every way.

ALCESTE: And I, Sir, am your most abject valet.

Scene 3 [PHILINTE, ALCESTE]

PHILINTE: Well, as you see, sincerity in excess
    Can get you into a very pretty mess;
    Oronte was hungry for appreciation. . . .

ALCESTE: Don't speak to me.

PHILINTE: What?

ALCESTE: No more conversation.

PHILINTE: Really, now . . .

ALCESTE: Leave me alone.

PHILINTE: If I . . .

ALCESTE: Out of my sight!

PHILINTE: But what . . .

ALCESTE: I won't listen.

PHILINTE: But . . .

ALCESTE: Silence!

PHILINTE: Now, is it polite . . .

ALCESTE: By heaven, I've had enough. Don't follow me.

PHILINTE: Ah, you're just joking. I'll keep you company.

ACT II

Scene 1 [ALCESTE, CÉLIMÈNE]

ALCESTE: Shall I speak plainly, Madam? I confess
    Your conduct gives me infinite distress,
    And my resentment's grown too hot to smother.
    Soon, I foresee, we'll break with one another.
    If I said otherwise, I should deceive you;
    Sooner or later, I shall be forced to leave you,
    And if I swore that we shall never part,
    I should misread the omens of my heart.

CÉLIMÈNE: You kindly saw me home, it would appear,
    So as to pour invectives in my ear.

ALCESTE: I've no desire to quarrel. But I deplore
    Your inability to shut the door
    On all these suitors who beset you so.
    There's what annoys me, if you care to know.

CÉLIMÈNE: Is it my fault that all these men pursue me?

Am I to blame if they're attracted to me?
And when they gently beg an audience,
Ought I to take a stick and drive them hence?
ALCESTE: Madam, there's no necessity for a stick;
A less responsive heart would do the trick.
Of your attractiveness I don't complain;
But those your charms attract, you then detain
By a most melting and receptive manner,
And so enlist their hearts beneath your banner.
It's the agreeable hopes which you excite
That keep these lovers round you day and night;
Were they less liberally smiled upon,
That sighing troop would very soon be gone.
But tell me, Madam, why it is that lately
This man Clitandre interests you so greatly?
Because of what high merits do you deem
Him worthy of the honor of your esteem?
Is it that your admiring glances linger
On the splendidly long nail of his little finger?
Or do you share the general deep respect
For the blond wig he chooses to affect?
Are you in love with his embroidered hose?
Do you adore his ribbons and his bows?
Or is it that this paragon bewitches
Your tasteful eye with his vast German breeches?
Perhaps his giggle, or his falsetto voice,
Makes him the latest gallant of your choice?
CÉLIMÈNE: You're much mistaken to resent him so.
Why I put up with him you surely know:
My lawsuit's very shortly to be tried,
And I must have his influence on my side.
ALCESTE: Then lose your lawsuit, Madam, or let it drop;
Don't torture me by humoring such a fop.
CÉLIMÈNE: You're jealous of the whole world, Sir.
ALCESTE: That's true,
Since the whole world is well-received by you.
CÉLIMÈNE: That my good nature is so unconfined
Should serve to pacify your jealous mind;
Were I to smile on one, and scorn the rest,
Then you might have some cause to be distressed.
ALCESTE: Well, if I mustn't be jealous, tell me, then,
Just how I'm better treated than other men.
CÉLIMÈNE: You know you have my love. Will that not do?

ALCESTE: What proof have I that what you say is true?
CÉLIMÈNE: I would expect, Sir, that my having said it
   Might give the statement a sufficient credit.
ALCESTE: But how can I be sure that you don't tell
   The selfsame thing to other men as well?
CÉLIMÈNE: What a gallant speech! How flattering to me!
   What a sweet creature you make me out to be!
   Well then, to save you from the pangs of doubt,
   All that I've said I hereby cancel out;
   Now, none but yourself shall make a monkey of you:
   Are you content?
ALCESTE: Why, why am I doomed to love you?
   I swear that I shall bless the blissful hour
   When this poor heart's no longer in your power!
   I make no secret of it: I've done my best
   To exorcise this passion from my breast;
   But thus far all in vain; it will not go;
   It's for my sins that I must love you so.
CÉLIMÈNE: Your love for me is matchless, Sir; that's clear.
ALCESTE: Indeed, in all the world it has no peer;
   Words can't describe the nature of my passion,
   And no man ever loved in such a fashion.
CÉLIMÈNE: Yes, it's a brand-new fashion, I agree:
   You show your love by castigating me,
   And all your speeches are enraged and rude.
   I've never been so furiously wooed.
ALCESTE: Yet you could calm that fury, if you chose.
   Come, shall we bring our quarrels to a close?
   Let's speak with open hearts, then, and begin . . .

Scene 2 [CÉLIMÈNE, ALCESTE, BASQUE]

CÉLIMÈNE: What is it?
BASQUE: Acaste is here.
CÉLIMÈNE: Well, send him in.

Scene 3 [CÉLIMÈNE, ALCESTE]

ALCESTE: What! Shall we never be alone at all?
   You're always ready to receive a call,
   And you can't bear, for ten ticks of the clock,
   Not to keep open house for all who knock.
CÉLIMÈNE: I couldn't refuse him: he'd be most put out.

ALCESTE: Surely that's not worth worrying about.
CÉLIMÈNE: Acaste would never forgive me if he guessed
  That I consider him a dreadful pest.
ALCESTE: If he's a pest, why bother with him then?
CÉLIMÈNE: Heavens! One can't antagonize such men;
  Why, they're the chartered gossips of the court,
  And have a say in things of every sort.
  One must receive them, and be full of charm;
  They're no great help, but they can do you harm,
  And though your influence be ever so great,
  They're hardly the best people to alienate.
ALCESTE: I see, dear lady, that you could make a case
  For putting up with the whole human race;
  These friendships that you calculate so nicely . . .

Scene 4 [ALCESTE, CÉLIMÈNE, BASQUE]

BASQUE: Madam, Clitandre is here as well.
ALCESTE: Precisely.
CÉLIMÈNE: Where are you going?
ALCESTE: Elsewhere.
CÉLIMÈNE: Stay.
ALCESTE: No, no.
CÉLIMÈNE: Stay, Sir.
ALCESTE: I can't.
CÉLIMÈNE: I wish it.
ALCESTE: No, I must go.
  I beg you, Madam, not to press the matter;
  You know I have no taste for idle chatter.
CÉLIMÈNE: Stay: I command you.
ALCESTE: No, I cannot stay.
CÉLIMÈNE: Very well; you have my leave to go away.

Scene 5 [ÉLIANTE, PHILINTE, ACASTE, CLITANDRE, ALCESTE, CÉLIMÈNE, BASQUE]

ÉLIANTE (*to* CÉLIMÈNE): The Marquesses have kindly come to call.
  Were they announced?
CÉLIMÈNE: Yes. Basque, bring chairs for all.

  (BASQUE *provides the chairs, and exits.*)

  (*To* ALCESTE.) You haven't gone?
ALCESTE: No; and I shan't depart

Till you decide who's foremost in your heart.

CÉLIMÈNE: Oh, hush.

ALCESTE: It's time to choose; take them, or me.

CÉLIMÈNE: You're mad.

ALCESTE: I'm not, as you shall shortly see.

CÉLIMÈNE: Oh?

ALCESTE: You'll decide.

CÉLIMÈNE: You're joking now, dear friend.

ALCESTE: No, no; you'll choose; my patience is at an end.

CLITANDRE: Madam, I come from court, where poor Cléonte
   Behaved like a perfect fool, as is his wont.
   Has he no friend to counsel him, I wonder,
   And teach him less unerringly to blunder?

CÉLIMÈNE: It's true, the man's a most accomplished dunce;
   His gauche behavior charms the eye at once;
   And every time one sees him, on my word,
   His manner's grown a trifle more absurd.

ACASTE: Speaking of dunces, I've just now conversed
   With old Damon, who's one of the very worst;
   I stood a lifetime in the broiling sun
   Before his dreary monologue was done.

CÉLIMÈNE: Oh, he's a wondrous talker, and has the power
   To tell you nothing hour after hour:
   If, by mistake, he ever came to the point,
   The shock would put his jawbone out of joint.

ÉLIANTE (to PHILINTE): The conversation takes its usual turn,
   And all our dear friends' ears will shortly burn.

CLITANDRE: Timante's a character, Madam.

CÉLIMÈNE: Isn't he, though?
   A man of mystery from top to toe,
   Who moves about in a romantic mist
   On secret missions which do not exist.
   His talk is full of eyebrows and grimaces;
   How tired one gets of his momentous faces;
   He's always whispering something confidential
   Which turns out to be quite inconsequential;
   Nothing's too slight for him to mystify;
   He even whispers when he says "good-by."

ACASTE: Tell us about Géralde.

CÉLIMÈNE: That tiresome ass.
   He mixes only with the titled class,
   And fawns on dukes and princes, and is bored
   With anyone who's not at least a lord.

    The man's obsessed with rank, and his discourses
    Are all of hounds and carriages and horses;
    He uses Christian names with all the great,
    And the word Milord, with him, is out of date.
CLITANDRE: He's very taken with Bélise, I hear.
CÉLIMÈNE: She is the dreariest company, poor dear.
    Whenever she comes to call, I grope about
    To find some topic which will draw her out,
    But, owing to her dry and faint replies,
    The conversation wilts, and droops, and dies.
    In vain one hopes to animate her face
    By mentioning the ultimate commonplace;
    But sun or shower, even hail or frost
    Are matters she can instantly exhaust.
    Meanwhile her visit, painful though it is,
    Drags on and on through mute eternities,
    And though you ask the time, and yawn, and yawn,
    She sits there like a stone and won't be gone.
ACASTE: Now for Adraste.
CÉLIMÈNE: Oh, that conceited elf
    Has a gigantic passion for himself;
    He rails against the court, and cannot bear it
    That none will recognize his hidden merit;
    All honors given to others give offense
    To his imaginary excellence.
CLITANDRE: What about young Cléon? His house, they say,
    Is full of the best society, night and day.
CÉLIMÈNE: His cook has made him popular, not he:
    It's Cléon's table that people come to see.
ÉLIANTE: He gives a splendid dinner, you must admit.
CÉLIMÈNE: But must he serve himself along with it?
    For my taste, he's a most insipid dish
    Whose presence sours the wine and spoils the fish.
PHILINTE: Damis, his uncle, is admired no end.
    What's your opinion, Madam?
CÉLIMÈNE: Why, he's my friend.
PHILINTE: He seems a decent fellow, and rather clever.
CÉLIMÈNE: He works too hard at cleverness, however.
    I hate to see him sweat and struggle so
    To fill his conversation with bons mots.
    Since he's decided to become a wit
    His taste's so pure that nothing pleases it;
    He scolds at all the latest books and plays,

Thinking that wit must never stoop to praise,
That finding fault's a sign of intellect,
That all appreciation is abject,
And that by damning everything in sight
One shows oneself in a distinguished light.
He's scornful even of our conversations:
Their trivial nature sorely tries his patience;
He folds his arms, and stands above the battle,
And listens sadly to our childish prattle.

ACASTE: Wonderful, Madam! You've hit him off precisely.

CLITANDRE: No one can sketch a character so nicely.

ALCESTE: How bravely, Sirs, you cut and thrust at all
These absent fools, till one by one they fall:
But let one come in sight, and you'll at once
Embrace the man you lately called a dunce,
Telling him in a tone sincere and fervent
How proud you are to be his humble servant.

CLITANDRE: Why pick on us? *Madame's* been speaking, Sir,
And you should quarrel, if you must, with her.

ALCESTE: No, no, by God, the fault is yours, because
You lead her on with laughter and applause,
And make her think that she's the more delightful
The more her talk is scandalous and spiteful.
Oh, she would stoop to malice far, far less
If no such claque approved her cleverness.
It's flatterers like you whose foolish praise
Nourishes all the vices of these days.

PHILINTE: But why protest when someone ridicules
Those you'd condemn, yourself, as knaves or fools?

CÉLIMÈNE: Why, Sir? Because he loves to make a fuss.
You don't expect him to agree with us,
When there's an opportunity to express
His heaven-sent spirit of contrariness?
What other people think, he can't abide;
Whatever they say, he's on the other side;
He lives in deadly terror of agreeing;
'Twould make him seem an ordinary being.
Indeed, he's so in love with contradiction,
He'll turn against his most profound conviction
And with a furious eloquence deplore it,
If only someone else is speaking for it.

ALCESTE: Go on, dear lady, mock me as you please;
You have your audience in ecstasies.

PHILINTE: But what she says is true: you have a way
 Of bridling at whatever people say;
 Whether they praise or blame, your angry spirit
 Is equally unsatisfied to hear it.
ALCESTE: Men, Sir, are always wrong, and that's the reason
 That righteous anger's never out of season;
 All that I hear in all their conversation
 Is flattering praise or reckless condemnation.
CÉLIMÈNE: But . . .
ALCESTE: No, no, Madam, I am forced to state
 That you have pleasures which I deprecate,
 And that these others, here, are much to blame
 For nourishing the faults which are your shame.
CLITANDRE: I shan't defend myself, Sir; but I vow
 I'd thought this lady faultless until now.
ACASTE: I see her charms and graces, which are many;
 But as for faults, I've never noticed any.
ALCESTE: I see them, Sir; and rather than ignore them,
 I strenuously criticize her for them.
 The more one loves, the more one should object
 To every blemish, every least defect.
 Were I this lady, I would soon get rid
 Of lovers who approved of all I did,
 And by their slack indulgence and applause
 Endorsed my follies and excused my flaws.
CÉLIMÈNE: If all hearts beat according to your measure,
 The dawn of love would be the end of pleasure;
 And love would find its perfect consummation
 In ecstasies of rage and reprobation.
ÉLIANTE: Love, as a rule, affects men otherwise,
 And lovers rarely love to criticize.
 They see their lady as a charming blur,
 And find all things commendable in her.
 If she has any blemish, fault, or shame,
 They will redeem it by a pleasing name.
 The pale-faced lady's lily-white, perforce;
 The swarthy one's a sweet brunette, of course;
 The spindly lady has a slender grace;
 The fat one has a most majestic pace;
 The plain one, with her dress in disarray,
 They classify as *beauté négligée;*
 The hulking one's a goddess in their eyes,
 The dwarf, a concentrate of Paradise;

The haughty lady has a noble mind;
The mean one's witty, and the dull one's kind;
The chatterbox has liveliness and verve,
The mute one has a virtuous reserve.
So lovers manage, in their passion's cause,
To love their ladies even for their flaws.

ALCESTE: But I still say . . .

CÉLIMÈNE: I think it would be nice
To stroll around the gallery once or twice.
What! You're not going, Sirs?

CLITANDRE AND ACASTE: No, Madam, no.

ALCESTE: You seem to be in terror lest they go.
Do what you will, Sirs; leave, or linger on,
But I shan't go till after you are gone.

ACASTE: I'm free to linger, unless I should perceive
Madame is tired, and wishes me to leave.

CLITANDRE: And as for me, I needn't go today
Until the hour of the King's *coucher*.

CÉLIMÈNE (*to* ALCESTE): You're joking, surely?

ALCESTE: Not in the least; we'll see
Whether you'd rather part with them, or me.

Scene 6 [ALCESTE, CÉLIMÈNE, ÉLIANTE, ACASTE, PHILINTE, CLITANDRE, BASQUE]

BASQUE (*to* ALCESTE): Sir, there's a fellow here who bids me state
That he must see you, and that it can't wait.

ALCESTE: Tell him that I have no such pressing affairs.

BASQUE: It's a long tailcoat that this fellow wears,
With gold all over.

CÉLIMÈNE (*to* ALCESTE): You'd best go down and see.
Or—have him enter.

Scene 7 [ALCESTE, CÉLIMÈNE, ÉLIANTE, ACASTE, PHILINTE, CLITANDRE, GUARD]

ALCESTE (*confronting the* GUARD): Well, what do you want with me?
Come in. Sir.

GUARD: I've a word, Sir, for your ear.

ALCESTE: Speak it aloud, Sir; I shall strive to hear.

GUARD: The Marshals have instructed me to say
You must report to them without delay.

ALCESTE: Who? Me, Sir?

GUARD: Yes, Sir; you.

ALCESTE: But what do they want?

PHILINTE (*to* ALCESTE): To scotch your silly quarrel with Oronte.

CÉLIMÈNE (*to* PHILINTE): What quarrel?

PHILINTE: Oronte and he have fallen out
  Over some verse he spoke his mind about;
  The Marshals wish to arbitrate the matter.

ALCESTE: Never shall I equivocate or flatter!

PHILINTE: You'd best obey their summons; come, let's go.

ALCESTE: How can they mend our quarrel, I'd like to know?
  Am I to make a cowardly retraction,
  And praise those jingles to his satisfaction?
  I'll not recant; I've judged that sonnet rightly.
  It's bad.

PHILINTE: But you might say so more politely. . . .

ALCESTE: I'll not back down; his verses make me sick.

PHILINTE: If only you could be more politic!
  But come, let's go.

ALCESTE: I'll go, but I won't unsay.
  A single word.

PHILINTE: Well, let's be on our way.

ALCESTE: Till I am ordered by my lord the King
  To praise that poem, I shall say the thing
  Is scandalous, by God, and that the poet
  Ought to be hanged for having the nerve to show it.

  (*To* CLITANDRE *and* ACASTE, *who are laughing.*)

  By heaven, Sirs, I really didn't know
  That I was being humorous.

CÉLIMÈNE: Go, Sir, go;
  Settle your business.

ALCESTE: I shall, and when I'm through,
  I shall return to settle things with you.

ACT III

Scene 1 [CLITANDRE, ACASTE]

CLITANDRE: Dear Marquess, how contented you appear;
  All things delight you, nothing mars your cheer.
  Can you, in perfect honesty, declare
  That you've a right to be so debonair?

ACASTE: By Jove, when I survey myself, I find
   No cause whatever for distress of mind.
   I'm young and rich; I can in modesty
   Lay claim to an exalted pedigree;
   And owing to my name and my condition
   I shall not want for honors and position.
   Then as to courage, that most precious trait,
   I seem to have it, as was proved of late
   Upon the field of honor, where my bearing,
   They say, was very cool and rather daring.
   I've wit, of course; and taste in such perfection
   That I can judge without the least reflection,
   And at the theater, which is my delight,
   Can make or break a play on opening night,
   And lead the crowd in hisses or bravos,
   And generally be known as one who knows.
   I'm clever, handsome, gracefully polite;
   My waist is small, my teeth are strong and white;
   As for my dress, the world's astonished eyes
   Assure me that I bear away the prize.
   I find myself in favor everywhere,
   Honored by men, and worshiped by the fair;
   And since these things are so, it seems to me
   I'm justified in my complacency.
CLITANDRE: Well, if so many ladies hold you dear,
   Why do you press a hopeless courtship here?
ACASTE: Hopeless, you say? I'm not the sort of fool
   That likes his ladies difficult and cool.
   Men who are awkward, shy, and peasantish
   May pine for heartless beauties, if they wish,
   Grovel before them, bear their cruelties,
   Woo them with tears and sighs and bended knees,
   And hope by dogged faithfulness to gain
   What their poor merits never could obtain.
   For men like me, however, it makes no sense
   To love on trust, and foot the whole expense.
   Whatever any lady's merits be,
   I think, thank God, that I'm as choice as she;
   That if my heart is kind enough to burn
   For her, she owes me something in return;
   And that in any proper love affair
   The partners must invest an equal share.
CLITANDRE: You think, then, that our hostess favors you?
ACASTE: I've reason to believe that that is true.

CLITANDRE: How did you come to such a mad conclusion?
    You're blind, dear fellow. This is sheer delusion.
ACASTE: All right, then: I'm deluded and I'm blind.
CLITANDRE: Whatever put the notion in your mind?
ACASTE: Delusion.
CLITANDRE: What persuades you that you're right?
ACASTE: I'm blind.
CLITANDRE: But have you any proofs to cite?
ACASTE: I tell you I'm deluded.
CLITANDRE: Have you, then,
    Received some secret pledge from Célimène?
ACASTE: Oh, no: she scorns me.
CLITANDRE: Tell me the truth, I beg.
ACASTE: She just can't bear me.
CLITANDRE: Ah, don't pull my leg.
    Tell me what hope she's given you, I pray.
ACASTE: I'm hopeless, and it's you who win the day.
    She hates me thoroughly, and I'm so vexed
    I mean to hang myself on Tuesday next.
CLITANDRE: Dear Marquess, let us have an armistice
    And make a treaty. What do you say to this?
    If ever one of us can plainly prove
    That Célimène encourages his love,
    The other must abandon hope, and yield,
    And leave him in possession of the field.
ACASTE: Now, there's a bargain that appeals to me;
    With all my heart, dear Marquess, I agree.
    But hush.

Scene 2 [CÉLIMÈNE, ACASTE, CLITANDRE]

CÉLIMÈNE: Still here?
CLITANDRE: 'Twas love that stayed our feet.
CÉLIMÈNE: I think I heard a carriage in the street.
    Whose is it? D'you know?

Scene 3 [CÉLIMÈNE, ACASTE, CLITANDRE, BASQUE]

BASQUE: Arsinoé is here,
    Madame.
CÉLIMÈNE: Arsinoé, you say? Oh, dear.
BASQUE: Éliante is entertaining her below.

CÉLIMÈNE: What brings the creature here, I'd like to know?
ACASTE: They say she's dreadfully prudish, but in fact
  I think her piety . . .
CÉLIMÈNE: It's all an act.
  At heart she's worldly, and her poor success
  In snaring men explains her prudishness.
  It breaks her heart to see the beaux and gallants
  Engrossed by other women's charms and talents,
  And so she's always in a jealous rage
  Against the faulty standards of the age.
  She lets the world believe that she's a prude
  To justify her loveless solitude,
  And strives to put a brand of moral shame
  On all the graces that she cannot claim.
  But still she'd love a lover; and Alceste
  Appears to be the one she'd love the best.
  His visits here are poison to her pride;
  She seems to think I've lured him from her side;
  And everywhere, at court or in the town,
  The spiteful, envious woman runs me down.
  In short, she's just as stupid as can be,
  Vicious and arrogant in the last degree,
  And . . .

Scene 4 [ARSINOÉ, CÉLIMÈNE, CLITANDRE, ACASTE]

CÉLIMÈNE: Ah! What happy chance has brought you here?
  I've thought about you ever so much, my dear.
ARSINOÉ: I've come to tell you something you should know.
CÉLIMÈNE: How good of you to think of doing so!

(CLITANDRE *and* ACASTE *go out, laughing.*)

Scene 5 [ARSINOÉ, CÉLIMÈNE]

ARSINOÉ: It's just as well those gentlemen didn't tarry.
CÉLIMÈNE: Shall we sit down?
ARSINOÉ: That won't be necessary.
  Madam, the flame of friendship ought to burn
  Brightest in matters of the most concern,
  And as there's nothing which concerns us more
  Than honor, I have hastened to your door
  To bring you, as your friend, some information

About the status of your reputation.
I visited, last night, some virtuous folk,
And, quite by chance, it was of you they spoke;
There was, I fear, no tendency to praise
Your light behavior and your dashing ways.
The quantity of gentlemen you see
And your by now notorious coquetry
Were both so vehemently criticized
By everyone, that I was much surprised.
Of course, I needn't tell you where I stood;
I came to your defense as best I could,
Assured them you were harmless, and declared
Your soul was absolutely unimpaired.
But there are some things, you must realize,
One can't excuse, however hard one tries,
And I was forced at last into conceding
That your behavior, Madam, is misleading,
That it makes a bad impression, giving rise
To ugly gossip and obscene surmise,
And that if you were more *overtly* good,
You wouldn't be so much misunderstood.
Not that I think you've been unchaste—no! no!
The saints preserve me from a thought so low!
But mere good conscience never did suffice:
One must avoid the outward show of vice.
Madam, you're too intelligent, I'm sure,
To think my motives anything but pure
In offering you this counsel—which I do
Out of a zealous interest in you.
CÉLIMÈNE: Madam, I haven't taken you amiss;
I'm very much obliged to you for this;
And I'll at once discharge the obligation
By telling you about *your* reputation.
You've been so friendly as to let me know
What certain people say of me, and so
I mean to follow your benign example
By offering you a somewhat similar sample.
The other day, I went to an affair
And found some most distinguished people there
Discussing piety, both false and true.
The conversation soon came round to you.
Alas! Your prudery and bustling zeal
Appeared to have a very slight appeal.

Your affectation of a grave demeanor,
Your endless talk of virtue and of honor,
The aptitude of your suspicious mind
For finding sin where there is none to find,
Your towering self-esteem, that pitying face
With which you contemplate the human race,
Your sermonizings and your sharp aspersions
On people's pure and innocent diversions—
All these were mentioned, Madam, and, in fact,
Were roundly and concertedly attacked.
"What good," they said, "are all these outward shows,
When everything belies her pious pose?
She prays incessantly; but then, they say,
She beats her maids and cheats them of their pay;
She shows her zeal in every holy place,
But still she's vain enough to paint her face;
She holds that naked statues are immoral,
But with a naked *man* she'd have no quarrel."
Of course, I said to everybody there
That they were being viciously unfair;
But still they were disposed to criticize you,
And all agreed that someone should advise you
To leave the morals of the world alone,
And worry rather more about your own.
They felt that one's self-knowledge should be great
Before one thinks of setting others straight;
That one should learn the art of living well
Before one threatens other men with hell,
And that the Church is best equipped, no doubt,
To guide our souls and root our vices out.
Madam, you're too intelligent, I'm sure,
To think my motives anything but pure
In offering you this counsel—which I do
Out of a zealous interest in you.

ARSINOÉ: I dared not hope for gratitude, but I
Did not expect so acid a reply;
I judge, since you've been so extremely tart,
That my good counsel pierced you to the heart.

CÉLIMÈNE: Far from it, Madam. Indeed, it seems to me
We ought to trade advice more frequently.
One's vision of oneself is so defective
That it would be an excellent corrective.
If you are willing, Madam, let's arrange

Shortly to have another frank exchange
In which we'll tell each other, *entre nous,*
What you've heard tell of me, and I of you.
ARSINOÉ: Oh, people never censure you, my dear;
It's me they criticize. Or so I hear.
CÉLIMÈNE: Madam, I think we either blame or praise
According to our taste and length of days.
There is a time of life for coquetry,
And there's a season, too, for prudery.
When all one's charms are gone, it is, I'm sure,
Good strategy to be devout and pure:
It makes one seem a little less forsaken.
Some day, perhaps, I'll take the road you've taken:
Time brings all things. But I have time aplenty,
And see no cause to be a prude at twenty.
ARSINOÉ: You give your age in such a gloating tone
That one would think I was an ancient crone;
We're not so far apart, in sober truth,
That you can mock me with a boast of youth!
Madam, you baffle me. I wish I knew
What moves you to provoke me as you do.
CÉLIMÈNE: For my part, Madam, I should like to know
Why you abuse me everywhere you go.
Is it my fault, dear lady, that your hand
Is not, alas, in very great demand?
If men admire me, if they pay me court
And daily make me offers of the sort
You'd dearly love to have them make to you,
How can I help it? What would you have me do?
If what you want is lovers, please feel free
To take as many as you can from me.
ARSINOÉ: Oh, come. D'you think the world is losing sleep
Over that flock of lovers which you keep,
Or that we find it difficult to guess
What price you pay for their devotedness?
Surely you don't expect us to suppose
Mere merit could attract so many beaux?
It's not your virtue that they're dazzled by;
Nor is it virtuous love for which they sigh.
You're fooling no one, Madam; the world's not blind;
There's many a lady heaven has designed
To call men's noblest, tenderest feelings out,
Who has no lovers dogging her about;

From which it's plain that lovers nowadays
Must be acquired in bold and shameless ways,
And only pay one court for such reward
As modesty and virtue can't afford.
Then don't be quite so puffed up, if you please,
About your tawdry little victories;
Try, if you can, to be a shade less vain,
And treat the world with somewhat less disdain.
If one were envious of your amours,
One soon could have a following like yours;
Lovers are no great trouble to collect
If one prefers them to one's self-respect.

CÉLIMÈNE: Collect them then, my dear; I'd love to see
You demonstrate that charming theory;
Who knows, you might . . .

ARSINOÉ: Now, Madam, that will do;
It's time to end this trying interview.
My coach is late in coming to your door,
Or I'd have taken leave of you before.

CÉLIMÈNE: Oh, please don't feel that you must rush away;
I'd be delighted, Madam, if you'd stay.
However, lest my conversation bore you,
Let me provide some better company for you;
This gentleman, who comes most apropos,
Will please you more than I could do, I know.

Scene 6 [ALCESTE, CÉLIMÈNE, ARSINOÉ]

CÉLIMÈNE: Alceste, I have a little note to write
Which simply must go out before tonight;
Please entertain *Madame*; I'm sure that she
Will overlook my incivility.

Scene 7 [ALCESTE, ARSINOÉ]

ARSINOÉ: Well, Sir, our hostess graciously contrives
For us to chat until my coach arrives;
And I shall be forever in her debt
For granting me this little tête-à-tête.
We women very rightly give our hearts
To men of noble character and parts,
And your especial merits, dear Alceste,
Have roused the deepest sympathy in my breast.

Oh, how I wish they had sufficient sense
At court, to recognize your excellence!
They wrong you greatly, Sir. How it must hurt you
Never to be rewarded for your virtue!
ALCESTE: Why, Madam, what cause have I to feel aggrieved?
What great and brilliant thing have I achieved?
What service have I rendered to the King
That I should look to him for anything?
ARSINOÉ: Not everyone who's honored by the State
Has done great services. A man must wait
Till time and fortune offer him the chance.
Your merit, Sir, is obvious at a glance,
And . . .
ALCESTE: Ah, forget my merit; I am not neglected.
The court, I think, can hardly be expected
To mine men's souls for merit, and unearth
Our hidden virtues and our secret worth.
ARSINOÉ: *Some* virtues, though, are far too bright to hide;
Yours are acknowledged, Sir, on every side.
Indeed, I've heard you warmly praised of late
By persons of considerable weight.
ALCESTE: This fawning age has praise for everyone,
And all distinctions, Madam, are undone.
All things have equal honor nowadays,
And no one should be gratified by praise.
To be admired, one only need exist,
And every lackey's on the honors list.
ARSINOÉ: I only wish, Sir, that you had your eye
On some position at court, however high;
You'd only have to hint at such a notion
For me to set the proper wheels in motion;
I've certain friendships I'd be glad to use
To get you any office you might choose.
ALCESTE: Madam, I fear that any such ambition
Is wholly foreign to my disposition.
The soul God gave me isn't of the sort
That prospers in the weather of a court.
It's all too obvious that I don't possess
The virtues necessary for success.
My one great talent is for speaking plain;
I've never learned to flatter or to feign;
And anyone so stupidly sincere
Had best not seek a courtier's career.

Outside the court, I know, one must dispense
With honors, privilege, and influence;
But still one gains the right, foregoing these,
Not to be tortured by the wish to please.
One needn't live in dread of snubs and slights,
Nor praise the verse that every idiot writes,
Nor humor silly Marquesses, nor bestow
Politic sighs on Madam So-and-So.

ARSINOÉ: Forget the court, then; let the matter rest.
But I've another cause to be distressed
About your present situation, Sir.
It's to your love affair that I refer.
She whom you love, and who pretends to love you,
Is, I regret to say, unworthy of you.

ALCESTE: Why, Madam? Can you seriously intend
To make so grave a charge against your friend?

ARSINOÉ: Alas, I must. I've stood aside too long
And let that lady do you grievous wrong;
But now my debt to conscience shall be paid:
I tell you that your love has been betrayed.

ALCESTE: I thank you, Madam; you're extremely kind.
Such words are soothing to a lover's mind.

ARSINOÉ: Yes, though she *is* my friend, I say again
You're very much too good for Célimène.
She's wantonly misled you from the start.

ALCESTE: You may be right; who knows another's heart?
But ask yourself if it's the part of charity
To shake my soul with doubts of her sincerity.

ARSINOÉ: Well, if you'd rather be a dupe than doubt her,
That's your affair. I'll say no more about her.

ALCESTE: Madam, you know that doubt and vague suspicion
Are painful to a man in my position;
It's most unkind to worry me this way
Unless you've some real proof of what you say.

ARSINOÉ: Sir, say no more: all doubts shall be removed,
And all that I've been saying shall be proved.
You've only to escort me home, and there
We'll look into the heart of this affair.
I've ocular evidence which will persuade you
Beyond a doubt, that Célimène's betrayed you.
Then, if you're saddened by that revelation,
Perhaps I can provide some consolation.

ACT IV

Scene 1 [ÉLIANTE, PHILINTE]

PHILINTE: Madam, he acted like a stubborn child;
  I thought they never would be reconciled;
  In vain we reasoned, threatened, and appealed;
  He stood his ground and simply would not yield.
  The Marshals, I feel sure, have never heard
  An argument so splendidly absurd.
  "No, gentlemen," said he, "I'll not retract.
  His verse is bad: extremely bad, in fact.
  Surely it does the man no harm to know it.
  Does it disgrace him, not to be a poet?
  A gentleman may be respected still,
  Whether he writes a sonnet well or ill.
  That I dislike his verse should not offend him;
  In all that touches honor, I commend him;
  He's noble, brave, and virtuous—but I fear
  He can't in truth be called a sonneteer.
  I'll gladly praise his wardrobe; I'll endorse
  His dancing, or the way he sits a horse;
  But, gentlemen, I cannot praise his rhyme.
  In fact, it ought to be a capital crime
  For anyone so sadly unendowed
  To write a sonnet, and read the thing aloud."
  At length he fell into a gentler mood
  And, striking a concessive attitude,
  He paid Oronte the following courtesies:
  "Sir, I regret that I'm so hard to please,
  And I'm profoundly sorry that your lyric
  Failed to provoke me to a panegyric."
  After these curious words, the two embraced,
  And then the hearing was adjourned—in haste.
ÉLIANTE: His conduct has been very singular lately;
  Still, I confess that I respect him greatly.
  The honesty in which he takes such pride
  Has—to my mind—its noble, heroic side.
  In this false age, such candor seems outrageous;
  But I could wish that it were more contagious.
PHILINTE: What most intrigues me in our friend Alceste
  Is the grand passion that rages in his breast.

The sullen humors he's compounded of
Should not, I think, dispose his heart to love;
But since they do, it puzzles me still more
That he should choose your cousin to adore.

ÉLIANTE: It does, indeed, belie the theory
That love is born of gentle sympathy,
And that the tender passion must be based
On sweet accords of temper and of taste.

PHILINTE: Does she return his love, do you suppose?

ÉLIANTE: Ah, that's a difficult question, Sir. Who knows?
How can we judge the truth of her devotion?
Her heart's a stranger to its own emotion.
Sometimes it thinks it loves, when no love's there;
At other times it loves quite unaware.

PHILINTE: I rather think Alceste is in for more
Distress and sorrow than he's bargained for;
Were he of my mind, Madam, his affection
Would turn in quite a different direction,
And we would see him more responsive to
The kind regard which he receives from you.

ÉLIANTE: Sir, I believe in frankness, and I'm inclined,
In matters of the heart, to speak my mind.
I don't oppose his love for her; indeed,
I hope with all my heart that he'll succeed,
And were it in my power, I'd rejoice
In giving him the lady of his choice.
But if, as happens frequently enough
In love affairs, he meets with a rebuff—
If Célimène should grant some rival's suit—
I'd gladly play the role of substitute;
Nor would his tender speeches please me less
Because they'd once been made without success.

PHILINTE: Well, Madam, as for me, I don't oppose
Your hopes in this affair; and heaven knows
That in my conversations with the man
I plead your cause as often as I can.
But if those two should marry, and so remove
All chance that he will offer you his love,
Then I'll declare my own, and hope to see
Your gracious favor pass from him to me.
In short, should you be cheated of Alceste,
I'd be most happy to be second best.

ÉLIANTE: Philinte, you're teasing.

PHILINTE: Ah, Madam, never fear;
   No words of mine were ever so sincere,
   And I shall live in fretful expectation
   Till I can make a fuller declaration.

Scene 2 [ALCESTE, ÉLIANTE, PHILINTE]

ALCESTE: Avenge me, Madam! I must have satisfaction,
   Or this great wrong will drive me to distraction!
ÉLIANTE: Why, what's the matter? What's upset you so?
ALCESTE: Madam, I've had a mortal, mortal blow.
   If Chaos repossessed the universe,
   I swear I'd not be shaken any worse.
   I'm ruined. . . . I can say no more. . . . My soul . . .
ÉLIANTE: Do try, Sir, to regain your self-control.
ALCESTE: Just heaven! Why were so much beauty and grace
   Bestowed on one so vicious and so base?
ÉLIANTE: Once more, Sir, tell us. . . .
ALCESTE: My world has gone to wrack;
   I'm—I'm betrayed; she's stabbed me in the back:
   Yes, Célimène (who would have thought it of her?)
   Is false to me, and has another lover.
ÉLIANTE: Are you quite certain? Can you prove these things?
PHILINTE: Lovers are prey to wild imaginings
   And jealous fancies. No doubt there's some mistake. . . .
ALCESTE: Mind your own business, Sir, for heaven's sake.

   (*To* ÉLIANTE.)

   Madam, I have the proof that you demand
   Here in my pocket, penned by her own hand.
   Yes, all the shameful evidence one could want
   Lies in this letter written to Oronte—
   Oronte! whom I felt sure she couldn't love,
   And hardly bothered to be jealous of.
PHILINTE: Still, in a letter, appearances may deceive;
   This may not be so bad as you believe.
ALCESTE: Once more I beg you, Sir, to let me be;
   Tend to your own affairs, leave mine to me.
ÉLIANTE: Compose yourself; this anguish that you feel . . .
ALCESTE: Is something, Madam, you alone can heal.
   My outraged heart, beside itself with grief,
   Appeals to you for comfort and relief.
   Avenge me on your cousin, whose unjust

And faithless nature has deceived my trust;
Avenge a crime your pure soul must detest.
ÉLIANTE: But how, Sir?
ALCESTE: Madam, this heart within my breast
  Is yours; pray take it; redeem my heart from her,
  And so avenge me on my torturer.
  Let her be punished by the fond emotion,
  The ardent love, the bottomless devotion,
  The faithful worship which this heart of mine
  Will offer up to yours as to a shrine.
ÉLIANTE: You have my sympathy, Sir, in all you suffer;
  Nor do I scorn the noble heart you offer;
  But I suspect you'll soon be mollified,
  And this desire for vengeance will subside.
  When some belovèd hand has done us wrong
  We thirst for retribution—but not for long;
  However dark the deed that she's committed,
  A lovely culprit's very soon acquitted.
  Nothing's so stormy as an injured lover,
  And yet no storm so quickly passes over.
ALCESTE: No, Madam, no—this is no lovers' spat;
  I'll not forgive her; it's gone too far for that;
  My mind's made up; I'll kill myself before
  I waste my hopes upon her any more.
  Ah, here she is. My wrath intensifies.
  I shall confront her with her tricks and lies,
  And crush her utterly, and bring you then
  A heart no longer slave to Célimène.

Scene 3 [CÉLIMÈNE, ALCESTE]

ALCESTE (aside): Sweet heaven, help me to control my passion.
CÉLIMÈNE (aside): Oh, Lord.

(To ALCESTE.)

                Why stand there staring in that fashion?
  And what d'you mean by those dramatic sighs,
  And that malignant glitter in your eyes?
ALCESTE: I mean that sins which cause the blood to freeze
  Look innocent beside your treacheries;
  That nothing Hell's or Heaven's wrath could do
  Ever produced so bad a thing as you.
CÉLIMÈNE: Your compliments were always sweet and pretty.

ALCESTE: Madam, it's not the moment to be witty.
  No, blush and hang your head; you've ample reason,
  Since I've the fullest evidence of your treason.
  Ah, this is what my sad heart prophesied;
  Now all my anxious fears are verified;
  My dark suspicion and my gloomy doubt
  Divined the truth, and now the truth is out.
  For all your trickery, I was not deceived;
  It was my bitter stars that I believed.
  But don't imagine that you'll go scot-free;
  You shan't misuse me with impunity.
  I know that love's irrational and blind;
  I know the heart's not subject to the mind,
  And can't be reasoned into beating faster;
  I know each soul is free to choose its master;
  Therefore had you but spoken from the heart,
  Rejecting my attentions from the start,
  I'd have no grievance, or at any rate
  I could complain of nothing but my fate.
  Ah, but so falsely to encourage me—
  That was a treason and a treachery
  For which you cannot suffer too severely,
  And you shall pay for that behavior dearly.
  Yes, now I have no pity, not a shred;
  My temper's out of hand; I've lost my head;
  Shocked by the knowledge of your double-dealings,
  My reason can't restrain my savage feelings;
  A righteous wrath deprives me of my senses,
  And I won't answer for the consequences.
CÉLIMÈNE: What does this outburst mean? Will you please explain?
  Have you, by any chance, gone quite insane?
ALCESTE: Yes, yes, I went insane the day I fell
  A victim to your black and fatal spell,
  Thinking to meet with some sincerity
  Among the treacherous charms that beckoned me.
CÉLIMÈNE: Pooh. Of what treachery can you complain?
ALCESTE: How sly you are, how cleverly you feign!
  But you'll not victimize me any more.
  Look: here's a document you've seen before.
  This evidence, which I acquired today,
  Leaves you, I think, without a thing to say.
CÉLIMÈNE: Is this what sent you into such a fit?
ALCESTE: You should be blushing at the sight of it.

CÉLIMÈNE: Ought I to blush? I truly don't see why.

ALCESTE: Ah, now you're being bold as well as sly;
   Since there's no signature, perhaps you'll claim . . .

CÉLIMÈNE: I wrote it, whether or not it bears my name.

ALCESTE: And you can view with equanimity
   This proof of your disloyalty to me!

CÉLIMÈNE: Oh, don't be so outrageous and extreme.

ALCESTE: You take this matter lightly, it would seem.
   Was it no wrong to me, no shame to you,
   That you should send Oronte this billet-doux?

CÉLIMÈNE: Oronte! Who said it was for him?

ALCESTE: Why, those
   Who brought me this example of your prose.
   But what's the difference? If you wrote the letter
   To someone else, it pleases me no better.
   My grievance and your guilt remain the same.

CÉLIMÈNE: But need you rage, and need I blush for shame,
   If this was written to a *woman* friend?

ALCESTE: Ah! Most ingenious. I'm impressed no end;
   And after that incredible evasion
   Your guilt is clear. I need no more persuasion.
   How dare you try so clumsy a deception?
   D'you think I'm wholly wanting in perception?
   Come, come, let's see how brazenly you'll try
   To bolster up so palpable a lie:
   Kindly construe this ardent closing section
   As nothing more than sisterly affection!
   Here, let me read it. Tell me, if you dare to,
   That this is for a woman . . .

CÉLIMÈNE: I don't care to.
   What right have you to badger and berate me,
   And so highhandedly interrogate me?

ALCESTE: Now, don't be angry; all I ask of you
   Is that you justify a phrase or two . . .

CÉLIMÈNE: No, I shall not, I utterly refuse,
   And you may take those phrases as you choose.

ALCESTE: Just show me how this letter could be meant
   For a woman's eyes, and I shall be content.

CÉLIMÈNE: No, no, it's for Oronte; you're perfectly right.
   I welcome his attentions with delight,
   I prize his character and his intellect,
   And everything is just as you suspect.
   Come, do your worst now; give your rage free rein;

But kindly cease to bicker and complain.
ALCESTE (*aside*): Good God! Could anything be more inhuman?
    Was ever a heart so mangled by a woman?
    When I complain of how she has betrayed me,
    She bridles, and commences to upbraid me!
    She tries my tortured patience to the limit;
    She won't deny her guilt; she glories in it!
    And yet my heart's too faint and cowardly
    To break these chains of passion, and be free,
    To scorn her as it should, and rise above
    This unrewarded, mad, and bitter love.

    (*To* CÉLIMÈNE.)

    Ah, traitress, in how confident a fashion
    You take advantage of my helpless passion,
    And use my weakness for your faithless charms
    To make me once again throw down my arms!
    But do at least deny this black transgression;
    Take back that mocking and perverse confession;
    Defend this letter and your innocence,
    And I, poor fool, will aid in your defense.
    Pretend, pretend, that you are just and true,
    And I shall make myself believe in you.
CÉLIMÈNE: Oh, stop it. Don't be such a jealous dunce,
    Or I shall leave off loving you at once.
    Just why should I *pretend*? What could impel me
    To stoop so low as that? And kindly tell me
    Why, if I loved another, I shouldn't merely
    Inform you of it, simply and sincerely!
    I've told you where you stand, and that admission
    Should altogether clear me of suspicion,
    After so generous a guarantee,
    What right have you to harbor doubts of me?
    Since women are (from natural reticence)
    Reluctant to declare their sentiments,
    And since the honor of our sex requires
    That we conceal our amorous desires,
    Ought any man for whom such laws are broken
    To question what the oracle has spoken?
    Should he not rather feel an obligation
    To trust that most obliging declaration?
    Enough, now. Your suspicions quite disgust me;
    Why should I love a man who doesn't trust me?

I cannot understand why I continue,
Fool that I am, to take an interest in you.
I ought to choose a man less prone to doubt,
And give you something to be vexed about.
ALCESTE: Ah, what a poor enchanted fool I am;
These gentle words, no doubt, were all a sham;
But destiny requires me to entrust
My happiness to you, and so I must.
I'll love you to the bitter end, and see
How false and treacherous you dare to be.
CÉLIMÈNE: No, you don't really love me as you ought.
ALCESTE: I love you more than can be said or thought;
Indeed, I wish you were in such distress
That I might show my deep devotedness.
Yes, I could wish that you were wretchedly poor,
Unloved, uncherished, utterly obscure;
That fate had set you down upon the earth
Without possessions, rank, or gentle birth;
Then, by the offer of my heart, I might
Repair the great injustice of your plight;
I'd raise you from the dust, and proudly prove
The purity and vastness of my love.
CÉLIMÈNE: This is a strange benevolence indeed!
God grant that I may never be in need. . . .
Ah, here's Monsieur Dubois, in quaint disguise.

Scene 4 [CÉLIMÈNE, ALCESTE, DUBOIS]

ALCESTE: Well, why this costume? Why those frightened eyes?
What ails you?
DUBOIS: Well, Sir, things are most mysterious.
ALCESTE: What do you mean?
DUBOIS: I fear they're very serious.
ALCESTE: What?
DUBOIS: Shall I speak more loudly?
ALCESTE: Yes; speak out.
DUBOIS: Isn't there someone here, Sir?
ALCESTE: Speak, you lout!
Stop wasting time.
DUBOIS: Sir, we must slip away.
ALCESTE: How's that?
DUBOIS: We must decamp without delay.

ALCESTE: Explain yourself.

DUBOIS: I tell you we must fly.

ALCESTE: What for?

DUBOIS: We mustn't pause to say good-by.

ALCESTE: Now what d'you mean by all of this, you clown?

DUBOIS: I mean, Sir, that we've got to leave this town.

ALCESTE: I'll tear you limb from limb and joint from joint
    If you don't come more quickly to the point.

DUBOIS: Well, Sir, today a man in a black suit,
    Who wore a black and ugly scowl to boot,
    Left us a document scrawled in such a hand
    As even Satan couldn't understand.
    It bears upon your lawsuit, I don't doubt;
    But all hell's devils couldn't make it out.

ALCESTE: Well, well, go on. What then? I fail to see
    How this event obliges us to flee.

DUBOIS: Well, Sir: an hour later, hardly more,
    A gentleman who's often called before
    Came looking for you in an anxious way.
    Not finding you, he asked me to convey
    (Knowing I could be trusted with the same)
    The following message. . . . Now, what *was* his name?

ALCESTE: Forget his name, you idiot. What did he say?

DUBOIS: Well, it was one of your friends, Sir, anyway.
    He warned you to begone, and he suggested
    That if you stay, you may well be arrested.

ALCESTE: What? Nothing more specific? Think, man, think!

DUBOIS: No, Sir. He had me bring him pen and ink,
    And dashed you off a letter which, I'm sure,
    Will render things distinctly less obscure.

ALCESTE: Well—let me have it!

CÉLIMÈNE: What *is* this all about?

ALCESTE: God knows; but I have hopes of finding out.
    How long am I to wait, you blitherer?

DUBOIS (*after a protracted search for the letter*): I must have left it on
       your table, Sir.

ALCESTE: I ought to . . .

CÉLIMÈNE: No, no, keep your self-control;
    Go find out what's behind his rigmarole.

ALCESTE: It seems that fate, no matter what I do,
    Has sworn that I may not converse with you;
    But, Madam, pray permit your faithful lover
    To try once more before the day is over.

ACT V

Scene 1 [ALCESTE, PHILINTE]

ALCESTE: No, it's too much. My mind's made up, I tell you.
PHILINTE: Why should this blow, however hard, compel you . . .
ALCESTE: No, no, don't waste your breath in argument;
   Nothing you say will alter my intent;
   This age is vile, and I've made up my mind
   To have no further commerce with mankind.
   Did not truth, honor, decency, and the laws
   Oppose my enemy and approve my cause?
   My claims were justified in all men's sight;
   I put my trust in equity and right;
   Yet, to my horror and the world's disgrace,
   Justice is mocked, and I have lost my case!
   A scoundrel whose dishonesty is notorious
   Emerges from another lie victorious!
   Honor and right condone his brazen fraud,
   While rectitude and decency applaud!
   Before his smirking face, the truth stands charmed,
   And virtue conquered, and the law disarmed!
   His crime is sanctioned by a court decree!
   And not content with what he's done to me,
   The dog now seeks to ruin me by stating
   That I composed a book now circulating,
   A book so wholly criminal and vicious
   That even to speak its title is seditious!
   Meanwhile Oronte, my rival, lends his credit
   To the same libelous tale, and helps to spread it!
   Oronte! a man of honor and of rank,
   With whom I've been entirely fair and frank;
   Who sought me out and forced me, willy-nilly,
   To judge some verse I found extremely silly;
   And who, because I properly refused
   To flatter him, or see the truth abused,
   Abets my enemy in a rotten slander!
   There's the reward of honesty and candor!
   The man will hate me to the end of time
   For failing to commend his wretched rhyme!
   And not this man alone, but all humanity
   Do what they do from interest and vanity;

They prate of honor, truth, and righteousness,
But lie, betray, and swindle nonetheless.
Come then: man's villainy is too much to bear;
Let's leave this jungle and this jackal's lair.
Yes! treacherous and savage race of men,
You shall not look upon my face again.

PHILINTE: Oh, don't rush into exile prematurely;
Things aren't as dreadful as you make them, surely.
It's rather obvious, since you're still at large,
That people don't believe your enemy's charge.
Indeed, his tale's so patently untrue
That it may do more harm to him than you.

ALCESTE: Nothing could do that scoundrel any harm:
His frank corruption is his greatest charm,
And, far from hurting him, a further shame
Would only serve to magnify his name.

PHILINTE: In any case, his bald prevarication
Has done no injury to your reputation,
And you may feel secure in that regard.
As for your lawsuit, it should not be hard
To have the case reopened, and contest
This judgment . . .

ALCESTE: No, no, let the verdict rest.
Whatever cruel penalty it may bring,
I wouldn't have it changed for anything.
It shows the times' injustice with such clarity
That I shall pass it down to our posterity
As a great proof and signal demonstration
Of the black wickedness of this generation.
It may cost twenty thousand francs; but I
Shall pay their twenty thousand, and gain thereby
The right to storm and rage at human evil,
And send the race of mankind to the devil.

PHILINTE: Listen to me. . . .

ALCESTE: Why? What can you possibly say?
Don't argue, Sir; your labor's thrown away.
Do you propose to offer lame excuses
For men's behavior and the times' abuses?

PHILINTE: No, all you say I'll readily concede:
This is a low, conniving age indeed;
Nothing but trickery prospers nowadays,
And people ought to mend their shabby ways.
Yes, man's a beastly creature; but must we then

Abandon the society of men?
Here in the world, each human frailty
Provides occasion for philosophy,
And that is virtue's noblest exercise;
If honesty shone forth from all men's eyes,
If every heart were frank and kind and just,
What could our virtues do but gather dust
(Since their employment is to help us bear
The villainies of men without despair)?
A heart well-armed with virtue can endure. . . .
ALCESTE: Sir, you're a matchless reasoner, to be sure;
Your words are fine and full of cogency;
But don't waste time and eloquence on me.
My reason bids me go, for my own good.
My tongue won't lie and flatter as it should;
God knows what frankness it might next commit,
And what I'd suffer on account of it.
Pray let me wait for Célimène's return
In peace and quiet. I shall shortly learn,
By her response to what I have in view,
Whether her love for me is feigned or true.
PHILINTE: Till then, let's visit Éliante upstairs.
ALCESTE: No, I am too weighed down with somber cares.
Go to her, do; and leave me with my gloom
Here in the darkened corner of this room.
PHILINTE: Why, that's no sort of company, my friend;
I'll see if Éliante will not descend.

Scene 2 [CÉLIMÈNE, ORONTE, ALCESTE]

ORONTE: Yes, Madam, if you wish me to remain
Your true and ardent lover, you must deign
To give me some more positive assurance.
All this suspense is quite beyond endurance.
If your heart shares the sweet desires of mine,
Show me as much by some convincing sign;
And here's the sign I urgently suggest:
That you no longer tolerate Alceste,
But sacrifice him to my love, and sever
All your relations with the man forever.
CÉLIMÈNE: Why do you suddenly dislike him so?
You praised him to the skies not long ago.
ORONTE: Madam, that's not the point. I'm here to find

Which way your tender feelings are inclined.
Choose, if you please, between Alceste and me,
And I shall stay or go accordingly.
ALCESTE (*emerging from the corner*): Yes, Madam, choose; this gentle-
man's demand
Is wholly just, and I support his stand.
I too am true and ardent; I too am here
To ask you that you make your feelings clear.
No more delays, now; no equivocation;
The time has come to make your declaration.
ORONTE: Sir, I've no wish in any way to be
An obstacle to your felicity.
ALCESTE: Sir, I've no wish to share her heart with you;
That may sound jealous, but at least it's true.
ORONTE: If, weighing us, she leans in your direction . . .
ALCESTE: If she regards you with the least affection . . .
ORONTE: I swear I'll yield her to you there and then.
ALCESTE: I swear I'll never see her face again.
ORONTE: Now, Madam, tell us what we've come to hear.
ALCESTE: Madam, speak openly and have no fear.
ORONTE: Just say which one is to remain your lover.
ALCESTE: Just name one name, and it will all be over.
ORONTE: What! Is it possible that you're undecided?
ALCESTE: What! Can your feelings possibly be divided?
CÉLIMÈNE: Enough: this inquisition's gone too far:
How utterly unreasonable you are!
Not that I couldn't make the choice with ease;
My heart has no conflicting sympathies;
I know full well which one of you I favor,
And you'd not see me hesitate or waver.
But how can you expect me to reveal
So cruelly and bluntly what I feel?
I think it altogether too unpleasant
To choose between two men when both are present;
One's heart has means more subtle and more kind
Of letting its affections be divined,
Nor need one be uncharitably plain
To let a lover know he loves in vain.
ORONTE: No, no, speak plainly; I for one can stand it.
I beg you to be frank.
ALCESTE: And I demand it.
The simple truth is what I wish to know,
And there's no need for softening the blow.

You've made an art of pleasing everyone,
But now your days of coquetry are done:
You have no choice now, Madam, but to choose,
For I'll know what to think if you refuse;
I'll take your silence for a clear admission
That I'm entitled to my worst suspicion.
ORONTE: I thank you for this ultimatum, Sir,
And I may say I heartily concur.
CÉLIMÈNE: Really, this foolishness is very wearing:
Must you be so unjust and overbearing?
Haven't I told you why I must demur?
Ah, here's Éliante; I'll put the case to her.

Scene 3 [ÉLIANTE, PHILINTE, CÉLIMÈNE, ORONTE, ALCESTE]

CÉLIMÈNE: Cousin, I'm being persecuted here
By these two persons, who, it would appear,
Will not be satisfied till I confess
Which one I love the more, and which the less,
And tell the latter to his face that he
Is henceforth banished from my company.
Tell me, has ever such a thing been done?
ÉLIANTE: You'd best not turn to me; I'm not the one
To back you in a matter of this kind:
I'm all for those who frankly speak their mind.
ORONTE: Madam, you'll search in vain for a defender.
ALCESTE: You're beaten, Madam, and may as well surrender.
ORONTE: Speak, speak, you must; and end this awful strain.
ALCESTE: Or don't, and your position will be plain.
ORONTE: A single word will close this painful scene.
ALCESTE: But if you're silent, I'll know what you mean.

Scene 4 [ARSINOÉ, CÉLIMÈNE, ÉLIANTE, ALCESTE, PHILINTE, ACASTE, CLITANDRE, ORONTE]

ACASTE (*to* CÉLIMÈNE): Madam, with all due deference, we two
Have come to pick a little bone with you.
CLITANDRE (*to* ORONTE *and* ALCESTE): I'm glad you're present, Sirs; as you'll
soon learn,
Our business here is also your concern.
ARSINOÉ (*to* CÉLIMÈNE): Madam, I visit you so soon again
Only because of these two gentlemen,

Who came to me indignant and aggrieved
About a crime too base to be believed.
Knowing your virtue, having such confidence in it,
I couldn't think you guilty for a minute,
In spite of all their telling evidence;
And, rising above our little difference,
I've hastened here in friendship's name to see
You clear yourself of this great calumny.

ACASTE: Yes, Madam, let us see with what composure
You'll manage to respond to this disclosure.
You lately sent Clitandre this tender note.

CLITANDRE: And this one, for Acaste, you also wrote.

ACASTE (to ORONTE and ALCESTE): You'll recognize this writing, Sirs, I
think;
The lady is so free with pen and ink
That you must know it all too well, I fear.
But listen: this is something you should hear.

"How absurd you are to condemn my lightheartedness in society,
and to accuse me of being happiest in the company of others. Nothing could be more unjust; and if you do not come to me instantly and
beg pardon for saying such a thing, I shall never forgive you as long
as I live. Our big bumbling friend the Viscount . . ."

What a shame that he's not here.

"Our big bumbling friend the Viscount, whose name stands first in
your complaint, is hardly a man to my taste; and ever since the day I
watched him spend three-quarters of an hour spitting into a well, so
as to make circles in the water, I have been unable to think highly of
him. As for the little Marquess . . ."

In all modesty, gentlemen, that is I.

"As for the little Marquess, who sat squeezing my hand for such a
long while yesterday, I find him in all respects the most trifling creature alive; and the only things of value about him are his cape and his
sword. As for the man with the green ribbons . . ."

(To ALCESTE.) It's your turn now, Sir.

"As for the man with the green ribbons, he amuses me now and
then with his bluntness and his bearish ill-humor; but there are many
times indeed when I think him the greatest bore in the world. And as
for the sonneteer . . ."

(To ORONTE.) Here's your helping.

"And as for the sonneteer, who has taken it into his head to be witty, and insists on being an author in the teeth of opinion, I simply cannot be bothered to listen to him, and his prose wearies me quite as much as his poetry. Be assured that I am not always so well-entertained as you suppose; that I long for your company, more than I dare to say, at all these entertainments to which people drag me; and that the presence of those one loves is the true and perfect seasoning to all one's pleasures."

CLITANDRE: And now for me.

"Clitandre, whom you mention, and who so pesters me with his saccharine speeches, is the last man on earth for whom I could feel any affection. He is quite mad to suppose that I love him, and so are you, to doubt that you are loved. Do come to your senses; exchange your suppositions for his; and visit me as often as possible, to help me bear the annoyance of his unwelcome attentions."

It's a sweet character that these letters show,
And what to call it, Madam, you well know.
Enough. We're off to make the world acquainted
With this sublime self-portrait that you've painted.
ACASTE: Madam, I'll make you no farewell oration;
No, you're not worthy of my indignation.
Far choicer hearts than yours, as you'll discover,
Would like this little Marquess for a lover.

Scene 5 [CÉLIMÈNE, ÉLIANTE, ARSINOÉ, ALCESTE, ORONTE, PHILINTE]

ORONTE: So! After all those loving letters you wrote,
You turn on me like this, and cut my throat!
And your dissembling, faithless heart, I find,
Has pledged itself by turns to all mankind!
How blind I've been! But now I clearly see;
I thank you, Madam, for enlightening me.
My heart is mine once more, and I'm content;
The loss of it shall be your punishment.

(*To* ALCESTE.)

Sir, she is yours; I'll seek no more to stand
Between your wishes and this lady's hand.

Scene 6 [CÉLIMÈNE, ÉLIANTE, ARSINOÉ, ALCESTE, PHILINTE]

ARSINOÉ (*to* CÉLIMÈNE): Madam, I'm forced to speak. I'm far too stirred
    To keep my counsel, after what I've heard.
    I'm shocked and staggered by your want of morals.
    It's not my way to mix in others' quarrels;
    But really, when this fine and noble spirit,
    This man of honor and surpassing merit,
    Laid down the offering of his heart before you,
    How *could* you . . .
ALCESTE: Madam, permit me, I implore you,
    To represent myself in this debate.
    Don't bother, please, to be my advocate.
    My heart, in any case, could not afford
    To give your services their due reward;
    And if I chose, for consolation's sake,
    Some other lady, 'twould not be you I'd take.
ARSINOÉ: What makes you think you could, Sir? And how dare you
    Imply that I've been trying to ensnare you?
    If you can for a moment entertain
    Such flattering fancies, you're extremely vain.
    I'm not so interested as you suppose
    In Célimène's discarded gigolos.
    Get rid of that absurd illusion, do.
    Women like me are not for such as you.
    Stay with this creature, to whom you're so attached;
    I've never seen two people better matched.

Scene 7 [CÉLIMÈNE, ÉLIANTE, ALCESTE, PHILINTE]

ALCESTE (*to* CÉLIMÈNE): Well, I've been still throughout this exposé,
    Till everyone but me has said his say.
    Come, have I shown sufficient self-restraint?
    And may I now . . .
CÉLIMÈNE: Yes, make your just complaint.
    Reproach me freely, call me what you will;
    You've every right to say I've used you ill.
    I've wronged you, I confess it; and in my shame
    I'll make no effort to escape the blame.
    The anger of those others I could despise;
    My guilt toward you I sadly recognize.

Your wrath is wholly justified, I fear;
I know how culpable I must appear,
I know all things bespeak my treachery,
And that, in short, you've grounds for hating me.
Do so; I give you leave.

ALCESTE: Ah, traitress—how,
How should I cease to love you, even now?
Though mind and will were passionately bent
On hating you, my heart would not consent.

(*To* ÉLIANTE *and* PHILINTE.)

Be witness to my madness, both of you;
See what infatuation drives one to;
But wait; my folly's only just begun,
And I shall prove to you before I'm done
How strange the human heart is, and how far
From rational we sorry creatures are.

(*To* CÉLIMÈNE.)

Woman, I'm willing to forget your shame,
And clothe your treacheries in a sweeter name;
I'll call them youthful errors, instead of crimes,
And lay the blame on these corrupting times.
My one condition is that you agree
To share my chosen fate, and fly with me
To that wild, trackless, solitary place
In which I shall forget the human race.
Only by such a course can you atone
For those atrocious letters; by that alone
Can you remove my present horror of you,
And make it possible for me to love you.

CÉLIMÈNE: What! *I* renounce the world at my young age,
And die of boredom in some hermitage?

ALCESTE: Ah, if you really loved me as you ought,
You wouldn't give the world a moment's thought;
Must you have me, and all the world beside?

CÉLIMÈNE: Alas, at twenty one is terrified
Of solitude. I fear I lack the force
And depth of soul to take so stern a course.
But if my hand in marriage will content you,
Why, there's a plan which I might well consent to,
And . . .

ALCESTE: No, I detest you now. I could excuse
   Everything else, but since you thus refuse
   To love me wholly, as a wife should do,
   And see the world in me, as I in you,
   Go! I reject your hand, and disenthrall
   My heart from your enchantments, once for all.

Scene 8 [ÉLIANTE, ALCESTE, PHILINTE]

ALCESTE (*to* ÉLIANTE): Madam, your virtuous beauty has no peer;
   Of all this world, you only are sincere;
   I've long esteemed you highly, as you know;
   Permit me ever to esteem you so,
   And if I do not now request your hand,
   Forgive me, Madam, and try to understand.
   I feel unworthy of it; I sense that fate
   Does not intend me for the married state,
   That I should do you wrong by offering you
   My shattered heart's unhappy residue,
   And that in short . . .
ÉLIANTE: Your argument's well taken:
   Nor need you fear that I shall feel forsaken.
   Were I to offer him this hand of mine,
   Your friend Philinte, I think, would not decline.
PHILINTE: Ah, Madam, that's my heart's most cherished goal,
   For which I'd gladly give my life and soul.
ALCESTE (*to* ÉLIANTE *and* PHILINTE): May you be true to all you now pro-
    fess,
   And so deserve unending happiness.
   Meanwhile, betrayed and wronged in everything,
   I'll flee this bitter world where vice is king,
   And seek some spot unpeopled and apart
   Where I'll be free to have an honest heart.
PHILINTE: Come, Madam, let's do everything we can
   To change the mind of this unhappy man.

When Molière's company first performed *The Misanthrope* in 1666 the success of the play was greater with the sophisticated literati at court than with the general audience. The same split response has attended most subsequent productions. Audiences and readers have felt that to understand the play is to be made uncomfortable rather than to be pleased and that Alceste is an interesting rather than an attractive character. Neither response is weakened by the likelihood that Alceste's fierce disgust with the polite shams of society was in part Molière's own at the time when he wrote the play.

The Palais Royal in Paris, Molière's theater, was a typical playhouse of French neoclassicism. From Italian stagecraft of the late Renaissance the theater of King Louis XIV took over and developed most of the features of the conventional modern theater: box stage within a proscenium arch, curtain, wings for movable sets, painted backdrop, artificial lighting, and women in women parts.

The play itself, however, observes the crucial neoclassical unities only in a somewhat casual manner. It is a comprehensive anatomy of social attitudes, an exposé of an entire milieu, and its action, accordingly, is static rather than dynamic, analytical and expository rather than narrative. Molière's singleness of intent has not left him much room for suspense or ordinary plot causality. He achieves his tart meanings less by means of events, singly or in structure, than by juxtapositions of characters, situations, and tones (almost the whole of Act II is an example). The gain in concentration on social manners is considerable: the whole series of episodes and confrontations of rivalries and animosities that substitutes for a coherent, climaxing plot exhibits the conflict between Alceste and society. This is true even of the only major scene in which Alceste himself is not on stage: the verbal duel between Célimène and Arsinoé, which, at the exact midpoint of the play, demonstrates what social intercourse would be like if Alceste's code of absolute frankness were to prevail.

The place throughout is a salon in Célimène's house, and the time appears to be limited to a single day, but neither place nor time is an active ingredient in the action, except insofar as a short time span strengthens psychological plausibility in a comedy that is based on a static concept of character. The setting is a neutral locale for visits and conversation. The time span is arbitrarily cut off at the beginning and the end (the opening conversation between Philinte and Alceste is a running start, and the ending is inconclusive) and could be any day in the usual routine of Célimène's idle and fashionable set. The absence of particulars about Alceste's and Célimène's lawsuits is another instance of indefiniteness. The cumulative effect of such nonparticularity is that the action seems "typical," a randomly selected illustration of a general pattern. Alceste becomes something like the Good Man Indignant.

The Misanthrope differs from several of Molière's other comedies in showing little influence from the *commedia dell' arte*, the vigorous, popular theater of contemporary Italy, in which professional companies performed semi-farces of stock plot, situation, and character, but of improvised dialogue. In Célimène there may be traces of the conventional stage courtesan, and Alceste's valet Dubois suggests the impertinent and stupid servant of standard farce. But Alceste himself belongs rather to the tradition of humor comedy, though here, too, Molière has modified convention. Society is under examination almost as much as the title character. Much of the action originates not in Alceste's eccentricity but in the foibles of his human environment: Oronte's literary vanity, Arsinoé's jealousy, and the Marquesses' foppish suit of Célimène.

The Misanthrope is the maturest of comedies of manners; that is, plays in which comedy results from the clash between a group code of upper-class social behavior and an individual deviating from the code. In simple specimens of the genre one or the other is felt to represent a sane norm and the antagonist a corresponding aberration which is exposed to laughter. In subtler kinds, right and wrong, approval and ridicule, are more evenly distributed. In The Misanthrope the ambivalence is carried to the point of paradox. The norm of the foolish and corrupt group code is opposed by the life-negating idiosyncrasy of the virtuous individual. The main audience problem becomes that of choosing sides between Alceste and society.

In the ambivalence resides the play's "darkness" as comedy, and it explains why, of all Molière's great comedies, it is the least gay and least popular and the most widely discussed. It has been called Molière's *Hamlet,* a label particularly fitting in the light of recent views of the Prince of Denmark as a homicidal neurotic. The "problem," in a narrow, technical sense, is that Alceste's character resists any effort to fit the play into the mold of Molière's other plays of comically deviant eccentrics. The jealous Arnolphe, the pious fraud Tartuffe, the miser Harpagon, and the would-be gentleman M. Jourdain are not fit company for the noble-minded Alceste. The Restoration playwright William Wycherley called his English adaptation *The Plain Dealer* and his hero Manly, and both title and name reflect a degree of unease with Alceste and his fate which Wycherley has not been alone in feeling.

Jean Jacques Rousseau, the French *philosophe* who godfathered Romantic individualism and "naturalness," may be taken to represent the opposition to Molière's treatment of Alceste. The real misanthrope, Rousseau argued, is not a man but a monster, "an enemy of the human race," an example of "natural depravity." But Alceste is very much a man—a good and honest man, unhappily in love with a charming but heartless coquette and opposed to her meretricious world. To affix the label of "misanthrope" to such a man and to show him behaving in a silly fashion is a betrayal of militant virtue.

The basis for Rousseau's attack is the theory that the function of literature is to teach good morals (if only implicitly, by showing models of exemplary behavior and attitude for the reader's emulation). Molière would have accepted the theory but differed on the degree of subtlety and indirection allowed the playwright in putting it to practice. The function of comedy has been defined as the eliciting of thoughtful laughter. By this definition The Misanthrope must be accounted at least a partial failure, for the spectacle of honest integrity in the role of furious and futile zeal may have provoked thought but hardly the liberating laughter of pure comedy—at most a wry and painful smile. And yet, the play's distinction as comedy rests on the impossibility of dismissing altogether the tragic alternative to the comic interpretation.

There is, on the one hand, the vital point of the comparison with Hamlet. Both plays give off a sense of life's dark ambiguities, of the disparity between social appearance and social reality. Both title characters are brooding and somber outsiders in a glittering company. In Hamlet the tragic irony is that in the rotten realm of Denmark the infection spreads to the noble Prince himself as he seeks to purify his heritage, paralyzing his will and poisoning his conscience with acts of rash injustice. In The Misanthrope there is the parallel irony that in an elegantly corrupt and superficially amiable society the blunt and virtuous hero necessarily appears absurd. The social evil of deception, murderous in the tragedy, frivolous in the comedy, not only opposes the uncompromising, heroic stance, but undermines it as well. And about Philinte, Alceste's friend and foil and the character who comes as close as any in the play to being Molière's spokesman (raisonneur), there hangs a curious air of tepid prig. If his reasonableness sets off Alceste's fanaticism, so does Alceste's idealism set off his compromise with the tainted world. And after his quaint love scene with Éliante in Act IV, in which both smother romance in good manners and selflessness, Philinte's common sense about social life appears less as wise conviction than as absence of strong feeling. The tone of the lovers' engagement scene at the end approaches that of parody:

ÉLIANTE [to ALCESTE]:   Your argument's well taken:
   Nor need you fear that I shall feel forsaken.
   Were I to offer him this hand of mine,
   Your friend Philinte, I think, would not decline.
PHILINTE: Ah, Madam, that's my heart's most cherished goal,
   For which I'd gladly give my life and soul.

The contrast with the spirited exchanges between Alceste and Célimène is obvious. With Éliante and Philinte ceremony is all. The quality of the peculiar sociality which the misanthrope rejects and which his friend wants him to accept is suggested by the fact that it does not involve a single family relationship. In the absence of ties of blood and marriage all social intimacy somehow seems precarious, transient, and shallow.

This is the play's (not Alceste's) case against society. But the play makes a case also against Alceste, and it is part of its subtle balance of values that this case is only partly also society's case. Alceste *is* impossible, and not just by the norms of a society that thrives on the pretense and the compromise entailed by good manners. He is also ridiculous. Act I serves to establish Alceste's position and the values he represents, but it also insinuates the vulnerability of both. We see him in double exposure vis-à-vis each of his three antagonists: the polite but insincere conventions of friends and acquaintances, the law that represents the contentious reality behind the affable surface of social life, and, finally, Célimène. There is the hint of temporizing in his repeated "I don't say that" in his comments on Oronte's sonnet—a hint all the more incongruous after his defense of frankness a few minutes earlier. (There is also the dubiousness of the critical judgment itself that prefers the artless "old love song" to Oronte's artificial but deft manipulation of a formally exacting set of paradoxes on love.) There is his cranky perverseness in welcoming the loss of his lawsuit for the sake of having his distrust of the court vindicated. Justice clearly means less to him than to be proved right in his cynicism. And there is, above all, the admitted unreason of his love for Célimène.

Throughout the play Alceste's naïveté, exposing him to furious and sometimes inarticulate disillusionment with each new instance of the world's hypocrisy, malice, fickleness, and affectation, is incongruous in a confirmed and self-confessed misanthrope. He never learns to expect the world to be as wicked as he says it is. And the cynicism which in theory is his armor against the slings and arrows of the world is never more easily penetrable than in his encounters with Célimène: he, tense with reluctant tenderness; she, thrilled with the risk of teasing her boorish lover. Against his better judgment and announced intentions he stoops again and again to vie with contemptible drones for her attention. Our sympathy is tempered by the spectacle of the self-declared hater of mankind in love with a flirtatious woman who aims to please indiscriminately. There is irony, both hilarious and touching, in the moment when his love wrings from him—from *him!*—this plea:

> Pretend, pretend, that you are just and true.

There is pathos in Alceste's fate, but his rigid pose in a pliable society is a comical rather than a tragical kind of *hubris*. It suggests petulant pride, childish self-indulgence, narcissistic love of an impressive attitude. We laugh, not at his virtue, or at his bluntness, or even at his lack of a sense of humor and self-irony, but at his monomania. The comic vision is committed to uphold even a flawed sociality in the face of however virtuous an isolating eccentricity, if only because it *is* eccentricity.

> . . . all you say I'll readily concede [says PHILINTE]:
> This is a low, conniving age indeed;
> Nothing but trickery prospers nowadays,
> And people ought to mend their shabby ways.
> Yes, man's a beastly creature; but must we then
> Abandon the society of men?

The voice that answers "no" is the voice of wisdom. Not the highest wisdom, not tragic wisdom, but the wisdom of the world in which it takes prudence and virtue to remain both uncorrupted and unbeguiled by corruption, and both tolerance and good nature to be able to see a gathering of gossiping prudes and coquettes, fops and witlings, as the regrettable but inevitable and rather amusing excrescence on a sophisticated court culture.

The comic spirit is the spirit that has learned to live with the fact of man's limitations. To this spirit Alceste represents a threat. No man's integrity or idealism is worth the disintegration of the social fabric, the bonds that tie man to man. Alceste's demand for instant and radical reform is the utopian dream of a ridiculous crank. The fanatic of virtue is just as much an enemy of the social system as any other kind of fanatic. The smallness, the stiffness, the frozen constriction, of his attitude qualify him for the wilderness he sets out for at the end. In Act I he had called it a "desert land, unfouled by humankind." The monstrosity of the phrase proves the justice of the title of the play, even on Rousseau's strict terms. Philinte's final reference to Alceste as an "unhappy man" is a piece of ironic charity, for the almost-tragic victim of virtue has, by resigning from the human family, made himself less than man.

The dramatized image of virtue as a potential destroyer, in an imperfect world, of man's humanity deepens and darkens the comical incongruity between what Alceste stands for and what his behavior actually makes him. Molière's control of tone and situation is largely a matter of his control of Alceste. He is given tirades to speak, not soliloquies; we always see him through the eyes of the group among whom he stalks. As a result, the latent tragedy of Alceste, the virtuous hero, never takes the play away from the overt comedy of the social misfit. Even our final glimpse of the solitude he seeks is comically tempered by the possibility that Philinte and Éliante may succeed in changing his mind. And Célimène in the wilderness is a less pleasing figure than Célimène elegantly at home. In the counterpoint effect, both witty and serious, rests the play's greatness as drama celebrating tact and tolerance, sanity, laughter, moderation, and breadth of spirit—in short, and preeminently, *civilization*.

Henrik Ibsen

Hedda Gabler

Translated by Otto Reinert

Characters

JØRGEN TESMAN *University Research Fellow in the History of Civilization*
HEDDA *his wife*
MISS JULIANE TESMAN *his aunt*
MRS. ELVSTED
JUDGE BRACK
EILERT LØVBORG
BERTE *the Tesmans' maid*

Scene: *The Tesmans' villa in a fashionable residential section of the town.*

A note on pronunciation

The approximate Norwegian pronunciation of names likely to be difficult to a speaker of English is suggested below (the syllable in capitals is accented; the unaccented e is close to English e in *quiet*).

JØRGEN   YUR-gen (g as in *bargain*)
JULLE   YOOL-le (short *oo*)
EILERT LØVBORG   AY-lert LUV-borg*
BERTE   BAIR-te

ACT I

(*A spacious, handsome, tastefully furnished room. Dark décor. In the rear, a wide doorway with open portieres. Beyond is a smaller room, furnished in the same style as the front room. A door, right, leads to the front hall. Left, French doors, with portieres drawn aside, through which can be seen a part of a roofed verandah and trees with autumn foliage. Front center, an oval table covered with a cloth. Chairs around it. Front right, a wide, dark, porcelain stove, a high-backed easy chair, a footstool with a pillow, and two ottomans. In the corner far right, a sofa and a small, round table. Front left, a sofa, set out from the wall. Far left, beyond the French doors, an upright piano. On both sides of the doorway, rear center, what-nots with knickknacks. Against the rear wall of the inner room, a sofa, and in front of it a table and two chairs. Above the sofa, a portrait of a handsome, elderly man in general's uniform. Over the table hangs a lamp with milky, white glass. There are several bouquets of flowers, in vases and glasses, in various places in the front room. Others are lying on the tables. Thick carpets on the floors of both rooms. The morning sun is shining through the French doors.*

MISS JULIANE TESMAN, *with hat and parasol, enters right, followed by* BERTE, *who carries a bouquet of flowers wrapped in paper.* MISS TESMAN *is a nice-looking woman of 65, of pleasant mien, neatly but not expensively dressed in a gray suit.* BERTE *is a middle-aged servant girl, of rather plain and countrified appearance.*)

MISS TESMAN (*stops inside the door, listens, says in a low voice*): On my word—I don't think they are even up yet!

BERTE (*also softly*): That's what I told you, miss. When you think how late the steamer got in last night. And afterwards—! Goodness!—all the stuff she wanted unpacked before she turned in.

MISS TESMAN: Well—just let them sleep. But fresh morning air—*that* we can give them when they come in here. (*Goes and opens the French doors wide.*)

*Løvborg means, literally, "leaf-castle"—a fact of possible bearing on the play's symbolism.

BERTE (*by the table, lost, still holding the flowers*): Please, miss—I just don't see a bit of space anywhere! I think I'd better put these over here. (*Puts the flowers down on the piano.*)

MISS TESMAN: Well, well, my dear Berte. So you've got yourself a new mistress now. The good Lord knows it was hard for me to let you go.

BERTE (*near tears*): What about me, then, miss! What shall *I* say? I who have served you and Miss Rina all these blessed years.

MISS TESMAN: We shall just have to make the best of it, Berte. That's all. Jørgen can't do without you, you know. He just can't. You've looked after him ever since he was a little boy.

BERTE: Yes, but miss—I'm ever so worried about leaving Miss Rina. The poor dear lying there all helpless. With that new girl and all! She'll never learn how to make things nice and comfortable for an invalid.

MISS TESMAN: Oh yes, you'll see. I'll teach her. And of course, you know, I'll do most of it myself. So don't you worry yourself about my poor· sister, Berte.

BERTE: Yes, but there's another thing, too, miss. I'm scared I won't be able to suit young Mrs. Tesman.

MISS TESMAN: Oh, well. Good heavens. So there is a thing or two—Right at first—

BERTE: For I believe she's ever so particular.

MISS TESMAN: Can you wonder? General Gabler's daughter? Just think of the kind of life she was used to when the General was alive. Do you remember when she rode by with her father? That long black riding habit she wore? And the feather in her hat?

BERTE: Oh, I remember, all right. But I'll be blessed if I ever thought she and the young master would make a pair of it.

MISS TESMAN: Nor did I. By the way, while I think of it, Berte. Jørgen has a new title now. From now on you should call him "the Doctor."

BERTE: Yes, the young mistress said something about that, too, last night. Soon as they were inside the door. Then it's really so, miss?

MISS TESMAN: It certainly is. Just think, Berte—they have made him a doctor abroad. During the trip, you know. I hadn't heard a thing about it till last night on the pier.

BERTE: Well, I daresay he could be anything he put his mind to, *he* could—smart as *he* is. But I must say I'd never thought he'd turn to doctoring people, too.

MISS TESMAN: Oh, that's not the kind of doctor he is. (*Nods significantly.*) And as far as that is concerned, there is no telling but pretty soon you may have to call him something grander yet.

BERTE: You don't say! What might that be, miss?

MISS TESMAN (*smiles*): Wouldn't you like to know! (*Moved.*) Ah yes, indeed—! If only dear Jochum could see from his grave what has become of his little boy! (*Looking around.*) But look, Berte—what's this for? Why have you taken off all the slip covers?

BERTE: She told me to. Said she can't stand slip covers on chairs.

MISS TESMAN: Do you think they mean to make this their everyday living room, then?

BERTE: It sure sounded that way. Mrs. Tesman did, I mean. For he—the doctor—he didn't say anything.

(JØRGEN TESMAN *enters from the right side of the inner room. He is humming to himself. He carries an open, empty suitcase. He is of medium height, youthful-looking, thirty-three years old; somewhat stoutish. Round, open, cheerful face. Blond hair and beard. He wears glasses and is dressed in a comfortable, rather casual suit.*)

MISS TESMAN: Good morning, good morning, Jørgen!

TESMAN (*in the doorway*): Auntie! Dearest Aunt Julle! (*Comes forward and shakes her hand.*) All the way out here—as early as this! Hm?

MISS TESMAN: Well—I just had to drop in for a moment. To see how you are getting along, you know.

TESMAN: Even though you haven't had a good night's sleep.

MISS TESMAN: Oh, that doesn't matter at all.

TESMAN: But you did get home from the pier all right, I hope. Hm?

MISS TESMAN: Oh yes, I certainly did, thank you. The Judge was kind enough to see me all the way to my door.

TESMAN: We were so sorry we couldn't give you a ride in our carriage. But you saw for yourself—all the boxes Hedda had.

MISS TESMAN: Yes, she certainly brought quite a collection.

BERTE (*to* TESMAN): Should I go and ask Mrs. Tesman if there's anything I can help her with?

TESMAN: No, thank you, Berte—you'd better not. She said she'll ring if she wants you.

BERTE (*going right*): Well, all right.

TESMAN: But, look—you might take this suitcase with you.

BERTE (*takes it*): I'll put it in the attic. (*Exits right.*)

TESMAN: Just think, Auntie—that whole suitcase was brimful of copies of old documents. You wouldn't believe me if I told you all the things I have collected from libraries and archives all over. Quaint old items nobody has known anything about.

MISS TESMAN: Well, no, Jørgen. I'm sure you haven't wasted your time on your honeymoon.

TESMAN: No, I think I may say I have not. But take your hat off, Auntie—for goodness' sake. Here! Let me untie the ribbon for you. Hm?

MISS TESMAN (*while he does so*): Ah, God forgive me, if this isn't just as if you were still at home with us!

TESMAN (*inspecting the hat*): My, what a fine-looking hat you've got yourself!

MISS TESMAN: I bought it for Hedda's sake.

TESMAN: For Hedda's sake? Hm?

MISS TESMAN: So she won't need to feel ashamed of me if we ever go out together.

TESMAN (*patting her cheek*): If you don't think of everything, Auntie! (*Puts the hat down on a chair by the table.*) And now—over here to the sofa—we'll just sit and chat for a while till Hedda comes.

(*They seat themselves. She places her parasol in the corner by the sofa.*)

MISS TESMAN (*takes both his hands in hers and gazes at him*): What a blessing it is to have you back again, Jørgen, big as life! You—Jochum's little boy!

TESMAN: For me, too, Aunt Julle. Seeing you again. For you have been both father and mother to me.

MISS TESMAN: Ah, yes—don't you think I know you'll always keep a spot in your heart for these two old aunts of yours!

TESMAN: So Aunt Rina isn't any better, hm?

MISS TESMAN: Oh no. We musn't look for improvement in her case, poor dear. She is lying there just as she has been all these years. Just the same, may the good Lord keep her for me a long time yet! For else I just wouldn't know what to do with myself, Jørgen. Especially now, when I don't have you to look after any more.

TESMAN (*pats her back*): There, there, now!

MISS TESMAN (*changing tone*): And to think that you are a married man, Jørgen! And that you were the one to walk off with Hedda Gabler. The lovely Hedda Gabler. Just think! As many admirers as she had!

TESMAN (*hums a little, smiles complacently*): Yes, I daresay I have quite a few good friends here in town who'd gladly be in my shoes, hm?

MISS TESMAN: And such a long and lovely honeymoon you had! More than five—almost six months!

TESMAN: Well, you know—for me it has been a kind of study tour as well. All the collections I had to go through. And the books I had to read!

MISS TESMAN: Yes, I suppose. (*More confidentially, her voice lowered a little.*) But listen, Jørgen—haven't you got something—something special to tell me?

TESMAN: About the trip?

MISS TESMAN: Yes.

TESMAN: No—I don't know of anything besides what I wrote in my letters. They gave me a doctor's degree down there—but I told you that last night; I'm sure I did.

MISS TESMAN: Well, yes, that sort of thing—What I mean is—don't you have certain—certain—expectations?

TESMAN: Expectations?

MISS TESMAN: Ah for goodness' sake, Jørgen! I am your old Auntie, after all!

TESMAN: Certainly I have expectations.

MISS TESMAN: Well!!

TESMAN: I fully expect to be made a professor one of these days.

MISS TESMAN: Professor—oh yes—

TESMAN: I may even say I am quite certain of it. But dear Aunt Julle—you know this just as well as I do!

MISS TESMAN (*laughing a little*): Of course I do. You're quite right. (*Changing topic.*) But about the trip. It must have cost a great deal of money—hm, Jørgen?

TESMAN: Well, now; you know that large stipend went quite a long way.

MISS TESMAN: I just don't see how you made it do for both of you, though.

TESMAN: No, I suppose that's not so easy to understand, hm?

MISS TESMAN: Particularly with a lady along. For I have always heard that is ever so much more expensive.

TESMAN: Well, yes, naturally. That *is* rather more expensive. But Hedda had to have this trip, Auntie! She really had to. Nothing less would do.

MISS TESMAN: No, I daresay. For a wedding journey is quite the thing these days. But now tell me—have you had a chance to look around here yet?

TESMAN: I certainly have. I have been up and about ever since dawn.

MISS TESMAN: And what do you think of it all?

TESMAN: Delightful! Perfectly delightful! The only thing is I don't see what we are going to do with the two empty rooms between the second sitting room in there and Hedda's bedroom.

MISS TESMAN (*with a chuckle*): Oh my dear Jørgen—you may find them useful enough—when the time comes!

TESMAN: Of course, you're right, Auntie! As my library expands, hm?

MISS TESMAN: Quite so, my dear boy. It was your library I was thinking of.

TESMAN: But I'm really most happy on Hedda's behalf. For you know, before we were engaged she used to say she wouldn't care to live anywhere but in Secretary Falk's house.

MISS TESMAN: Yes, just think—wasn't that a lucky coincidence, that it was up for sale right after you had left?

TESMAN: Yes, Aunt Julle. We've certainly been lucky. Hm?

MISS TESMAN: But it will be expensive, my dear Jørgen. Terribly expensive—all this.

TESMAN (*looks at her, a bit crestfallen*): Yes, I daresay it will, Auntie.

MISS TESMAN: Heavens, yes!

TESMAN: How much, do you think? Roughly. Hm?

MISS TESMAN: No, I couldn't possibly say till all the bills arrive.

TESMAN: Well, anyway, Judge Brack managed to get very reasonable terms for us. He said so himself in a letter to Hedda.

MISS TESMAN: Yes, and I won't have you uneasy on that account, Jørgen. Besides, I have given security for the furniture and the carpets.

TESMAN: Security? You? But dear Aunt Julle—what kind of security could you give?

MISS TESMAN: The annuity.

TESMAN (*jumps up*): What! Your and Aunt Rina's annuity?

MISS TESMAN: Yes. I didn't know what else to do, you see.

TESMAN (*standing before her*): But are you clear out of your mind, Auntie! That annuity—that's all the two of you have to live on!

MISS TESMAN: Oh well, there's nothing to get so excited about, I'm sure. It's all just a matter of form, you know. That's what the Judge said, too. For he was kind enough to arrange the whole thing for me. Just a matter of form—those were his words.

TESMAN: That's all very well. Still—

MISS TESMAN: For now you'll have your own salary, you know. And, goodness—what if we do have a few expenses—Help out a bit right at first—? That would only be a joy for us—

TESMAN: Oh, Auntie! When will you ever stop making sacrifices for my sake!

MISS TESMAN (*gets up, puts her hands on his shoulders*): But what other happiness do I have in this world than being able to smooth your way a little, my own dear boy? Orphan as you were, with no one to lean on but us? And now the goal is in sight, Jørgen. Things may have looked black at times. But heaven be praised; now you've arrived!

TESMAN: Yes, it's really quite remarkable the way things have worked out.

MISS TESMAN: Yes—and those who were against you—who tried to block your way—now they are tasting defeat. They are down, Jørgen! He, the most dangerous of them all, his fall was the greatest! He made his bed, and now he is lying in it—poor, lost wretch that he is!

TESMAN: Have you had any news about Eilert? Since I went away, I mean?

MISS TESMAN: Just that he is supposed to have published a new book.

TESMAN: What? Eilert Løvborg? Recently? Hm?

MISS TESMAN: That's what they say. But I wonder if there can be much to it. What do you think? Ah—but when *your* new book comes, that will be something quite different, Jørgen! What is it going to be about?

TESMAN: It deals with the domestic industries of Brabant during the Middle Ages.

MISS TESMAN: Just think—being able to write about something like that!

TESMAN: But as far as that is concerned, it may be quite some time before it is ready. I have all these collections to put in order first, you see.

MISS TESMAN: Yes, collecting and putting things in order—you certainly know how to do that. In that you are your father's own son.

TESMAN: Well, I must say I am looking forward to getting started. Particularly now, that I've got my own delightful home to work in.

MISS TESMAN: And most of all now that you have the one your heart desired, dear Jørgen.

TESMAN (*embracing her*): Oh yes, yes, Aunt Julle! Hedda—she is the most wonderful part of it all! (*Looks toward the doorway.*) There—I think she is coming now, hm?

(HEDDA *enters from the left side of the inner room. She is twenty-nine years old. Both features and figure are noble and elegant. Pale, ivory complexion. Steel-gray eyes, expressive of cold, clear calm. Beautiful brown hair, though not particularly ample. She is dressed in a tasteful, rather loose-fitting morning costume.*)

MISS TESMAN (*going toward her*): Good morning, my dear Hedda! A very happy morning to you!

HEDDA (*giving her hand*): Good morning, dear Miss Tesman! So early a call? That is most kind.

MISS TESMAN (*seems slightly embarrassed*): And—has the little lady of the house slept well the first night in her new home?

HEDDA: Passably, thank you.

TESMAN (*laughs*): Passably! You are a good one, Hedda! You were sleeping like a log when I got up.

HEDDA: Fortunately. And then, of course, Miss Tesman, it always takes time to get used to new surroundings. That has to come gradually. (*Looks left.*) Oh dear. The maid has left the verandah doors wide open. There's a veritable flood of sunlight in here.

MISS TESMAN (*toward the doors*): Well, then, we'll just close them.

HEDDA: No, no, not that. Tesman, dear, please pull the curtains. That will give a softer light.

TESMAN (*over by the French doors*): Yes, dear. There, now! Now you have both shade and fresh air, Hedda.

HEDDA: We certainly can use some air in here. Such loads of flowers— But, Miss Tesman, please—won't you be seated?

MISS TESMAN: No thanks. I just wanted to see if everything was all right—and so it is, thank goodness. I had better get back to Rina. I know she is waiting for me, poor thing.

TESMAN: Be sure to give her my love, Auntie. And tell her I'll be around to see her later today.

MISS TESMAN: I'll certainly do that!—Oh my! I almost forgot! (*Searches the pocket of her dress.*) I have something for you, Jørgen. Here.

TESMAN: What's that, Auntie? Hm?

MISS TESMAN (*pulls out a flat parcel wrapped in newspaper and gives it to him*): Here you are, dear.

TESMAN (*opens the parcel*): Well, well, well! So you took care of them for me, Aunt Julle! Hedda! Now, isn't that sweet, hm?

HEDDA (*by the whatnot, right*): If you'd tell me what it is—

TESMAN: My old slippers! *You* know!

HEDDA: Oh really? I remember you often talked about them on the trip.

TESMAN: Yes, for I missed them so. (*Walks over to her.*) Here—now you can see what they're like, Hedda.

HEDDA (*crosses toward stove*): Thanks. I don't know that I really care.

TESMAN (*following*): Just think—Aunt Rina embroidered these slippers for me. Ill as she was. You can't imagine how many memories they hold for me!

HEDDA (*by the table*): Hardly for me.

MISS TESMAN: That's true, you know, Jørgen.

TESMAN: Yes, but—I just thought that now that she's one of the family—

HEDDA (*interrupting*): I don't think we'll get on with that maid, Tesman.

MISS TESMAN: Not get on with Berte?

TESMAN: Whatever makes you say that, dear? Hm?

HEDDA (*points*): Look—she has left her old hat on the chair over there.

TESMAN (*appalled, drops the slippers*): But Hedda—!

HEDDA: What if somebody were to come and see it!

TESMAN: No, no, Hedda—that's Aunt Julle's hat!

HEDDA: Oh?

MISS TESMAN (*picking up the hat*): Yes, indeed it is. And it isn't old either, my dear young lady.

HEDDA: I really didn't look that closely—

MISS TESMAN (*tying the ribbons*): I want you to know that this is the first time I have had it on my head. On my word it is!

TESMAN: And very handsome it is, too. Really a splendid-looking hat!

MISS TESMAN: Oh, I don't know that it is anything so special, Jørgen. (*Looks around.*) My parasol—? Ah, here it is. (*Picks it up.*) For that is mine, too. (*Mutters.*) Not Berte's.

TESMAN: New hat and new parasol! What do you think of that, Hedda!

HEDDA: Very nice indeed.

TESMAN: Yes, don't you think so? Hm? But, Auntie, take a good look at Hedda before you leave. See how pretty and blooming she looks.

MISS TESMAN: Dear me, Jørgen; that's nothing new. Hedda has been lovely all her days. (*She nods and walks right.*)

TESMAN (*following*): Yes, but have you noticed how full-figured and healthy she looks after the trip? How she has filled out?

HEDDA (*crossing*): Oh—stop it!

MISS TESMAN (*halts, turns around*): Filled out?

TESMAN: Yes, Aunt Julle. You can't see it so well now when she wears that dress. But I, who have the opportunity—

HEDDA (*by the French doors, impatiently*): Oh, you haven't any opportunities at all!

TESMAN: It must be the mountain air in Tyrol.

HEDDA (*curtly interrupting*): I am just as I was when I left.

TESMAN: Yes, so you say. I just don't think you're right. What do you think, Auntie?

MISS TESMAN (*has folded her hands, gazes at* HEDDA): Lovely—lovely—lovely; that is what Hedda is. (*Goes over to her, inclines her head forward with both her hands, and kisses her hair.*) God bless and keep Hedda Tesman. For Jørgen's sake.

HEDDA (*gently freeing herself*): There, there. Now let me go.

MISS TESMAN (*in quiet emotion*): Every single day I'll be over and see you two.

TESMAN: Yes, please do, Auntie. Hm?

MISS TESMAN: Goodbye, goodbye!

(*She leaves through door, right.* TESMAN *sees her out. The door remains ajar.* TESMAN *is heard repeating his greetings for* AUNT RINA *and his thanks for the slippers. In the meantime,* HEDDA *paces up and down, raises her arms, clenching her fists, as in quiet rage. Opens the curtains by the French doors and stands looking out. In a few moments,* TESMAN *re-enters and closes the door behind him.*)

TESMAN (*picking up the slippers*): What are you looking at, Hedda?

HEDDA (*once again calm and controlled*): Just the leaves. They are so yellow. And withered.

TESMAN (*wrapping the slippers in their paper, putting the parcel down on the table*): Well, you know—we're in September now.

HEDDA (*again restless*): Yes—just think. It's already—September.

TESMAN: Don't you think Aunt Julle acted strange, Hedda? Almost solemn. I wonder why. Hm?

HEDDA: I hardly know her, you see. Isn't she often like that?

TESMAN: Not the way she was today.

HEDDA (*turning away from the French doors*): Do you think she minded that business with the hat?

TESMAN: Oh, I don't think so. Not much. Perhaps a little bit right at the moment—

HEDDA: Well, I'm sorry, but I must say it strikes me as very odd—putting her hat down here in the living room. One just doesn't do that.

TESMAN: Well, you may be sure Aunt Julle won't ever do it again.

HEDDA: Anyway, I'll make it up to her, somehow.

TESMAN: Oh yes, Hedda; if only you would!

HEDDA: When you go over there today, why don't you ask her over for tonight?

TESMAN: I'll certainly do that. And then there is one other thing you could do that she'd appreciate ever so much.

HEDDA: What?

TESMAN: If you could just bring yourself to call her Auntie. For my sake, Hedda, hm?

HEDDA: No, Tesman, no. You really mustn't ask me to do that. I have already told you I can't. I'll try to call her Aunt Juliane. That will have to do.

TESMAN: All right, if you say so. I just thought that now that you're in the family—

HEDDA: Hmmm—I don't know about that—(*She walks toward the doorway.*)

TESMAN (*after a brief pause*): Anything the matter, Hedda? Hm?

HEDDA: I'm just looking at my old piano. It doesn't quite go with the other furniture in here.

TESMAN: As soon as I get my first paycheck we'll have it traded in.

HEDDA: No—I don't want to do that. I want to keep it. But let's put it in this inner room and get another one for out here. Whenever it's convenient, I mean.

TESMAN (*a little taken back*): Well—yes—we could do that—

HEDDA (*picks up the bouquet from the piano*): These flowers weren't here last night.

TESMAN: I suppose Aunt Julle brought them for you.

HEDDA (*looking at the flowers*): There's a card here. (*Takes it out and reads.*) "Will be back later." Can you guess who it's from?

TESMAN: No. Who? Hm?

HEDDA: Thea Elvsted.

TESMAN: No, really? Mrs. Elvsted! Miss Rysing that was.

HEDDA: That's right. The one with that irritating head of hair she used to show off with. An old flame of yours, I understand.

TESMAN (*laughs*): Well, now—that didn't last long! Anyway, that was before I knew you, Hedda. Just think—her being in town.

HEDDA: Strange, that she'd call on us. I have hardly seen her since we went to school together.

TESMAN: As far as that goes, I haven't seen her either for—God knows how long. I don't see how she can stand living in that out-of-the-way place. Hm?

HEDDA (*suddenly struck by a thought*): Listen, Tesman—isn't it some place near there that he lives—what's his name—Eilert Løvborg?

TESMAN: Yes, that's right. He is up there, too.

(BERTE *enters right*.)

BERTE: Ma'am, she's here again, that lady who brought those flowers a while back. (*Pointing*.) The flowers you're holding in your hand, ma'am.

HEDDA: Ah, she is? Well, show her in, please.

(BERTE *opens the door for* MRS. ELVSTED *and exits*. MRS. ELVSTED *is of slight build, with a pretty, soft face. Her eyes are light blue, large, round, rather prominent, of a timid and querying expression. Her hair is strikingly light in color, almost whitish, and unusually rich and wavy. She is a couple of years younger than* HEDDA. *She is dressed in a dark visiting dress, tasteful, but not quite in the most recent fashion*.)

HEDDA (*walks toward her. Friendly*): Good morning, my dear Mrs. Elvsted. How very nice to see you again.

MRS. ELVSTED (*nervous, trying not to show it*): Well, yes, it is quite some time since we met.

TESMAN (*shaking hands*): And we, too. Hm?

HEDDA: Thank you for your lovely flowers—

MRS. ELVSTED: Please, don't—I would have come here yesterday afternoon. But I was told you were still traveling—

TESMAN: You've just arrived in town, hm?

MRS. ELVSTED: I got here yesterday, at noon. Oh, I was quite desperate when I learned you weren't home.

HEDDA: Desperate? But why?

TESMAN: But my dear Mrs. Rysing—I mean Mrs. Elvsted—

HEDDA: There is nothing wrong, I hope?

MRS. ELVSTED: Yes there is. And I don't know a single soul other than you that I can turn to here.

HEDDA (*putting the flowers down on the table*): Come—let's sit down here on the sofa.

MRS. ELVSTED: Oh, I'm in no mood to sit!

HEDDA: Of course you are. Come on. (*She pulls* MRS. ELVSTED *over to the sofa and sits down next to her*.)

TESMAN: Well, now, Mrs.—? Exactly what—?

HEDDA: Has something—special happened at home?

MRS. ELVSTED: Well, yes—and no. Oh, but I am so afraid you won't understand!

HEDDA: In that case, it seems to me you ought to tell us exactly what has
happened, Mrs. Elvsted.

TESMAN: After all, that's why you are here. Hm?

MRS. ELVSTED: Yes, yes, of course. Well, then, maybe you already know—
Eilert Løvborg is in town.

HEDDA: Is Løvborg—!

TESMAN: No! You don't say! Just think, Hedda—Løvborg's back!

HEDDA: All right. I can hear.

MRS. ELVSTED: He has been here a week already. Imagine—a whole week!
In this dangerous place. Alone! With all that bad company around.

HEDDA: But my dear Mrs. Elvsted—why is he a concern of yours?

MRS. ELVSTED (*with an apprehensive look at her, says quickly*): He tutored
the children.

HEDDA: Your children?

MRS. ELVSTED: My husband's. I don't have any.

HEDDA: In other words, your stepchildren.

MRS. ELVSTED: Yes.

TESMAN (*with some hesitation*): But was he—I don't quite know how to
put this—was he sufficiently—regular—in his way of life to be thus
employed? Hm?

MRS. ELVSTED: For the last two years, there hasn't been a thing to object
to in his conduct.

TESMAN: No, really? Just think, Hedda!

HEDDA: I hear.

MRS. ELVSTED: Not the least little bit, I assure you! Not in any respect. And
yet—knowing he's here—in the big city—And with all that money,
too! I'm scared to death!

TESMAN: But in that case, why didn't he remain with you and your husband? Hm?

MRS. ELVSTED: After his book came out, he was too restless to stay.

TESMAN: Ah yes, that's right. Aunt Julle said he has published a new book.

MRS. ELVSTED: Yes, a big new book, about the course of civilization in
general. It came out about two weeks ago. And since it has had such
big sales and been discussed so much and made such a big splash—

TESMAN: It has, has it? I suppose this is something he has had lying
around from better days?

MRS. ELVSTED: You mean from earlier?

TESMAN: Yes.

MRS. ELVSTED: No; it's all been written since he came to stay with us. During this last year.

TESMAN: Well now! That's very good news, Hedda! Just think!

MRS. ELVSTED: Yes, if it only would last!

HEDDA: Have you seen him since you came to town?

MRS. ELVSTED: No, not yet. I had a great deal of trouble finding his address. But this morning I finally tracked him down.

HEDDA (*looks searchingly at her*): Isn't it rather odd that your husband—hm—

MRS. ELVSTED (*with a nervous start*): My husband! What about him?

HEDDA: That he sends you to town on such an errand? That he doesn't go and look after his friend himself?

MRS. ELVSTED: Oh, no, no—my husband doesn't have time for things like that. Besides, I have some—some shopping to do, anyway.

HEDDA (*with a slight smile*): Well, in that case, of course—

MRS. ELVSTED (*getting up, restlessly*): And now I beg of you, Mr. Tesman—won't you please receive Eilert Løvborg nicely if he calls on you? And I am sure he will. After all—such good friends as you two used to be. And then you both do the same kind of work—the same field of study, as far as I know.

TESMAN: We used to, at any rate.

MRS. ELVSTED: Yes. And that's why I implore you to please, please, try to keep an eye on him—you too. You'll do that, Mr. Tesman, won't you? Promise?

TESMAN: With the greatest pleasure, Mrs. Rysing.

HEDDA: Elvsted.

TESMAN: I'll gladly do as much for Eilert as I possibly can. You may certainly count on that.

MRS. ELVSTED: Oh, how good and kind you are! (*Clasps his hands.*) Thank you, thank you, thank you! (*Nervously.*) You see, my husband is so very fond of him.

HEDDA (*getting up*): You ought to write him a note, Tesman. Maybe he won't come without an invitation.

TESMAN: Yes, I suppose that would be the right thing to do, Hedda. Hm?

HEDDA: The sooner the better. Right away, *I* think.

MRS. ELVSTED (*pleadingly*): If only you would!

TESMAN: I'll write this minute. Do you have his address, Mrs.—Mrs. Elvsted?

MRS. ELVSTED: Yes. (*Pulls a slip of paper from her bag and gives it to him.*) Here it is.

TESMAN: Very good. Well, then, if you'll excuse me—(*Looks around.*) By the way—the slippers? Ah, here we are. (*Leaving with the parcel.*)

HEDDA: Be sure you write a nice, warm, friendly letter, Tesman. And a long one, too.

TESMAN: Certainly, certainly.

MRS. ELVSTED: But not a word that it is I who—!

TESMAN: No, that goes without saying, I should think. Hm? (*Goes out right through inner room.*)

HEDDA (*goes over to* MRS. ELVSTED, *smiles, says in a low voice*): There! We just killed two birds with one stone.

MRS. ELVSTED: What do you mean?

HEDDA: Didn't you see I wanted him out of the room?

MRS. ELVSTED: Yes, to write that letter—

HEDDA: And to speak to you alone.

MRS. ELVSTED (*flustered*): About this same thing?

HEDDA: Exactly.

MRS. ELVSTED (*anxious*): But there *is* nothing more, Mrs. Tesman! Really, there isn't!

HEDDA: Oh yes, there is. There is considerably more. I can see that much. Over here—We are going to have a real, nice, confidential talk, you and I. (*She forces* MRS. ELVSTED *down in the easy chair and seats herself on one of the ottomans.*)

MRS. ELVSTED (*worried, looks at her watch*): But my dear Mrs. Tesman—I had really thought I would be on my way now.

HEDDA: Oh I am sure there is no rush. Now, then. Tell me about yourself. How are things at home?

MRS. ELVSTED: That is just what I don't want to talk about.

HEDDA: But to me—! After all, we are old schoolmates.

MRS. ELVSTED: But you were a year ahead of me. And I used to be so scared of you!

HEDDA: Scared of me?

MRS. ELVSTED: Terribly. For when we met on the stairs, you always ruffled my hair.

HEDDA: Did I really?

MRS. ELVSTED: Yes. And once you said you were going to burn it off.

HEDDA: Oh, but you know—I wasn't serious!

MRS. ELVSTED: No, but I was such a silly, then. Anyway, afterwards we drifted far apart. Our circles are so very different, you know.

HEDDA: All the more reason for getting close again. Listen. In school we called each other by our first names.

MRS. ELVSTED: Oh I'm sure you're wrong—

HEDDA: I'm sure I'm not! I remember it quite clearly. And now we want to be open with one another, just the way we used to. (*Moves the ottoman closer.*) There, now! (*Kisses her cheek.*) You call me Hedda.

MRS. ELVSTED (*seizes her hands*): Oh, you are so good and kind! I'm not used to that.

HEDDA: There, there! And I'll call you my dear Thora, just as in the old days.

MRS. ELVSTED: My name is Thea.

HEDDA: So it is. Of course. I meant Thea. (*Looks at her with compassion.*) So you're not much used to goodness and kindness, Thea? Not in your own home?

MRS. ELVSTED: If I even had a home! But I don't. I never have had one.

HEDDA (*looks at her for a moment*): I thought there might be something like this.

MRS. ELVSTED (*helplessly, looking straight ahead*): Yes—yes—yes—

HEDDA: I am not sure if I quite remember—Didn't you first come to your husband as his housekeeper?

MRS. ELVSTED: I was really hired as governess. But his wife—his first wife—was ailing already then and practically bedridden. So I had to take charge of the household as well.

HEDDA: But in the end you became his wife.

MRS. ELVSTED (*dully*): So I did.

HEDDA: Let's see. How long ago is that?

MRS. ELVSTED: Since my marriage?

HEDDA: Yes.

MRS. ELVSTED: About five years.

HEDDA: Right. It must be that long.

MRS. ELVSTED: Oh, those five years! Or mostly the last two or three! Oh, Mrs. Tesman—if you could just imagine!

HEDDA (*slaps her hand lightly*): Mrs. Tesman? Shame on you!

MRS. ELVSTED: Oh yes; all right, I'll try. Yes—if you could just—conceive—understand—

HEDDA (*casually*): And Eilert Løvborg has been living near you for some three years or so, hasn't he?

MRS. ELVSTED (*looks at her uncertainly*): Eilert Løvborg? Yes—he has.

HEDDA: Did you know him before? Here in town?

MRS. ELVSTED: Hardly at all. That is, of course I did in a way. I mean, I knew *of* him.

HEDDA: But up there—You saw a good deal of him; did you?

MRS. ELVSTED: Yes, he came over to us every day. He was supposed to tutor the children, you see. For I just couldn't do it all by myself.

HEDDA: Of course not. And your husband—? I suppose he travels quite a bit.

MRS. ELVSTED: Well, yes, Mrs. Tes—Hedda—as a public magistrate, you know, he very often has to travel all over his district.

HEDDA (*leaning against the armrest on the easy chair*): Thea—poor, sweet Thea—now you have to tell me everything—just as it is.

MRS. ELVSTED: You'd better ask me, then.

HEDDA: How *is* your husband, Thea? I mean—you know—*really?* To be with. What kind of person is he? Is he good to you?

MRS. ELVSTED (*evasively*): I believe he thinks he does everything for the best.

HEDDA: But isn't he altogether too old for you? He is more than twenty years older, isn't he?

MRS. ELVSTED (*with irritation*): Yes, there is that, too. But there isn't just one thing. Every single little thing about him repels me! We don't have a thought in common, he and I. Not a thing in the world!

HEDDA: But isn't he fond of you all the same? I mean in his own way?

MRS. ELVSTED: I don't know. I think I am just useful to him. And I don't use much money. I am inexpensive.

HEDDA: That is foolish of you.

MRS. ELVSTED (*shakes her head*): Can't be changed. Not with him. I don't think he cares for anybody much except himself. Perhaps the children a little.

HEDDA: And Eilert Løvborg, Thea.

MRS. ELVSTED (*looks at her*): Eilert Løvborg? What makes you think that?

HEDDA: Well, it seems to me that when he sends you all the way to town to look after him—(*With an almost imperceptible smile.*) Besides, you said so yourself. To Tesman.

MRS. ELVSTED (*with a nervous twitch*): Did I? I suppose I did. (*With a muted outburst.*) No! I might as well tell you now as later. For it's bound to come out, anyway.

HEDDA: But my dear Thea—?

MRS. ELVSTED: All right. My husband doesn't know I'm gone!

HEDDA: What! He doesn't know?

MRS. ELVSTED: He wasn't even home. He's away again. Oh, I just couldn't take it any longer, Hedda! It had become utterly impossible. All alone as I was.

HEDDA: So what did you do?

MRS. ELVSTED: I packed some of my things. Just the most necessary. Without telling anybody. And left.

HEDDA: Just like that?

MRS. ELVSTED: Yes. And took the next train to town.

HEDDA: But dearest Thea—how did you dare to do a thing like that!

MRS. ELVSTED (*rises, walks*): What else could I do?

HEDDA: But what do you think your husband will say when you go back?

MRS. ELVSTED (*by the table; looks at her*): Go back to him?

HEDDA: Yes!

MRS. ELVSTED: I'll never go back.

HEDDA (*rises, approaches her slowly*): So you have really, seriously—left everything?

MRS. ELVSTED: Yes. It seemed to me there was nothing else I could do.

HEDDA: And quite openly, too.

MRS. ELVSTED: You can't keep a thing like that secret, anyway.

HEDDA: But what do you think people will say, Thea?

MRS. ELVSTED: In God's name, let them say whatever they like. (*Sits down on the sofa, dully, tired.*) For I have only done what I had to do.

HEDDA (*after a brief silence*): And what do you plan to do with yourself? What sort of work will you do?

MRS. ELVSTED: I don't know yet. I only know I have to live where Eilert Løvborg is. If I am to live at all.

HEDDA (*moves a chair from the table closer to* MRS. ELVSTED, *sits down, strokes her hands*): Thea—tell me. How did this—this friendship between you and Eilert Løvborg—how did it begin?

MRS. ELVSTED: Oh, it grew little by little. I got some sort of power over him.

HEDDA: Oh?

MRS. ELVSTED: He dropped his old ways. Not because I asked him to. I never dared to do that. But I think he must have noticed how I felt about that kind of life. So he changed.

HEDDA (*quickly suppresses a cynical smile*): So you have—rehabilitated him, as they say. Haven't you, Thea?

MRS. ELVSTED: At least, that's what *he* says. On the other hand, he has turned me into a real human being. Taught me to think—and understand—all sorts of things.

HEDDA: Maybe he tutored you, too?

MRS. ELVSTED: No, not tutored exactly. But he talked to me. About so many, many things. And then came that lovely, lovely time when I could share his work with him. He let me help him!

HEDDA: He did?

MRS. ELVSTED: Yes! Whatever he wrote, he wanted us to be together about it.

HEDDA: Just like two good comrades.

MRS. ELVSTED (*with animation*): Comrades!—that's it! Imagine, Hedda—that's just what he called it, too. Oh, I really ought to feel so happy. But I can't. For you see, I don't know if it will last.

HEDDA: You don't trust him any more than that?

MRS. ELVSTED (*heavily*): The shadow of a woman stands between Eilert Løvborg and me.

HEDDA (*tensely, looks at her*): Who?

MRS. ELVSTED: I don't know. Somebody or other from—his past. I don't think he has ever really forgotten her.

HEDDA: What has he told you about it?

MRS. ELVSTED: He has mentioned it only once—just casually.

HEDDA: And what did he say?

MRS. ELVSTED: He said that when they parted she was going to kill him with a gun.

HEDDA (*cold, controlled*): Oh, nonsense. People don't do that sort of thing here.

MRS. ELVSTED: No, I know. And that is why I think it must be that red-headed singer he used to—

HEDDA: Yes, I suppose so.

MRS. ELVSTED: For I remember people said she carried a loaded gun.

HEDDA: Well, then I'm sure it's she.

MRS. ELVSTED (*wringing her hands*): Yes, but just think, Hedda—now I hear that she—that singer—that she's here in town again, too! Oh, I'm just desperate—!

HEDDA (*with a glance toward the inner room*): Shhh! Here's Tesman. (*Rises and whispers.*) Not a word about all this to anybody, Thea!

MRS. ELVSTED (*jumps up*): No, no. For God's sake—!

(TESMAN, *carrying a letter, enters from the right side of the inner room.*)

TESMAN: There, now—here's the missive, all ready to go!

HEDDA: Good. But I believe Mrs. Elvsted wants to be on her way. Wait a moment. I'll see you to the garden gate.

TESMAN: Say, Hedda—do you think Berte could take care of this?

HEDDA (*takes the letter*): I'll tell her.

(BERTE *enters right.*)

BERTE: Judge Brack is here and wants to know if you're receiving.

HEDDA: Yes, ask the Judge please to come in. And—here—drop this in a mailbox, will you?

BERTE (*takes the letter*): Yes, ma'am.

(*She opens the door for* JUDGE BRACK *and exits. The* JUDGE *is forty-five years of age. Rather thickset, but well-built and with brisk, athletic movements. Roundish face, aristocratic profile. His hair is short, still almost completely black, very neatly dressed. Lively, sparkling eyes. Thick eyebrows and mustache with cut-off points. He is dressed in an elegant suit, a trifle youthful for his age. He wears pince-nez glasses, attached to a string, and lets them drop from time to time.*)

JUDGE BRACK (*hat in hand, salutes*): May one pay one's respects as early as this?

HEDDA: One certainly may.

TESMAN (*shaking his hand*): You are always welcome. (*Introducing.*) Judge Brack—Miss Rysing—

(HEDDA *groans.*)

BRACK (*bowing*): Delighted!

HEDDA (*looks at him, laughs*): How nice it is to see you in daylight, Judge!

BRACK: You find me changed, perhaps?

HEDDA: A bit younger, I think.

BRACK: Much obliged.

TESMAN: But what do you think of Hedda? Hm? Did you ever see her in such bloom? She positively—

HEDDA: Will you please leave me out of this? You had better thank the Judge for all the trouble he has taken.

BRACK: Oh, nonsense. It's been a pleasure.

HEDDA: Yes, you are indeed a faithful soul. But my friend here is dying to be off. Don't leave, Judge. I'll be back in a minute.

(*Mutual goodbyes.* MRS. ELVSTED *and* HEDDA *exit, right.*)

BRACK: Well, now—your wife—is she tolerably satisfied?

TESMAN: Yes, indeed, and we really can't thank you enough. That is, I understand there will have to be some slight changes made here and there. And there are still a few things—just a few trifles—we'll have to get.

BRACK: Oh? Really?

TESMAN: But we certainly don't want to bother you with that. Hedda said she's going to take care of it herself. But do sit down, hm?

BRACK: Thanks. Maybe just for a moment—(*Sits down by the table.*) There's one thing I'd like to talk to you about, my dear Tesman.

TESMAN: Oh? Ah, I see! (*Sits down.*) I suppose it's the serious part of the festivities that's beginning now. Hm?

BRACK: Oh—there's no great rush as far as the money is concerned. Though I must say I wish we could have established ourselves a trifle more economically.

TESMAN: Out of the question, my dear fellow! Remember, it's all for Hedda! You, who know her so well—! After all, I couldn't put her up like any little middle-class housewife—

BRACK: No, I suppose—That's just it.

TESMAN: Besides—fortunately—it can't be long now before I receive my appointment.

BRACK: Well, you know—things like that have a way of hanging fire.

TESMAN: Perhaps you have heard something? Something definite? Hm?

BRACK: No, nothing certain—(*Interrupting himself.*) But that reminds me. I have some news for you.

TESMAN: Oh?

BRACK: Your old friend Eilert Løvborg is back in town.

TESMAN: I know that already.

BRACK: So? Who told you?

TESMAN: The lady who just left.

BRACK: I see. What did you say her name was again? I didn't quite catch—

TESMAN: Mrs. Elvsted.

BRACK: Ah yes—the Commissioner's wife. Yes, it's up in her part of the country that Løvborg has been staying, too.

TESMAN: And just think. I am so glad to hear it. He is quite respectable again.

BRACK: Yes, so they say.

TESMAN: And he has published a new book, hm?

BRACK: Oh yes.

TESMAN: Which is making quite a stir.

BRACK: Quite an unusual stir.

TESMAN: Just think! Isn't that just wonderful! He—with his remarkable gifts. And I was so sure he'd gone under for good.

BRACK: That seems to have been the general opinion.

TESMAN: What I don't understand, though, is what he is going to do with himself. What sort of living can he make? Hm?

(*During the last remark* HEDDA *re-enters, right.*)

HEDDA (*to* BRACK, *with a scornful little laugh*): Tesman is forever worrying about how people are going to make a living.

TESMAN: Well, you see, we are talking about poor Eilert Løvborg, Hedda.

HEDDA (*with a quick look at him*): You are? (*Sits down in the easy chair by the stove and asks casually.*) What is the matter with him?

TESMAN: Well, you see, I believe he's run through his inheritance a long time ago. And I don't suppose he can write a new book every year. Hm? So I really must ask how he is going to make out.

BRACK: Maybe I could help you answer that.

TESMAN: Yes?

BRACK: Remember, he has relatives with considerable influence.

TESMAN: Ah—unfortunately, those relatives have washed their hands of him long ago.

BRACK: Just the same, they used to call him the hope of the family.

TESMAN: Yes, before! But he has ruined all that.

HEDDA: Who knows? (*With a little smile.*) I hear the Elvsteds have rehabilitated him.

BRACK: And then this book—

TESMAN: Well, I certainly hope they will help him to find something or other. I just wrote him a letter. Hedda, dear, I asked him to come out here tonight.

BRACK: Oh dear, I am sorry. Don't you remember—you're supposed to come to my little stag dinner tonight? You accepted last night on the pier, you know.

HEDDA: Had you forgotten, Tesman?

TESMAN: So I had.

BRACK: Oh well, I'm sure he won't come, so it doesn't really make any difference.

TESMAN: Why is that? Hm?

BRACK (*gets up somewhat hesitantly, rests his hands on the back of the chair*): Dear Tesman—and you, too, Mrs. Tesman—I cannot in good conscience let you remain in ignorance of something, which—which—

TESMAN: Something to do with Eilert?

BRACK: With both you and him.

TESMAN: But my dear Judge, do speak!

BRACK: You must be prepared to find that your appointment will not come through as soon as you hope and expect.

TESMAN (*jumps up, nervously*): Something's happened? Hm?

BRACK: It may conceivably be made contingent upon the result of a competition.

TESMAN: Competition! Just think, Hedda!

HEDDA (*leaning farther back in her chair*): Ah—I see, I see—!

TESMAN: But with whom? Don't tell me with—?

BRACK: Precisely. With Eilert Løvborg.

TESMAN (*claps his hands together*): No, no! This can't be! It is unthinkable! Quite impossible! Hm?

BRACK: All the same, that's the way it may turn out.

TESMAN: No, but Judge, this would amount to the most incredible callousness toward me! (*Waving his arms.*) For just think—I'm a married man! We married on the strength of these prospects, Hedda and I. Got ourselves deep in debt. Borrowed money from Aunt Julle, too. After all, I had practically been promised the post, you know. Hm?

BRACK: Well, well. I daresay you'll get it in the end. If only after a competition.

HEDDA (*motionless in her chair*): Just think, Tesman. It will be like a kind of contest.

TESMAN: But dearest Hedda, how can you be so unconcerned!

HEDDA (*still without moving*): I'm not at all unconcerned. I'm dying to see who wins.

BRACK: In any case, Mrs. Tesman, I'm glad you know the situation as it is. I mean—before you proceed to make the little additional purchases I understand you threaten us with.

HEDDA: This makes no difference as far as that is concerned.

BRACK: Really? Well, in that case, of course—Goodbye! (*To* TESMAN.) I'll pick you up on my afternoon walk.

TESMAN: What? Oh yes, yes, of course. I'm sorry; I'm just all flustered.

HEDDA (*without getting up, gives her hand*): Goodbye, Judge. Come back soon.

BRACK: Thanks. Goodbye, goodbye.

TESMAN (*sees him to the door*): Goodbye, my dear Judge. You really must excuse me—

(JUDGE BRACK *exits, right.*)

TESMAN (*pacing the floor*): Oh, Hedda, Hedda! One should never venture into fairyland. Hm?

HEDDA (*looks at him, smiles*): Do *you* do that?

TESMAN: Well, yes—it can't be denied—it was most venturesome of me to rush into marriage and set up a home on the strength of mere prospects.

HEDDA: Well, maybe you're right.

TESMAN: Anyway—we do have our own nice, comfortable home, now. Just think, Hedda—the very home both of us dreamed about. Set our hearts on, I may almost say. Hm?

HEDDA (*rises, slowly, tired*): The agreement was that we were to maintain a certain position—entertain—

TESMAN: Don't I know it! Dearest Hedda—I have been so looking forward to seeing you as hostess in a select circle! Hm? Well, well, well! In the meantime, we'll just have to be content with one another. See Aunt Julle once in a while. Nothing more. And you were meant for such a different kind of life, altogether!

HEDDA: I suppose a footman is completely out of the question.

TESMAN: I'm afraid so. Under the circumstances, you see—we couldn't possibly—

HEDDA: And as for getting my own riding horse—

TESMAN (*aghast*): Riding horse!

HEDDA: I suppose I mustn't even think of that.

TESMAN: Good heavens, no! That goes without saying, I hope!

HEDDA (*walking*): Well—at least I have one thing to amuse myself with in the meantime.

TESMAN (*overjoyed*): Oh thank goodness for that! And what *is* that, Hedda, hm?

HEDDA (*in the doorway, looks at him with suppressed scorn*): My guns— Jørgen!

TESMAN (*in fear*): Your guns!

HEDDA (*with cold eyes*): General Gabler's guns. (*She exits left, through the inner room.*)

TESMAN (*runs up to the doorway, calls after her*): But Hedda! Good gracious! Hedda, dear! Please don't touch those dangerous things! For my sake, Hedda! Hm?

ACT II

(*The same room at the TESMANS'. The piano has been moved out and replaced by an elegant little writing desk. A small table has been placed near the sofa, left. Most of the flowers have been removed. MRS. ELVSTED'S bouquet is on the big table front center. Afternoon.*

HEDDA, *dressed to receive callers, is alone. She is standing near the open French doors, loading a revolver. Its mate is lying in an open case on the desk.*)

HEDDA (*looking down into the garden, calls*): Hello there, Judge! Welcome back!

JUDGE BRACK (*off stage*): Thanks, Mrs. Tesman!

HEDDA (*raises the gun, sights*): I am going to shoot you, Judge Brack!

BRACK (*calls off stage*): No—no—no! Don't point the gun at me like that!

HEDDA: That's what you get for sneaking in the back door! (*Fires.*)

BRACK (*closer*): Are you out of your mind—!

HEDDA: Oh dear—did I hit you?

BRACK (*still off stage*): Stop that nonsense!

HEDDA: Come on in, then.

(JUDGE BRACK, *dressed for dinner, enters, left. He carries a light overcoat over his arm.*)

BRACK: Dammit! Do you still fool around with that thing? What are you shooting at, anyway?

HEDDA: Oh—just firing off into blue air.

BRACK (*gently but firmly taking the gun away from her*): With your permission, Mrs. Tesman. (*Looks at it.*) Ah yes, I remember this gun very well. (*Looks around.*) Where is the case? Ah, here we are. (*Puts the gun in the case and closes it.*) That's enough of that silliness for today.

HEDDA: But in the name of heaven, what do you expect me to do with myself?

BRACK: No callers?

HEDDA (*closing the French doors*): Not a soul. All my close friends are still out of town, it seems.

BRACK: And Tesman is out, too, perhaps?

HEDDA (*by the desk, puts the gun case in a drawer*): Yes. He took off for the aunts' right after lunch. He didn't expect you so early.

BRACK: I should have thought of that. That was stupid of me.

HEDDA (*turns her head, looks at him*): Why stupid?

BRACK: I would have come a little—sooner.

HEDDA (*crossing*): If you had, you wouldn't have found anybody home. For I have been in my room ever since lunch, changing my clothes.

BRACK: And isn't there the tiniest little opening in the door for negotiations?

HEDDA: You forgot to provide one.

BRACK: Another stupidity.

HEDDA: So we'll have to stay in here. And wait. For I don't think Tesman will be back for some time.

BRACK: By all means. I'll be very patient.

(HEDDA *sits on the sofa in the corner.* BRACK *puts his overcoat over the back of the nearest chair and sits down, keeping his hat in his hand. Brief silence. They look at one another.*)

HEDDA: Well?

BRACK (*in the same tone*): Well?

HEDDA: I said it first.

BRACK (*leans forward a little*): All right. Let's have a nice little chat, Mrs. Tesman.

HEDDA (*leans back*): Don't you think it's an eternity since last time we talked! I don't count last night and this morning. That was nothing.

BRACK: You mean—just the two of us?

HEDDA: Mmm. If you like.

BRACK: There hasn't been a day I haven't wished you were back again.

HEDDA: My feelings, exactly.

BRACK: Yours? Really, Mrs. Tesman? And I have been assuming you were having such a wonderful time.

HEDDA: I'd say!

BRACK: All Tesman's letters said so.

HEDDA: Oh yes, he! He's happy just poking through old collections of books. And copying old parchments—or whatever they are.

BRACK (*with a touch of malice*): Well, that's his calling, you know. Partly, anyway.

HEDDA: Yes, so it is. And in that case I suppose—But I! Oh, Judge! You've no idea how bored I've been.

BRACK (*with sympathy*): Really? You're serious?

HEDDA: Surely you can understand that? For a whole half year never to see anyone who knows even a little bit about our circle? And talks our language?

BRACK: Yes, I think I would find that trying, too.

HEDDA: And then the most unbearable thing of all—

BRACK: Well?

HEDDA: —everlastingly to be in the company of the same person—

BRACK (*nods in agreement*): Both early and late—yes. I can imagine—at all possible times—

HEDDA: I said everlastingly.

BRACK: All right. Still, it seems to me that with as excellent a person as our Tesman, it ought to be possible—

HEDDA: My dear Judge—Tesman is a specialist.

BRACK: Granted.

HEDDA: And specialists are not at all entertaining travel companions. Not in the long run, at any rate.

BRACK: Not even—the specialist—one happens to love?

HEDDA: Bah! That nauseating word!

BRACK (*puzzled*): Really, now, Mrs. Tesman—?

HEDDA (*half laughing, half annoyed*): *You* ought to try it some time! Listening to talk about the history of civilization, early and late—

BRACK: Everlastingly—

HEDDA: All right. And then this business about the domestic industry in the Middle Ages—! That's the ghastliest part of it all!

BRACK (*looking searchingly at her*): But in that case—tell me—how am I to explain—?

HEDDA: That Jørgen Tesman and I made a pair of it, you mean?

BRACK: If you want to put it that way—yes.

HEDDA: Come now. Do you really find that so strange?

BRACK: Both yes and no—Mrs. Tesman.

HEDDA: I had danced myself tired, my dear Judge. My season was over—(*Gives a slight start.*) No, no—I don't really mean that. Won't think it, either!

BRACK: Nor do you have the slightest reason to, I am sure.

HEDDA: Oh—as far as reasons are concerned—(*Looks at him as if trying to read his mind.*) And, after all, Jørgen Tesman must be said to be a most proper young man in all respects.

BRACK: Both proper and substantial. Most certainly.

HEDDA: And one can't say there is anything exactly comical about him. Do you think there is?

BRACK: Comical? No—o. I wouldn't say that—

HEDDA: All right, then. And he is a most assiduous collector. Nobody can deny that. I think it is perfectly possible he may go quite far, after all.

BRACK (*looks at her rather uncertainly*): I assumed that you, like everybody else, thought he'll in time become an exceptionally eminent man?

HEDDA (*with a weary expression*): Yes, I did. And then, you see—there he was, wanting so desperately to be allowed to provide for me—I don't know why I shouldn't have accepted?

BRACK: No, certainly. From that point of view—

HEDDA: For you know, Judge, that was considerably more than my other admirers were willing to do.

BRACK (*laughs*): Well! Of course I can't answer for all the others. But as far as I am concerned, I have always had a certain degree of—respect for the bonds of matrimony. You know—as a general proposition, Mrs. Tesman.

HEDDA (*lightly*): Well, I never really counted very heavily on *you*—

BRACK: All I want is a nice, confidential circle, in which I can be of service, both in deed and in counsel. Be allowed to come and go like a true and trusted friend—

HEDDA: You mean, of the master of the house—?

BRACK (*with a slight bow*): To be perfectly frank—rather of the mistress. But by all means—the master, too, of course. Do you know, that kind of—shall I say, triangular?—relationship can really be a great comfort to all parties involved.

HEDDA: Yes, many were the times I missed a second travel companion. To be twosome in the compartment—brrr!

BRACK: Fortunately, the wedding trip is over.

HEDDA (*shakes her head*): There's a long journey ahead. I've just arrived at a station on the way.

BRACK: Well, at the station one gets out and moves around a bit, Mrs. Tesman.

HEDDA: I never get out.

BRACK: Really?

HEDDA: No. For there's always someone around, who—

BRACK (*laughs*):—looks at one's legs; is that it?

HEDDA: Exactly.

BRACK: Oh well, really, now—

HEDDA (*with a silencing gesture*): I won't have it! Rather stay in my seat—once I'm seated. Twosome and all.

BRACK: I see. But what if a third party were to join the couple?

HEDDA: Well, now—*that* would be something altogether different!

BRACK: A proven, understanding friend—

HEDDA:—entertaining in all sorts of lively ways—

BRACK:—and not at all a specialist!

HEDDA (*with audible breath*): Yes, that would indeed be a comfort.

BRACK (*hearing the front door open, looking at her*): The triangle is complete.

HEDDA (*half aloud*): And the train goes on.

(TESMAN, *in gray walking suit and soft hat, enters, right. He carries a pile of paperbound books under his arm. Others are stuffed in his pockets.*)

TESMAN (*as he walks up to the table in front of the corner sofa*): Puuhh—! Quite some load to carry, all this—and in this heat, too. (*Puts the books down.*) I am positively perspiring, Hedda. Well, well. So you're here already, my dear Judge. Hm? And Berte didn't tell me.

BRACK (*rises*): I came through the garden.

HEDDA: What are all those books?

TESMAN (*leafing through some of them*): Just some new publications in my special field.

HEDDA: Special field, hm?

BRACK: Ah yes—professional publications, Mrs. Tesman.

(BRACK *and* HEDDA *exchange knowing smiles.*)

HEDDA: Do you still need more books?

TESMAN: Yes, my dear. There is no such thing as having too many books in one's special field. One has to keep up with what is being written and published, you know.

HEDDA: I suppose.

TESMAN (*searching among the books*): And look. Here is Eilert Løvborg's new book, too. (*Offers it to her.*) Want to take a look at it, Hedda? Hm?

HEDDA: No—thanks just the same. Or perhaps later.

TESMAN: I glanced at it on my way home.

BRACK: And what do you think of it? As a specialist yourself?

TESMAN: It is remarkable for its sobriety. He never wrote like that before. (*Gathers up all the books.*) I just want to take these into my study. I am so much looking forward to cutting them open! And then I'll change. (*To* BRACK.) I assume there's no rush to be off, is there?

BRACK: Not at all. We have plenty of time.

TESMAN: In that case, I think I'll indulge myself a little. (*On his way out with the books he halts in the doorway and turns.*) By the way, Hedda—Aunt Julle won't be out to see you tonight, after all.

HEDDA: No? Is it that business with the hat, do you think?

TESMAN: Oh, no—not at all. How can you believe a thing like that about Aunt Julle! Just think! No, it's Aunt Rina. She's feeling very poorly.

HEDDA: Isn't she always?

TESMAN: Yes, but it's especially bad today, poor thing.

HEDDA: Well, in that case I suppose she ought to stay home. I shall have to put up with it; that's all.

TESMAN: And you have no idea how perfectly delighted Aunt Julle was, even so. Because of how splendid you look after the trip, Hedda!

HEDDA (*half aloud, rising*): Oh, these everlasting aunts!

TESMAN: Hm?

HEDDA (*walks over to the French doors*): Nothing.

TESMAN: No? All right. Well, excuse me. (*Exits right, through inner room.*)

BRACK: What is this about a hat?

HEDDA: Oh, something with Miss Tesman this morning. She had put her hat down on the chair over there. (*Looks at him, smiles.*) So I pretended to think it was the maid's.

BRACK (*shakes his head*): But my dear Mrs. Tesman—how could you do a thing like that! And to that excellent old lady, too!

HEDDA (*nervously pacing the floor*): Well, you see—something just takes hold of me at times. And then I can't help myself—(*Throws herself down in the easy chair near the stove.*) Oh I can't explain it even to myself.

BRACK (*behind her chair*): You aren't really happy—that's the trouble.

HEDDA (*staring into space*): I don't know any reason why I should be. Do you?

BRACK: Well, yes—partly because you've got the home you've always wanted.

HEDDA (*looks up at him and laughs*): So you too believe that story about my great wish?

BRACK: You mean, there is nothing to it?

HEDDA: Well, yes, there is *something* to it.

BRACK: Well?

HEDDA: There is this much to it, that last summer I used Tesman to see me home from evening parties.

BRACK: Unfortunately—my route was in quite a different direction.

HEDDA: True. You walked on other roads last summer.

BRACK (*laughs*): Shame on you, Mrs. Tesman! So, all right—you and Tesman—?

HEDDA: One evening we passed by here. And Tesman, poor thing, was practically turning himself into knots trying to find something to talk about. So I felt sorry for all that erudition—

BRACK (*with a doubting smile*): You did? Hm—

HEDDA: I really did. So, just to help him out of his misery, I happened to say that I'd like to live in this house.

BRACK: Just that?

HEDDA: That was all—*that* evening.

BRACK: But afterwards—?

HEDDA: Yes, my frivolity had consequences, Judge.

BRACK: Unfortunately—that's often the way with frivolities. It happens to all of us, Mrs. Tesman.

HEDDA: Thanks! So in our common enthusiasm for Mr. Secretary Falk's villa Tesman and I found each other, you see! The result was engagement and wedding and honeymoon abroad and all the rest of it. Well, yes, my dear Judge—I've made my bed—I almost said.

BRACK: But this is priceless! And you didn't really care for the house at all?

HEDDA: Certainly not.

BRACK: Not even now? After all, we've set up quite a comfortable home for you here, haven't we?

HEDDA: Oh—it seems to me I smell lavender and rose sachets in all the rooms. But maybe that's a smell Aunt Julle brought with her.

BRACK (*laughs*): My guess is rather the late lamented Secretary's wife.

HEDDA: It smells of mortality, whoever it is. Like corsages—the next day. (*Clasps her hands behind her neck, leans back, looks at him.*) Judge, you have no idea how dreadfully bored I'll be—out here.

BRACK: But don't you think life may hold some task for you, too, Mrs. Tesman?

HEDDA: A task? With any kind of appeal?

BRACK: Preferably that, of course.

HEDDA: Heaven knows what kind of task that might be. There are times when I wonder if—(*Interrupts herself.*) No; I'm sure that wouldn't work, either.

BRACK: Who knows? Tell me.

HEDDA: It has occurred to me that maybe I could get Tesman to enter politics.

BRACK (*laughs*): Tesman! No, really—I must confess that—politics doesn't strike me as being exactly Tesman's line.

HEDDA: I agree. But suppose I were to prevail on him, all the same?

BRACK: What satisfaction could you possibly find in that? If he can't succeed—why do you want him even to try?

HEDDA: Because I am bored, I tell you! (*After a brief pause.*) So you think it's quite out of the question that Tesman could ever become prime minister?

BRACK: Well, you see, Mrs. Tesman—to do that he'd first of all have to be a fairly wealthy man.

HEDDA (*getting up, impatiently*): Yes! There we are! These shabby circumstances I've married into! (*Crosses the floor.*) That's what makes life so mean. So—so—ridiculous! For that's what it is, you know.

BRACK: Personally I believe something else is to blame.

HEDDA: What?

BRACK: You've never been through anything that's really stirred you.

HEDDA: Something serious, you mean?

BRACK: If you like. But maybe it's coming now.

HEDDA (*with a toss of her head*): You are thinking of that silly old professorship! That's Tesman's business. I refuse to give it a thought.

BRACK: As you wish. But now—to put it in the grand style—now when a solemn challenge of responsibility is being posed? Demands made on you? (*Smiles.*) New demands, Mrs. Tesman.

HEDDA (*angry*): Quiet! You'll never see anything of the kind.

BRACK (*cautiously*): We'll talk about this a year from now—on the outside.

HEDDA (*curtly*): I'm not made for that sort of thing, Judge! No demands for me!

BRACK: But surely you, like most women, are made for a duty, which—

HEDDA (*over by the French doors*): O, do be quiet! Often it seems to me there's only one thing in the world that I am made for.

BRACK (*coming close*): And may I ask what that is?

HEDDA (*looking out*): To be bored to death. Now you know. (*Turns, looks toward the inner room, laughs.*) Just as I thought. Here comes the professor.

BRACK (*warningly, in a low voice*): Steady, now, Mrs. Tesman!

(TESMAN, *dressed for a party, carrying his hat and gloves, enters from the right side of the inner room.*)

TESMAN: Hedda, any word yet from Eilert Løvborg that he isn't coming, hm?

HEDDA: No.

TESMAN: In that case, I wouldn't be a bit surprised if we have him here in a few minutes.

BRACK: You really think he'll come?

TESMAN: I am almost certain he will. For I'm sure it's only idle gossip what you told me this morning.

BRACK: Oh?

TESMAN: Anyway, that's what Aunt Julle said. She doesn't for a moment believe he'll stand in my way. Just think!

BRACK: I'm very glad to hear that.

TESMAN (*puts his hat and his gloves down on a chair, right*): But you must let me wait for him as long as possible.

BRACK: By all means. We have plenty of time. Nobody will arrive at my place before seven—seven-thirty, or so.

TESMAN: And in the meantime we can keep Hedda company. Take our time. Hm?

HEDDA (*carrying BRACK's hat and coat over to the sofa in the corner*): And if worst comes to worst, Mr. Løvborg can stay here with me.

BRACK (*trying to take the things away from her*): Let me, Mrs. Tesman— What do you mean—"if worst comes to worst?"

HEDDA: If he doesn't want to go with you and Tesman.

TESMAN (*looks dubiously at her*): But, dearest Hedda—do you think that will quite do? He staying here with you? Hm? Remember, Aunt Julle won't be here.

HEDDA: No, but Mrs. Elvsted will. The three of us will have a cup of tea together.

TESMAN: Oh yes; *that* will be perfectly all right!

BRACK (*with a smile*): And perhaps the wiser course of action for him.

HEDDA: What do you mean?

BRACK: Begging your pardon, Mrs. Tesman—you've often enough looked askance at my little stag dinners. It's been your opinion that only men of the firmest principles ought to attend.

HEDDA: I should think Mr. Løvborg is firm-principled enough now. A reformed sinner—

(BERTE *appears in door, right.*)

BERTE: Ma'am—there's a gentleman here who asks if—

HEDDA: Show him in, please.

TESMAN (*softly*): I'm sure it's he! Just think!

(EILERT LØVBORG *enters, right. He is slim, gaunt. Of* TESMAN'S *age, but he looks older and somewhat dissipated. Brown hair and beard. Pale, longish face, reddish spots on the cheekbones. Dressed for visiting in elegant, black, brand-new suit. He carries a silk hat and dark gloves in his hand. He remains near the door, makes a quick bow. He appears a little embarrassed.*)

TESMAN (*goes over to him, shakes his hand*): My dear Eilert—at last we meet again!

EILERT LØVBORG (*subdued voice*): Thanks for your note, Jørgen! (*Approaching* HEDDA.) Am I allowed to shake your hand, too, Mrs. Tesman?

HEDDA (*accepting his proffered hand*): I am very glad to see you, Mr. Løvborg. (*With a gesture.*) I don't know if you two gentlemen—

LØVBORG (*with a slight bow*): Judge Brack, I believe.

BRACK (*also bowing lightly*): Certainly. Some years ago—

TESMAN (*to* LØVBORG, *both hands on his shoulders*): And now I want you to feel quite at home here, Eilert! Isn't that right, Hedda? For you plan to stay here in town, I understand. Hm?

LØVBORG: Yes, I do.

TESMAN: Perfectly reasonable. Listen—I just got hold of your new book, but I haven't had a chance to read it yet.

LØVBORG: You may save yourself the trouble.

TESMAN: Why do you say that?

LØVBORG: There's not much to it.

TESMAN: Just think—you saying that!

BRACK: Nevertheless, people seem to have very good things to say about it.

LØVBORG: That's exactly why I wrote it—so everybody would like it.

BRACK: Very wise of you.

TESMAN: Yes, but Eilert—!

LØVBORG: For I am trying to rebuild my position. Start all over again.

TESMAN (*with some embarrassment*): Yes, I suppose you are, aren't you? Hm?

LØVBORG (*smiles, puts his hat down, pulls a parcel out of his pocket*): When *this* appears—Jørgen Tesman—this you must read. For this is the real thing. This is me.

TESMAN: Oh really? And what is it?

LØVBORG: The continuation.

TESMAN: Continuation? Of what?

LØVBORG: Of the book.

TESMAN: Of the new book?

LØVBORG: Of course.

TESMAN: But Eilert—you've carried the story all the way up to the present!

LØVBORG: So I have. And this is about the future.

TESMAN: The future! But, heavens—we don't know a thing about the future!

LØVBORG: No, we don't. But there are a couple of things to be said about it all the same. (*Unwraps the parcel.*) Here, let me show you—

TESMAN: But that's not your handwriting.

LØVBORG: I have dictated it. (*Leafs through portions of the manuscript.*) It's in two parts. The first is about the forces that will shape the civilization of the future. And the second (*riffling through more pages*)—about the course which that future civilization will take.

TESMAN: How remarkable! It would never occur to me to write anything like that.

HEDDA (*over by the French doors, her fingers drumming the pane*): Hmm—I dare say—

LØVBORG (*replacing the manuscript in its wrappings and putting it down on the table*): I brought it along, for I thought maybe I'd read parts of it aloud to you this evening.

TESMAN: That's very good of you, Eilert. But this evening—? (*Looks at* BRACK.) I'm not quite sure how to arrange that—

LØVBORG: Some other time, then. There's no hurry.

BRACK: You see, Mr. Løvborg, there's a little get-together over at my house tonight. Mainly for Tesman, you know—

LØVBORG (*looking for his hat*): In that case, I certainly won't—

BRACK: No, listen. Won't you do me the pleasure to join us?

LØVBORG (*firmly*): No, I won't. But thanks all the same.

BRACK: Oh come on! Why don't you do that? We'll be a small, select circle. And I think I can promise you a fairly lively evening, as Hed—as Mrs. Tesman would say.

LØVBORG: I don't doubt that. Nevertheless—

BRACK: And you may bring your manuscript along and read aloud to Tesman over at my house. I have plenty of room.

TESMAN: Just think, Eilert! Wouldn't that be nice, hm?

HEDDA (*intervening*): But can't you see that Mr. Løvborg doesn't want to? I'm sure he would rather stay here and have supper with me.

LØVBORG (*looks at her*): With you, Mrs. Tesman?

HEDDA: And with Mrs. Elvsted.

LØVBORG: Ah—! (*Casually.*) I ran into her at noon today.

HEDDA: Oh? Well, she'll be here tonight. So you see your presence is really required, Mr. Løvborg. Otherwise she won't have anybody to see her home.

LØVBORG: True. All right, then, Mrs. Tesman—I'll stay, thank you.

HEDDA: Good, I'll just tell the maid. (*She rings for* BERTE *over by the door, right.*)

(BERTE *appears just off stage.* HEDDA *talks with her in a low voice, points toward the inner room.* BERTE *nods and exits.*)

TESMAN (*while* HEDDA *and* BERTE *are talking, to* LØVBORG): Tell me, Eilert—is it this new subject—about the future—is that what you plan to lecture on?

LØVBORG: Yes.

TESMAN: For the bookseller told me you have announced a lecture series for this fall.

LØVBORG: Yes, I have. I hope you won't mind too much.

TESMAN: Of course not! But—

LØVBORG: For of course I realize it is rather awkward for you.

TESMAN (*unhappily*): Oh well—I certainly can't expect—that just for my sake—

LØVBORG: But I will wait till you receive your appointment.

TESMAN: Wait? But—but—but—you mean you aren't going to compete with me? Hm?

LØVBORG: No. Just triumph over you. In people's opinion.

TESMAN: Oh, for goodness' sake! Then Aunt Julle was right, after all! I knew it all the time. Hedda! Do you hear that! Just think—Eilert Løvborg isn't going to stand in our way after all.

HEDDA (*tersely*): *Our?* I have nothing to do with this.

(HEDDA *walks into the inner room, where* BERTE *is bringing in a tray with decanters and glasses.* HEDDA *nods her approval and comes forward again.*)

TESMAN (*during the foregoing business*): How about that, Judge? What do you say to this? Hm?

BRACK: I say that moral victory and all that—hm—may be glorious enough and beautiful enough—

TESMAN: Oh, I agree. All the same—

HEDDA (*looks at* TESMAN *with a cold smile*): You look thunderstruck.

TESMAN: Well, I am—pretty much—I really believe—

BRACK: After all, Mrs. Tesman, that was quite a thunderstorm that just passed over.

HEDDA (*points to the inner room*): How about a glass of cold punch, gentlemen?

BRACK (*looks at his watch*): A stirrup cup. Not a bad idea.

TESMAN: Splendid, Hedda. Perfectly splendid. In such a lighthearted mood as I am now—

HEDDA: Please. You, too, Mr. Løvborg.

LØVBORG (*with a gesture of refusal*): No, thanks. Really. Nothing for me.

BRACK: Good heavens, man! Cold punch isn't poison, you know!

LØVBORG: Perhaps not for everybody.

HEDDA: I'll keep Mr. Løvborg company in the meantime.

TESMAN: All right, Hedda. You do that.

(*He and* BRACK *go into the inner room, sit down, drink punch, smoke cigarettes, and engage in lively conversation during the next scene.* EILERT LØVBORG *remains standing near the stove.* HEDDA *walks over to the desk.*)

HEDDA (*her voice a little louder than usual*): I'll show you some pictures, if you like. You see—Tesman and I, we took a trip through Tyrol on our way back.

(*She brings an album over to the table by the sofa. She sits down in the far corner of the sofa.* LØVBORG *approaches, stops, looks at her. He takes a chair and sits down at her left, his back toward the inner room.*)

HEDDA (*opens the album*): Do you see these mountains, Mr. Løvborg? They are the Ortler group. Tesman has written their name below. Here it is: "The Ortler group near Meran."

LØVBORG (*has looked steadily at her all this time. Says slowly*): Hedda—Gabler!

HEDDA (*with a quick glance sideways*): Not that! Shhh!

LØVBORG (*again*): Hedda Gabler!

HEDDA (*looking at the album*): Yes, that used to be my name. When—when we two knew each other.

LØVBORG: And so from now on—for the whole rest of my life—I must get used to never again saying Hedda Gabler.

HEDDA (*still occupied with the album*): Yes, you must. And you might as well start right now. The sooner the better, I think.

LØVBORG (*with indignation*): Hedda Gabler married? And married to—Jørgen Tesman!

HEDDA: Yes—that's the way it goes.

LØVBORG: Oh, Hedda, Hedda—how could you throw yourself away like that!

HEDDA (*with a fierce glance at him*): What's this? I won't have any of that!

LØVBORG: What do you mean?

(TESMAN *enters from the inner room.*)

HEDDA (*hears him coming and remarks casually*): And this here, Mr. Løvborg, this is from somewhere in the Ampezzo valley. Just look at those peaks over there. (*With a kindly look at* TESMAN.) What did you say those peaks were called, dear?

TESMAN: Let me see. Oh, they—they are the Dolomites.

HEDDA: Right. Those are the Dolomites, Mr. Løvborg.

TESMAN: Hedda, I thought I'd just ask you if you don't want me to bring you some punch, after all? For you, anyway? Hm?

HEDDA: Well, yes; thanks. And a couple of cookies, maybe.

TESMAN: No cigarettes?

HEDDA: No.

TESMAN: All right.

(*He returns to the inner room, then turns right.* BRACK *is in there, keeping an eye on* HEDDA *and* LØVBORG *from time to time.*)

LØVBORG (*still in a low voice*): Answer me, Hedda. How could you do a thing like that?

HEDDA (*apparently engrossed in the album*): If you keep on using my first name I won't talk to you.

LØVBORG: Not even when we're alone?

HEDDA: No. You may think it, but you must not say it.

LØVBORG: I see. It offends your love for —Jørgen Tesman.

HEDDA (*glances at him, smiles*): Love? That's a good one!

LØVBORG: Not love, then.

HEDDA: But no infidelities, either! I won't have it.

LØVBORG: Hedda—answer me just this one thing—

HEDDA: Shhh!

(TESMAN *enters with a tray from the inner room.*)

TESMAN: Here! Here are the goodies. (*Puts the tray down.*)

HEDDA: Why don't you get Berte to do it?

TESMAN (*pouring punch*): Because I think it's so much fun waiting on you, Hedda.

HEDDA: But you've filled both glasses. And Mr. Løvborg didn't want any—

TESMAN: I know, but Mrs. Elvsted will soon be here, won't she?

HEDDA: That's right. So she will.

TESMAN: Had you forgotten about her? Hm?

HEDDA: We've been so busy looking at this. (*Shows him a picture.*) Remember that little village?

TESMAN: That's the one just below the Brenner Pass, isn't it? We spent the night there—

HEDDA:—and ran into that lively crowd of summer guests.

TESMAN: Right! Just think—if we only could have had you with us. Eilert! Oh well.

(*Returns to the inner room, sits down, and resumes his conversation with* BRACK.)

LØVBORG: Just tell me this, Hedda—

HEDDA: What?

LØVBORG: Wasn't there love in your feelings for me, either? Not a touch—not a shimmer of love? Wasn't there?

HEDDA: I wonder. To me, we seemed to be simply two good comrades. Two close friends. (*Smiles.*) You, particularly, were very frank.

LØVBORG: You wanted it that way.

HEDDA: And yet—when I look back upon it now, there was something beautiful, something thrilling, something brave, I think, about the secret frankness—that comradeship that not a single soul so much as suspected.

LØVBORG: Yes, wasn't there, Hedda? Wasn't there? When I called on your father in the afternoons—And the General sat by the window with his newspapers—his back turned—

HEDDA: And we two in the sofa in the corner—

LØVBORG:—always with the same illustrated magazine—

HEDDA:—for want of an album, yes—

LØVBORG: Yes, Hedda—and then when I confessed to you—! Told you all about myself, things the others didn't know. Sat and told you about my orgies by day and night. Dissipation day in and day out! Oh, Hedda—what sort of power in you was it that forced me to tell you things like that?

HEDDA: You think there was some power in me?

LØVBORG: How else can I explain it? And all those veiled questions you asked—

HEDDA:—which you understood so perfectly well—

LØVBORG: That you could ask such questions! With such complete frankness!

HEDDA: *Veiled,* if you please.

LØVBORG: But frankly all the same. All about—that!

HEDDA: And to think that you answered, Mr. Løvborg!

LØVBORG: Yes, that's just what I can't understand—now, afterwards. But tell me, Hedda; wasn't love at the bottom of our whole relationship? Didn't you feel some kind of urge to—purify me—when I came to you in confession? Wasn't that it?

HEDDA: No, not quite.

LØVBORG: Then what made you do it?

HEDDA: Do you find it so very strange that a young girl—when she can do so, without anyone knowing—

LØVBORG: Yes—?

HEDDA:—that she wants to take a peek into a world which—

LØVBORG:—which—?

HEDDA:—she is not supposed to know anything about?

LØVBORG: So that was it!

HEDDA: That, too. That, too—I think—

LØVBORG: Companionship in the lust for life. But why couldn't *that* at least have continued?

HEDDA: That was your own fault.

LØVBORG: You were the one who broke off.

HEDDA: Yes, when reality threatened to enter our relationship. Shame on you, Eilert Løvborg! How could you want to do a thing like that to your frank and trusting comrade!

LØVBORG (*clenching his hands*): Oh, why didn't you do it! Why didn't you shoot me down, as you said you would!

HEDDA: Because I'm scared of scandal.

LØVBORG: Yes, Hedda. You are really a coward.

HEDDA: A terrible coward. (*Changing her tone.*) But that was your good luck, wasn't it? And now the Elvsteds have healed your broken heart very nicely.

LØVBORG: I know what Thea has told you.

HEDDA: Perhaps you have told her about us?

LØVBORG: Not a word. She is too stupid to understand.

HEDDA: Stupid?

LØVBORG: In things like that.

HEDDA: And I'm a coward. (*Leans forward, without looking in his eyes, whispers.*) But now *I* am going to confess something to *you.*

LØVBORG (*tense*): What?

HEDDA: That I didn't dare to shoot—?

LØVBORG: Yes—?

HEDDA:—that was not the worst of my cowardice that night.

LØVBORG (*looks at her a moment, understands, whispers passionately*): Oh, Hedda! Hedda Gabler! Now I begin to see what was behind the companionship! You and I! So it *was* your lust for life—!

HEDDA (*in a low voice, with an angry glance*): Take care! Don't you believe it!

(*Darkness is falling. The door, right, is opened by* BERTE, *who remains invisible.*)

HEDDA (*closing the album, calls out, smiling*): At last! So there you are, dearest Thea! Come in!

(MRS. ELVSTED *enters. She is dressed for a party. The door is closed behind her.*)

HEDDA (*on the sofa, reaching out for* MRS. ELVSTED): Sweetest Thea, you have no idea how I've waited for you.

(*In passing,* MRS. ELVSTED *exchanges quick greetings with* TESMAN *and* BRACK *in the inner room. She walks up to the table and shakes* HEDDA'S *hand.* EILERT LØVBORG *rises. He and* MRS. ELVSTED *greet one another with a silent nod.*)

MRS. ELVSTED: Shouldn't I go in and say hello to your husband?

HEDDA: No, never mind that. Leave them alone. They're soon leaving, anyway.

MRS. ELVSTED: Leaving?

HEDDA: They're going out to drink.

MRS. ELVSTED (*quickly, to* LØVBORG): Not you?

LØVBORG: No.

HEDDA: Mr. Løvborg stays here with us.

MRS. ELVSTED (*pulls up a chair, is about to sit down next to* LØVBORG): Oh, how wonderful it is to be here!

HEDDA: Oh no, little Thea. Not that. Not there. Over here by me, please. *I* want to be in the middle.

MRS. ELVSTED: Just as you like. (*She walks in front of the table and seats herself on the sofa, on* HEDDA'S *right.* LØVBORG *sits down again on his chair.*)

LØVBORG (*after a brief pause, to* HEDDA): Isn't she lovely to look at?

HEDDA (*gently stroking her hair*): Just to look at?

LØVBORG: Yes. For you see—she and I—we are real comrades. We have absolute faith in one another. And we can talk together in full freedom.

HEDDA: Unveiled, Mr. Løvborg?

LØVBORG: Well—

MRS. ELVSTED (*in a low voice, clinging to* HEDDA): Oh, I am so happy, Hedda! For just think—he also says I have inspired him!

HEDDA (*looks at her with a smile*): No, really! He says that?

LØVBORG: And she has such courage, Mrs. Tesman! Such courage of action.

MRS. ELVSTED: Oh, my God—courage—! I!

LØVBORG: Infinite courage—when it concerns the comrade.

HEDDA: Yes, courage—if one only had that.

LØVBORG: What then?

HEDDA: Then maybe life would be tolerable, after all. (*Changing her tone.*) But now, dearest Thea, you want a glass of nice, cold punch.

MRS. ELVSTED: No, thanks. I never drink things like that.

HEDDA: Then what about you, Mr. Løvborg?

LØVBORG: Thanks, Nothing for me, either.

MRS. ELVSTED: No, nothing for him, either.

HEDDA (*looks firmly at him*): If I say so?

LØVBORG: Makes no difference.

HEDDA (*laughs*): Oh dear! So I have no power over you at all. Is that it?

LØVBORG: Not in that respect.

HEDDA: Seriously, though; I really think you should. For your own sake.

MRS. ELVSTED: No, but Hedda—!

LØVBORG: Why so?

HEDDA: Or rather for people's sake.

LØVBORG: Oh?

HEDDA: For else they might think you don't really trust yourself— That you lack self-confidence—

MRS. ELVSTED (*softly*): Don't, Hedda!

LØVBORG: People may think whatever they like for all I care—for the time being.

MRS. ELVSTED (*happy*): Exactly!

HEDDA: I could easily tell from watching Judge Brack just now.

LØVBORG: Tell what?

HEDDA: He smiled so contemptuously when you didn't dare to join them in there.

LØVBORG: Didn't I dare to! It's just that I'd much rather stay here and talk with you!

MRS. ELVSTED: But that's only natural, Hedda.

HEDDA: The Judge had no way of knowing that. And I also noticed he smiled and looked at Tesman when you didn't dare to go to his silly old party.

LØVBORG: Didn't dare! Are you saying I didn't dare?

HEDDA: *I* am not. But that's how Judge Brack understood it.

LØVBORG: Let him.

HEDDA: So you're not going?

LØVBORG: I'm staying here with you and Thea.

MRS. ELVSTED: Of course, he is, Hedda!

HEDDA (*smiles, nods approvingly*): That's what I call firm foundations. Principled forever; that's the way a man ought to be! (*Turning to* MRS. ELVSTED, *stroking her cheek.*) What did I tell you this morning—when you came here, quite beside yourself—?

LØVBORG (*puzzled*): Beside herself?

MRS. ELVSTED (*in terror*): Hedda—Hedda—don't!

HEDDA: Now do you see? There was no need at all for that mortal fear of yours—(*Interrupting herself.*) There now! Now we can all three relax and enjoy ourselves.

LØVBORG (*startled*): What's all this, Mrs. Tesman?

MRS. ELVSTED: Oh, God, Hedda—what are you saying? What are you doing?

HEDDA: Please be quiet. That horrible Judge is looking at you.

LØVBORG: In mortal fear? So that's it. Because of me.

MRS. ELVSTED (*softly, wailing*): Oh, Hedda—if you only knew how utterly miserable you have made me!

LØVBORG (*stares at her for a moment. His face is distorted.*): So that was the comrade's happy confidence in me!

MRS. ELVSTED: Oh, my dearest friend—listen to me first—!

LØVBORG (*picks up one of the glasses of punch, raises it, says hoarsely*): Here's to you, Thea! (*Empties the glass, puts it down, picks up the other one.*)

MRS. ELVSTED (*softly*): Hedda, Hedda—why did you want to do this?

HEDDA: Want to! I! Are you mad?

LØVBORG: And here's to you, too, Mrs. Tesman! Thanks for telling me the truth. Long live the truth! (*He drains the glass and is about to fill it again.*)   •

HEDDA (*restrains him*): That's enough for now. Remember you are going to a party.

MRS. ELVSTED: No, no, no!

HEDDA: Shhh! They are looking at you.

LØVBORG (*puts his glass down*): Listen, Thea—tell me the truth—

MRS. ELVSTED: I will, I will!

LØVBORG: Did your husband know you were coming after me?

MRS. ELVSTED (*wringing her hands*): Oh, Hedda—do you hear what he's asking?

LØVBORG: Did the two of you agree that you were to come here and look after me? Maybe it was his idea, even? Did he send you? Ah, I know what it was—he missed me in the office, didn't he? Or was it at the card table?

MRS. ELVSTED (*softly, in agony*): Oh, Løvborg, Løvborg!

LØVBORG (*grabs a glass and is about to fill it*): Here's to the old Commissioner, too!

HEDDA (*stops him*): No more now. You're supposed to read aloud for Tesman tonight—remember?

LØVBORG (*calm again, puts the glass down*): This was silly of me, Thea. I'm sorry. Taking it this way. Please, don't be angry with me. You'll see—both you and all those others—that even if I have been down—! With your help, Thea—dear comrade.

MRS. ELVSTED (*beaming*): Oh, thank God—!

(*In the meantime, BRACK has looked at his watch. He and TESMAN get up and come forward.*)

BRACK (*picking up his coat and hat*): Well, Mrs. Tesman; our time is up.

HEDDA: I suppose it is.

LØVBORG (*rising*): Mine, too, Judge.

MRS. ELVSTED (*softly, pleadingly*): Oh, Løvborg—don't do it!

HEDDA (*pinches her arm*): They can hear you!

MRS. ELVSTED (*with a soft exclamation*): Ouch!

LØVBORG (*to BRACK*): You were good enough to ask me—

BRACK: So you're coming, after all?

LØVBORG: If I may.

BRACK: I'm delighted.

LØVBORG (*picks up his manuscript and says to TESMAN*): For there are a couple of things here I'd like to show you before I send it off.

TESMAN: Just think! Isn't that nice! But—dearest Hedda—? In that case, how are you going to get Mrs. Elvsted home? Hm?

HEDDA: We'll manage somehow.

LØVBORG (*looking at the two women*): Mrs. Elvsted? I'll be back to pick her up, of course. (*Coming closer.*) About ten o'clock, Mrs. Tesman? Is that convenient?

HEDDA: Certainly. That will be fine.

TESMAN: Then everything is nice and settled. But don't expect me that early, Hedda.

HEDDA: You just stay as long as—as long as you want to, dear.

MRS. ELVSTED (*in secret fear*): I'll be waiting for you here, then, Mr. Løvborg.

LØVBORG (*hat in hand*): Of course, Mrs. Elvsted.

BRACK: All aboard the pleasure train, gentlemen! I hope we'll have a lively evening—as a certain fair lady would say.

HEDDA: Ah—if only the fair lady could be present. Invisibly.

BRACK: Why invisibly?

HEDDA: To listen to some of your unadulterated liveliness, Judge.

BRACK (*laughs*): I shouldn't advise the fair lady to do that!

TESMAN (*also laughing*): You're a good one, Hedda! Just think!

BRACK: Well—good night, ladies!

LØVBORG (*with a bow*): Till about ten, then.

(BRACK, LØVBORG, *and* TESMAN *go out, right. At the same time* BERTE *enters from the inner room with a lighted lamp, which she places on the table, front center. She goes out the same way.*)

MRS. ELVSTED (*has risen and paces restlessly up and down*): Hedda, Hedda—how do you think all this will end?

HEDDA: At ten o'clock he'll be here. I see him already. With vine leaves in his hair. Flushed and confident.

MRS. ELVSTED: I only hope you're right.

HEDDA: For then, you see, he'll have mastered himself. And be a free man for all the days of his life.

MRS. ELVSTED: Dear God—how I hope you are right! That he'll come back like that.

HEDDA: That is the way he will come. No other way. (*She rises and goes closer to* MRS. ELVSTED.) *You* may doubt as long as you like. I believe in him. And now we'll see—

MRS. ELVSTED: There is something behind all this, Hedda. Some hidden purpose.

HEDDA: Yes, there is! For once in my life I want to have power over a human destiny.

MRS. ELVSTED: But don't you already?

HEDDA: I don't and I never have.

MRS. ELVSTED: But your husband—?

HEDDA: You think that's worth the trouble? Oh, if you knew how poor I am! And you got to be so rich! (*Embraces her passionately.*) I think I'll have to burn your hair off, after all!

MRS. ELVSTED: Let me go! Let me go! You scare me, Hedda!

BERTE (*in the doorway*): Supper is served, ma'am.

HEDDA: Good. We're coming.

MRS. ELVSTED: No, no, no! I'd rather go home by myself! Right now!

HEDDA: Nonsense! You'll have your cup of tea first, you little silly. And then—at ten o'clock—Eilert Løvborg comes—with vine leaves in his hair! (*She almost pulls* MRS. ELVSTED *toward the doorway.*)

ACT III

(*The same room at the* TESMANS'. *The doorway and the French windows both have their portieres closed. The lamp, turned half down, is still on the table. The stove is open. Some dying embers can be seen.*)

MRS. ELVSTED, *wrapped in a big shawl, is in the easy chair near the stove, her feet on a footstool.* HEDDA, *also dressed, is lying on the sofa, covered by a blanket.*)

MRS. ELVSTED (*after a while suddenly sits up, listens anxiously; then she wearily sinks back in her chair, whimpers softly*): Oh my God, my God—not yet!

(BERTE *enters cautiously, right, carrying a letter.*)

MRS. ELVSTED (*turns and whispers tensely*): Well—has anybody been here?
BERTE (*in a low voice*): Yes. Just now there was a girl with this letter.
MRS. ELVSTED (*quickly, reaches for it*): A letter! Give it to me.
BERTE: No, ma'am. It's for the Doctor.
MRS. ELVSTED: I see.
BERTE: Miss Tesman's maid brought it. I'll leave it here on the table.
MRS. ELVSTED: All right.
BERTE (*puts the letter down*): I'd better put out the lamp. It just reeks.
MRS. ELVSTED: Yes, do that. It must be daylight soon, anyway.
BERTE (*putting out the lamp*): It's light already, ma'am.
MRS. ELVSTED: Light already! And still not back!
BERTE: No, so help us. Not that I didn't expect as much—
MRS. ELVSTED: You did?
BERTE: Yes, when I saw a certain character was back in town. Taking off with him. We sure heard enough about him in the old days!
MRS. ELVSTED: Not so loud. You are waking up Mrs. Tesman.
BERTE (*looks toward the sofa, sighs*): God forbid—Let her sleep, poor thing. Do you want me to get the fire going again?
MRS. ELVSTED: Not on my account, thank you.
BERTE: All right. (*Exits quietly, right.*)
HEDDA (*awakened by the closing door*): What's that?
MRS. ELVSTED: Just the maid.
HEDDA (*looks around*): Why in here—? Oh, I remember! (*Sits up, rubs her eyes, stretches.*) What time is it, Thea?
MRS. ELVSTED (*looks at her watch*): Past seven.
HEDDA: When did Tesman get home?
MRS. ELVSTED: He didn't.
HEDDA: Not home yet!
MRS. ELVSTED (*getting up*): Nobody's come.
HEDDA: And we waited till four!
MRS. ELVSTED (*wringing her hands*): And *how* we waited!
HEDDA (*her hand covering a yawn*): We—ll. We could have saved ourselves that trouble.
MRS. ELVSTED: Did you get any sleep at all?

HEDDA: Yes, I slept pretty well, I think. Didn't you?

MRS. ELVSTED: Not a wink. I just couldn't, Hedda! It was just impossible.

HEDDA (*rises, walks over to her*): Well, now! There's nothing to worry about, for heaven's sake. I know exactly what's happened.

MRS. ELVSTED: Then tell me please. Where do you think they are?

HEDDA: Well, first of all, I'm sure they were terribly late leaving the Judge's—

MRS. ELVSTED: Dear, yes. I'm sure you're right. Still—

HEDDA:—and so Tesman didn't want to wake us up in the middle of the night. (*Laughs.*) Maybe he didn't want us to see him, either—after a party like that.

MRS. ELVSTED: But where do you think he has gone?

HEDDA: To the aunts', of course. His old room is still there, all ready for him.

MRS. ELVSTED: No, he can't be there. Just a few minutes ago there came a letter for him from Miss Tesman. It's over there.

HEDDA: Oh? (*looks at the envelope.*) So it is—Auntie Julle herself. In that case, I suppose he's still at Brack's. And there's Eilert Løvborg, too—reading aloud, with vine leaves in his hair.

MRS. ELVSTED: Oh Hedda—you're only saying things you don't believe yourself.

HEDDA: My, what a little imbecile you really are, Thea!

MRS. ELVSTED: Yes, I suppose I am.

HEDDA: And you look dead tired, too.

MRS. ELVSTED: I *am* dead tired.

HEDDA: Why don't you do as I say. Go into my room and lie down.

MRS. ELVSTED: No, no—I wouldn't be able to go to sleep, anyway.

HEDDA: Of course, you would.

MRS. ELVSTED: And your husband is bound to be home any minute now. And I have to know right away.

HEDDA: I'll let you know as soon as he gets here.

MRS. ELVSTED: You promise me that, Hedda?

HEDDA: I do. You just go to sleep.

MRS. ELVSTED: Thanks. At least I'll try. (*Exits through inner room.*)

(HEDDA *goes to the French doors, opens the portieres. The room is now in full daylight. She picks up a little hand mirror from the desk, looks at herself, smooths her hair. Walks over to door, right, rings the bell for the maid.* BERTE *presently appears.*)

BERTE: You want something, ma'am?

HEDDA: Yes. You'll have to start the fire again. I'm cold.

BERTE: Yes, ma'am! I'll get it warm in no time. (*Rakes the embers together and puts in another piece of wood. Then she suddenly listens.*) There's the doorbell, ma'am.

HEDDA: All right. See who it is. I'll take care of the stove myself.

BERTE: You'll have a nice blaze going in a minute. (*Exits right.*)

(HEDDA *kneels on the footstool and puts in more pieces of wood. Presently* TESMAN *enters, right. He looks tired and somber. He tiptoes toward the doorway and is about to disappear between the portieres.*)

HEDDA (*by the stove, without looking up*): Good morning.

TESMAN (*turning*): Hedda! (*Comes closer.*) For heaven's sake—you up already! Hm?

HEDDA: Yes, I got up very early this morning.

TESMAN: And I was sure you'd still be sound asleep! Just think!

HEDDA: Not so loud. Mrs. Elvsted is asleep in my room.

TESMAN: Mrs. Elvsted stayed here all night?

HEDDA: Yes. Nobody came for her, you know.

TESMAN: No, I suppose—

HEDDA (*closes the stove, rises*): Well, did you have a good time at the Judge's?

TESMAN: Were you worried about me? Hm?

HEDDA: I'd never dream of worrying about you. I asked if you had a good time.

TESMAN: Yes, indeed. Nice for a change, anyway. But I think I liked it best early in the evening. For then Eilert read to me. Just think—we were more than an hour early! And Brack, of course, had things to see to. So Eilert read.

HEDDA (*sits down at the right side of the table*): So? Tell me all about it.

TESMAN (*sits down on an ottoman near the stove*): Oh Hedda, you'll never believe what a book that will be! It must be just the most remarkable thing ever written! Just think!

HEDDA: Yes, but I don't really care about that—

TESMAN: I must tell you, Hedda—I have a confession to make. As he was reading—something ugly came over me—

HEDDA: Ugly?

TESMAN: I sat there envying Eilert for being able to write like that! Just think, Hedda!

HEDDA: All right. I'm thinking!

TESMAN: And yet, with all his gifts—he's incorrigible, after all.

HEDDA: I suppose you mean he has more courage for life than the rest of you?

TESMAN: No, no—I don't mean that. I mean that he's incapable of exercising moderation in his pleasures.

HEDDA: What happened—in the end?

TESMAN: Well—*I* would call it a bacchanal, Hedda.

HEDDA: Did he have vine leaves in his hair?

TESMAN: Vine leaves? No, I didn't notice any vine leaves. But he gave a long, muddled speech in honor of the woman who had inspired him in his work. Those were his words.

HEDDA: Did he mention her name?

TESMAN: No, he didn't. But I'm sure it must be Mrs. Elvsted. You just wait and see if I'm not right!

HEDDA: And where did you and he part company?

TESMAN: On the way back to town. We left—the last of us did—at the same time. And Brack came along, too, to get some fresh air. Then we decided we'd better see Eilert home. You see, he had had altogether too much to drink!

HEDDA: I can imagine.

TESMAN: But then the strangest thing of all happened, Hedda! Or maybe I should say the saddest. I'm almost ashamed—on Eilert's behalf—even talking about it.

HEDDA: Well—?

TESMAN: You see, on the way back I happened to be behind the others a little. Just for a minute or two—you know—

HEDDA: All right, all right—!

TESMAN: And when I hurried to catch up with them, can you guess what I found by the roadside? Hm?

HEDDA: How can I possibly—?

TESMAN: You mustn't tell this to a living soul, Hedda! Do you hear! Promise me that, for Eilert's sake. (*Pulls a parcel out of his coat pocket.*) Just think—I found this!

HEDDA: Isn't that what he had with him here yesterday?

TESMAN: Yes! It's his whole, precious, irreplaceable manuscript! And he had dropped it—just like that! Without even noticing! Just think, Hedda! Isn't that awfully sad?

HEDDA: But why didn't you give it back to him?

TESMAN: In the condition he was in! Dear—I just didn't dare to.

HEDDA: And you didn't tell any of the others that you had found it, either?

TESMAN: Of course not. I didn't want to, for Eilert's sake—don't you see?

HEDDA: So nobody knows that you have Eilert Løvborg's papers?

TESMAN: Nobody. And nobody must know, either.

HEDDA: And what did you and he talk about afterwards?

TESMAN: I didn't have a chance to talk to him at all after that. For when we came into town, he and a couple of the others simply vanished. Just think!

HEDDA: Oh? I expect they took him home.

TESMAN: I suppose that must be it. And Brack took off on his own, too.

HEDDA: And what have you been doing with yourself since then?

TESMAN: Well, you see, I and some of the others went home with one of the younger fellows and had a cup of early morning coffee. Or night coffee maybe, rather. Hm? And now, after I've rested a bit and poor Eilert's had some sleep, I'll take this back to him.

HEDDA (*reached for the parcel*): No—don't do that! Not right away, I mean. Let me look at it first.

TESMAN: Dearest Hedda—honestly, I just don't dare to.

HEDDA: Don't you dare to?

TESMAN: No, for I'm sure you realize how utterly desperate he'll be when he wakes up and finds that the manuscript is gone. For he hasn't a copy, you know. He said so himself.

HEDDA (*looks searchingly at him*): But can't a thing like that be written over again?

TESMAN: Hardly. I really don't think so. For, you see—the inspiration—

HEDDA: Yes, I daresay that's the main thing. (*Casually.*) By the way, here's a letter for you.

TESMAN: Imagine!

HEDDA (*gives it to him*): It came early this morning.

TESMAN: It's from Aunt Julle, Hedda! I wonder what it can be. (*Puts the manuscript down on the other ottoman, opens the letter, skims the content, jumps up.*) Oh Hedda! She says here that poor Aunt Rina is dying!

HEDDA: You know we had to expect that.

TESMAN: And if I want to see her again I had better hurry. I'll rush over right away.

HEDDA (*suppressing a smile*): You'll rush?

TESMAN: Dearest Hedda of mine—if only you could bring yourself to come along! Hm?

HEDDA (*rises, weary, with an air of refusal*): No, no. You mustn't ask me that. I don't want to look at death and disease. I don't want anything to do with ugliness.

TESMAN: Well, all right—(*Scurrying around.*) My hat? My coat? Oh—out here in the hall. I just hope I won't be too late, Hedda. Hm?

HEDDA: Oh I'm sure that if you rush—

(BERTE *appears in the door, right.*)

BERTE: Judge Brack is here and wants to know if he may see you.

TESMAN: At this hour! No, no. I can't possibly see him now!

HEDDA: But *I* can. (*To* BERTE.) Tell the Judge please to come in.

(BERTE *exits.*)

HEDDA (*with a quick whisper*): Tesman! The package! (*She grabs it from the ottoman.*)

TESMAN: Yes! Give it to me!

HEDDA: No, no. I'll hide it for you till later.

(*She walks over to the desk and sticks the parcel in among the books on the shelf. In his hurry* TESMAN *is having difficulties getting his gloves on.* JUDGE BRACK *enters, right.*)

HEDDA (*nods to him*): If *you* aren't an early bird—
BRACK: Yes, don't you think so? (*To* TESMAN.) You're going out, too?
TESMAN: Yes, I must go and see the aunts. Just think, the invalid—she's dying!
BRACK: Oh, I'm terribly sorry! In that case, don't let me keep you. At such a moment—
TESMAN: Yes, I really must run. Goodbye, goodbye! (*Hurries out, right.*)
HEDDA (*approaching* BRACK): It appears that things were quite lively last night over at your house.
BRACK: Indeed, Mrs. Tesman—I didn't get to bed at all.
HEDDA: You didn't either?
BRACK: As you see. But tell me—what has Tesman told you about the night's adventures?
HEDDA: Just some tiresome story about having coffee with somebody someplace—
BRACK: I believe I know all about that coffee. Eilert Løvborg wasn't one of them, was he?
HEDDA: No, they had taken him home first.
BRACK: Tesman, too?
HEDDA: No. Some of the others, he said.
BRACK (*smiles*): Jørgen Tesman is really an ingenuous soul, you know.
HEDDA: He certainly is. But why do you say that? Is there something more to all this?
BRACK: Yes, there is.
HEDDA: Well! In that case, why don't we make ourselves comfortable, Judge. You'll tell your story better, too.

(*She sits down at the left side of the table,* BRACK *near her at the adjacent side.*)

HEDDA: All right?
BRACK: For reasons of my own I wanted to keep track of my guests' movements last night. Or, rather—some of my guests.
HEDDA: Eilert Løvborg was one of them, perhaps?
BRACK: As a matter of fact—he was.
HEDDA: Now you are really making me curious.
BRACK: Do you know where he and a couple of the others spent the rest of the night, Mrs. Tesman?
HEDDA: No—tell me. If it can be told.

BRACK: Oh, certainly. They turned up at an exceptionally gay early morning gathering.

HEDDA: Of the lively kind?

BRACK: Of the liveliest.

HEDDA: A little more about this, Judge.

BRACK: Løvborg had been invited beforehand. I knew about that. But he had declined. He is a reformed character, you know.

HEDDA: As of his stay with the Elvsteds—yes. But he went after all?

BRACK: Well, yes, you see, Mrs. Tesman—unfortunately, the spirit moved him over at my house last evening.

HEDDA: Yes, I understand he became inspired.

BRACK: Quite violently inspired. And that, I gather, must have changed his mind. You know, we men don't always have as much integrity as we ought to have.

HEDDA: Oh, I'm sure you're an exception, Judge Brack. But about Løvborg—?

BRACK: To make a long story short—he ended up at Miss Diana's establishment.

HEDDA: Miss Diana's?

BRACK: She was the hostess at this gathering—a select circle of intimate friends, male and female.

HEDDA: Is she a redhead, by any chance?

BRACK: That's correct.

HEDDA: And a singer—of sorts?

BRACK: Yes—that, too. And a mighty huntress—of men, Mrs. Tesman. You seem to have heard of her. Eilert Løvborg used to be one of her most devoted protectors in his more affluent days.

HEDDA: And how did it all end?

BRACK: Not in a very friendly fashion, apparently. It seems that after the tenderest reception Miss Diana resorted to brute force—

HEDDA: Against Løvborg?

BRACK: Yes. He accused her or her women friends of having stolen something of his. Said his wallet was gone. And other things, too. In brief, he's supposed to have started a pretty wicked row.

HEDDA: And—?

BRACK: Well—there was a general free-for-all—men and women both. Fortunately, the police stepped in—

HEDDA: The police—!

BRACK: Yes. But I'm afraid this will be an expensive escapade for Eilert Løvborg, crazy fool that he is.

HEDDA: Well!

BRACK: It appears that he made quite violent objection—struck an officer in the ear and tore his coat. So they had to take him along.

HEDDA: How do you know all this?

BRACK: From the police.

HEDDA (*staring straight ahead*): So that's how it was. No vine leaves in his hair.

BRACK: Vine leaves, Mrs. Tesman?

HEDDA (*changing her tone*): But tell me, Judge Brack—why did you keep such a close watch on Eilert Løvborg?

BRACK: Well—for one thing, it is obviously of some concern to me if he testifies that he came straight from my party.

HEDDA: So you think there will be an investigation?

BRACK: Naturally. But I suppose that doesn't really matter too much. However, as a friend of the house I considered it my duty to give you and Tesman a full account of his night-time exploits.

HEDDA: Yes, but why?

BRACK: Because I very strongly suspect that he intends to use you as·a kind of screen.

HEDDA: Really! Why do you think that?

BRACK: Oh, come now, Mrs. Tesman! We can use our eyes, can't we? This Mrs. Elvsted—she isn't leaving town right away, you know.

HEDDA: Well, even if there should be something going on between those two, I'd think there would be plenty of other places they could meet.

BRACK: But no home. After last night, every respectable house will once again be closed to Eilert Løvborg.

HEDDA: And so should mine, you mean?

BRACK: Yes. I admit I would find it more than embarrassing if the gentleman were to become a daily guest here, Mrs. Tesman. If he, as an outsider—a highly dispensable outsider—if he were to intrude himself—

HEDDA:—into the triangle?

BRACK: Precisely. It would amount to homelessness for me.

HEDDA (*smiling*): Sole cock-o'-the-walk—so, that's your goal, is it, Judge?

BRACK (*nods slowly, lowers his voice*): Yes. That is my goal. And for that I will fight with every means at my disposal.

HEDDA (*her smile fading*): You're really a dangerous person, you know—when you come right down to it.

BRACK: You think so?

HEDDA: Yes. I am beginning to think so now. And I must say I am exceedingly glad you don't have any kind of hold on me.

BRACK (*with a noncommittal laugh*): Well, well, Mrs. Tesman! Maybe there is something to what you are saying, at that. Who knows what I might do if I did.

HEDDA: Really, now, Judge Brack! Are you threatening me?

BRACK (*rising*):—Nonsense! For the triangle, you see—is best maintained on a voluntary basis.

HEDDA: My sentiments, exactly.

BRACK: Well, I have said what I came to say. And now I should get back to town. Goodbye, Mrs. Tesman! (*Walks toward the French doors.*)

HEDDA (*rises*): You're going through the garden?

BRACK: Yes. For me that's a short cut.

HEDDA: Yes, and then it's a back way.

BRACK: Quite true. I have nothing against back ways. There are times when they are most intriguing.

HEDDA: You mean when real ammunition is used?

BRACK (*in the doorway, laughs back at her*): Oh good heavens! I don't suppose one shoots one's tame roosters!

HEDDA (*laughs also*): No—not if one has only one—!

(*They nod to each other, both still laughing. He leaves. She closes the door behind him. For a few moments she remains by the door, quite serious now, looking into the garden. Then she walks over to the doorway and opens the portieres wide enough to look into the inner room. Goes to the desk, pulls* LØVBORG'S *manuscript from the bookshelf and is about to read in it when* BERTE'S *voice, very loud, is heard from the hall, right.* HEDDA *turns around, listens. She hurriedly puts the manuscript into the drawer of the desk and puts the key down on its top.* EILERT LØVBORG, *wearing his coat and with his hat in his hand, flings open the door, right. He looks somewhat confused and excited.*)

LØVBORG (*turned toward the invisible* BERTE *in the hall*):—And I say I must! You can't stop me! (*He closes the door, turns, sees* HEDDA, *immediately controls himself, greets her.*)

HEDDA (*by the desk*): Well, well, Mr. Løvborg—aren't you a trifle late coming for Thea?

LØVBORG: Or a trifle early for calling on you. I apologize.

HEDDA: How do you know she is still here?

LØVBORG: The people she is staying with told me she's been gone all night.

HEDDA (*walks over to the table*): Did they seem—strange—when they said it?

LØVBORG (*puzzled*): Strange?

HEDDA: I mean, did they seem to find it a little—unusual?

LØVBORG (*suddenly understands*): Ah, I see what you mean! Of course! I'm dragging her down with me. No, as a matter of fact, I didn't notice anything. I suppose Tesman isn't up yet?

HEDDA: I—I don't think so—

LØVBORG: When did he get home?

HEDDA: Very late.

LØVBORG: Did he tell you anything?

HEDDA: Yes, he said you'd all had quite a time over at Brack's.

LØVBORG: Just that?

HEDDA: I think so. But I was so awfully sleepy—

(*Mrs.* ELVSTED *enters through portieres in the rear.*)

MRS. ELVSTED (*toward him*): Oh, Løvborg! At last!

LØVBORG: Yes, at last. And too late.

MRS. ELVSTED (*in fear*): What is too late?

LØVBORG: Everything is too late now. It's all over with me.

MRS. ELVSTED: Oh no, no! Don't say things like that!

LØVBORG: You'll say the same yourself when you hear—

MRS. ELVSTED: I don't want to hear—!

HEDDA: Maybe you'd rather talk with her alone? I'll leave.

LØVBORG: No, stay—you, too. I beg you to.

MRS. ELVSTED: But I don't want to listen, do you hear?

LØVBORG: It isn't last night I want to talk about.

MRS. ELVSTED: What about, then?

LØVBORG: We'll have to part, Thea.

MRS. ELVSTED: Part!

HEDDA (*involuntarily*): I knew it!

LØVBORG: For I don't need you any more.

MRS. ELVSTED: And you can stand there and tell me a thing like that! Don't need me! Why can't I help you the way I did before? Aren't we going to keep on working together?

LØVBORG: I don't intend to work any more.

MRS. ELVSTED (*desperately*): What am I going to do with my life, then?

LØVBORG: You'll have to try to live your life as if you'd never known me.

MRS. ELVSTED: But I can't do that!

LØVBORG: Try, Thea. Go back home.

MRS. ELVSTED (*agitated*): Never again! Where you are I want to be! And you can't chase me away just like that. I want to stay right here! Be with you when the book appears.

HEDDA (*in a tense whisper*): Ah—yes—the book!

LØVBORG (*looks at her*): My book—and Thea's. For that's what it is.

MRS. ELVSTED: That's what I feel, too. And that's why I have the right to be with you when it comes out. I want to see all the honor and all the fame you'll get. And the joy—I want to share the joy, too.

LØVBORG: Thea, our book is never going to come out.

HEDDA: Ah!

MRS. ELVSTED: It won't!

LØVBORG: *Can't* ever appear.

MRS. ELVSTED (*with fearful suspicion*): Løvborg, what have you done with the manuscript?

HEDDA (*watching him tensely*): Yes—what about the manuscript?

MRS. ELVSTED: Where is it?

LØVBORG: Oh Thea—please, don't ask me about that!

MRS. ELVSTED: Yes, yes,—I want to be told! I have the right to know—right now!

LØVBORG: All right. I've torn it to pieces.

MRS. ELVSTED (*screams*): Oh, no! No!

HEDDA (*involuntarily*): But that's not—!

LØVBORG (*looks at her*): Not true, you think?

HEDDA (*composing herself*): Well, of course, if you say so. You should know. It just sounds so—so unbelievable.

LØVBORG: All the same, it's true.

MRS. ELVSTED (*hands clenched*): Oh God—oh God, Hedda. He has torn his own work to pieces!

LØVBORG: I have torn my whole life to pieces, so why not my life's work as well?

MRS. ELVSTED: And that's what you did last night?

LØVBORG: Yes, I tell you! In a thousand pieces. And scattered them in the fjord. Far out—where the water is clean and salty. Let them drift there, with wind and current. Then they'll sink. Deep, deep down. Like me, Thea.

MRS. ELVSTED: Do you know, Løvborg—this thing you've done to the book—all the rest of my life I'll think of it as killing a little child.

LØVBORG: You are right. It is like murdering a child.

MRS. ELVSTED: But then, how could you? For the child was mine, too!

HEDDA (*almost soundlessly*): The child—

MRS. ELVSTED (*with a deep sigh*): So it's all over. I'll go now, Hedda.

HEDDA: But you aren't leaving town?

MRS. ELVSTED: Oh, I don't know myself what I'll do. There's only darkness before me. (*Exits, right.*)

HEDDA (*waits for a moment*): Aren't you going to see her home, Mr. Løvborg?

LØVBORG: I? Through the streets? Letting people see her with me?

HEDDA: Of course, I don't know what else may have happened last night. But is it really so absolutely irreparable—?

LØVBORG: Last night is not the end of it. That I know. And yet, I don't really care for that kind of life any more. Not again. She has broken all the courage for life and all the defiance that was in me.

HEDDA (*staring ahead*): So that sweet little goose has had her hand in a human destiny. (*Looks at him.*) But that you could be so heartless, even so!

LØVBORG: Don't tell me I was heartless!

HEDDA: To ruin everything that's filled her soul for such a long time! You don't call that heartless!

LØVBORG: Hedda—to you I can tell the truth.

HEDDA: The truth?

LØVBORG: But first promise me—give me your word you'll never let Thea know what I'm going to tell you now.

HEDDA: You have it.

LØVBORG: All right. It isn't true, what I just told her.

HEDDA: About the manuscript?

LØVBORG: Yes. I have not torn it up. Not thrown it in the sea, either.

HEDDA: But then—where is it?

LØVBORG: I've destroyed it just the same. Really, I have, Hedda!

HEDDA: I don't understand.

LØVBORG: Thea said that what I had done seemed to her like murdering a child.

HEDDA: Yes—she did.

LØVBORG: But killing a child, that's not the worst thing a father can do to it.

HEDDA: No?

LØVBORG: No. And the worst is what I don't want Thea to know.

HEDDA: What *is* the worst?

LØVBORG: Hedda—suppose a man, say, early in the morning, after a stupid, drunken night—suppose he comes home to his child's mother and says: Listen, I've been in such and such a place. I've been here— and I've been there. And I had our child with me. In all those places. And the child is lost. Gone. Vanished. I'll be damned if I know where it is. Who's got hold of it—

HEDDA: Yes—but when all is said and done—it is only a book, you know.

LØVBORG: Thea's pure soul was in that book.

HEDDA: I realize that.

LØVBORG: Then you surely also realize that she and I can have no future together.

HEDDA: Where do you go from here?

LØVBORG: Nowhere. Just finish everything off. The sooner the better.

HEDDA (*a step closer*): Listen—Eilert Løvborg—Couldn't you make sure it's done beautifully?

LØVBORG: Beautifully? (*Smiles.*) With vine leaves in the hair, as you used to say.

HEDDA: Oh no. I don't believe in vine leaves any more. But still beautifully! For once. Goodbye. Go now. And don't come back.

LØVBORG: Goodbye, Mrs. Tesman. Give my regards to Jørgen Tesman. (*He is about to leave.*)

HEDDA: Wait! I want to give you something—a remembrance. (*Goes to the desk, opens the drawer, takes out the gun case. Returns to LØVBORG with one of the revolvers.*)

LØVBORG: The gun? That's the remembrance?

HEDDA (*nods slowly*): Do you recognize it? It was pointed at you once.

LØVBORG: You should have used it then.

HEDDA: Take it! *You* use it.

LØVBORG (*pockets the gun*): Thanks!

HEDDA: And beautifully, Eilert Løvborg! That's all I ask!

LØVBORG: Goodbye, Hedda Gabler. (*Exits, right.*)

(HEDDA *listens by the door for a moment. Then she crosses to the desk, takes out the manuscript, glances inside the cover, pulls some of the pages halfway out and looks at them. Carries the whole manuscript over to the chair by the stove. She sits down with the parcel in her lap. After a moment she opens the stove and then the manuscript.*)

HEDDA (*throws a bundle of sheets into the fire, whispers*): Now I'm burning your child, Thea. You—curlyhead! (*Throws more sheets in.*) Your and Eilert Løvborg's child. (*Throws all the rest of the manuscript into the stove.*) I am burning—I am burning your child.

ACT IV

(*The same rooms at the* TESMANS'. *Evening. The front room is dark. The inner room is lighted by the ceiling lamp over the table. Portieres cover the French doors.*

HEDDA, *in black, is walking up and down in the dark of the front room. She goes into the inner room, turning left in the doorway. She is heard playing a few bars on the piano. She reappears and comes forward again.* BERTE *enters from the right side of the inner room. She carries a lighted lamp, which she puts down on the table in front of the corner sofa. Her eyes show signs of weeping; she wears black ribbons on her uniform. She exits quietly, right.* HEDDA *goes over to the French windows, looks between the portieres into the dark. Presently* MISS TESMAN, *in mourning, with hat and veil, enters, right.* HEDDA *walks over to meet her, gives her her hand.*)

MISS TESMAN: Yes, my dearest Hedda—here you see me in my garb of grief. For now at last my poor sister has fought her fight to the end.

HEDDA: I already know—as you see. Tesman sent word.

MISS TESMAN: Yes, he promised he'd do that. But I thought that to you, Hedda—here in the house of life—I really ought to bring you the tidings of death myself.

HEDDA: That is very kind of you.

MISS TESMAN: Ah, but Rina shouldn't have died just now. There should be no mourning in Hedda's house at this time.

HEDDA (*changing the topic*): I understand she had a very quiet end.

MISS TESMAN: Oh so beautiful, so peaceful! She left us so quietly! And then the unspeakable happiness of seeing Jørgen one more time! To say goodbye to him to her heart's content! Isn't he back yet?

HEDDA: No. He wrote I mustn't expect him back very soon. But do sit down.

MISS TESMAN: No—no, thanks, my dear, blessed Hedda. Not that I wouldn't like to. But I don't have much time. I must go back and prepare her as best I can. I want her to look right pretty when she goes into her grave.

HEDDA: Is there anything I can help you with?

MISS TESMAN: I won't have you as much as think of it! That's not for Hedda Tesman to lend a hand to. Or lend thoughts to, either. Not now, of all times!

HEDDA: Oh—thoughts! We can't always control our thoughts—

MISS TESMAN (*still preoccupied*): Ah yes—such is life. At home we're making a shroud for Rina. And here, too, there'll be sewing to do soon, I expect. But of quite a different kind, thank God!

(TESMAN *enters, right.*)

HEDDA: Finally!

TESMAN: You here, Aunt Julle? With Hedda? Just think!

MISS TESMAN: I am just about to leave, Jørgen dear. Well—did you do all the things you promised me you'd do?

TESMAN: No, I'm afraid I forgot half of them, Auntie. I'd better run in again tomorrow. I'm all confused today. I can't seem to keep my thoughts together.

MISS TESMAN: But dearest Jørgen—you mustn't take it this way!

TESMAN: Oh, I mustn't? How do you mean?

MISS TESMAN: You ought to be joyful in the midst of your sorrow. Glad for what's happened. The way I am.

TESMAN: Oh yes, of course. You're thinking of Aunt Rina.

HEDDA: You're going to feel lonely now, Miss Tesman.

MISS TESMAN: The first few days, yes. But I hope that won't last long. Dear Rina's little parlor won't be empty for long, if I can help it!

TESMAN: Oh? And who do you want to move in there. Hm?

MISS TESMAN: Ah—it's not very hard to find some poor soul who needs nursing and comfort.

HEDDA: And you really want to take on such a burden all over again?

MISS TESMAN: Heavens! God forgive you, child—burden? It has not been a burden to me.

HEDDA: Still—a stranger, who—

MISS TESMAN: Oh, it's easy to make friends with sick people. And I need somebody to live for, too. Well, the Lord be praised, maybe soon there'll be a thing or two an old aunt can turn her hand to here.

HEDDA: Oh, never mind us—

TESMAN: Yes, just think—how lovely it would be for the three of us, if only—

HEDDA: If only—?

TESMAN (*uneasy*): Oh, nothing. I daresay it will all work out. Let's hope it will, hm?

MISS TESMAN: Well, well. I can see that you two have something to talk about. (*With a smile.*) And perhaps Hedda has something to tell *you,* Jørgen! Goodbye! I'm going home to Rina, now. (*Turns around in the door.*) Dear, dear—how strange to think—Now Rina is both with me and with Jochum!

TESMAN: Yes, just think, Aunt Julle! Hm?

(MISS TESMAN *exits, right.*)

HEDDA (*coldly scrutinizing* TESMAN): I wouldn't be at all surprised if you aren't more affected by this death than she is.

TESMAN: Oh, it isn't just Aunt Rina's death, Hedda. It's Eilert I worry about.

HEDDA (*quickly*): Any news about him?

TESMAN: I went over to his room this afternoon to tell him the manuscript is safe.

HEDDA: Well? And didn't you see him?

TESMAN: No. He wasn't home. But I ran into Mrs. Elvsted and she told me he'd been here early this morning.

HEDDA: Yes, right after you'd left.

TESMAN: And he said he'd torn up the manuscript? Did he really say that?

HEDDA: Yes. So he claimed.

TESMAN: But dear God—in that case he really must have been out of his mind! So I assume you didn't give it to him either, hm, Hedda?

HEDDA: No. He didn't get it.

TESMAN: But you told him we had it, of course?

HEDDA: No. (*Quickly.*) Did you tell Mrs. Elvsted?

TESMAN: No, I didn't want to. But you ought to have told him, Hedda. Just think—what if he does something rash—something to hurt himself! Give me the manuscript, Hedda! I want to rush down to him with it right this minute. Where is it?

HEDDA (*cold, motionless, one arm resting on the chair*): I haven't got it any more.

TESMAN: You haven't got it! What do you mean by that?

HEDDA: I burned it—the whole thing.

TESMAN (*jumps up*): Burned it! Burned Eilert's book!

HEDDA: Don't shout. The maid might hear you.

TESMAN: Burned it? But good God—no, no, no—! This can't be—!

HEDDA: It is, all the same.

TESMAN: But do you realize what you've done, Hedda? It's illegal! Willful destruction of lost property! You just ask Judge Brack! He'll tell you!

HEDDA: You'd better not talk about this to anyone—the Judge or anybody else.

TESMAN: But how could you do a thing like that! I never heard anything like it! What came over you? What can possibly have been going on in your head? Answer me! Hm?

HEDDA (*suppresses an almost imperceptible smile*): I did it for your sake, Jørgen.

TESMAN: For my sake!

HEDDA: When you came back this morning and told me he had read aloud to you—

TESMAN: Yes, yes! What then?

HEDDA: You admitted you were jealous of him for having written such a book.

TESMAN: But good gracious—! I didn't mean it as seriously as all that!

HEDDA: All the same. I couldn't stand the thought that somebody else was to overshadow you.

TESMAN (*in an outburst of mingled doubt and joy*): Hedda—oh Hedda! Is it true what you're saying! But—but—but—I never knew you loved me like that! Just think!

HEDDA: In that case, I might as well tell you—that—just at this time— (*Breaks off, vehemently.*) No, no! You can ask Aunt Julle. She'll tell you.

TESMAN: I almost think I know what you mean, Hedda! (*Claps his hands.*) For goodness' sake! Can that really be so! Hm?

HEDDA: Don't shout so! The maid can hear you.

TESMAN (*laughing with exuberant joy*): The maid! Well, if you don't take the prize, Hedda! The maid—but that's Berte! I'm going to tell Berte myself this very minute!

HEDDA (*her hands clenched in despair*): Oh I'll die—I'll die, in all this!

TESMAN: In what, Hedda? Hm?

HEDDA (*cold and composed*): In all this—ludicrousness, Jørgen.

TESMAN: Ludicrous? That I'm so happy? Still—maybe I oughtn't to tell Berte, after all.

HEDDA: Oh, go ahead. What difference does it make?

TESMAN: No, not yet. But on my word—Aunt Julle must be told. And that you've started to call me "Jørgen," too! Just think! She'll be ever so happy—Aunt Julle will!

HEDDA: Even when you tell her that I have burned Eilert Løvborg's papers?

TESMAN: No, oh no! That's true! That about the manuscript—nobody must know about that. But to think that you'd burn for me, Hedda—I certainly want to tell *that* to Aunt Julle! I wonder now—is that sort of thing usual with young wives, hm?

HEDDA: Why don't you ask Aunt Julle about that, too?

TESMAN: I shall—I certainly shall, when I get the chance. (*Looks uneasy and disturbed again.*) But the manuscript! Good God—I don't dare to think what this is going to do to poor Eilert!

(MRS. ELVSTED, *dressed as on her first visit, wearing hat and coat, enters, right.*)

MRS. ELVSTED (*gives a hurried greeting, is obviously upset*): Oh Hedda, you must forgive me for coming here again!

HEDDA: What has happened, Thea?

TESMAN: Something to do with Eilert Løvborg again? Hm?

MRS. ELVSTED: Yes, yes—I'm so terribly afraid something's happened to him.

HEDDA (*seizing her arm*): Ah—you think so?

TESMAN: Oh dear—why do you think that, Mrs. Elvsted?

MRS. ELVSTED: I heard them talking about him in the boarding house, just as I came in. And people are saying the most incredible things about him today.

TESMAN: Yes, imagine! I heard that, too! And I can testify that he went straight home to bed! Just think!

HEDDA: And what did they say in the boarding house?

MRS. ELVSTED: Oh, I didn't find out anything. Either they didn't know any details or—They all became silent when they saw me. And I didn't dare to ask.

TESMAN (*pacing the floor uneasily*): We'll just have to hope—to hope that you heard wrong, Mrs. Elvsted!

MRS. ELVSTED: No, no. I'm sure it was he they were talking about. And somebody said something about the hospital or—

TESMAN: The hospital—!

HEDDA: Surely, that can't be so!

MRS. ELVSTED: I got so terribly frightened! So I went up to his room and asked for him there.

HEDDA: Could you bring yourself to do that, Thea?

MRS. ELVSTED: What else could I do? For I felt I just couldn't stand the uncertainty any longer.

TESMAN: But I suppose you didn't find him in, either, did you? Hm?

MRS. ELVSTED: No. And the people there didn't know anything about him. He hadn't been home since yesterday afternoon, they said.

TESMAN: Yesterday! Just think! How could they say that!

MRS. ELVSTED: I don't know what else to think—something bad must have happened to him!

TESMAN: Hedda, dear—? What if I were to walk downtown and ask around for him—?

HEDDA: No, no—don't you go and get mixed up in all this.

(JUDGE BRACK, *hat in hand, enters through the door, right, which* BERTE *opens and closes for him. He looks serious and greets the others in silence.*)

TESMAN: So here you are, Judge, hm?

BRACK: Yes. I had to see you this evening.

TESMAN: I can see you got Aunt Julle's message.

BRACK: That, too—yes.

TESMAN: Isn't it sad, though?

BRACK: Well, my dear Tesman—that depends on how you look at it.

TESMAN (*looks at him uncertainly*): Has something else happened?

BRACK: Yes.

HEDDA (*tense*): Something sad, Judge Brack?

BRACK: That, too, depends on how you look at it, Mrs. Tesman.

MRS. ELVSTED (*bursting out*): Oh, I'm sure it has something to do with Eilert Løvborg!

BRACK (*looks at her for a moment*): Why do you think that, Mrs. Elvsted? Maybe you already know something—?

MRS. ELVSTED (*confused*): No, no; not at all. It's just—

TESMAN: For heaven's sake, Brack, out with it!

BRACK (*shrugging his shoulders*): Well—unfortunately, Eilert Løvborg's in the hospital. Dying.

MRS. ELVSTED (*screams*): Oh God, oh God!

TESMAN: In the hospital! And dying!

HEDDA (*without thinking*): So soon—!

MRS. ELVSTED (*wailing*): And we didn't even part as friends, Hedda!

HEDDA (*whispers*): Thea, Thea—for heaven's sake—!

MRS. ELVSTED (*paying no attention to her*): I want to see him! I want to see him alive!

BRACK: Won't do you any good, Mrs. Elvsted. Nobody can see him.

MRS. ELVSTED: Then tell me what's happened to him! What?

TESMAN: For, surely, he hasn't himself—!

HEDDA: I'm sure he has.

TESMAN: Hedda! How can you—!

BRACK (*observing her all this time*): I am sorry to say that your guess is absolutely correct, Mrs. Tesman.

MRS. ELVSTED: Oh, how awful!

TESMAN: Did it himself! Just think!

HEDDA: Shot himself!

BRACK: Right again, Mrs. Tesman.

MRS. ELVSTED (*trying to pull herself together*): When did this happen, Judge?

BRACK: This afternoon. Between three and four.

TESMAN: But dear me—where can he have done a thing like that? Hm?

BRACK (*a little uncertain*): Where? Well—I suppose in his room. I don't really know—

MRS. ELVSTED: No, it can't have been there. For I was up there sometime between six and seven.

BRACK: Well, then, some other place. I really can't say. All I know is that he was found. He had shot himself—in the chest.

MRS. ELVSTED: Oh, how horrible to think! That he was to end like that!

HEDDA (*to* BRACK): In the chest?

BRACK: Yes—as I just told you.

HEDDA: Not the temple?

BRACK: In the chest, Mrs. Tesman.

HEDDA: Well, well—the chest is a good place, too.

BRACK: How is that, Mrs. Tesman?

HEDDA (*turning him aside*): Oh—nothing.

TESMAN: And you say the wound is fatal? Hm?

BRACK: No doubt about it—absolutely fatal. He's probably dead already.

MRS. ELVSTED: Yes, yes! I feel you're right! It's over! It's all over! Oh, Hedda!

TESMAN: But tell me—how do *you* know all this?

BRACK (*tersely*): A man on the force told me. One I had some business with.

HEDDA (*loudly*): At last a deed!

TESMAN (*appalled*): Oh dear—what are you saying, Hedda!

HEDDA: I am saying there is beauty in this.

BRACK: Well, now—Mrs. Tesman—

TESMAN: Beauty—! Just think!

MRS. ELVSTED: Oh, Hedda—how can you talk about beauty in a thing like this!

HEDDA: Eilert Løvborg has settled his account with himself. He has had the courage to do—what had to be done.

MRS. ELVSTED: But you mustn't believe it happened that way! He did it when he was not himself!

TESMAN: In despair! That's how!

HEDDA: He did not. I am certain of that.

MRS. ELVSTED: Yes he did! He was not himself! That's the way he tore up the book, too!

BRACK (*puzzled*): The book? You mean the manuscript? Has he torn it up?

MRS. ELVSTED: Yes, last night.

TESMAN (*whispers*): Oh, Hedda—we'll never get clear of all this!

BRACK: That is strange.

TESMAN (*walking the floor*): To think that this was to be the end of Eilert! Not to leave behind him anything that would have preserved his name—

MRS. ELVSTED: Oh, if only it could be put together again!

TESMAN: Yes, if only it could. I don't know what I wouldn't give—

MRS. ELVSTED: Maybe it can, Mr. Tesman.

TESMAN: What do you mean?

MRS. ELVSTED (*searching her dress pocket*): Look, I have kept these little slips he dictated from.

HEDDA (*a step closer*): Ah—!

TESMAN: You've kept them, Mrs. Elvsted? Hm?

MRS. ELVSTED: Yes. Here they are. I took them with me when I left. And I've had them in my pocket ever since—

TESMAN: Please, let me see—

MRS. ELVSTED (*gives him a pile of small paper slips*): But it's such a mess. Without any kind of system or order—!

TESMAN: But just think if we could make sense out of them, all the same! Perhaps if we helped each other—

MRS. ELVSTED: Oh yes! Let's try, anyway!

TESMAN: It will work! It *has* to work! I'll stake my whole life on this!

HEDDA: You, Jørgen? Your life?

TESMAN: Yes, or at any rate all the time I can set aside. My own collections can wait. Hedda, you understand—don't you? Hm? This is something I owe Eilert's memory.

HEDDA: Maybe so.

TESMAN: And now, my dear Mrs. Elvsted, we want to get to work. Good heavens, there's no point brooding over what's happened. Hm? We'll just have to acquire sufficient peace of mind to—

MRS. ELVSTED: All right, Mr. Tesman. I'll try to do my best.

TESMAN: Very well, then. Come over here. Let's look at these slips right away. Where can we sit? Here? No, it's better in the other room. If you'll excuse us, Judge! Come along, Mrs. Elvsted.

MRS. ELVSTED: Oh dear God—if only it were possible—!

(TESMAN *and* MRS. ELVSTED *go into the inner room. She takes off her hat and coat. Both sit down at the table under the hanging lamp and ab-*

sorb themselves in the slips. HEDDA *walks over toward the stove and sits down in the easy chair. After a while,* BRACK *walks over to her.*)

HEDDA (*in a low voice*): Ah, Judge—what a liberation there is in this thing with Eilert Løvborg!

BRACK: Liberation, Mrs. Tesman? Well, yes, for him perhaps one may say there was liberation of a kind—

HEDDA: I mean for me. There is liberation in knowing that there is such a thing in the world as an act of free courage. Something which becomes beautiful by its very nature.

BRACK (*smiles*): Well—dear Mrs. Tesman—

HEDDA: Oh I know what you're going to say! For you see—you really are a kind of specialist, too!

BRACK (*looks at her fixedly*): Eilert Løvborg has meant more to you than perhaps you're willing to admit, even to yourself. Or am I wrong?

HEDDA: I won't answer such questions. All I know is that Eilert Løvborg had the courage to live his own life. And then now—this—magnificence! The beauty of it! Having the strength and the will to get up and leave life's feast—so early—

BRACK: Believe me, Mrs. Tesman, this pains me, but I see it is necessary that I destroy a pretty illusion—

HEDDA: An illusion?

BRACK: Which could not have been maintained for very long, anyway.

HEDDA: And what is that?

BRACK: He didn't shoot himself—of his own free will.

HEDDA: Not of his own—!

BRACK: No. To tell the truth, the circumstances of Eilert Løvborg's death aren't exactly what I said they were.

HEDDA (*tense*): You've held something back? What?

BRACK: For the sake of poor Mrs. Elvsted I used a few euphemisms.

HEDDA: What?

BRACK: First—he is already dead.

HEDDA: In the hospital.

BRACK: Yes. And without regaining consciousness.

HEDDA: What else haven't you told?

BRACK: That fact that it didn't happen in his room.

HEDDA: Well, does that really make much difference?

BRACK: Some. You see—Eilert Løvborg was found shot in Miss Diana's bedroom.

HEDDA (*is about to jump up, but sinks back*): That's impossible, Judge Brack! He can't have been there again today!

BRACK: He was there this afternoon. He came to claim something he said they had taken from him. Spoke some gibberish about a lost child—

HEDDA: So that's why—!

BRACK: I thought maybe he meant his manuscript. But now I hear he has destroyed that himself. So I suppose it must have been something else.

HEDDA: I suppose. So it was there—so they found him there?

BRACK: Yes. With a fired gun in his pocket. Mortally wounded.

HEDDA: Yes—in the chest.

BRACK: No—in the gut.

HEDDA (*looks at him with an expression of disgust*): That, too! What is this curse that turns everything I touch into something ludicrous and low!

BRACK: There is something else, Mrs. Tesman. Something I'd call—nasty.

HEDDA: And what is that?

BRACK: The gun they found—

HEDDA (*breathless*): What about it?

BRACK: He must have stolen it.

HEDDA (*jumps up*): Stolen! That's not true! He didn't!

BRACK: Anything else is impossible. He *must* have stolen it.—Shhh!

(TESMAN *and* MRS. ELVSTED *have risen from the table and come forward into the front room.*)

TESMAN (*with papers in both hands*): D'you know, Hedda—you can hardly see in there with that lamp! Just think!

HEDDA: I am thinking.

TESMAN: I wonder if you'd let us use your desk, hm?

HEDDA: Certainly, if you like. (*Adds quickly.*) Wait a minute, though! Let me clear it off a bit first.

TESMAN: Ah, there's no need for that, Hedda. There's plenty of room.

HEDDA: No, no. I want to straighten it up. I'll carry all this in here. I'll put it on top of the piano for the time being.

(*She has pulled an object, covered by note paper, out of the bookcase. She puts several other sheets of paper on top of it and carries the whole pile into the left part of the inner room.* TESMAN *puts the papers down on the desk and moves the lamp from the corner table over to the desk. He and* MRS. ELVSTED *sit down and resume their work.* HEDDA *returns.*)

HEDDA (*behind* MRS. ELVSTED'S *chair, softly ruffling her hair*): Well, little Thea—how is Eilert Løvborg's memorial coming along?

MRS. ELVSTED (*looks up at her, discouraged*): Oh God—I'm sure it's going to be terribly hard to make anything out of all this.

TESMAN: But we have to. We just don't have a choice. And putting other people's papers in order—that's just the thing for me.

(HEDDA *walks over to the stove and sits down on one of the ottomans.* BRACK *stands over her, leaning on the easy chair.*)

HEDDA (*whispers*): What were you saying about the gun?

BRACK (*also softly*): That he must have stolen it.

HEDDA: Why, necessarily?

BRACK: Because any other explanation ought to be out of the question, Mrs. Tesman.

HEDDA: Oh?

BRACK (*looks at her for a moment*): Eilert Løvborg was here this morning, of course. Isn't that so?

HEDDA: Yes.

BRACK: Were you alone with him?

HEDDA: Yes, for a while.

BRACK: You didn't leave the room while he was here?

HEDDA: No.

BRACK: Think. Not at all? Not even for a moment?

HEDDA: Well—maybe just for a moment—out in the hall.

BRACK: And where was the gun case?

HEDDA: In the—

BRACK: Mrs. Tesman?

HEDDA: On the desk.

BRACK: Have you looked to see if both guns are still there?

HEDDA: No.

BRACK: You needn't bother. I saw the gun they found on Løvborg, and I knew it immediately. From yesterday—and from earlier occasions, too.

HEDDA: Perhaps you have it?

BRACK: No, the police do.

HEDDA: What are the police going to do with it?

BRACK: Try to find the owner.

HEDDA: Do you think they will?

BRACK (*leans over her, whispers*): No, Hedda Gabler—not as long as I keep quiet.

HEDDA (*with a hunted look*): And if you don't?

BRACK (*shrugs his shoulders*): Of course, there's always the chance that the gun was stolen.

HEDDA (*firmly*): Rather die!

BRACK (*smiles*): People *say* things like that. They don't *do* them.

HEDDA (*without answering*): And if the gun was not stolen—and if they find the owner—then what happens?

BRACK: Well, Hedda—then comes the scandal!

HEDDA: The scandal!

BRACK: Yes—the scandal. That you are so afraid of. You will of course be required to testify. Both you and Miss Diana. Obviously, she'll have to explain how the whole thing happened. Whether it was accident or homicide. Did he try to pull the gun out of his pocket to threaten her? And did it fire accidentally? Or did she grab the gun away from him, shoot him, and put it back in his pocket? She might just possibly have done that. She's a pretty tough girl—Miss Diana.

HEDDA: But this whole disgusting mess has nothing to do with me.

BRACK: Quite so. But you'll have to answer the question: Why did you give Eilert Løvborg the gun? And what inferences will be drawn from the fact that you did?

HEDDA (*lowers her head*): That's true. I hadn't thought of that.

BRACK: Well—luckily, there's nothing to worry about as long as I don't say anything.

HEDDA (*looks up at him*): So then I'm in your power, Judge. From now on you can do anything you like with me.

BRACK (*in an even softer whisper*): Dearest Hedda—believe me, I'll not misuse my position.

HEDDA: In your power, all the same. Dependent on your will. Servant to your demands. Not free. Not free! (*Rises suddenly.*) No—I can't stand that thought! Never!

BRACK (*looks at her, half mockingly*): Most people submit to the inevitable.

HEDDA (*returning his glance*): Perhaps. (*Walks over to the desk. Suppresses a smile and mimics* TESMAN'S *way of speaking.*) Well? Do you think you can do it, Jørgen? Hm?

TESMAN: Lord knows, Hedda. Anyway, I can already see it will take months.

HEDDA (*still mimicking*): Just think! (*Runs her hands lightly through* MRS. ELVSTED'S *hair.*) Doesn't this seem strange to you, Thea? Sitting here with Tesman—just the way you used to with Eilert Løvborg?

MRS. ELVSTED: Oh dear—if only I could inspire your husband, too!

HEDDA: Oh, I'm sure that will come—in time.

TESMAN: Well, yes—do you know, Hedda? I really think I begin to feel something of the kind. But why don't you go and talk to the Judge again?

HEDDA: Isn't there anything you two can use me for?

TESMAN: No, not a thing, dear. (*Turns around.*) From now on, you must be good enough to keep Hedda company, my dear Judge!

BRACK (*glancing at* HEDDA): I'll be only too delighted.

HEDDA: Thank you. But I'm tired tonight. I think I'll go and lie down for a while.

TESMAN: Yes, you do that, dear; why don't you? Hm?

(HEDDA *goes into the inner room, closes the portieres behind her. Brief pause. Suddenly, she is heard playing a frenzied dance tune on the piano.*)

MRS. ELVSTED (*jumps up*): Oh God! What's that!

TESMAN (*running to the doorway*): But dearest Hedda—you mustn't play dance music tonight, for goodness' sake! Think of Aunt Rina! And Eilert, too!

HEDDA (*peeks in from between the portieres*): And Aunt Julle. And everybody. I'll be quiet. (*She pulls the portieres shut again.*)

TESMAN (*back at the desk*): I don't think it's good for her to see us at such a melancholy task. I'll tell you what, Mrs. Elvsted. You move in with Aunt Julle, and then I'll come over in the evenings. Then we can sit and work over there. Hm?

MRS. ELVSTED: Maybe that would be better—

HEDDA (*from the inner room*): I hear every word you're saying, Tesman. And how am I going to spend my evenings?

TESMAN (*busy with the papers*): Oh, I'm sure Judge Brack will be good enough to come out and see you, anyway.

BRACK (*in the easy chair, calls out gaily*): Every single night, as far as I'm concerned, Mrs. Tesman! I'm sure we're going to have a lovely time, you and I!

HEDDA (*loud and clear*): Yes, don't you think that would be nice, Judge Brack? You—sole cock-o-the walk—

(*A shot is heard from the inner room.* TESMAN, MRS. ELVSTED, *and* JUDGE BRACK *all jump up.*)

TESMAN: There she is, fooling with those guns again.

(*He pulls the portieres apart and runs inside.* MRS. ELVSTED *also.* HEDDA, *lifeless, is lying on the sofa. Cries and confusion.* BERTE, *flustered, enters, right.*)

TESMAN (*shouts to* BRACK): She's shot herself! In the temple! Just think!

BRACK (*half stunned in the easy chair*): But, merciful God—! One just doesn't *do* that!

During the second half of his playwriting career Ibsen produced plays almost exactly on a two-year schedule and by the daily work habits of a punctilious clerk. The genius that revolutionized the nineteenth-century theater apparently worked best by the discipline of both clock and calendar.

After the completion of one play his mind lay fallow for a year, slowly generating new motifs. Actual work on a new play began with note-taking and sketching of character descriptions and fragments of dialogue. The writing itself took only a few months of summer and fall. The last month or so Ibsen revised his first draft, rarely altering basics in theme or plot but often adding telling details of imagery and characterization. In *Hedda Gabler* Tesman's fussy "just think"'s and "hm?"'s, the slipper episode in Act I, Hedda's phrase "vine leaves in the hair," and the many references to her and Thea Elvsted's hair, were all added during revision. The second draft, executed in a meticulous hand, was sent off to the printer in Copenhagen, to be published in time for the Christmas trade. In addition to being a bit of a philistine and pedant Ibsen was also an excellent businessman.

The genesis of *Hedda Gabler* followed this general scheme. The play was written between July–August and November, 1890, published on December 16, and first performed (in Munich) on January 31, 1891.

It was not an unqualified success. By 1890, both critical and popular consensus had decided that Ibsen was a problem playwright of implicit social and moral reform. One walked away from his plays disturbed or even possibly irritated and scandalized, but salutarily provoked to serious thought about oneself and one's society, one's moral sensitivity alerted and refined. With this preconception it was a little difficult to know exactly what one was supposed to make of this story of "a pointless suicide ending a useless life," as one critic summed it up. Here was no obvious problem—beyond, possibly, that of what the bourgeois housewife is to do with her time—no moral, not even a provocative slogan like *Rosmersholm's* "joyous guiltlessness" and *The Lady of the Sea's* "freedom with responsibility." There was only a Bacchic image, mystifying and a little lost in the contemporary drawing room. To observe that Brack's final speech was Ibsen's retort to critics who had presumed to find certain of his earlier plays implausible—"One just doesn't *do* that!"—was clever, but it clearly did not account for the *play*. Interpretation would have to come to grips with Hedda herself.

Is she a sardonic sequel to Nora in *A Doll's House*, a twisted product of wifely emancipation, the caged pet turned beast of the jungle? Does she, like Oswald in *Ghosts*, belong to Ibsen's "huge family of victims of bourgeois morality," her *joie de vivre* perverted by conventional hypocrisy to cowardly spite, her passions to prurient curiosity? Is she the eternal female incarnate, "splendidly immoral"? Is the play an allegory on woman's nature, with Hedda, Thea, Aunt Julle, and Miss Diana representing, respectively, woman's Will, Soul, Heart, and Body? Is it "pure psychological drama," a study in frigidity and irrational obsession, a portrait of an abnormal lady? And as such, is it, as Chekhov suggested, shallow melodrama, because the much deeper real-life tragedy is that a Hedda Gabler does *not* shoot herself? And does Hedda herself, whatever her larger significance, come across the footlights as a believable human being? Gerhard Gran, a contemporary Norwegian critic, did not think so:

> My imagination cannot grasp her as . . . one, single, integrated person. She falls apart in contradictions, and I don't find the common denominator. . . . When I think of her now, a few weeks after reading the play, I think of a rather odd woman, who astonished me with her strange behavior, who excited my curiosity without capturing my interest.

The critical difficulty is not to separate valid from invalid in this welter of views, but to apprehend their several truths as something other than an amorphous aggregate of opinion. The difficulty is compounded by our tendency to make the play coextensive with the title character. This probably underlies Gran's bewilderment. It has made of the play a wonderful, if sometimes rather showy, vehicle for great actresses, and it has helped to conceal such glaring dramatic flaws as the pretentiously demoniac doom of the Byronic Løvborg, unconvincing alike as genius of sociology and as conqueror of women, and the air of strain and contrivance that surrounds the checkered fortune of his manuscript (including Ibsen's amusing concept of scholarship as a pocket full of notes). But it has also isolated Hedda from her dramatic context. She has become a case history. Critics ask how she became what she has become and ignore what happens in the play.

This is not to deny that Hedda is both a fascinating and a consummate psychological portrait or that she represents a type of general validity, and of validity perhaps more urgent today than in the 1890's. But it is to insist that Hedda, as individual and type, emerges from the traffic on the stage and is not a preconceived postulate of psychology, exhibited, for greater vividness, in her natural habitat. In her, Ibsen prefigured a psyche felt to be peculiarly modern: the atomized self, the alienated identity. He anticipated a major theme—*the* major theme?—of contemporary drama. But whereas the expressionists and the semi-surrealistic absurdists put the fragments of the broken personality on stage as separate characters, scenically objectifying the soul's war with itself, somewhat in the manner of the medieval morality play, Ibsen achieved the same end within the limiting realist conventions of stage illusion and plot coherence—given the theme, a far more difficult achievement. Hedda's case is that of the modern existentialist anti-hero who witnesses his own dereliction and disintegration in a meaningless world made boring by overstimulation and violent with inarticulateness. As relativist skeptics of absolutes and formulas we are less likely than some of the positivist critics of the '90's or the Freudians and the social conscience school of the 1920's and '30's to consider *Hedda Gabler* a failure because Hedda herself is a riddle the solution to which Ibsen failed to embody in his play. We respond to the play to the extent to which we can sense Hedda as a stage presence, a kind of modern Medea, but the force of that presence is a function of the pervasive patterns of ironies, of images of words and actions, of juxtapositions of moral values and of moments of farce, melodrama, and tragedy, in which it exists.

Hedda's fatal crisis plays itself out in a sequence of calls. Visiting as recurrent stage event not only establishes the upper-class milieu that has shaped her personality and causes the middle-class manners of Tesman and Aunt Julle to set her teeth on edge. It also serves as plausible pretext for keeping several people coming and going within a single setting and ironically emphasizes Hedda's position as hostess "at home." The other characters come and go, active beyond the September smell of mortality in the late Mrs. Falk's rooms. They are rooms that never turn into a home for Hedda. She is trapped in the drawing room she seems to dominate. Early in Act I Aunt Julle and Berte evoke for us a picture of Hedda on horseback. The contrast between the aristocratic girl rider's free and graceful movements and her present situation as bored and restless passenger on a train endlessly journeying through middle-class domesticity lends pathos to the somewhat obvious point of the title: that she is her father's daughter rather than her husband's wife.

Three kinds of people move in and out of her enclosed existence, each associated with a different realm of values. There is Brack's world of elegant sophistication, a world of wit, grace, social form, and ruthless libertinism. There is the decent and cozy world of the aunts, its virtues genuine though tame, its narrow horizons stable, its kindly concerns trivial. Tesman, bookful blockhead, well-meaning and slippered, is its characteristic product. And there is the triply oriented world of Løvborg, part brilliant intellectual vistas (though Ibsen never lets us share them), part manly rehabilitation under the influence of a good woman, part debauch with demimondaines. Hedda is in the middle of the triangle, homeless in her new home, dislocated, in search of an identity fragmentized by the pressures—for propriety, for marriage—which imparted attitudes have exerted on her Dionysiac personality. Identityless, she is in the grip of impulses she neither comprehends nor controls. Seeking to live vicariously through Løvborg, she succeeds only in killing both him and herself. Her mania for manipulating men's lives—and Tesman in politics is even more grotesque than Løvborg with vine leaves in his hair—is a symptom of her inner emptiness. By birth and background she belongs to Brack, by temperament and her own half-understood ideology to Løvborg, by matrimony to Tesman. The split corrupts her. In tense boredom she can only define herself by fierce devotion to manners and prudence. She substitutes convention for morality. She refuses to have her legs looked at but calmly contemplates a discreet affair. She excites passionate men and ends up married to an old maid. Life's primary realities, sex, pregnancy, birth, and death, are all hateful to her. Her two decisive actions in the play both entail infanticide, one symbolic, the other real. Her erotic frustration precedes her marriage. Two of the three or four glimpses we get of her past show her in destructive poses: the schoolgirl on a staircase threatening to burn off her friend's beautiful hair, the affronted young lady threatening her overeager lover with a gun. It is one of the play's many ironic paradoxes that Thea, a life force of pure femininity (the contrasting symbolic values that attach to her and Hedda's hair are relevant in this connection), whose emblem is a little child, is literally childless, whereas Hedda, deadly as her pistols, is pregnant. That "lively" is Hedda's favorite adjective is another.

As in just about every one of Ibsen's plays of social realism the action is set in motion by an arrival/return, here the newlywed Tesmans' and Mrs. Elvsted's and Løvborg's. The past returning explosively in the present is the core action in Ibsen's dramas, evidence, perhaps, both that he shared the century's sense of causality and continuum in human affairs and that he rejected its prevailing belief in progress. Acts I and II take place in the morning and evening, respectively, of one day; Acts III and IV repeat the same pattern for the following day. But although the morning of Act III is earlier than that of Act I and the evening of Act IV later than that of Act II, the last two acts taken together are shorter than the first two. It is as if the tempo of Hedda's life accelerates after the sunny hush of the opening through scenes of more and more hectic social activity to the final gunshot. She is adrift on a river rushing toward its deadly rapids.

Consider another example of Ibsen's use of patterned action as vehicle for crucial meanings. In the beginning of Act IV Aunt Julle reports the death of the invalid Aunt Rina to Hedda. The occasion, as she says, represents a visit from the house of death to the house of life. But at the end of the act the contrast has been reversed. Thea will move into Aunt Rina's room, and there she and Tesman will resurrect her "child," whereas Hedda's suicide means that the empty rooms in the Tesman villa will not become nurseries. With their larger ramifications Aunt Rina's and Hedda's deaths, flanking Act IV, not only juxtapose two kinds of paralysis, one physical and one emotional, they also suggest the central moral polarity in the play: between the virtuous and unselfish world of the aunts, to which Berte already belongs, Thea naturally moves, and the erring Tesman at the end returns, and the negative world of the selfish hedonists, Hedda, Brack, and Løvborg.

If the play is thought of as dramatic pattern rather than as a polemic against the prudish upbringing of young Victorian ladies or a study in psychopathology, we see Hedda also as the main participant in a sequence of interlocking rivalries that maintains tension throughout the play and is an action–image of the flux and disharmony that characterize its social climate. Hedda and Thea are rivals for Løvborg already in Act I. Brack considers Løvborg a threat to his own hoped-for liaison with Hedda. There is talk of a competition for a professorship between Tesman and Løvborg. Although Tesman does not know it both his friends threaten his domestic felicity. At the end Thea and Hedda are once again rivals for the same man—Tesman, this time.

Their rivalry frames the entire action and is its ironic center. Hedda takes Løvborg away from Thea, but the sordid manner of his death nullifies her triumph. Upon this flawed success follows unmitigated defeat, as Hedda's husband, by virtue of the very quality she finds most ludicrous in him, his indefatigable scholarship, is about to become the second father of Thea's book-child with Løvborg. That Hedda does not love Tesman and therefore hardly takes his and Thea's intimacy much to heart is immaterial in this connection; it is the pattern that counts, the pattern manifest in Hedda's question, "Isn't there anything you two can use me for?" and Tesman's answer, "No, not a thing, dear." It spells

Thea's double triumph: as "mother" and as inspiring soul mate. Cleverer than her rival, Hedda yet loses to her on all fronts. The would-be liberator is herself caught. Realizing her defeat she disappears into the back room where the General's portrait hangs like an altarpiece over the sofa on which she is about to perform, in self-immolation, the deed of beauty and courage of which Løvborg has cheated her. She veils the sanctum from the sight of the others, plays out her frustrated love of life and freedom in one, last, wild burst of dance music, promises to be quiet—and fires her gun. If she is not allowed to break the decorous quiet by playing she can do so by dying.

In another way, also, the suicide scene gathers up the entire play in its imagery. Hedda escapes both Brack and scandal by doing exactly what Brack, with his "specialist's" assurance, had assumed "people don't do." The phrase haunts the play. Hedda herself uses it twice: once, apropos of Aunt Julle's hapless hat on the drawing-room chair, a second time apropos of the girl-with-the-gun from Løvborg's past. Thus, verbal echoes associate Hedda's death with two other, mutually contrasting, kinds of unconventionality: Aunt Julle's (actually Tesman's) gaucheries, and Miss Diana's (actually Hedda's own) erotic flamboyance. The curtain drops on a comical–grisly tableau, on the death of a neurotic woman, but also on the defeat of the social expertise, the moral evil, and the unscrupulous use of a constrictive convention, which Hedda, her impossible dream intact, frustrates by dying.

Miss Diana never appears on stage. Is it—also—because she represents the suppressed part of Hedda's psyche, the vital component in the complete and fulfilled woman she might have become in another kind of society? Their plot connection, at any rate, takes on a mythological resonance. Hedda shares with Miss Diana the role of Løvborg's *femme fatale*. She, too, once leveled one of General Gabler's guns at him, and in his death society lady and "tough girl," frigid wife and bohemian mistress, merge in the figure of the changeable goddess of the moon, fiercely and fatally asserting her virginally inviolate nature.

Anton Chekhov

The Cherry Orchard

Translated by Stark Young

Characters

RANEVSKAYA, LYUBOFF ANDREEVNA a *landowner*
ANYA *her daughter, seventeen years old*
VARYA *her adopted daughter, twenty-four years old*
GAYEFF, LEONID ANDREEVICH *brother of Ranevskaya*
LOPAHIN, YERMOLAY ALEXEEVICH a *merchant*
TROFIMOFF, PYOTR SERGEEVICH a *student*
SEMYONOFF-PISHTCHIK, BORIS BORISOVICH a *landowner*
CHARLOTTA IVANOVNA a *governess*
EPIHODOFF, SEMYON PANTELEEVICH a *clerk*
DUNYASHA a *maid*
FIERS a *valet, an old man of eighty-seven*
YASHA a *young valet*
A PASSERBY or STRANGER
THE STATIONMASTER
A POST-OFFICE CLERK
VISITORS, SERVANTS

Scene: *The action takes place on the estate of* L. A. RANEVSKAYA.

ACT I

(*A room that is still called the nursery. One of the doors leads into* ANYA'S *room. Dawn, the sun will soon be rising. It is May, the cherry trees are in blossom but in the orchard it is cold, with a morning frost.*

The windows in the room are closed. Enter DUNYASHA *with a candle and* LOPAHIN *with a book in his hand.*)

LOPAHIN: The train got in, thank God! What time is it?

DUNYASHA: It's nearly two. (*Blows out her candle.*) It's already daylight.

LOPAHIN: But how late was the train? Two hours at least. (*Yawning and stretching.*) I'm a fine one, I am, look what a fool thing I did! I drove here on purpose just to meet them at the station, and then all of a sudden I'd overslept myself! Fell asleep in my chair. How provoking!— You could have waked me up.

DUNYASHA: I thought you had gone. (*Listening.*) Listen, I think they are coming now.

LOPAHIN (*listening*): No—No, there's the luggage and one thing and another. (*A pause.*) Lyuboff Andreevna has been living abroad five years. I don't know what she is like now—She is a good woman. An easy-going, simple woman. I remember when I was a boy about fifteen, my father, who is at rest—in those days he ran a shop here in the village—hit me in the face with his fist, my nose was bleeding—We'd come to the yard together for something or other, and he was a little drunk. Lyuboff Andreevna, I can see her now, still so young, so slim, led me to the washbasin here in this very room. in the nursery. "Don't cry," she says, "little peasant, it will be well in time for your wedding"—(*A pause.*) Yes, little peasant—My father was a peasant truly, and here I am in a white waistcoat and yellow shoes. Like a pig rooting in a pastry shop—I've got this rich, lots of money, but if you really stop and think of it, I'm just a peasant—(*Turning the pages of a book.*) Here I was reading a book and didn't get a thing out of it. Reading and went to sleep. (*A pause.*)

DUNYASHA: And all night long the dogs were not asleep, they know their masters are coming.

LOPAHIN: What is it, Dunyasha, you're so—

DUNYASHA: My hands are shaking. I'm going to faint.

LOPAHIN: You're just so delicate, Dunyasha. And all dressed up like a lady, and your hair all done up! Mustn't do that. Must know your place.

(*Enter* EPIHODOFF, *with a bouquet: he wears a jacket and highly polished boots with a loud squeak. As he enters he drops the bouquet.*)

EPIHODOFF (*picking up the bouquet*): Look, the gardener sent these, he says to put them in the dining room. (*Giving the bouquet to* DUNYASHA.)

LOPAHIN: And bring me some kvass.

DUNYASHA: Yes, sir. (*Goes out.*)

EPIHODOFF: There is a morning frost now, three degrees of frost (*sighing*) and the cherries all in bloom. I cannot approve of our climate—I cannot. Our climate can never quite rise to the occasion. Listen, Yermolay Alexeevich, allow me to subtend, I bought myself, day before yesterday, some boots and they, I venture to assure you, squeak so that it is impossible. What could I grease them with?

LOPAHIN: Go on. You annoy me.

EPIHODOFF: Every day some misfortune happens to me. But I don't complain, I am used to it and I even smile.

(DUNYASHA *enters, serves* LOPAHIN *the kvass.*)

EPIHODOFF: I'm going. (*Stumbling over a chair and upsetting it.*) There (*as if triumphant*), there, you see, pardon the expression, a circumstance like that, among others—It is simply quite remarkable. (*Goes out.*)

DUNYASHA: And I must tell you, Yermolay Alexeevich, that Epihodoff has proposed to me.

LOPAHIN: Ah!

DUNYASHA: I don't know really what to—He is a quiet man but sometimes when he starts talking, you can't understand a thing he means. It's all very nice, and full of feeling, but just doesn't make any sense. I sort of like him. He loves me madly. He's a man that's unfortunate, every day there's something or other. They tease him around here, call him twenty-two misfortunes—

LOPAHIN (*cocking his ear*): Listen, I think they are coming—

DUNYASHA: They are coming! But what's the matter with me—I'm cold all over.

LOPAHIN: They're really coming. Let's go meet them. Will she recognize me? It's five years we haven't seen each other.

DUNYASHA (*excitedly*): I'm going to faint this very minute. Ah, I'm going to faint!

(*Two carriages can be heard driving up to the house.* LOPAHIN *and* DUNYASHA *hurry out. The stage is empty. In the adjoining rooms a noise begins.* FIERS *hurries across the stage, leaning on a stick; he has been to meet* LYUBOFF ANDREEVNA, *and wears an old-fashioned livery and a high hat; he mutters something to himself, but you cannot understand a word of it. The noise offstage gets louder and louder. A voice: "Look! Let's go through here—"* LYUBOFF ANDREEVNA, ANYA *and* CHARLOTTA IVANOVNA, *with a little dog on a chain, all of them dressed for traveling,* VARYA, *in a coat and kerchief,* GAYEFF, SEMYONOFF-PISHTCHIK, LOPAHIN, DUNYASHA, *with a bundle and an umbrella,* SERVANTS *with pieces of luggage—all pass through the room.*)

ANYA: Let's go through here. Mama, do you remember what room this is?

LYUBOFF ANDREEVNA (*happily, through her tears*): The nursery!

VARYA: How cold it is, my hands are stiff. (*To* LYUBOFF ANDREEVNA.) Your rooms, the white one and the violet, are just the same as ever, Mama.

LYUBOFF ANDREEVNA: The nursery, my dear beautiful room—I slept here when I was little—(*Crying.*) And now I am like a child—(*Kisses her brother and* VARYA, *then her brother again.*) And Varya is just the same as ever, looks like a nun. And I knew Dunyasha—(*Kisses* DUNYASHA.)

GAYEFF: The train was two hours late. How's that? How's that for good management?

CHARLOTTA (*to* PISHTCHIK): My dog he eats nuts too.

PISHTCHIK (*astonished*): Think of that!

(*Everybody goes out except* ANYA *and* DUNYASHA.)

DUNYASHA: We waited so long—(*Taking off* ANYA'S *coat and hat.*)

ANYA: I didn't sleep all four nights on the way. And now I feel so chilly.

DUNYASHA: It was Lent when you left, there was some snow then, there was frost, and now? My darling (*laughing and kissing her*), I waited so long for you, my joy, my life—I'm telling you now, I can't keep from it another minute.

ANYA (*wearily*): There we go again—

DUNYASHA: The clerk, Epihodoff, proposed to me after Holy Week.

ANYA: You're always talking about the same thing—(*Arranging her hair.*) I've lost all my hairpins—(*She is tired to the point of staggering.*)

DUNYASHA: I just don't know what to think. He loves me, loves me so!

ANYA (*looks in through her door, tenderly*): My room, my windows, it's just as if I had never been away. I'm home! Tomorrow morning I'll get up, I'll run into the orchard—Oh, if I only could go to sleep! I haven't slept all the way, I was tormented by anxiety.

DUNYASHA: Day before yesterday, Pyotr Sergeevich arrived.

ANYA (*joyfully*): Petya!

DUNYASHA: He's asleep in the bathhouse, he lives there. I am afraid, he says, of being in the way. (*Taking her watch from her pocket and looking at it.*) Somebody ought to wake him up. It's only that Varvara Mikhailovna told us not to. Don't you wake him up, she said.

VARYA (*enter* VARYA *with a bunch of keys at her belt*): Dunyasha, coffee, quick—Mama is asking for coffee.

DUNYASHA: This minute. (*Goes out.*)

VARYA: Well, thank goodness, you've come back. You are home again. (*Caressingly.*) My darling is back! My precious is back!

ANYA: I've had such a time.

VARYA: I can imagine!

ANYA: I left during Holy Week, it was cold then. Charlotta talked all the way and did her tricks. Why did you fasten Charlotta on to me—?

VARYA: But you couldn't have traveled alone, darling; not at seventeen!

ANYA: We arrived in Paris, it was cold there and snowing. I speak terrible French. Mama lived on the fifth floor; I went to see her; there were some French people in her room, ladies, an old priest with his prayer book, and the place was full of tobacco smoke—very dreary. Suddenly I began to feel sorry for Mama, so sorry, I drew her to me, held her close and couldn't let her go. Then Mama kept hugging me, crying—yes—

VARYA (*tearfully*): Don't—oh, don't—

ANYA: Her villa near Mentone she had already sold, she had nothing left, nothing. And I didn't have a kopeck left. It was all we could do to get here. And Mama doesn't understand! We sit down to dinner at a station and she orders, insists on the most expensive things and gives the waiters rouble tips. Charlotta does the same. Yasha too demands his share; it's simply dreadful. Mama has her butler, Yasha, we've brought him here—

VARYA: I saw the wretch.

ANYA: Well, how are things? Has the interest on the mortgage been paid?

VARYA: How could we?

ANYA: Oh, my God, my God—!

VARYA: In August the estate is to be sold—

ANYA: My God—!

LOPAHIN (*looking in through the door and mooing like a cow*): Moo-o-o—(*Goes away.*)

VARYA (*tearfully*): I'd land him one like that—(*Shaking her fist.*)

ANYA (*embracing* VARYA *gently*): Varya, has he proposed? (VARYA *shakes her head.*) But he loves you—Why don't you have it out with him, what are you waiting for?

VARYA: I don't think anything will come of it for us. He is very busy, he hasn't any time for me—And doesn't notice me. God knows, it's painful for me to see him—Everybody talks about our marriage, everybody congratulates us, and the truth is, there's nothing to it—it's all like a dream—(*In a different tone.*) You have a brooch looks like a bee.

ANYA (*sadly*): Mama bought it. (*Going toward her room, speaking gaily, like a child.*) And in Paris I went up in a balloon!

VARYA: My darling is back! My precious is back! (DUNYASHA *has returned with the coffee pot and is making coffee.* VARYA *is standing by the door.*) Darling, I'm busy all day long with the house and I go around thinking things. If only you could be married to a rich man, I'd be more at peace too, I would go all by myself to a hermitage—then to Kiev—to Moscow, and I'd keep going like that from one holy place to another—I would go on and on. Heavenly!

ANYA: The birds are singing in the orchard. What time is it now?

VARYA: It must be after two. It's time you were asleep, darling (*Going into* ANYA'S *room.*) Heavenly!

YASHA (YASHA *enters with a lap robe and a traveling bag. Crossing the stage airily*): May I go through here?

DUNYASHA: We'd hardly recognize you, Yasha; you've changed so abroad!

YASHA: Hm—And who are you?

DUNYASHA: When you left here, I was like that—(*Her hand so high from the floor.*) I'm Dunyasha, Fyodor Kozoyedoff's daughter. You don't remember!

YASHA: Hm—You little peach! (*Looking around before he embraces her; she shrieks and drops a saucer;* YASHA *hurries out.*)

VARYA (*at the door, in a vexed tone*): And what's going on here?

DUNYASHA (*tearfully*): I broke a saucer—

VARYA: That's good luck.

ANYA (*emerging from her room*): We ought to tell Mama beforehand: Petya is here—

VARYA: I told them not to wake him up.

ANYA (*pensively*): Six years ago our father died, a month later our brother Grisha was drowned in the river, such a pretty little boy, just seven. Mama couldn't bear it, she went away, went away without ever looking back—(*Shuddering.*) How I understand her, if she only knew I did. (*A pause.*) And Petya Trofimoff was Grisha's tutor, he might remind—

FIERS (*enter* FIERS; *he is in a jacket and white waistcoat. Going to the coffee urn, busy with it*): The mistress will have her breakfast here—(*Putting on white gloves.*) Is the coffee ready? (*To* DUNYASHA, *sternly.*) You! What about the cream?

DUNYASHA: Oh, my God—(*Hurrying out.*)

FIERS (*busy at the coffee urn*): Oh, you good-for-nothing—! (*Muttering to himself.*) Come back from Paris—And the master used to go to Paris by coach—(*Laughing.*)

VARYA: Fiers, what are you—?

FIERS: At your service. (*Joyfully.*) My mistress is back! It's what I've been waiting for! Now I'm ready to die—(*Crying for joy.*)

(LYUBOFF ANDREEVNA, GAYEFF and SEMYONOFF-PISHTCHIK *enter;* SEMYONOFF-PISHTCHIK *is in a podyovka of fine cloth and sharovary.* GAYEFF *enters; he makes gestures with his hands and body as if he were playing billiards.*)

LYUBOFF ANDREEVNA: How is it? Let me remember—Yellow into the corner! Duplicate in the middle!

GAYEFF: I cut into the corner. Sister, you and I slept here in this very room once, and now I am fifty-one years old, strange as that may seem—

LOPAHIN: Yes, time passes.

GAYEFF: What?

LOPAHIN: Time, I say, passes.

GAYEFF: And it smells like patchouli here.

ANYA: I'm going to bed. Good night, Mama. (*Kissing her mother.*)

LYUBOFF ANDREEVNA: My sweet little child. (*Kissing her hands.*) You're glad you are home? I still can't get myself together.

ANYA: Good-by, Uncle.

GAYEFF (*kissing her face and hands*): God be with you. How like your mother you are! (*To his sister.*) Lyuba, at her age you were exactly like her.

(ANYA *shakes hands with* LOPAHIN *and* PISHTCHIK, *goes out and closes the door behind her.*)

LYUBOFF ANDREEVNA: She's very tired.

PISHTCHIK: It is a long trip, I imagine.

VARYA (*to* LOPAHIN *and* PISHTCHIK): Well, then, sirs? It's going on three o'clock, time for gentlemen to be going.

LYUBOFF ANDREEVNA (*laughing*): The same old Varya. (*Drawing her to her and kissing her.*) There, I'll drink my coffee, then we'll all go. (FIERS *puts a small cushion under her feet.*) Thank you, my dear. I am used to coffee. Drink it day and night. Thank you, my dear old soul. (*Kissing* FIERS.)

VARYA: I'll go see if all the things have come. (*Goes out.*)

LYUBOFF ANDREEVNA: Is it really me sitting here? (*laughing.*) I'd like to jump around and wave my arms. (*Covering her face with her hands.*) But I may be dreaming! God knows I love my country, love it deeply, I couldn't look out of the car window, I just kept crying. (*Tearfully.*) However, I must drink my coffee. Thank you, Fiers, thank you, my dear old friend. I'm so glad you're still alive.

FIERS: Day before yesterday.

GAYEFF: He doesn't hear well.

LOPAHIN: And I must leave right now. It's nearly five o'clock in the morning, for Kharkov. What a nuisance! I wanted to look at you—talk—You are as beautiful as ever.

PISHTCHIK (*breathing heavily*): Even more beautiful—In your Paris clothes—It's a feast for the eyes—

LOPAHIN: Your brother, Leonid Andreevich here, says I'm a boor, a peasant money grubber, but that's all the same to me, absolutely. Let him say it. All I wish is you'd trust me as you used to, and your wonderful, touching eyes would look at me as they did. Merciful God! My father was a serf; belonged to your grandfather and your father; but you, your own self, you did so much for me once that I've forgotten all that and love you like my own kin—more than my kin.

LYUBOFF ANDREEVNA: I can't sit still—I can't. (*Jumping up and walking about in great excitement.*) I'll never live through this happiness—Laugh at me, I'm silly—My own little bookcase—! (*Kissing the bookcase.*) My little table!

GAYEFF: And in your absence the nurse here died.

LYUBOFF ANDREEVNA (*sitting down and drinking coffee*): Yes, may she rest in Heaven! They wrote me.

GAYEFF: And Anastasy died. Cross-eyed Petrushka left me and lives in town now at the police officer's. (*Taking out of his pocket a box of hard candy and sucking a piece.*)

PISHTCHIK: My daughter, Dashenka—sends you her greetings—

LOPAHIN: I want to tell you something very pleasant, cheerful. (*Glancing at his watch.*) I'm going right away. There's no time for talking. Well, I'll make it two or three words. As you know, your cherry orchard is to be sold for your debts; the auction is set for August twenty-second, but don't worry, my dear, you just sleep in peace, there's a way out of it. Here's my plan. Please listen to me. Your estate is only thirteen miles from town. They've run the railroad by it. Now if the cherry orchard and the land along the river were cut up into building lots and leased for summer cottages, you'd have at the very lowest twenty-five thousand roubles per year income.

GAYEFF: Excuse me, what rot!

LYUBOFF ANDREEVNA: I don't quite understand you, Yermolay Alexeevich.

LOPAHIN: At the very least you will get from the summer residents twenty-five roubles per year for a two-and-a-half acre lot, and if you post a notice right off, I'll bet you anything that by autumn you won't have a single patch of land free, everything will be taken. In a word, my congratulations, you are saved. The location is wonderful, the river's so deep. Except, of course, it all needs to be tidied up, cleared—For instance, let's say, tear all the old buildings down and this house, which is no good any more, and cut down the old cherry orchard—

LYUBOFF ANDREEVNA: Cut down? My dear, forgive me, you don't understand at all. If there's one thing in the whole province that's interesting—not to say remarkable—it's our cherry orchard.

LOPAHIN: The only remarkable thing about this cherry orchard is that it's very big. There's a crop of cherries once every two years and even that's hard to get rid of. Nobody buys them.

GAYEFF: This orchard is even mentioned in the encyclopedia.

LOPAHIN (*glancing at his watch*): If we don't cook up something and don't get somewhere, the cherry orchard and the entire estate will be sold at auction on the twenty-second of August. Do get it settled then! I swear there is no other way out. Not a one!

FIERS: There was a time, forty-fifty years ago when the cherries were dried, soaked, pickled, cooked into jam and it used to be—

GAYEFF: Keep quiet, Fiers.

FIERS: And it used to be that the dried cherries were shipped by the wagon-load to Moscow and to Kharkov. And the money there was! And the dried cherries were soft then, juicy, sweet, fragrant—They had a way of treating them then—

LYUBOFF ANDREEVNA: And where is that way now?

FIERS: They have forgotten it. Nobody remembers it.

PISHTCHIK (*to* LYUBOFF ANDREEVNA): What's happening in Paris? How is everything? Did you eat frogs?

LYUBOFF ANDREEVNA: I ate crocodiles.

PISHTCHIK: Think of it—!

LOPAHIN: Up to now in the country there have been only the gentry and the peasants, but now in summer the villa people too are coming in. All the towns, even the least big ones, are surrounded with cottages. In about twenty years very likely the summer resident will multiply enormously. He merely drinks tea on the porch now, but it might well happen that on this two-and-a-half acre lot of his, he'll go in for farming, and then your cherry orchard would be happy, rich, splendid—

GAYEFF (*getting hot*): What rot!

(*Enter* VARYA *and* YASHA.)

VARYA: Here, Mama. Two telegrams for you. (*Choosing a key and opening the old bookcase noisily.*) Here they are.

LYUBOFF ANDREEVNA: From Paris (*Tearing up the telegrams without reading them.*) Paris, that's all over—

GAYEFF: Do you know how old this bookcase is, Lyuba? A week ago I pulled out the bottom drawer and looked, and there the figures were burned on it. The bookcase was made exactly a hundred years ago. How's that? Eh? You might celebrate its jubilee. It's an inanimate object, but all the same, be that as it may, it's a bookcase.

PISHTCHIK (*in astonishment*): A hundred years—! Think of it—!

GAYEFF: Yes—quite something—(*Shaking the bookcase.*) Dear, honored bookcase! I saluted your existence, which for more than a hundred years has been directed toward the clear ideals of goodness and justice; your silent appeal to fruitful endeavor has not flagged in all the course of a hundred years, sustaining (*tearfully*) through the generations of our family, our courage and our faith in a better future and nurturing in us ideals of goodness and of a social consciousness.

(*A pause.*)

LOPAHIN: Yes.

LYUBOFF ANDREEVNA: You're the same as ever, Lenya.

GAYEFF (*slightly embarrassed*): Carom to the right into the corner pocket. I cut into the side pocket!

LOPAHIN (*glancing at his watch*): Well, it's time for me to go.

YASHA (*handing medicine to* LYUBOFF ANDREEVNA): Perhaps you'll take the pills now—

PISHTCHIK: You should never take medicaments, dear madam—They do neither harm nor good—Hand them here, dearest lady. (*He takes the pillbox, shakes the pills out into his palm, blows on them, puts them in his mouth and washes them down with kvass.*) There! Now!

LYUBOFF ANDREEVNA (*startled*): Why, you've lost your mind!

PISHTCHIK: I took all the pills.

LOPAHIN: Such a glutton!

(*Everyone laughs.*)

FIERS: The gentleman stayed with us during Holy Week, he ate half a bucket of pickles—(*Muttering.*)

LYUBOFF ANDREEVNA: What is he muttering about?

VARYA: He's been muttering like that for three years. We're used to it.

YASHA: In his dotage.

(CHARLOTTA IVANOVNA *in a white dress—she is very thin, her corset laced very tight—with a lorgnette at her belt, crosses the stage.*)

LOPAHIN: Excuse me, Charlotta Ivanovna, I haven't had a chance yet to welcome you. (*Trying to kiss her hand.*)

CHARLOTTA (*drawing her hand away*): If I let you kiss my hand, 'twould be my elbow next, then my shoulder—

LOPAHIN: No luck for me today. (*Everyone laughs.*) Charlotta Ivanovna, show us a trick!

CHARLOTTA: No. I want to go to bed. (*Exit.*)

LOPAHIN: In three weeks we shall see each other. (*Kissing* LYUBOFF ANDREEVNA'S *hand.*) Till then, good-by. It's time. (*To* GAYEFF.) See you soon. (*Kissing* PISHTCHIK.) See you soon. (*Shaking* VARYA'S *hand, then* FIERS' *and* YASHA'S.) I don't feel like going. (*To* LYUBOFF ANDREEVNA.) If you think it over and make up your mind about the summer cottages, let me know and I'll arrange a loan of something like fifty thousand roubles. Think it over seriously.

VARYA (*angrily*): Do go on, anyhow, will you!

LOPAHIN: I'm going, I'm going—(*Exit.*)

GAYEFF: Boor. However, pardon—Varya is going to marry him, it's Varya's little fiancé.

VARYA: Don't talk too much, Uncle.

LYUBOFF ANDREEVNA: Well, Varya, I should be very glad. He's a good man.

PISHTCHIK: A man, one must say truthfully—A most worthy—And my

Dashenka—says also that—she says all sorts of things—(*Snoring but immediately waking up.*) Nevertheless, dearest lady, oblige me— With a loan of two hundred and forty roubles—Tomorrow the interest on my mortgage has got to be paid—

VARYA (*startled*): There's not any money, none at all.

LYUBOFF ANDREEVNA: Really, I haven't got anything.

PISHTCHIK: I'll find it, somehow. (*Laughing.*) I never give up hope. There, I think to myself, all is lost, I am ruined and lo and behold—a railroad is put through my land and—they paid me. And then, just watch, something else will turn up—if not today, then tomorrow—Dashenka will win two hundred thousand—She has a ticket.

LYUBOFF ANDREEVNA: We've finished the coffee, now we can go to bed.

FIERS (*brushing GAYEFF's clothes, reprovingly*): You put on the wrong trousers again. What am I going to do with you!

VARYA (*softly*): Anya is asleep. (*Opening the window softly.*) Already the sun's rising—it's not cold. Look, Mama! What beautiful trees! My Lord, what air! The starlings are singing!

GAYEFF (*opening another window*): The orchard is all white. You haven't forgotten, Lyuba? That long lane there runs straight—as a strap stretched out. It glistens on moonlight nights. Do you remember? You haven't forgotten it?

LYUBOFF ANDREEVNA (*looking out of the window on to the orchard*): Oh, my childhood, my innocence! I slept in this nursery and looked out on the orchard from here, every morning happiness awoke with me, it was just as it is now, then, nothing has changed. (*Laughing with joy.*) All, all white! Oh, my orchard! After a dark, rainy autumn and cold winter, you are young again and full of happiness. The heavenly angels have not deserted you—If I only could lift the weight from my breast, from my shoulders, if I could only forget my past!

GAYEFF: Yes, and the orchard will be sold for debt, strange as that may seem.

LYUBOFF ANDREEVNA: Look, our dear mother is walking through the orchard—In a white dress! (*Laughing happily.*) It's she.

GAYEFF: Where?

VARYA: God be with you, Mama!

LYUBOFF ANDREEVNA: There's not anybody, it only seemed so. To the right, as you turn to the summerhouse, a little white tree is leaning there, looks like a woman—(*Enter TROFIMOFF, in a student's uniform, well worn, and glasses.*) What a wonderful orchard! The white masses of blossoms, the sky all blue.

TROFIMOFF: Lyuboff Andreevna! (*She looks around at him.*) I will just greet you and go immediately. (*Kissing her hand warmly.*) I was told to wait until morning, but I hadn't the patience—

(LYUBOFF ANDREEVNA *looks at him puzzled.*)

VARYA (*tearfully*): This is Petya Trofimoff—

TROFIMOFF: Petya Trofimoff, the former tutor of your Grisha—Have I really changed so?

(LYUBOFF ANDREEVNA *embraces him; and crying quietly.*)

GAYEFF (*embarrassed*): There, there, Lyuba.

VARYA (*crying*): I told you, Petya, to wait till tomorrow.

LYUBOFF ANDREEVNA: My Grisha—My boy—Grisha—Son—

VARYA: What can we do, Mama? It's God's will.

TROFIMOFF (*in a low voice, tearfully*): There, there—

LYUBOFF ANDREEVNA (*weeping softly*): My boy was lost, drowned—Why, Why, my friend? (*More quietly.*) Anya is asleep there, and I am talking so loud—Making so much noise—But why, Petya? Why have you lost your looks? Why do you look so much older?

TROFIMOFF: A peasant woman on the train called me a mangy-looking gentleman.

LYUBOFF ANDREEVNA: You were a mere boy then, a charming young student, and now your hair's not very thick any more and you wear glasses. Are you really a student still? (*Going to the door.*)

TROFIMOFF: Very likely I'll be a perennial student.

LYUBOFF ANDREEVNA (*kissing her brother, then* VARYA): Well, go to bed— You've grown older too, Leonid.

PISHTCHIK (*following her*): So that's it, we are going to bed now. Oh, my gout! I'm staying here—I'd like, Lyuboff Andreevna, my soul, tomorrow morning—Two hundred and forty roubles—

GAYEFF: He's still at it.

PISHTCHIK: Two hundred and forty roubles—To pay interest on the mortgage.

LYUBOFF ANDREEVNA: I haven't any money, my dove.

PISHTCHIK: I'll pay it back, my dear—It's a trifling sum—

LYUBOFF ANDREEVNA: Oh, very well, Leonid will give—You give it to him, Leonid.

GAYEFF: Oh, certainly, I'll give it to him. Hold out your pockets.

LYUBOFF ANDREEVNA: What can we do, give it, he needs it—He'll pay it back.

(LYUBOFF ANDREEVNA, TROFIMOFF, PISHTCHIK *and* FIERS *go out.* GAYEFF, VARYA *and* YASHA *remain.*)

GAYEFF: My sister hasn't yet lost her habit of throwing money away. (*To* YASHA.) Get away, my good fellow, you smell like hens.

YASHA (*with a grin*): And you are just the same as you used to be, Leonid Andreevich.

GAYEFF: What? (*To* VARYA.) What did he say?

VARYA (*to* YASHA): Your mother has come from the village, she's been sitting in the servants' hall ever since yesterday, she wants to see you—

YASHA: The devil take her!

VARYA: Ach, shameless creature!

YASHA: A lot I need her! She might have come tomorrow. (*Goes out.*)

VARYA: Mama is just the same as she was, she hasn't changed at all. If she could, she'd give away everything she has.

GAYEFF: Yes—If many remedies are prescribed for an illness, you may know the illness is incurable. I keep thinking, I rack my brains, I have many remedies, a great many, and that means, really, I haven't any at all. It would be fine to inherit a fortune from somebody, it would be fine to marry off our Anya to a very rich man, it would be fine to go to Yaroslavl and try our luck with our old aunt, the Countess. Auntie is very, very rich.

VARYA (*crying*): If God would only help us!

GAYEFF: Don't bawl! Auntie is very rich but she doesn't like us. To begin with, Sister married a lawyer, not a nobleman—(ANYA *appears at the door.*) Married not a nobleman and behaved herself, you could say, not very virtuously. She is good, kind, nice, I love her very much, but no matter how much you allow for the extenuating circumstances, you must admit she's a depraved woman. You feel it in her slightest movement.

VARYA (*whispering*): Anya is standing in the door there.

GAYEFF: What? (*A pause.*) It's amazing, something got in my right eye. I am beginning to see poorly. And on Thursday, when I was in the District Court—

(ANYA *enters.*)

VARYA: But why aren't you asleep, Anya?

ANYA: I don't feel like sleeping. I can't.

GAYEFF: My little girl—(*Kissing* ANYA's *face and hands.*) My child—(*Tearfully.*) You are not my niece, you are my angel, you are everything to me. Believe me, believe—

ANYA: I believe you, Uncle. Everybody loves you, respects you—But dear Uncle, you must keep quiet, just keep quiet—What were you saying, just now, about my mother, about your own sister? What did you say that for?

GAYEFF: Yes, yes—(*Putting her hand up over his face.*) Really, it's terrible! My God! Oh, God, save me! And today I made a speech to the bookcase—So silly! And it was only when I finished it that I could see it was silly.

VARYA: It's true, Uncle, you ought to keep quiet. Just keep quiet. That's all.

ANYA: If you kept quiet, you'd have more peace.

GAYEFF: I'll keep quiet. (*Kissing* ANYA's *and* VARYA's *hands.*) I'll keep quiet. Only this, it's about business. On Thursday I was in the District Court; well, a few of us gathered around and a conversation began about this and that, about lots of things; apparently it will be possible to arrange a loan on a promissory note to pay the bank the interest due.

VARYA: If the Lord would only help us!

GAYEFF: Tuesday I shall go and talk it over again. (*To* VARYA.) Don't bawl! (*To* ANYA. Your mother will talk to Lopahin; of course, he won't refuse her . . . And as soon as you rest up, you will go to Yaroslavl to your great-aunt, the Countess. There, that's how we will move from three directions, and the business is in the bag. We'll pay the interest. I am convinced of that—(*Putting a hard candy in his mouth.*) On my honor I'll swear, by anything you like, that the estate shall not be sold! (*Excitedly.*) By my happiness, I swear! Here's my hand, call me a worthless, dishonorable man, if I allow it to come up for auction! With all my soul I swear it!

ANYA (*a quieter mood returns to her; she is happy*): How good you are, Uncle, how clever! (*Embracing her uncle.*) I feel easy now! I feel easy! I'm happy!

FIERS (FIERS *enters, reproachfully*): Leonid Andreevich, have you no fear of God? When are you going to bed?

GAYEFF: Right away, right away. You may go, Fiers. For this once I'll undress myself. Well, children, beddy bye—More details tomorrow, and now, go to bed. (*Kissing* ANYA *and* VARYA.) I am a man of the eighties—It is a period that's not admired, but I can say, nevertheless, that I've suffered no little for my convictions in the course of my life. It is not for nothing that the peasant loves me. One must know the peasant! One must know from what—

ANYA: Again, Uncle!

VARYA: You, Uncle dear, keep quiet.

FIERS (*angrily*): Leonid Andreevich!

GAYEFF: I'm coming, I'm coming—Go to bed. A double bank into the side pocket! A clean shot—(*Goes out,* FIERS *hobbling after him.*)

ANYA: I feel easy now. I don't feel like going to Yaroslavl; I don't like Great-aunt, but still I feel easy. Thanks to Uncle. (*Sits down.*)

VARYA: I must get to sleep. I'm going. And there was unpleasantness here during your absence. In the old servants' quarters, as you know, live only the old servants: Yephemushka, Polya, Yevstignay, well, and Karp. They began to let every sort of creature spend the night with them—I didn't say anything. But then I hear they've spread the rumor

that I'd given orders to feed them nothing but beans. Out of stingi-
ness, you see—And all that from Yevstignay—Very well, I think to myself. If that's the way it is, I think to myself, then you just wait. I call
in Yevstignay—(*Yawning.*) He comes—How is it, I say, that you,
Yevstignay—You're such a fool—(*Glancing at* ANYA.) Anitchka!—(*A
pause.*) Asleep! (*Takes* ANYA *by her arm.*) Let's go to bed—Come
on!—(*Leading her.*) My little darling fell asleep! Come on—(*They go.
Far away beyond the orchard a shepherd is playing on a pipe.*
TROFIMOFF *walks across the stage and, seeing* VARYA *and* ANYA, *stops.*)
Shh—She is asleep—asleep—Let's go, dear.

ANYA (*softly, half dreaming*): I'm so tired—All the bells!—Uncle
—dear—And Mama and Uncle—Varya.

VARYA: Come on, my dear, come on. (*They go into* ANYA'S *room.*)

TROFIMOFF (*tenderly*): My little sun! My spring!

ACT II

(*A field. An old chapel, long abandoned, with crooked walls, near it
a well, big stones that apparently were once tombstones, and an old
bench. A road to the estate of* GAYEFF *can be seen. On one side poplars
rise, casting their shadows, the cherry orchard begins there. In the
distance a row of telegraph poles; and far, far away, faintly traced on
the horizon, is a large town, visible only in the clearest weather. The
sun will soon be down.* CHARLOTTA, YASHA *and* DUNYASHA *are sitting on
the bench;* EPIHODOFF *is standing near and playing the guitar; everyone
sits lost in thought.* CHARLOTTA *wears an old peak cap* (fourrage); *she
has taken a rifle from off her shoulders and is adjusting the buckle on
the strap.*)

CHARLOTTA (*pensively*): I have no proper passport, I don't know how old
I am—it always seems to me I'm very young. When I was a little girl,
my father and mother traveled from fair to fair and gave performances, very good ones. And I did *salto mortale* and different tricks.
And when Papa and Mama died, a German lady took me to live with
her and began teaching me. Good. I grew up. And became a governess. But where I came from and who I am I don't know—Who my
parents were, perhaps they weren't even married—I don't know.
(*Taking a cucumber out of her pocket and beginning to eat it.*) I don't
know a thing. (*A pause.*) I'd like so much to talk but there's not anybody. I haven't anybody.

EPIHODOFF (*playing the guitar and singing*): "What care I for the noisy
world, what care I for friends and foes."—How pleasant it is to play
the mandolin!

DUNYASHA: That's a guitar, not a mandolin. (*Looking into a little mirror and powdering her face.*)

EPIHODOFF: For a madman who is in love this is a mandolin—(*Singing.*) "If only my heart were warm with the fire of requited love."

(YASHA *sings with him.*)

CHARLOTTA: How dreadfully these people sing—Phooey! Like jackals.

DUNYASHA (*to* YASHA): All the same, what happiness to have been abroad.

YASHA: Yes, of course. I cannot disagree with you. (*Yawning and then lighting a cigar.*)

EPIHODOFF: That's easily understood. Abroad everything long since attained its complete development.

YASHA: That's obvious.

EPIHODOFF: I am a cultured man. I read all kinds of remarkable books, but the trouble is I cannot discover my own inclinations, whether to live or to shoot myself, but nevertheless, I always carry a revolver on me. Here it is—(*Showing a revolver.*)

CHARLOTTA: That's done. Now I am going. (*Slinging the rifle over her shoulder.*) You are a very clever man, Epihodoff, and a very terrible one; the women must love you madly. Brrrr-r-r-r! (*Going.*) These clever people are all so silly, I haven't anybody to talk with. I'm always alone, alone, I have nobody and—Who I am, why I am, is unknown—(*Goes out without hurrying.*)

EPIHODOFF: Strictly speaking, not touching on other subjects, I must state about myself, in passing, that fate treats me mercilessly, as a storm does a small ship. If, let us suppose, I am mistaken, then why, to mention one instance, do I wake up this morning, look, and there on my chest is a spider of terrific size—There, like that. (*Showing the size with both hands.*) And also I take some kvass to drink and in it I find something in the highest degree indecent, such as a cockroach. (*A pause.*) Have you read Buckle? (*A pause.*) I desire to trouble you, Avdotya Feodorovna, with a couple of words.

DUNYASHA: Speak.

EPIHODOFF: I have a desire to speak with you alone—(*Sighing.*)

DUNYASHA (*embarrassed*): Very well—But bring me my cape first—by the cupboard—It's rather damp here—

EPIHODOFF: Very well—I'll fetch it—Now I know what I should do with my revolver—(*Takes the guitar and goes out playing.*)

YASHA: Twenty-two misfortunes! Between us he's a stupid man, it must be said. (*Yawning.*)

DUNYASHA: God forbid he should shoot himself. (*A pause.*) I've grown so uneasy, I'm always fretting. I was only a girl when I was taken into the master's house, and now I've lost the habit of simple living—and here are my hands white, white as a lady's. I've become so delicate, fragile, ladylike, afraid of everything—Frightfully so. And, Yasha, if you deceive me, I don't know what will happen to my nerves.

YASHA (*kissing her*): You little cucumber! Of course every girl must behave properly. What I dislike above everything is for a girl to conduct herself badly.

DUNYASHA: I have come to love you passionately, you are educated, you can discuss anything. (*A pause.*)

YASHA (*yawning*): Yes, sir—To my mind it is like this: If a girl loves someone, it means she is immoral. (*A pause.*) It is pleasant to smoke a cigar in the clear air—(*Listening.*) They are coming here—It is the ladies and gentlemen—

(DUNYASHA *impulsively embraces him.*)

YASHA: Go to the house, as though you had been to bathe in the river, go by this path, otherwise, they might meet you and suspect me of making a rendezvous with you. That I cannot tolerate.

DUNYASHA (*with a little cough*): Your cigar has given me the headache. (*Goes out.*)

(YASHA *remains, sitting near the chapel.* LYUBOFF ANDREEVNA, GAYEFF *and* LOPAHIN *enter.*)

LOPAHIN: We must decide definitely, time doesn't wait. Why, the matter's quite simple. Are you willing to lease your land for summer cottages or are you not? Answer in one word, yes or no? Just one word!

LYUBOFF ANDREEVNA: Who is it smokes those disgusting cigars out here—? (*Sitting down.*)

GAYEFF: The railroad running so near is a great convenience. (*Sitting down.*) We made a trip to town and lunched there—Yellow in the side pocket! Perhaps I should go in the house first and play one game—

LYUBOFF ANDREEVNA: You'll have time.

LOPAHIN: Just one word! (*Imploringly.*) Do give me your answer!

GAYEFF (*yawning*): What?

LYUBOFF ANDREEVNA (*looking in her purse*): Yesterday there was lots of money in it. Today there's very little. My poor Varya! For the sake of economy she feeds everybody milk soup, and in the kitchen the old people get nothing but beans, and here I spend money—senselessly— (*Dropping her purse and scattering gold coins.*) There they go scattering! (*She is vexed.*)

YASHA: Allow me, I'll pick them up in a second. (*Picking up the coins.*)

LYUBOFF ANDREEVNA: If you will, Yasha. And why did I go in town for lunch—? Your restaurant with its music is trashy, the tablecloths smell of soap—Why drink so much, Lyonya? Why eat so much? Why talk so much? Today in the restaurant you were talking a lot again, and all of it beside the point. About the seventies, about the decadents. And to whom? Talking to waiters about the decadents!

LOPAHIN: Yes.

GAYEFF (*waving his hand*): I am incorrigible, that's evident—(*To* YASHA, *irritably.*) What is it?—You are forever swirling around in front of us!

YASHA (*laughing*): I cannot hear your voice without laughing.

GAYEFF (*to his sister*): Either I or he—

LYUBOFF ANDREEVNA: Go away, Yasha, Go on—

YASHA (*giving* LYUBOFF ANDREEVNA *her purse*): I am going right away. (*Barely suppressing his laughter.*) This minute. (*Goes out.*)

LOPAHIN: The rich Deriganoff intends to buy your estate. They say he is coming personally to the auction.

LYUBOFF ANDREEVNA: And where did you hear that?

LOPAHIN: In town they are saying it.

GAYEFF: Our Yaroslavl aunt promised to send us something, but when and how much she will send, nobody knows—

LOPAHIN: How much will she send? A hundred thousand? Two hundred?

LYUBOFF ANDREEVNA: Well—maybe ten, fifteen thousand—we'd be thankful for that.

LOPAHIN: Excuse me, but such light-minded people as you are, such odd, unbusinesslike people, I never saw. You are told in plain Russian that your estate is being sold up and you just don't seem to take it in.

LYUBOFF ANDREEVNA: But what are we to do? Tell us what?

LOPAHIN: I tell you every day. Every day I tell you the same thing. Both the cherry orchard and the land have got to be leased for summer cottages, it has to be done right now, quick—The auction is right under your noses. Do understand! Once you finally decide that there are to be summer cottages, you will get all the money you want, and then you'll be saved.

LYUBOFF ANDREEVNA: Summer cottages and summer residents—it is so trivial, excuse me.

GAYEFF: I absolutely agree with you.

LOPAHIN: I'll either burst out crying, or scream, or faint. I can't bear it! You are torturing me! (*To* GAYEFF.) You're a perfect old woman!

GAYEFF: What?

LOPAHIN: A perfect old woman! (*About to go.*)

LYUBOFF ANDREEVNA (*alarmed*): No, don't go, stay, my lamb, I beg you. Perhaps we will think of something!

LOPAHIN: What is there to think about?

LYUBOFF ANDREEVNA: Don't go, I beg you. With you here it is more cheerful anyhow—(*A pause.*) I keep waiting for something, as if the house were about to tumble down on our heads.

GAYEFF (*deep in thought*): Double into the corner pocket—Bank into the side pocket—

LYUBOFF ANDREEVNA: We have sinned so much—

LOPAHIN: What sins have you—?

GAYEFF (*puts a hard candy into his mouth*): They say I've eaten my fortune up in hard candies—(*Laughing.*)

LYUBOFF ANDREEVNA: Oh, my sins—I've always thrown money around like mad, recklessly, and I married a man who accumulated nothing but debts. My husband died from champagne—he drank fearfully—and to my misfortune I fell in love with another man. I lived with him, and just at that time—it was my first punishment—a blow over the head: right here in the river my boy was drowned and I went abroad—went away for good, never to return, never to see this river again—I shut my eyes, ran away, beside myself, and he after me—mercilessly, brutally. I bought a villa near Menton, because he fell ill there, and for three years I knew no rest day or night, the sick man exhausted me, my soul dried up. And last year when the villa was sold for debts, I went to Paris and there he robbed me of everything, threw me over, took up with another woman; I tried to poison myself—so stupid, so shameful—And suddenly I was seized with longing for Russia, for my own country, for my little girl—(*Wiping away her tears.*) Lord, Lord, have mercy, forgive me my sins! Don't punish me any more! (*Getting a telegram out of her pocket.*) I got this today from Paris, he asks forgiveness, begs me to return—(*Tears up the telegram.*) That sounds like music somewhere. (*Listening.*)

GAYEFF: It is our famous Jewish orchestra. You remember, four violins, a flute and double bass.

LYUBOFF ANDREEVNA: Does it still exist? We ought to get hold of it sometime and give a party.

LOPAHIN (*listening*): Can't hear it—(*Singing softly.*) "And for money the Germans will frenchify a Russian." (*Laughing.*) What a play I saw yesterday at the theatre, very funny!

LYUBOFF ANDREEVNA: And most likely there was nothing funny about it. You shouldn't look at plays, but look oftener at yourselves. How gray all your lives are, what a lot of idle things you say!

LOPAHIN: That's true. It must be said frankly this life of ours is idiotic—(*A pause.*) My father was a peasant, an idiot, he understood nothing, he taught me nothing, he just beat me in his drunken fits and always with a stick. At bottom I am just as big a dolt and idiot as he was. I wasn't taught anything, my handwriting is vile, I write like a pig—I am ashamed for people to see it.

LYUBOFF ANDREEVNA: You ought to get married, my friend.

LOPAHIN: Yes—That's true.

LYUBOFF ANDREEVNA: To our Varya, perhaps. She is a good girl.

LOPAHIN: Yes.

LYUBOFF ANDREEVNA: She comes from simple people, and she works all day long, but the main thing is she loves you. And you, too, have liked her a long time.

LOPAHIN: Why not? I am not against it—She's a good girl. (*A pause.*)

GAYEFF: They are offering me a position in a bank. Six thousand a year— Have you heard that?

LYUBOFF ANDREEVNA: Not you! You stay where you are—

FIERS (FIERS *enters, bringing an overcoat. To* GAYEFF): Pray, Sir, put this on, it's damp.

GAYEFF (*putting on the overcoat*): You're a pest, old man.

FIERS: That's all right—This morning you went off without letting me know. (*Looking him over.*)

LYUBOFF ANDREEVNA: How old you've grown, Fiers!

FIERS: At your service.

LOPAHIN: She says you've grown very old!

FIERS: I've lived a long time. They were planning to marry me off before your papa was born. (*Laughing.*) And at the time the serfs were freed I was already the head footman. I didn't want to be freed then, I stayed with the masters—(*A pause.*) And I remember, everybody was happy, but what they were happy about they didn't know themselves.

LOPAHIN: In the old days it was fine. At least they flogged.

FIERS (*not hearing*): But, of course. The peasants stuck to the masters, the masters stuck to the peasants, and now everything is all smashed up, you can't tell about anything.

GAYEFF: Keep still, Fiers. Tomorrow I must go to town. They have promised to introduce me to a certain general who might make us a loan.

LOPAHIN: Nothing will come of it. And you can rest assured you won't pay the interest.

LYUBOFF ANDREEVNA: He's just raving on. There aren't any such generals.

(TROFIMOFF, ANYA *and* VARYA *enter.*)

GAYEFF: Here they come.

ANYA: There is Mama sitting there.

LYUBOFF ANDREEVNA (*tenderly*): Come, come—My darlings—(*Embracing* ANYA *and* VARYA.) If you only knew how I love you both! Come sit by me—there—like that.

(*Everybody sits down.*)

LOPAHIN: Our perennial student is always strolling with the young ladies.

TROFIMOFF: It's none of your business.

LOPAHIN: He will soon be fifty and he's still a student.

TROFIMOFF: Stop your stupid jokes.

LOPAHIN: But why are you so peevish, you queer duck?

TROFIMOFF: Don't you pester me.

LOPAHIN (*laughing*): Permit me to ask you, what do you make of me?

TROFIMOFF: Yermolay Alexeevich, I make this of you: you are a rich man, you'll soon be a millionaire. Just as it is in the metabolism of nature, a wild beast is needed to eat up everything that comes his way; so you, too, are needed.

(*Everyone laughs.*)

VARYA: Petya, you'd better tell us about the planets.

LYUBOFF ANDREEVNA: No, let's go on with yesterday's conversation.

TROFIMOFF: What was it about?

GAYEFF: About the proud man.

TROFIMOFF: We talked a long time yesterday, but didn't get anywhere. In a proud man, in your sense of the word, there is something mystical. Maybe you are right, from your standpoint, but if we are to discuss it in simple terms, without whimsy, then what pride can there be, is there any sense in it, if man physiologically is poorly constructed, if in the great majority he is crude, unintelligent, profoundly miserable. One must stop admiring oneself. One must only work.

GAYEFF: All the same, you will die.

TROFIMOFF: Who knows? And what does it mean—you will die? Man may have a hundred senses, and when he dies only the five that are known to us may perish, and the remaining ninety-five go on living.

LYUBOFF ANDREEVNA: How clever you are, Petya!

LOPAHIN (*ironically*): Terribly!

TROFIMOFF: Humanity goes forward, perfecting its powers. Everything that's unattainable now will some day become familiar, understandable; it is only that one must work and must help with all one's might those who seek the truth. With us in Russia so far only a very few work. The great majority of the intelligentsia that I know are looking for nothing, doing nothing, and as yet have no capacity for work. They call themselves intelligentsia, are free and easy with the servants, treat the peasants like animals, educate themselves poorly, read nothing seriously, do absolutely nothing; about science they just talk and about art they understand very little. Every one of them is serious, all have stern faces; they all talk of nothing but important things, philosophize, and all the time everybody can see that the workmen eat abominably, sleep without any pillows, thirty or forty to a room, and everywhere there are bedbugs, stench, dampness, moral uncleanness—And apparently with us, all the fine talk is only to divert the attention of ourselves and of others. Show me where we have the day nurseries they are always talking so much about, where are the reading rooms? They only write of these in novels, for the truth is there are not any at all. There is only filth, vulgarity, orientalism—I am afraid of very serious faces and dislike them. I'm afraid of serious conversations. Rather than that let's just keep still.

LOPAHIN: You know I get up before five o'clock in the morning and work from morning till night. Well, I always have money, my own and other people's, on hand, and I see what the people around me are. One has only to start doing something to find out how few honest and decent people there are. At times when I can't go to sleep, I think: Lord, thou gavest us immense forests, unbounded fields and the widest horizons, and living in the midst of them we should indeed by giants—

LYUBOFF ANDREEVNA: You feel the need for giants—They are good only in fairy tales, anywhere else they only frighten us.

(*At the back of the stage* EPIHODOFF *passes by, playing the guitar.*)

LYUBOFF ANDREEVNA (*lost in thought*): Epihodoff is coming—

ANYA (*lost in thought*): Epihodoff is coming.

GAYEFF: The sun has set, ladies and gentlemen.

TROFIMOFF: Yes.

GAYEFF (*not loud and as if he were declaiming*): Oh, Nature, wonderful, you gleam with eternal radiance, beautiful and indifferent, you, whom we call Mother, combine in yourself both life and death, you give life and you take it away.

VARYA (*beseechingly*): Uncle!

ANYA: Uncle, you're doing it again!

TROFIMOFF: You'd better bank the yellow into the side pocket.

GAYEFF: I'll be quiet, quiet.

(*All sit absorbed in their thoughts. There is only the silence.* FIERS *is heard muttering to himself softly. Suddenly a distant sound is heard, as if from the sky, like the sound of a snapped string, dying away, mournful.*)

LYUBOFF ANDREEVNA: What's that?

LOPAHIN: I don't know. Somewhere far off in a mine shaft a bucket fell. But somewhere very far off.

GAYEFF: And it may be some bird—like a heron.

TROFIMOFF: Or an owl—

LYUBOFF ANDREEVNA (*shivering*): It's unpleasant, somehow. (*A pause.*)

FIERS: Before the disaster it was like that. The owl hooted and the samovar hummed without stopping, both.

GAYEFF: Before what disaster?

FIERS: Before the emancipation. (*A pause.*)

LYUBOFF ANDREEVNA: You know, my friends, let's go. Twilight is falling. (*To* ANYA.) You have tears in your eyes—What is it, my dear little girl? (*Embracing her.*)

ANYA: It's just that, Mama. It's nothing.

TROFIMOFF: Somebody is coming.

(*A stranger appears in a shabby white cap, and an overcoat; he is a little drunk.*)

THE STRANGER: Allow me to ask you, can I go straight through here to the station?

GAYEFF: You can. Go by that road.

THE STRANGER: I am heartily grateful to you. (*Coughing.*) The weather is splendid—(*Declaiming.*) Brother of mine, suffering brother—Go out to the Volga, whose moans—(*To* VARYA.) Mademoiselle, grant a hungry Russian man some thirty kopecks—

(VARYA *is frightened and gives a shriek.*)

LOPAHIN (*angrily*): There's a limit to everything.

LYUBOFF ANDREEVNA (*flustered*): Take this—Here's this for you—(*Searching in her purse.*) No silver—It's all the same, here's a gold piece for you—

THE STRANGER: I am heartily grateful to you. (*Goes out. Laughter.*)

VARYA (*frightened*): I'm going—I'm going—Oh, Mama, you poor little Mama! There's nothing in the house for people to eat, and you gave him a gold piece.

LYUBOFF ANDREEVNA: What is to be done with me, so silly? I shall give you all I have in the house. Yermolay Alexeevich, you will lend me some this once more!—

LOPAHIN: Agreed.

LYUBOFF ANDREEVNA: Let's go, ladies and gentlemen, it's time. And here, Varya, we have definitely made a match for you, I congratulate you.

VARYA (*through her tears*): Mama, that's not something to joke about.

LOPAHIN: Achmelia, get thee to a nunnery.

GAYEFF: And my hands are trembling; it is a long time since I have played billiards.

LOPAHIN: Achmelia, oh, nymph, in thine orisons be all my sins remember'd—

LYUBOFF ANDREEVNA: Let's go, my dear friends, it will soon be suppertime.

VARYA: He frightened me. My heart is thumping so!

LOPAHIN: I remind you, ladies and gentlemen: August twenty-second the cherry orchard will be auctioned off. Think about that!—Think!—

(*All go out except* TROFIMOFF *and* ANYA.)

ANYA (*laughing*): My thanks to the stranger, he frightened Varya, now we are alone.

TROFIMOFF: Varya is afraid we might begin to love eath other and all day long she won't leave us to ourselves. With her narrow mind she cannot understand that we are above love. To sidestep the petty and illusory, which prevent our being free and happy, that is the aim and meaning of our life. Forward! We march on irresistibly toward the bright star that burns there in the distance. Forward! Do not fall behind, friends!

ANYA (*extending her arms upward*): How well you talk! (*A pause.*) It's wonderful here today!

TROFIMOFF: Yes, the weather is marvelous.

ANYA: What have you done to me, Petya, why don't I love the cherry orchard any longer the way I used to? I loved it so tenderly, it seemed to me there was not a better place on earth than our orchard.

TROFIMOFF: All Russia is our orchard. The earth is immense and beautiful, and on it are many wonderful places. (*A pause.*) Just think, Anya: your grandfather, great-grandfather and all your ancestors were slave owners, in possession of living souls, and can you doubt that from every cherry in the orchard, from every leaf, from every trunk, human beings are looking at you, can it be that you don't hear their voices? To possess living souls, well, that depraved all of you who lived before and who are living now, so that your mother and you, and your uncle no longer notice that you live by debt, at somebody else's expense, at the expense of those very people whom you wouldn't let past your front door—We are at least two hundred years behind the times, we have as yet absolutely nothing, we have no definite attitude toward the past, we only philosophize, complain of our sadness or drink vodka. Why, it is quite clear that to begin to live in the present we must first atone for our past, must be done with it; and we can atone for it only through suffering, only through uncommon, incessant labor. Understand that, Anya.

ANYA: The house we live in ceased to be ours long ago, and I'll go away, I give you my word.

TROFIMOFF: If you have the household keys, throw them in the well and go away. Be free as the wind.

ANYA (*transported*): How well you said that!

TROFIMOFF: Believe me, Anya, believe me! I am not thirty yet, I am young, I am still a student, but I have already borne so much! Every winter I am hungry, sick, anxious, poor as a beggar, and—where has destiny not chased me, where haven't I been! And yet, my soul has always, every minute, day and night, been full of inexplicable premonitions. I have a premonition of happiness, Anya, I see it already—

ANYA (*pensively*): The moon is rising.

(EPIHODOFF *is heard playing on the guitar, always the same sad song. The moon rises. Somewhere near the poplars* VARYA *is looking for* ANYA *and calling: "Anya! Where are you?"*)

TROFIMOFF: Yes, the moon is rising. (*A pause.*) Here is happiness, here it comes, comes always nearer and nearer, I hear its footsteps now. And if we shall not see it, shall not come to know it, what does that matter? Others will see it!

VARYA (*off*): Anya! Where are you?

TROFIMOFF: Again, that Varya! (*Angrily.*) It's scandalous!

ANYA: Well, let's go to the river. It's lovely there.

TROFIMOFF: Let's go. (*They go out.*)

VARYA (*off*): Anya! Anya!

ACT III

(*The drawing room, separated by an arch from the ballroom. A chandelier is lighted. A Jewish orchestra is playing—the same that was mentioned in Act Two. Evening. In the ballroom they are dancing grand rond. The voice of* SEMYONOFF-PISHTCHIK: *"Promenade à une paire!" They enter the drawing room; in the first couple are* PISHTCHIK *and* CHARLOTTA IVANOVNA; *in the second,* TROFIMOFF *and* LYUBOFF ANDREEVNA; *in the third,* ANYA *with the* POST-OFFICE CLERK; *in the fourth,* VARYA *with the* STATIONMASTER, *et cetera—*VARYA *is crying softly and wipes away her tears while she is dancing,* DUNYASHA *is in the last couple through the drawing room,* PISHTCHIK *shouts: "Grand rond, balancez!" and "Les Cavaliers à genoux et remerciez vos dames!"*
    FIERS *in a frock coat goes by with seltzer water on a tray.* PISHTCHIK *and* TROFIMOFF *come into the drawing room.*)

PISHTCHIK: I am full-blooded, I have had two strokes already, and dancing is hard for me, but as they say, if you are in a pack of dogs, you may bark and bark, but you must still wag your tail. At that, I have the health of a horse. My dear father—he was a great joker—may he dwell in Heaven—used to talk as if our ancient line, the Semyonoff-Pishtchiks, were descended from the very horse that Caligula made a Senator—(*Sitting down.*) But here's my trouble: I haven't any money. A hungry dog believes in nothing but meat—(*Snoring but waking at once.*) And the same way with me—I can't talk about anything but money.

TROFIMOFF: Well, to tell you the truth, there is something of a horse about your figure.

PISHTCHIK: Well—a horse is a fine animal—You can sell a horse—

(*The sound of playing billiards comes from the next room.* VARYA *appears under the arch to the ballroom.*)

TROFIMOFF (*teasing*): Madam Lopahin! Madam Lopahin!

VARYA (*angrily*): A mangy-looking gentleman!

TROFIMOFF: Yes, I am a mangy-looking gentleman, and proud of it!

VARYA (*in bitter thought*): Here we have gone and hired musicians and what are we going to pay them with? (*Goes out.*)

TROFIMOFF (*to* PISHTCHIK): If the energy you have wasted in the course of your life trying to find money to pay the interest had gone into something else, you could very likely have turned the world upside down before you were done with it.

PISHTCHIK: Nietzsche—the philosopher—the greatest—the most celebrated—a man of tremendous mind—says in his works that one may make counterfeit money.

TROFIMOFF: And have you read Nietzsche?

PISHTCHIK: Well—Dashenka told me. And I'm in such a state now that I could make counterfeit money myself—Day after tomorrow three hundred and ten roubles must be paid—one hundred and thirty I've on hand—(*Feeling in his pockets, alarmed.*) The money is gone! I have lost the money! (*Tearfully.*) Where is the money? (*Joyfully.*) Here it is, inside the lining—I was in quite a sweat—

(LYUBOFF ANDREEVNA *and* CHARLOTTA IVANOVNA *come in.*)

LYUBOFF ANDREEVNA (*humming lazginka, a Georgian dance*): Why does Leonid take so long? What's he doing in town? (*To* DUNYASHA.) Dunyasha, offer the musicians some tea—

TROFIMOFF: In all probability the auction did not take place.

LYUBOFF ADREEVNA: And the musicians came at an unfortunate moment and we planned the ball at an unfortunate moment—Well, it doesn't matter. (*Sitting down and singing softly.*)

CHARLOTTA (*gives* PISHTCHIK *a deck of cards*): Here is a deck of cards for you, think of some one card.

PISHTCHIK: I have thought of one.

CHARLOTTA: Now, shuffle the deck. Very good. Hand it here; oh, my dear Monsieur Pishtchik. *Ein, zwei, drei!* Now look for it, it's in your coat pocket—

PISHTCHIK (*getting a card out of his coat pocket*): The Eight of Spades, that's absolutely right! (*Amazed.*) Fancy that!

CHARLOTTA (*holding a deck of cards in her palm; to* TROFIMOFF): Tell me quick now, which card is on top?

TROFIMOFF: What is it? Well—the Queen of Spades.

CHARLOTTA: Right! (*To* PISHTCHIK.) Well? Which card's on top?

PISHTCHIK: The Ace of Hearts.

CHARLOTTA: Right! (*Strikes the deck against her palm; the deck of cards disappears.*) And what beautiful weather we are having today!

(*A mysterious feminine voice answers her, as if from under the floor: "Oh, yes. The weather is splendid, madame." "You are so nice, you're my ideal—" The voice: "Madame, you too please me greatly."*)

THE STATIONMASTER (*applauding*): Madam Ventriloquist, bravo!

PISHTCHIK (*amazed*): Fancy that! Most charming Charlotte Ivanovna— I am simply in love with you.

CHARLOTTA: In love? (*Shrugging her shoulders.*) Is it possible that you can love? *Guter mensch aber schlächter musikant.*

TROFIMOFF (*slapping* PISHTCHIK *on the shoulder*): You horse, you—

CHARLOTTA: I beg your attention, one more trick. (*Taking a lap robe from the chair.*) Here is a very fine lap robe—I want to sell it—(*Shaking it out.*) Wouldn't somebody like to buy it?

PISHTCHIK (*amazed*): Fancy that!

CHARLOTTA: *Ein, zwei, drei!*

(*She quickly raises the lowered robe, behind it stands* ANYA, *who curtseys, runs to her mother, embraces her and runs back into the ballroom amid the general delight.*)

LYUBOFF ANDREEVNA (*applauding*): Bravo, bravo—!

CHARLOTTA: Now again! *Ein, zwei, drei!*

(*Lifting the robe: behind it stands* VARYA, *she bows.*)

PISHTCHIK (*amazed*): Fancy that!

CHARLOTTA: That's all. (*Throwing the robe at* PISHTCHIK, *curtseying and running into the ballroom.*)

PISHTCHIK (*hurrying after her*): You little rascal—What a girl! What a girl! (*Goes out.*)

LYUBOFF ANDREEVNA: And Leonid is not here yet. What he's doing in town so long, I don't understand! Everything is finished there, either the estate is sold by now, or the auction didn't take place. Why keep it from us so long?

VARYA (*trying to comfort her*): Uncle has bought it, I am sure of that.

TROFIMOFF (*mockingly*): Yes.

VARYA: Great-aunt sent him power of attorney to buy it in her name and transfer the debt. She did this for Anya. And I feel certain, God willing, that Uncle will buy it.

LYUBOFF ANDREEVNA: Our Yaroslavl great-aunt has sent fifteen thousand to buy the estate in her name—She doesn't trust us, but that wouldn't be enough to pay the interest even—(*Covering her face with her hands.*) Today my fate will be decided, my fate—

TROFIMOFF (*teasing* VARYA): Madam Lopahin!

VARYA (*angrily*): Perennial student! You have already been expelled from the University twice.

LYUBOFF ANDREEVNA: But why are you angry, Varya? He teases you about Lopahin, what of it? Marry Lopahin if you want to, he is a good man, interesting. If you don't want to, don't marry him; darling, nobody is making you do it.

VARYA: I look at this matter seriously, Mama, one must speak straight out. He's a good man, I like him.

LYUBOFF ANDREEVNA: Then marry him. What there is to wait for I don't understand!

VARYA: But I can't propose to him myself, Mama. It's two years now; everyone has been talking to me about him, everyone talks, and he either remains silent or jokes. I understand. He's getting rich, he's busy with his own affairs, and has no time for me. If there were money, ever so little, even a hundred roubles, I would drop everything, and go far away. I'd go to a nunnery.

TROFIMOFF: How saintly!

VARYA (*to* TROFIMOFF): A student should be intelligent! (*In a low voice, tearfully.*) How homely you have grown, Petya, how old you've got. (*To* LYUBOFF ANDREEVNA, *no longer crying.*) It is just that I can't live without working, Mama, I must be doing something every minute.

YASHA (YASHA *enters. Barely restraining his laughter.*): Epihodoff has broken a billiard cue!—(*Goes out.*)

VARYA: But why is Epihodoff here? Who allowed him to play billiards? I don't understand these people—(*Goes out.*)

LYUBOFF ANDREEVNA: Don't tease her, Petya; you can see she has troubles enough without that.

TROFIMOFF: She is just too zealous. Sticking her nose into things that are none of her business. All summer she gave us no peace, neither me nor Anya; she was afraid a romance would spring up between us. What business is that of hers? And besides I haven't shown any signs of it. I am so remote from triviality. We are above love!

LYUBOFF ANDREEVNA: Well, then, I must be beneath love. (*Very anxiously.*) Why isn't Leonid here? Just to tell us whether the estate is sold or not? Calamity seems to me so incredible that I don't know what to think, I'm lost—I could scream this minute—I could do something insane. Save me, Petya. Say something, do say. . . .

TROFIMOFF: Whether the estate is sold today or is not sold—is it not the same? There is no turning back, the path is all grown over. Calm yourself, my dear, all that was over long ago. One mustn't deceive oneself, one must for once at least in one's life look truth straight in the eye.

LYUBOFF ANDREEVNA: What truth? You see where the truth is and where the untruth is, but as for me, it's as if I had lost my sight, I see nothing. You boldly decide all important questions, but tell me, my dear boy, isn't that because you are young and haven't had time yet to suffer through any one of your problems? You look boldly ahead, and isn't that because you don't see and don't expect anything terrible, since life is still hidden from your young eyes? You are braver, more honest, more profound than we are, but stop and think, be magnanimous, have a little mercy on me, just a little. Why, I was born here. My father and mother lived here and my grandfather. I love this house, I can't imagine my life without the cherry orchard and if it is very necessary to sell it, then sell me along with the orchard—(*Embracing* TROFIMOFF *and kissing him on the forehead.*) Why, my son was drowned here—(*Crying.*) Have mercy on me, good, kind man.

TROFIMOFF: You know I sympathize with you from the bottom of my heart.

LYUBOFF ANDREEVNA: But that should be said differently, differently—(*Taking out her handkerchief; a telegram falls on the floor.*) My heart is heavy today, you can't imagine how heavy. It is too noisy for me here, my soul trembles at every sound, I tremble all over and yet I can't go off to myself, when I am alone the silence frightens me. Don't blame me, Petya—I love you as one of my own. I should gladly have given you Anya's hand, I assure you, only, my dear, you must study and finish your course. You do nothing. Fate simply flings you about from place to place, and that's so strange—Isn't that so? Yes? And you must do something about your beard, to make it grow somehow—(*Laughing.*) You look funny!

TROFIMOFF (*picking up the telegram*): I do not desire to be beautiful.

LYUBOFF ANDREEVNA: This telegram is from Paris. I get one every day. Yesterday and today too. That wild man has fallen ill again, something is wrong again with him—He asks forgiveness, begs me to come, and really I ought to make a trip to Paris and stay awhile near him. Your face looks stern, Petya, but what is there to do, my dear, what am I to do, he is ill, he is alone, unhappy and who will look after him there, who will keep him from doing the wrong thing, who will give him his medicine on time? And what is there to hide or keep still about? I love him, that's plain. I love him, love him—It's a stone about my neck, I'm sinking to the bottom with it, but I love that stone and live without it I cannot. (*Pressing* TROFIMOFF'S *hand.*) Don't think harshly of me, Petya, don't say anything to me, don't—

TROFIMOFF (*tearfully*): Forgive my frankness, for God's sake! Why, he picked your bones.

LYUBOFF ANDREEVNA: No, no, no, you must not talk like that. (*Stopping her ears.*)

TROFIMOFF: But he is a scoundrel, only you, you are the only one that doesn't know it. He is a petty scoundrel, a nonentity—

LYUBOFF ANDREEVNA (*angry but controlling herself*): You are twenty-six years old or twenty-seven, but you are still a schoolboy in the second grade!

TROFIMOFF: Very well!

LYUBOFF ANDREEVNA: You should be a man—at your age you should understand people who love. And you yourself should love someone— you should fall in love! (*Angrily.*) Yes, yes! And there is no purity in you; you are simply smug, a ridiculous crank, a freak—

TROFIMOFF (*horrified*): What is she saying!

LYUBOFF ANDREEVNA: "I am above love!" You are not above love, Petya, you are, as our Fiers would say, just a good-for-nothing. Imagine, at your age, not having a mistress—!

TROFIMOFF (*horrified*): This is terrible! What is she saying! (*Goes quickly into the ballroom, clutching his head.*) This is horrible—I can't bear it, I am going—(*Goes out but immediately returns.*) All is over between us. (*Goes out into the hall.*)

LYUBOFF ANDREEVNA (*shouting after him*): Petya, wait! You funny creature, I was joking! Petya! (*In the hall you hear someone running up the stairs and suddenly falling back down with a crash. You hear* ANYA *and* VARYA *scream but immediately you hear laughter.*) What's that?

ANYA (ANYA *runs in. Laughing*): Petya fell down the stairs! (*Runs out.*)

LYUBOFF ANDREEVNA: What a funny boy that Petya is—! (*The* STATION-MASTER *stops in the center of the ballroom and begins to recite "The Sinner" by A. Tolstoi. They listen to him but he has recited only a few lines when the strains of a waltz are heard from the hall and the recitation is broken off. They all dance.* TROFIMOFF, ANYA, VARYA *and* LYUBOFF ANDREEVNA *come in from the hall.*) But, Petya—but, dear soul—I beg your forgiveness—Let's go dance. (*She dances with* TROFIMOFF. ANYA *and* VARYA *dance.* FIERS *enters, leaving his stick by the side door.* YASHA *also comes into the drawing room and watches the dancers.*)

YASHA: What is it, Grandpa?

FIERS: I don't feel very well. In the old days there were generals, barons, admirals dancing at our parties, and now we send for the post-office clerk and the stationmaster, and even they are none too anxious to come. Somehow I've grown feeble. The old master, the grandfather, treated everybody with sealing-wax for all sicknesses. I take sealing-wax every day, have done so for twenty-odd years or more; it may be due to that that I'm alive.

YASHA: You are tiresome, Grandpa. (*Yawning.*) Why don't you go off and die?

FIERS: Aw, you—good-for-nothing!—(*Muttering.*)

(TROFIMOFF *and* LYUBOFF ANDREEVNA *dance in the ballroom and then in the drawing room.*)

LYUBOFF ANDREEVNA: *Merci.* I'll sit down awhile—(*Sitting down.*) I'm tired.

ANYA (ANYA *enters. Agitated*): And just now in the kitchen some man was saying that the cherry orchard had been sold today.

LYUBOFF ANDREEVNA: Sold to whom?

ANYA: He didn't say who to. He's gone.

(*Dancing with* TROFIMOFF, *they pass into the ballroom.*)

YASHA: It was some old man babbling there. A stranger.

FIERS: And Leonid Andreevich is still not here, he has not arrived. The overcoat he has on is light, midseason—let's hope he won't catch cold. Ach, these young things!

LYUBOFF ANDREEVNA: I shall die this minute. Go, Yasha, find out who it was sold to.

YASHA: But he's been gone a long time, the old fellow. (*Laughing.*)

LYUBOFF ANDREEVNA (*with some annoyance*): Well, what are you laughing at? What are you so amused at?

YASHA: Epihodoff is just too funny. An empty-headed man. Twenty-two misfortunes!

LYUBOFF ANDREEVNA: Fiers, if the estate is sold, where will you go?

FIERS: Wherever you say, there I'll go.

LYUBOFF ANDREEVNA: Why do you look like that? Aren't you well? You know you ought to go to bed—

FIERS: Yes—(*With a sneer.*) I go to bed and without me who's going to serve, who'll take care of things? I'm the only one in the whole house.

YASHA (*to* LYUBOFF ANDREEVNA): Lyuboff Andreevna, let me ask a favor of you, do be so kind! If you ever go back to Paris, take me with you, please do! It's impossible for me to stay here. (*Looking around him, and speaking in a low voice.*) Why talk about it? You can see for yourself it's an uncivilized country, an immoral people and not only that, there's the boredom of it. The food they give us in that kitchen is abominable and there's that Fiers, too, walking about and muttering all kinds of words that are out of place. Take me with you, be so kind!

PISHTCHIK (*enters*): Allow me to ask you—for a little waltz, most beautiful lady—(LYUBOFF ANDREEVNA *goes with him.*) Charming lady, I must borrow a hundred and eighty roubles from you—will borrow—(*dancing*) a hundred and eighty roubles—(*They pass into the ballroom.*)

YASHA (*singing low*): "Wilt thou know the unrest in my soul!"

(*In the ballroom a figure in a gray top hat and checked trousers waves both hands and jumps about; there are shouts of "Bravo, Charlotta Ivanovna!"*)

DUNYASHA (*stopping to powder her face*): The young lady orders me to dance—there are a lot of gentlemen and very few ladies—but dancing makes my head swim and my heart thump. Fiers Nikolaevich, the post-office clerk said something to me just now that took my breath away.

(*The music plays more softly.*)

FIERS: What did he say to you?
DUNYASHA: You are like a flower, he says.
YASHA (*yawning*): What ignorance—! (*Goes out.*)
DUNYASHA: Like a flower—I am such a sensitive girl, I love tender words awfully.
FIERS: You'll be getting your head turned.

(EPIHODOFF *enters.*)

EPIHODOFF: Avdotya Feodorovna, you don't want to see me—It's as if I were some sort of insect. (*Sighing.*) Ach, life!
DUNYASHA: What do you want?
EPIHODOFF: Undoubtedly you may be right. (*Sighing.*) But of course, if one considers it from a given point of view, then you, I will allow myself so to express it, forgive my frankness, absolutely led me into a state of mind. I know my fate, every day some misfortune happens to me, but I have long since become accustomed to that, and so I look on my misfortunes with a smile. You gave me your word and, although I—
DUNYASHA: I beg you, we'll talk later on, but leave me now in peace. I'm in a dream now. (*Playing with her fan.*)
EPIHODOFF: I have something wrong happens every day—I will allow myself so to express it—I just smile, I even laugh.
VARYA (*enters from the ballroom*): You are not gone yet, Semyon? What a really disrespectful man you are! (*To* DUNYASHA.) Get out of here, Dunyasha. (*To* EPIHODOFF.) You either play billiards and break a cue or you walk about the drawing room like a guest.
EPIHODOFF: Allow me to tell you, you cannot make any demands on me.
VARYA: I'm not making any demands on you, I'm talking to you. All you

know is to walk from place to place but not do any work. We keep a clerk, but what for, nobody knows.

EPIHODOFF (*offended*): Whether I work, whether I walk, whether I eat, or whether I play billiards are matters to be discussed only by people of understanding and my seniors.

VARYA: You dare to say that to me! (*Flying into a temper.*) You dare? So I don't understand anything? Get out of here! This minute!

EPIHODOFF (*alarmed*): I beg you to express yourself in a delicate manner.

VARYA (*beside herself*): This very minute, get out of here! Get out! (*He goes to the door; she follows him.*) Twenty-two misfortunes! Don't you dare breathe in here! Don't let me set eyes on you! (EPIHODOFF *has gone out, but his voice comes from outside the door: "I shall complain about you."*) Ah, you are coming back? (*Grabbing the stick that* FIERS *put by the door.*) Come on, come—come on, I'll show you—Ah, you are coming? You are coming? Take that then—!

(*She swings the stick, at the very moment when* LOPAHIN *is coming in.*)

LOPAHIN: Most humbly, I thank you.

VARYA (*angrily and ironically*): I beg your pardon!

LOPAHIN: It's nothing at all. I humbly thank you for the pleasant treat.

VARYA: It isn't worth your thanks. (*Moving away, then looking back and asking gently.*) I haven't hurt you?

LOPAHIN: No, it's nothing. There's a great bump coming, though.

(*Voices in the ballroom: "Lopahin has come back." "Yermolay Alexeevich!"*)

PISHTCHIK (*enters*): See what we see, hear what we hear—! (*He and* LOPAHIN *kiss one another.*) You smell slightly of cognac, my dear, my good old chap. And we are amusing ourselves here too.

LYUBOFF ANDREEVNA (*enters*): Is that you, Yermolay Alexeevich? Why were you so long? Where is Leonid?

LOPAHIN: Leonid Andreevich got back when I did, he's coming.

LYUBOFF ANDREEVNA (*agitated*): Well, what? Was there an auction? Do speak!

LOPAHIN (*embarrassed, afraid of showing the joy he feels*): The auction was over by four o'clock—We were late for the train, had to wait till half-past nine. (*Sighing heavily.*) Ugh, my head's swimming a bit!

(GAYEFF *enters; with his right hand he carries his purchases, with his left he wipes away his tears.*)

LYUBOFF ANDREEVNA: Lyona, what? Lyona, eh? (*Impatiently, with tears in her eyes.*) Quick, for God's sake—

GAYEFF (*not answering her, merely waving his hand; to* FIERS, *crying*):

Here, take it—There are anchovies, some Kertch herrings—I haven't eaten anything all day—What I have suffered! (*The door into the billiard room is open; you hear the balls clicking and* YASHA'S *voice: "Seven and eighteen!"* GAYEFF'S *expression changes, he is no longer crying.*) I'm terribly tired. You help me change, Fiers. (*Goes to his room through the ballroom,* FIERS *behind him.*)

PISHTCHIK: What happened at the auction? Go on, tell us!

LYUBOFF ANDREEVNA: Is the cherry orchard sold?

LOPAHIN: It's sold.

LYUBOFF ANDREEVNA: Who bought it?

LOPAHIN: I bought it. (*A pause.* LYUBOFF ANDREEVNA *is overcome. She would have fallen had she not been standing near the chair and table.* VARYA *takes the keys from her belt, throws them on the floor in the middle of the drawing room and goes out.*) I bought it. Kindly wait a moment, ladies and gentlemen, everything is muddled up in my head, I can't speak—(*Laughing.*) We arrived at the auction, Deriganoff was already there. Leonid Andreevich had only fifteen thousand and Deriganoff right off bids thirty over and above indebtedness. I see how things are, I match him with forty thousand. He forty-five. I fifty-five. That is to say he raises it by fives, I by tens—So it ended. Over and above the indebtedness, I bid up to ninety thousand, it was knocked down to me. The cherry orchard is mine now. Mine! (*Guffawing.*) My God, Lord, the cherry orchard is mine! Tell me I'm drunk, out of my head, that I'm imagining all this—(*Stamps his feet.*) Don't laugh at me! If only my father and grandfather could rise from their graves and see this whole business, see how their Yermolay, beaten, half-illiterate Yermolay, who used to run around barefoot in winter, how that very Yermolay has bought an estate that nothing in the world can beat. I bought the estate where grandfather and father were slaves, where you wouldn't even let me in the kitchen. I am asleep, it's only some dream of mine, it only seems so to me—That's nothing but the fruit of your imagination, covered with the darkness of the unknown—(*Picking up the keys, with a gentle smile.*) She threw down the keys, wants to show she is not mistress any more—(*Jingling the keys.*) Well, it's all the same. (*The orchestra is heard tuning up.*) Hey, musicians, play, I want to hear you! Come on, everybody, and see how Yermolay Lopahin will swing the ax in the cherry orchard, how the trees will fall to the ground! We are going to build villas and our grandsons and great-grandsons will see a new life here—Music, play! (*The music is playing.* LYUBOFF ANDREEVNA *has sunk into a chair, crying bitterly.* LOPAHIN *reproachfully.*) Why, then, didn't you listen to me? My poor dear, it can't be undone now. (*With tears.*) Oh, if this could all be over soon, if somehow our awkward, unhappy life would be changed!

PISHTCHIK (*taking him by the arm, in a low voice*): She is crying. Come on in the ballroom, let her be by herself—Come on—(*Taking him by the arm and leading him into the ballroom.*)

LOPAHIN: What's the matter? Music, there, play up! (*Sarcastically.*) Everything is to be as I want it! Here comes the new squire, the owner of the cherry orchard. (*Quite accidentally, he bumps into the little table, and very nearly upsets the candelabra.*) I can pay for everything!

(*Goes out with PISHTCHIK. There is nobody left either in the ballroom or the drawing room but LYUBOFF ANDREEVNA, who sits all huddled up and crying bitterly. The music plays softly. ANYA and TROFIMOFF enter hurriedly. ANYA comes up to her mother and kneels in front of her. TROFIMOFF remains at the ballroom door.*)

ANYA: Mama—! Mama, you are crying? My dear, kind, good Mama, my beautiful, I love you—I bless you. The cherry orchard is sold, it's not ours any more, that's true, true; but don't cry, Mama, you've your life still left you, you've your good, pure heart ahead of you—Come with me, come on, darling, away from here, come on—We will plant a new orchard, finer than this one, you'll see it, you'll understand; and joy, quiet, deep joy will sink into your heart, like the sun at evening, and you'll smile, Mama! Come, darling, come on!

ACT IV

(*The same setting as in Act One. There are neither curtains on the windows nor are there any pictures on the walls. Only a little furniture remains piled up in one corner as if for sale. A sense of emptiness is felt. Near the outer door, at the rear of the stage, is a pile of suitcases, traveling bags, and so on. The door on the left is open, and through it VARYA'S and ANYA'S voices are heard. LOPAHIN is standing waiting. YASHA is holding a tray with glasses of champagne. In the hall EPI-HODOFF is tying up a box, offstage at the rear there is a hum. It is the peasants who have come to say good-by. GAYEFF'S voice: "Thanks, brothers, thank you."*)

YASHA: The simple folk have come to say good-by. I am of the opinion, Yermolay Alexeevich, that the people are kind enough but don't understand anything.

(*The hum subsides. LYUBOFF ANDREEVNA enters through the hall with GAYEFF; she is not crying, but is pale, her face quivers, she is not able to speak.*)

GAYEFF: You gave them your purse, Lyuba. Mustn't do that! Mustn't do that!

LYUBOFF ANDREEVNA: I couldn't help it! I couldn't help it!

(*Both go out.*)

LOPAHIN (*calling through the door after them*): Please, I humbly beg you! A little glass at parting. I didn't think to bring some from town, and at the station I found just one bottle. Please! (*A pause.*) Well, then, ladies and gentlemen! You don't want it? (*Moving away from the door.*) If I'd known that, I wouldn't have bought it. Well, then I won't drink any either. (YASHA *carefully sets the tray down on a chair.*) At least, you have some, Yasha.

YASHA: To those who are departing! Pleasant days to those who stay behind! (*Drinking.*) This champagne is not the real stuff, I can assure you.

LOPAHIN: Eight roubles a bottle. (*A pause.*) It's devilish cold in here.

YASHA: They didn't heat up today, we are leaving anyway. (*Laughing.*)

LOPAHIN: What are you laughing about?

YASHA: For joy.

LOPAHIN: Outside it's October, but it's sunny and still, like summer. Good for building. (*Looking at his watch, then through the door.*) Ladies and gentlemen, bear in mind we have forty-six minutes in all till train time! Which means you have to go to the station in twenty minutes. Hurry up a little.

TROFIMOFF (*in an overcoat, entering from outside*): Seems to me it is time to go. The carriages are ready. The devil knows where my rubbers are. They've disappeared. (*In the door.*) Anya, my rubbers are not here! I can't find them.

LOPAHIN: And I have to go to Harkoff. I'm going on the same train with you. I'm going to live in Harkoff all winter. I've been dillydallying along with you, I'm tired of doing nothing. I can't be without work, look, I don't know what to do with my hands here, see, they are dangling somehow, as if they didn't belong to me.

TROFIMOFF: We are leaving right away, and you'll set about your useful labors again.

LOPAHIN: Here, drink a glass.

TROFIMOFF: I shan't.

LOPAHIN: It's to Moscow now?

TROFIMOFF: Yes. I'll see them off to town, and tomorrow to Moscow.

LOPAHIN: Yes—Maybe the professors are not giving their lectures. I imagine they are waiting till you arrive.

TROFIMOFF: That's none of your business.

LOPAHIN: How many years is it you've been studying at the University?

TROFIMOFF: Think of something newer. This is old and flat. (*Looking for his rubbers.*) You know, perhaps, we shall not see each other again; therefore, permit me to give you one piece of advice at parting! Don't wave your arms! Cure yourself of that habit—of arm waving. And also of building summer cottages, figuring that the summer residents will in time become individual landowners; figuring like that is arm waving too—Just the same, however, I like you. You have delicate soft fingers like an artist, you have a delicate soft heart—

LOPAHIN (*embracing him*): Good-by, my dear boy. Thanks for everything. If you need it, take some money from me for the trip.

TROFIMOFF: Why should I? There's no need for it.

LOPAHIN: But you haven't any.

TROFIMOFF: I have. Thank you. I got some for a translation. Here it is in my pocket. (*Anxiously.*) But my rubbers are gone.

VARYA (*from another room*): Take your nasty things! (*Throws a pair of rubbers on to the stage.*)

TROFIMOFF: But what are you angry about, Varya? Hm—Why, these are not my rubbers.

LOPAHIN: In the spring I planted twenty-seven hundred acres of poppies and now I've made forty thousand clear. And when my poppies were in bloom, what a picture it was! So look, as I say, I've made forty thousand, which means I'm offering you a loan because I can afford to. Why turn up your nose? I'm a peasant—I speak straight out.

TROFIMOFF: Your father was a peasant, mine—an apothecary—and from that absolutely nothing follows. (LOPAHIN *takes out his wallet.*) Leave it alone, leave it alone—If you gave me two hundred thousand even, I wouldn't take it. I am a free man. And everything that you all value so highly and dearly, both rich man and beggars, has not the slightest power over me, it's like a mere feather floating in the air. I can get along without you, I can pass you by, I am strong and proud. Humanity is moving toward the loftiest truth, toward the loftiest happiness that is possible on earth and I am in the front ranks.

LOPAHIN: Will you get there?

TROFIMOFF: I'll get there. (*A pause.*) I'll get there, or I'll show the others the way to get there.

(*In the distance is heard the sound of an ax on a tree.*)

LOPAHIN: Well, good-by, my dear boy. It's time to go. We turn up our noses at one another, but life keeps on passing. When I work a long time without stopping, my thoughts are clearer, and it seems as if I, too, know what I exist for, and, brother, how many people are there in Russia who exist, nobody knows for what? Well, all the same, it's not that that keeps things circulating. Leonid Andreevich, they say, has accepted a position—he'll be in a bank, six thousand a year—the only thing is he won't stay there, he's very lazy—

ANYA (*in the doorway*): Mama begs of you until she's gone, not to cut down the orchard.

TROFIMOFF: Honestly, haven't you enough tact to—(*Goes out through the hall.*)

LOPAHIN: Right away, right away—What people, really! (*Goes out after him.*)

ANYA: Has Fiers been sent to the hospital?

YASHA: I told them to this morning. They must have sent him.

ANYA (*to* EPIHODOFF, *who is passing through the room*): Semyon Panteleevich, please inquire whether or not they have taken Fiers to the hospital.

YASHA (*huffily*): This morning, I told Igor. Why ask ten times over!

EPIHODOFF: The venerable Fiers, according to my conclusive opinion, is not worth mending, he ought to join his forefathers. And I can only envy him. (*Putting a suitcase on a hatbox and crushing it.*) Well, there you are, of course. I knew it. (*Goes out.*)

YASHA (*mockingly*): Twenty-two misfortunes—

VARYA (*on the other side of the door*): Have they taken Fiers to the hospital?

ANYA: They have.

VARYA: Then why didn't they take the letter to the doctor?

ANYA: We must send it on after them—(*Goes out.*)

VARYA (*from the next room*): Where is Yasha? Tell him his mother has come, she wants to say good-by to him.

YASHA (*waving his hand*): They merely try my patience.

(DUNYASHA *has been busying herself with the luggage; now when* YASHA *is left alone, she goes up to him.*)

DUNYASHA: If you'd only look at me once, Yasha. You are going away—leaving me—(*Crying and throwing herself on his neck.*)

YASHA: Why are you crying? (*Drinking champagne.*) In six days I'll be in Paris again. Tomorrow we will board the express train and dash off out of sight; somehow, I can't believe it. *Vive la France!* It doesn't suit me here—I can't live here—Can't help that. I've seen enough ignorance—enough for me. (*Drinking champagne.*) Why do you cry? Behave yourself properly, then you won't be crying.

DUNYASHA (*powdering her face, looking into a small mirror*): Send me a letter from Paris. I loved you, Yasha, you know, loved you so! I am a tender creature, Yasha!

YASHA: They are coming here. (*Bustling about near the suitcases, humming low.*)

(LYUBOFF ANDREEVNA, GAYEFF, ANYA and CHARLOTTA IVANOVNA enter.)

GAYEFF: We should be going. There is very little time left. (*Looking at* YASHA.) Who is it smells like herring!

LYUBOFF ANDREEVNA: In about ten minutes let's be in the carriage—(*Glancing around the room.*) Good-by, dear house, old Grandfather. Winter will pass, spring will be here, but you won't be here any longer, they'll tear you down. How much these walls have seen! (*Kissing her daughter warmly.*) My treasure, you are beaming, your eyes are dancing like two diamonds. Are you happy? Very?

ANYA: Very! It's the beginning of a new life, Mama!

GAYEFF (*gaily*): Yes, indeed, everything is fine now. Before the sale of the cherry orchard, we all were troubled, distressed, and then when the question was settled definitely, irrevocably, we all calmed down and were even cheerful—I'm a bank official. I am a financier now—Yellow ball into the side pocket, anyway, Lyuba, you look better, no doubt about that.

LYUBOFF ANDREEVNA: Yes. My nerves are better, that's true. (*They hand her her hat and coat.*) I sleep well. Carry out my things, Yasha. It's time. (*To* ANYA.) My little girl, we shall see each other again soon—I am going to Paris, I shall live there on the money your Yaroslavl great-aunt sent for the purchase of the estate—long live Great-aunt! But that money won't last long.

ANYA: Mama, you'll come back soon, soon—Isn't that so? I'll prepare myself, pass the examination at high school, and then I'll work, I will help you. We'll read all sorts of books together. Mama, isn't that so? (*Kissing her mother's hands.*) We'll read in the autumn evenings, read lots of books, and a new, wonderful world will open up before us—(*Daydreaming.*) Mama, do come—

LYUBOFF ANDREEVNA: I'll come, my precious. (*Embracing her daughter.*)

(LOPAHIN enters with CHARLOTTA who is softly humming a song.)

GAYEFF: Lucky Charlotta: she's singing!

CHARLOTTA (*taking a bundle that looks like a baby wrapped up*): My baby, bye, bye—(*A baby's cry is heard: Ooah, ooah—!*) Hush, my darling, my dear little boy. (*Ooah, ooah—!*) I am so sorry for you! (*Throwing the bundle back.*) Will you please find me a position? I cannot go on like this.

LOPAHIN: We will find something, Charlotta Ivanovna, don't worry.

GAYEFF: Everybody is dropping us, Varya is going away.—All of a sudden we are not needed.

CHARLOTTA: I have no place in town to live. I must go away. (*Humming.*) It's all the same—

(PISHTCHIK *enters.*)

LOPAHIN: The freak of nature—!

PISHTCHIK (*out of breath*): Ugh, let me catch my breath—I'm exhausted— My honored friends—Give me some water—

GAYEFF: After money, I suppose? This humble servant will flee from sin! (*Goes out.*)

PISHTCHIK: It's a long time since I was here—Most beautiful lady—(*To* LOPAHIN.) You here—? Glad to see you—a man of the greatest intellect—Here—Take it—(*Giving* LOPAHIN *some money.*) Four hundred roubles—That leaves eight hundred and forty I still owe you—

LOPAHIN (*with astonishment, shrugging his shoulders*): I must be dreaming. But where did you get it?

PISHTCHIK: Wait—I'm hot—Most extraordinary event. Some Englishmen came and found on my land some kind of white clay—(*To* LYUBOFF ANDREEVNA.) And four hundred for you—Beautiful lady—Wonderful lady—(*Handing over the money.*) The rest later. (*Taking a drink of water.*) Just now a young man was saying on the train that some great philosopher recommends jumping off roofs—"Jump!" he says, and "therein lies the whole problem." (*With astonishment.*) You don't say! Water!

LOPAHIN: And what Englishmen were they?

PISHTCHIK: I leased them the parcel of land with the clay for twenty-four years—And now, excuse me, I haven't time—I must run along—I'm going to Znoykoff's—To Kardamonoff's—I owe everybody— (*Drinking.*) I wish you well—I'll drop in on Thursday—

LYUBOFF ANDREEVNA: We are moving to town right away, and tomorrow I'm going abroad—

PISHTCHIK: What? (*Alarmed.*) Why to town? That's why I see furniture— Suitcases—Well, no matter—(*Tearfully.*) No matter—Men of the greatest minds—those Englishmen—No matter—Good luck! God will help you—No matter—Everything in this world comes to an end— (*Kissing* LYUBOFF ANDREEVNA'S *hand.*) And should the report reach you that my end has come, think of that well-known horse and say: "There was once on earth a so and so—Semyonoff Pishtchik—The kingdom of Heaven be his." Most remarkable weather—yes—(*Going out greatly disconcerted, but immediately returning and speaking from the door.*) Dashenka sends her greetings! (*Goes out.*)

LYUBOFF ANDREEVNA: And now we can go. I am leaving with two worries. First, that Fiers is sick. (*Glancing at her watch.*) We still have five minutes—

ANYA: Mama, Fiers has already been sent to the hospital. Yasha sent him off this morning.

LYUBOFF ANDREEVNA: My second worry—is Varya. She is used to getting up early and working, and now without any work she is like a fish out of water. She has grown thin, pale and cries all the time, poor thing—(*A pause.*) You know this, Yermolay Alexeevich: I dreamed—of marrying her to you. And there was every sign of your getting married. (*Whispering to* ANYA, *who beckons to* CHARLOTTA; *both go out.*) She loves you, you are fond of her, and I don't know, don't know why it is you seem to avoid each other—I don't understand it!

LOPAHIN: I don't understand it either, I must confess. It's all strange somehow—If there's still time, I am ready right now even—Let's finish it up—and *basta,* but without you I feel I won't propose.

LYUBOFF ANDREEVNA: But that's excellent. Surely it takes only a minute. I'll call her at once.

LOPAHIN: And to fit the occasion there's the champagne. (*Looking at the glasses.*) Empty, somebody has already drunk them. (YASHA *coughs.*) That's what's called lapping it up—

LYUBOFF ANDREEVNA (*vivaciously*): Splendid! We'll go out—Yasha, *allez!* I'll call her—(*Through the door.*) Varya, drop everything and come here. Come on! (*Goes out with* YASHA.)

LOPAHIN (*looking at his watch*): Yes—

(*A pause. Behind the door you hear smothered laughter, whispering, finally* VARYA *enters.*)

VARYA (*looking at the luggage a long time*): That's strange, I just can't find it—

LOPAHIN: What are you looking for?

VARYA: I packed it myself and don't remember where. (*A pause.*)

LOPAHIN: Where do you expect to go now, Varvara Mikhailovna?

VARYA: I? To Regulin's. I agreed to go there to look after the house—As a sort of housekeeper.

LOPAHIN: That's in Yashnevo? It's nigh on to seventy miles. (*A pause.*) And here ends life in this house—

VARYA (*examining the luggage*): But where is it? Either I put it in the trunk, perhaps—Yes, life in this house is ended—it won't be any more—

LOPAHIN: And I am going to Harkoff now—By the next train. I've a lot to do. And I am leaving Epihodoff—on the ground here—I've hired him.

VARYA: Well!

LOPAHIN: Last year at this time it had already been snowing, if you remember, and now it's quiet, it's sunny. It's only that it's cold, about three degrees of frost.

VARYA: I haven't noticed. (*A pause.*) And besides our thermometer is broken—(*A pause. A voice from the yard through the door.*) Yermolay Alexeevich—

LOPAHIN (*as if he had been expecting this call for a long time*): This minute! (*Goes out quickly.*)

(VARYA, *sitting on the floor, putting her head on a bundle of clothes, sobs quietly. The door opens,* LYUBOFF ANDREEVNA *enters cautiously.*)

VARYA (*she is not crying any longer, and has wiped her eyes*): Yes, it's time, Mama. I can get to Regulin's today, if we are just not too late for the train—(*Through the door.*) Anya, put your things on! (ANYA, *then* GAYEFF *and* CHARLOTTA IVANOVNA *enter.* GAYEFF *has on a warm overcoat, with a hood. The servants gather, also the drivers.* EPIHODOFF *busies himself with the luggage.*) Now we can be on our way.

ANYA (*joyfully*): On our way!

GAYEFF: My friends, my dear, kind friends! Leaving this house forever, can I remain silent, can I restrain myself from expressing, as we say, farewell, those feelings that fill now my whole being—

ANYA (*beseechingly*): Uncle!

VARYA: Dear Uncle, don't!

GAYEFF (*dejectedly*): Bank the yellow into the side pocket—I am silent—

(TROFIMOFF *and then* LOPAHIN *enter.*)

TROFIMOFF: Well, ladies and gentlemen, it's time to go!

LOPAHIN: Epihodoff, my coat!

LYUBOFF ANDREEVNA: I'll sit here just a minute more. It's as if I had never seen before what the walls in this house are like, what kind of ceilings, and now I look at them greedily, with such tender love—

GAYEFF: I remember when I was six years old, on Trinity Day, I sat in this window and watched my father going to Church—

LYUBOFF ANDREEVNA: Are all the things taken out?

LOPAHIN: Everything, I think. (*Putting on his overcoat. To* EPIHODOFF.) Epihodoff, you see that everything is in order.

EPIHODOFF (*talking in a hoarse voice*): Don't worry, Yermolay Alexeevich!

LOPAHIN: Why is your voice like that?

EPIHODOFF: Just drank some water, swallowed something.

YASHA (*with contempt*): The ignorance—

LYUBOFF ANDREEVNA: We are going and there won't be a soul left here—

LOPAHIN: Till spring.

VARYA (*she pulls an umbrella out from a bundle, it looks as if she were going to hit someone;* LOPAHIN *pretends to be frightened*): What do you, what do you—I never thought of it.

TROFIMOFF: Ladies and gentlemen, let's get in the carriages—It's time! The train is coming any minute.

VARYA: Petya, here they are, your rubbers, by the suitcase. (*Tearfully.*) And how dirty yours are, how old—!

TROFIMOFF (*putting on the rubbers*): Let's go, ladies and gentlemen!

GAYEFF (*greatly embarrassed, afraid he will cry*): The train—The station—Cross into the side, combination off the white into the corner—

LYUBOFF ANDREEVNA: Let's go!

LOPAHIN: Everybody here? Nobody there? (*Locking the side door on the left.*) Things are stored here, it must be locked up, let's go!

ANYA: Good-by, house! Good-by, the old life!

TROFIMOFF: Long live the new life!

(*Goes out with* ANYA. VARYA *casts a glance around the room, and without hurrying, goes out.* YASHA *and* CHARLOTTA, *with her dog, go out.*)

LOPAHIN: And so, till spring. Out, ladies and gentlemen—Till we meet. (*Goes out.*)

(LYUBOFF ANDREEVNA *and* GAYEFF *are left alone. As if they had been waiting for this, they throw themselves on one another's necks sobbing, but smothering their sobs as if afraid of being heard.*)

GAYEFF (*in despair*): Oh, Sister, Sister—

LYUBOFF ANDREEVNA: Oh, my dear, my lovely, beautiful orchard! My life, my youth, my happiness, good-by!

ANYA (ANYA'S *voice, gaily, appealingly*): Mama—!

TROFIMOFF (TROFIMOFF'S *voice, gaily, excitedly*): Aaooch!

LYUBOFF ANDREEVNA: For the last time, just to look at the walls, at the window—My dear mother used to love to walk around in this room—

GAYEFF: Oh, Sister, Sister—!

ANYA (ANYA'S *voice*): Mama—!

TROFIMOFF (TROFIMOFF'S *voice*): Aaooch—!

LYUBOFF ANDREEVNA: We are coming! (*They go out.*)

(*The stage is empty. You hear the keys locking all the doors, then the carriages drive off. It grows quiet. In the silence you hear the dull thud of an ax on a tree, a lonely, mournful sound. Footsteps are heard. From the door on the right* FIERS *appears. He is dressed as usual, in a jacket and a white waistcoat, slippers on his feet. He is sick.*)

FIERS (*going to the door and trying the knob*): Locked. They've gone. (*Sitting down on the sofa.*) They forgot about me—No matter—I'll sit here awhile—And Leonid Andreevich, for sure, didn't put on his fur coat, he went off with his topcoat—(*Sighing anxiously.*) And I didn't see to it—The young saplings! (*He mutters something that cannot be understood.*) Life has gone by, as if I hadn't lived at all—(*Lying down.*) I'll lie down awhile—You haven't got any strength, nothing is left, nothing—Ach, you—good-for-nothing—(*He lies still.*)

(*There is a far-off sound as if out of the sky, the sound of a snapped string, dying away, sad. A stillness falls, and there is only the thud of an ax on a tree, far away in the orchard.*)

The beginning of the second act of *The Cherry Orchard* is a particularly concise collocation of characteristics found in all of Chekhov's last four plays. Since the plays are so often misunderstood and since a main cause of misunderstanding is the failure to realize what Chekhov was doing and the assumption that he was trying to do something else, the passage may repay a closer look.

Its four characters are all employed in the Ranevskaya household, and all are minor: Charlotta, a governess of indeterminate youthfulness and cosmopolitan circus background; Epihodoff, a foolish clerk, whose dignity of speech and bearing continually collapses in pratfalls and jammed syntax; the maid Dunyasha, with whom Epihodoff is in love; and the brash young valet Yasha, Epihodoff's successful rival. They are together for no particular purpose. There is a touch of pathos in Charlotta's situation and perhaps in Epihodoff's, but none of the four is really an attractive character. They do not know each other very well and do not establish any close rapport. Their words bound off other words or drop, echoless, in a void of indifference and self-absorption. When Charlotta ends her opening monologue with a plea for human contact, Epihodoff breaks into song on the all-sufficiency of love. He is joined in singing by his rival Yasha. Dunyasha tells them they sound "like jackals." Alone with Yasha Dunyasha tells him she loves him. Yasha replies that he considers a girl who is in love immoral. Talk is desultory, punctuated by pauses and yawns. The constant changes in topic are incoherent: foreign travel, suicide, a cockroach in a glass of beer, an early Victorian philosopher. The setting is desolate: sunset among forgotten tombstones near an abandoned chapel, the cherry orchard on one side and a large town looming on the horizon.

One hesitates calling such a passage a "scene," because "scene" suggests a distinct unit within a larger plot dynamic. But no plot is furthered by this casual group, no phase of action marked, no issue raised or concluded, no climax prepared. The impression of aimless and listless small talk remains even when the passage is seen in the context of the whole play. At its end Charlotta is as lost and lonely as she is here, and Epihodoff neither kills himself nor ever stops stumbling over or crushing things or tangling his sentences. Neither her rifle nor his revolver is ever mentioned again, let alone fired—as if in deliberate repudiation of Chekhov's own early dictum that "if in the first act you hang a pistol on the wall, then in the last act it must be shot off. Otherwise you do not hang it there." The Epihodoff-Dunyasha-Yasha triangle ends in stalemate, like the other two tentative romances in the play, Lopahin's and Varya's, and Anya's and Trofimoff's. None of the four characters here influences the issue of whether or not the estate is to be sold or otherwise affects the destiny of the major characters.

To people used to the taut, significant action patterns of Western drama from Sophocles through Shakespeare and Ibsen, Chekhov's status as major dramatist may seem puzzling. The tension between Mme. Ranevskaya and her equally vague and ineffectual brother Gayeff on the one hand and the concerned and practical merchant Lopahin on the other on how to save the mortgaged estate provides *The Cherry Orchard* with more suspense and plot coherence than Chekhov's other important plays. Nevertheless, what coherence the play possesses is rather in the nature of frame than of substance. As in *The Sea-Gull, Uncle Vanya,* and *Three Sisters* most of the drama proceeds, like our sample passage, by incongruent juxtapositions of little banalities and irrelevancies, fatuities and incoherences—random fragments of life lifted on stage from a continuing flow of trivia to make an irregular, languid rhythm of inconsequence. Take the episode in Act I when Pishtchik swallows Mme. Ranevskaya's (Lyuboff Andreevna's) pills.

PISHTCHIK: You should never take medicaments, dear madam—They do neither harm nor good—Hand them here, dearest lady. (*He takes the pillbox, shakes the pills out into his palm, blows on them, puts them in his mouth and washes them down with kvass.*) There! Now!
LYUBOFF ANDREEVNA (*startled*): Why, you've lost your mind!
PISHTCHIK: I took all the pills.
LOPAHIN: Such a glutton!
(*Everyone laughs.*)

And that is the end of the episode. The pills are not missed, we are never told what Mme. Ranevskaya takes pills for, Pishtchik does not get sick, they do not alter his behavior in any way, nobody ever refers to them again. By the rules of sound play construction one should be shocked by such casualness and waste and demand to know the relevance of the incident. But its relevance is its nonrelevance to anything beyond its own inanity. Of such isolated bits of humdrum life, as startling as they are pointless, is Chekhov's world made. No wonder he found Ibsen "too simple" and disliked him for not "knowing life." To judge by his own plays, what he objected to in the Norwegian was his reduction of the rich and chaotic complexity of experience to tightly plotted melodrama of thematic import, in which every event is a link in a causal chain and every speech reveals character or contributes to the theme. Economy of means to a significant end is the Ibsen hallmark. Chekhov is lavish with apparently useless character and incident. His plays are not unplanned, and their quality of improvised rambling is the result of scrupulous craftsmanship, but his realism is of the inclusive kind that not only can afford but needs items that have no other function than to make a moment of live drama. Near the close of Act II there is heard, "as if from the sky," a "mournful" sound, "like the sound of a snapped string." A few moments later, a drunken beggar appears. If only because of mere proximity, is there a connection between sound and man? What do they mean? How do they function in the drama? The questions are unanswerable, even—in the sense in which they usually are asked—impertinent. We can only say that without the sound and the beggar a dimension of reality would be gone from the scene. Instead of Ibsen's stripped and strictly functional casts Chekhov prodigally peoples the Ranevskaya estate with a chorus of semi-grotesque retainers and hangers-on, for whom there is no more a definite function in the plot than there appears to be in the running of the household. The quartet in the opening of Act II are just four of them. He further diffuses the outline of his cast with unseen characters in a kind of ghostly attendance on those on stage: Mme. Ranevskaya's dead little boy Grisha, her Paris lover, Gayeff's rich old aunt in Yaroslavl, Pishtchik's clever daughter Dashenka. Swayed by the dead and the absent, the characters we *do* see appear more real and less strong.

Thus, Chekhov builds drama by a kind of pointillism. If we look too close we see only specks of reality, but at a distance a pattern emerges. As sentiment is about to become pathos and tension approaches tragic intensity, a sudden incongruity deflates theme and mood—a moment of slapstick, a change in tempo, an unattuned image or speech, a new topic of conversation. In Act I, when Varya tells Anya of the family's precarious financial position—"In August the estate is to be sold"—Lopahin suddenly sticks his head through the door and moos like a cow. "I'd land him one like that," threatens Varya tearfully, shaking her fist. In Act III she does almost exactly that, by unlucky timing hitting him over the head with a broomstick just as he enters to tell the family that he has bought the estate. In Chekhov, typically, farce impinges on the peripety of the main drama. Lopahin's allusions to Hamlet and Ophelia represent the third coordinate in the system that defines his and Varya's abortive romance in terms partly farcical and partly poignant. Just as Lopahin, the serf's son, impatient with procrastination and a businessman of action himself, is no Prince Hamlet, so is the Ranevskaya estate which he seeks to set right both a more innocent and a pettier world than the realm of Denmark. And poor Varya is only a formidable and rather foolish nun. Tragic grandeur is further deflated by Lopahin's consistent failure to remember Ophelia's name.*

From such discord and ambivalence the play builds its larger patterns. Old Fiers considers the emancipation of the serfs in 1863 a disaster. In contrast, Trofimoff, the muddled revolutionary idealist, envisions a brighter Russian future built by liberty and dignified labor. Between past and future the present moves by ceaseless ebb and flow. In Act I, Mme. Ranevskaya comes home; in Act IV she goes away. Arrival-departure frames the collection of discordant moments here as in Chekhov's other late plays. But departure is not conclusion. Though something passes, something also comes. The cherry trees fall by the blows of the ax that new enterprise wields. But how great is the loss? After all, the old recipe for drying cherries and keeping them "soft, . . . juicy, sweet, fragrant" is forgotten. But, then, is the main value of the orchard commercial? The beauty of the old order, but also its foolishness and gentle decadence, give way to Lopahin, the entrepreneur, the reluctant heir of the feudal past, including his own childhood and—though he does not know it—the old serf Fiers.

The pattern of change is framed by a still larger pattern. The play

---

*He also misquotes Shakespeare's lines, a fact which the English translation here does not take notice of. See David Magarshack, *Chekhov the Dramatist* (New York, 1960), pp. 278–279.

begins with Lopahin waking up and ends with Fiers falling asleep. What happens in the interval?

> We are such stuff
> As dreams are made on, and our little life
> Is rounded with a sleep.

That is, nothing—and everything. Is it just another odd fact that the first and the last act both take place in a room called "the Nursery" and that it is furnished in Act I and bare in Act IV? To Fiers at the end it is as if life has gone by and left him with a feeling of not having lived at all. Is *The Cherry Orchard* Chekhov's *Tempest* in a deeper sense than by being his last play? Lopahin has been taken to represent the new economic man, the proletarian become a rising merchant, a bourgeois forerunner of the Soviet revolution. Perhaps he is. There certainly is irony in his unawareness of his artistic inclinations and in his inability to escape his serf origin long enough to get himself a genteel wife, either Varya or her foster mother, Mme. Ranevskaya herself, who is—as certain of his speeches hint—the woman he really loves. But to seize upon socio-economic symbolism or on Lopahin's psychology as main theme is to lock Chekhov's kaleidoscope in one or the other of only two of its myriad constellations. Life may be "little" in Chekhov, as it is for most people, but the drama in which it is recorded is not impoverished. When people complain that "nothing happens" in Chekhov, one may agree to see what they have in mind. But they are quite wrong.

What is true, however, is that Chekhov's manner of drama is one that makes heavy demands on the *reader*. Few great playwrights gain more from performance than he. His distinctive tonality is muted on the page. In the absence of exciting scenes and strong plot, interest has to depend on imaginative evocation of spectacle, movement, and voice, and this, for most of us, is a new and difficult challenge. If we fail to meet it, bewilderment first and then boredom may follow. The strangeness and the number of the Russian names are further obstacles.

But even in the theater there are people who find Chekhov too wanly elegiac, slow, and indefinite. Chekhov realized the danger himself and quarreled with the two directors of the Moscow Art Theater for not guarding sufficiently against it. One of them was Konstantin Stanislavsky, whose naturalistic staging of *The Sea-Gull* in 1898 had established Chekhov's reputation as a dramatist and whose painstaking rehearsals, emphasis on ensemble acting, and insistence that the actor engage himself imaginatively and emotionally in his part (we call all this "Method" acting today) were to make him the single most important influence on modern acting. But to Chekhov he was the man who had "ruined" his *Cherry Orchard.* In an effort, perhaps, to avert the disaster he saw was coming he wrote to Stanislavsky's wife even before rehearsals began, in October, 1903: "I'm afraid my play has turned out to be not a drama but a comedy, and in places even a farce, and I fear Nemirovich-Danchenko [the literary director of the Theater] will never forgive me for that." What actually happened was, from Chekhov's point of view, even worse. So far from feeling any need for forgiving Chekhov for having written a comedy, it did not even occur to the two directors that he had not written a tragedy. Some weeks after the first performance of *The Cherry Orchard* in January, 1904, and about four months before his death, Chekhov wrote to his wife about the Stanislavsky production:

> Take my *Cherry Orchard.* Is it my *Cherry Orchard?* With the exception of one or two parts nothing in it is mine. I am describing life, ordinary life, and not blank despondency. They either make me into a cry-baby or a bore. They invent something about me out of their own heads, anything they like, something I never thought of or dreamed about. This is beginning to make me angry.

There is in principle no reason why Stanislavsky and Nemirovich-Danchenko cannot have perceived the nature of *The Cherry Orchard* more clearly than Chekhov himself. But did they? Most producers have heeded the playwright's protests against a tragic *Cherry Orchard,* but few have staged it as a comedy or agreed with Chekhov that Lopahin's part is comical and the whole play "gay and frivolous." For most people, on either side of the footlights, Chekhov remains the twilight voice of old Russia, a bittersweet realist poet of mood and atmosphere, the sympathetic–ironic chronicler of the heartaches and frustrations and failures of decent but foolishly weak and confused people. What comedy there is in Chekhov is in a very minor key indeed, at most arch and acid, very rarely hearty. Trofimoff, for example, is an undoubted fool, and yet he is made the spokesman of genuine values: the blessings of work and love. Other visionary idealists in Chekhov are also presented as fatuous escapists into vague and wordy optimism.

From the vantage point of today we may wonder whether Chekhov, were he still alive, would have persisted in using "comedy" and "farce" as labels for *The Cherry Orchard*. To turn again to the opening of Act II, consider the following exchange:

CHARLOTTA: . . . Who my parents were, perhaps they weren't even married—I don't know. (*Taking a cucumber out of her pocket and beginning to eat it.*) I don't know a thing. (*A pause.*) I'd like so much to talk but there's not anybody. I haven't anybody.

EPIHODOFF (*playing the guitar and singing*): "What care I for the noisy world, what care I for friends and foes."—How pleasant it is to play the mandolin!

DUNYASHA: That's a guitar, not a mandolin. (*Looking into a little mirror and powdering her face.*)

EPIHODOFF: For a madman who is in love this is a mandolin—(*Singing.*) "If only my heart were warm with the fire of requited love."

(YASHA *sings with him.*)

This is quintessential Chekhov, but it might have come from a contemporary play of the absurd theater. Without a "proper passport" and with her sense of lostness and isolation in a meaningless existence—"Who I am, why I am, is unknown"—Charlotta becomes an almost Kafkaesque figure in a parable of modern man's existential agony. In her military cap, tinkering with a rifle, eating a cucumber, holding forth in unhappy monologue, she is a figure of pathetic farce as well. The incongruity is "absurd" in the modern, literary, sense. She and Epihodoff are equally lonely, but their monodies produce only discord. The scenic and verbal imagery of guitar and cigar, guns and pocket mirror, jackals, spider, cockroach, and a serving-maid's lily-white, ladylike hands belongs in an odd, vaguely disturbing dream. "Absurd" also is people's failure to relate through language. Charlotta's sudden vaudeville tricks come to seem less like farcical interruptions than like symptoms of an isolation desperately battered by the inarticulate prisoner within. Epihodoff reads important books he cannot understand and which fail to convince him that life is worth living. For lack of human respondents Gayeff apostrophizes bookcases and Nature and hides his embarrassment in billiard jargon and candy. As means to overcome a breakdown in communication his antics resemble Charlotta's tricks. Since experience is wholly subjective, there can be no stable relationship between word and meaning:

DUNYASHA: That's a guitar, not a mandolin. . . .
EPIHODOFF: For a madman who is in love this is a mandolin— . . .

Even the lovers fail to communicate:

DUNYASHA: I have come to love you passionately, you are educated, you can discuss anything. (*A pause.*)
YASHA (*yawning*): Yes sir— . . .

Certainly there is comedy here, even farce, but is that *all* there is?

The point is not that Chekhov anticipated the absurd theater some sixty years ago or that today's absurdists are indebted to him—not even, though this is true, that the absurd manner is not the invention of existential playwrights of the last decade. The point of Chekhov's "absurdity" is the more general one that art always "is" and does not "mean" and that modern art has made a fetish and a program of what previous generations of artists tacitly took for granted.

Not that Chekhov, of course, is "meaningless"—literally—any more than are playwrights like Beckett and Genet. Art cannot be "meaningless"—literally—and still remain art (which is why people who make nothing of the absurdists quite properly deny them status as dramatists). "Absurd" is a silly epithet for drama that takes reality too seriously to presume to subject it to interpretation or judgment or to arrangement by laws of narrative. The dictum that art be without meaning means that its meaning should be inviolately implicit and centripetal. The artist's image of reality does not derive its authority from a nonart original and does not justify itself by any intention of altering such an original, for however commendable an end. Chekhov was occasionally provoked into claiming for his plays a pragmatic value for lethargic, end-of-the-century Russian intelligentsia—object lessons in how *not* to manage the business of life—but their uncompromising objectivity suggests that the claim was only an effort to speak a language that dull producers could understand. With reference to this specific case: in the opening of Act II of *The Cherry Orchard* Chekhov is not telling us that life is trivial, futile, and solitary or asking us to do something about it. He is showing us some trivial, futile, and solitary moments in a scenic imitation of life. The distinction is all-important: ultimately that between an election poster and Rembrandt. "You ask me what life is?" he once wrote to his wife. "It is like asking what a carrot is. A carrot is a carrot; that's all we know." The artist records facts: people, places, things, words. But held in the artist's vision, they catch the comical or frightening but always vulnerable human pose—"the lust of the flesh and the soul's incurable loneliness"—between the quaint, incontrovertible events of birth and death. Our most vital drama, old and contemporary, claims to do no more and no less.

Tennessee Williams

The Glass Menagerie

Nobody, not even the rain, has such small hands.

Characters

AMANDA WINGFIELD *the mother*
LAURA WINGFIELD *her daughter*
TOM WINGFIELD *her son*
JIM O'CONNOR *the gentleman caller*

Scene: *An alley in St. Louis.*

Part I. *Preparation for a Gentleman Caller.*
Part II. *The Gentleman Calls.*

Time: *Now and the Past.*

SCENE I

(*The Wingfield apartment is in the rear of the building, one of those vast hive-like conglomerations of cellular living-units that flower as warty growths in overcrowded urban centers of lower middle-class population and are symptomatic of the impulse of this largest and fundamentally enslaved section of American society to avoid fluidity and differentiation and to exist and function as one interfused mass of automatism.*

The apartment faces an alley and is entered by a fire-escape, a structure whose name is a touch of accidental poetic truth, for all of these huge buildings are always burning with the slow and implacable fires of human desperation. The fire-escape is included in the set—that is, the landing of it and steps descending from it.

The scene is memory and is therefore nonrealistic. Memory takes a lot of poetic license. It omits some details; others are exaggerated, according to the emotional value of the articles it touches, for memory is seated predominantly in the heart. The interior is therefore rather dim and poetic.

At the rise of the curtain, the audience is faced with the dark, grim rear wall of the Wingfield tenement. This building, which runs parallel to the footlights, is flanked on both sides by dark, narrow alleys which run into murky canyons of tangled clotheslines, garbage cans and the sinister latticework of neighboring fire-escapes. It is up and down these side alleys that exterior entrances and exits are made, during the play. At the end of TOM'S opening commentary, the dark tenement wall slowly reveals (by means of a transparency) the interior of the ground floor Wingfield apartment.

Downstage is the living room, which also serves as a sleeping room for LAURA, *the sofa unfolding to make her bed. Upstage, center, and divided by a wide arch or second proscenium with transparent faded portieres (or second curtain), is the dining room. In an old-fashioned what-not in the living room are seen scores of transparent glass animals. A blown-up photograph of the father hangs on the wall of the living room, facing the audience, to the left of the archway. It is the face of a very handsome young man in a doughboy's First World War cap. He is gallantly smiling, ineluctably smiling, as if to say, "I will be smiling forever."*

The audience hears and sees the opening scene in the dining room through both the transparent fourth wall of the building and the transparent gauze portieres of the dining-room arch. It is during this revealing scene that the fourth wall slowly ascends, out of sight. This transparent exterior wall is not brought down again until the very end of the play, during TOM'S *final speech.*

The narrator is an undisguised convention of the play. He takes whatever license with dramatic convention as is convenient to his purposes.

TOM *enters dressed as a merchant sailor from alley, stage left, and strolls across the front of the stage to the fire-escape. There he stops and lights a cigarette. He addresses the audience.*)

TOM: Yes, I have tricks in my pocket, I have things up my sleeve. But I am the opposite of a stage magician. He gives you illusion that has the appearance of truth. I give you truth in the pleasant disguise of illusion. To begin with, I turn back time. I reverse it to that quaint period, the thirties, when the huge middle class of America was matriculating in a school for the blind. Their eyes had failed them, or they had failed their eyes, and so they were having their fingers pressed forcibly down on the fiery Braille alphabet of a dissolving economy. In Spain there was revolution. Here there was only shouting and confusion. In Spain there was Guernica. Here there were disturbances of labor, sometimes pretty violent, in otherwise peaceful cities such as Chicago, Cleveland, Saint Louis. . . . This is the social background of the play.

(MUSIC.)

The play is memory. Being a memory play, it is dimly lighted, it is sentimental, it is not realistic. In memory everything seems to happen to music. That explains the fiddle in the wings. I am the narrator of the play, and also a character in it. The other characters are my mother, Amanda, my sister, Laura, and a gentleman caller who appears in the final scenes. He is the most realistic character in the play, being an emissary from a world of reality that we were somehow set apart from. But since I have a poet's weakness for symbols, I am using this character also as a symbol; he is the long delayed but always expected something that we live for. There is a fifth character in the play who doesn't appear except in this larger-than-life photograph over the mantel. This is our father who left us a long time ago. He was a telephone man who fell in love with long distances; he gave up his job with the telephone company and skipped the light fantastic out of town . . . The last we heard of him was a picture post-card from Mazatlan, on the Pacific coast of Mexico, containing a message of two words—"Hello—Good-bye!" and no address. I think the rest of the play will explain itself. . . .

(AMANDA'S *voice becomes audible through the portieres.*)

(LEGEND ON SCREEN: "OÙ SONT LES NEIGES.")

(*He divides the portieres and enters the upstage area.*)

(AMANDA *and* LAURA *are seated at a drop-leaf table. Eating is indicated by gestures without food or utensils.* AMANDA *faces the audience.* TOM *and* LAURA *are seated in profile.*)

(*The interior has lit up softly and through the scrim we see* AMANDA *and* LAURA *seated at the table in the upstage area.*)

AMANDA (*calling*): Tom?

TOM: Yes, Mother.

AMANDA: We can't say grace until you come to the table!

TOM: Coming, Mother. (*He bows slightly and withdraws, reappearing a few moments later in his place at the table.*)

AMANDA (*to her son*): Honey, don't *push* with your *fingers*. If you have to push with something, the thing to push with is a crust of bread. And chew—chew! Animals have sections in their stomachs which enable them to digest food without mastication, but human beings are supposed to chew their food before they swallow it down. Eat food leisurely, son, and really enjoy it. A well-cooked meal has lots of delicate flavors that have to be held in the mouth for appreciation. So chew your food and give your salivary glands a chance to function!

(TOM *deliberately lays his imaginary fork down and pushes his chair back from the table.*)

TOM: I haven't enjoyed one bite of this dinner because of your constant directions on how to eat it. It's you that makes me rush through meals with your hawk-like attention to every bite I take. Sickening—spoils my appetite—all this discussion of animals' secretion—salivary glands—mastication!

AMANDA (*lightly*): Temperament like a Metropolitan star! (*He rises and crosses downstage.*) You're not excused from the table.

TOM: I'm getting a cigarette.

AMANDA: You smoke too much.

(LAURA *rises.*)

LAURA: I'll bring in the blanc mange.

(*He remains standing with his cigarette by the portieres during the following.*)

AMANDA (*rising*): No, sister, no, sister—you be the lady this time and I'll be the darky.

LAURA: I'm already up.

AMANDA: Resume your seat, little sister—I want you to stay fresh and pretty—for gentlemen callers!

LAURA: I'm not expecting any gentlemen callers.

AMANDA (*crossing out to kitchenette. Airily*): Sometimes they come

when they are least expected! Why, I remember one Sunday afternoon in Blue Mountain—(*Enters kitchenette.*)

TOM: I know what's coming!

LAURA: Yes. But let her tell it.

TOM: Again?

LAURA: She loves to tell it.

(AMANDA *returns with bowl of dessert.*)

AMANDA: One Sunday afternoon in Blue Mountain—your mother received—*seventeen!*—gentlemen callers! Why, sometimes there
weren't chairs enough to accommodate them all. We had to send the
nigger over to bring in folding chairs from the parish house.

TOM (*remaining at portieres*): How did you entertain those gentlemen
callers?

AMANDA: I understood the art of conversation!

TOM: I bet you could talk.

AMANDA: Girls in those days *knew* how to talk, I can tell you.

TOM: Yes?

(IMAGE: AMANDA AS A GIRL ON A PORCH, GREETING CALLERS.)

AMANDA: They knew how to entertain their gentlemen callers. It wasn't
enough for a girl to be possessed of a pretty face and a graceful figure—although I wasn't slighted in either respect. She also needed to
have a nimble wit and a tongue to meet all occasions.

TOM: What did you talk about?

AMANDA: Things of importance going on in the world! Never anything
coarse or common or vulgar. (*She addresses* TOM *as though he were
seated in the vacant chair at the table though he remains by portieres.
He plays this scene as though he held the book.*) My callers were
gentlemen—all! Among my callers were some of the most prominent
young planters of the Mississippi Delta—planters and sons of planters!

(TOM *motions for music and a spot of light on* AMANDA.)

(*Her eyes lift, her face glows, her voice becomes rich and elegiac.*)

(SCREEN LEGEND: "OÙ SONT LES NEIGES.")

There was young Champ Laughlin who later became vice-president
of the Delta Planters Bank. Hadley Stevenson who was drowned in
Moon Lake and left his widow one hundred and fifty thousand in
Government bonds. There were the Cutrere brothers, Wesley and
Bates. Bates was one of my bright particular beaux! He got in a quarrel
with that wild Wainright boy. They shot it out on the floor of Moon

Lake Casino. Bates was shot through the stomach. Died in the ambulance on his way to Memphis. His widow was also well-provided for, came into eight or ten thousand acres, that's all. She married him on the rebound—never loved her—carried my picture on him the night he died! And there was that boy that every girl in the Delta had set her cap for! That beautiful, brilliant young Fitzhugh boy from Greene County!

TOM: What did he leave his widow?

AMANDA: He never married! Gracious, you talk as though all of my old admirers had turned up their toes to the daisies!

TOM: Isn't this the first you've mentioned that still survives?

AMANDA: That Fitzhugh boy went North and made a fortune—came to be known as the Wolf of Wall Street! He had the Midas touch, whatever he touched turned to gold! And I could have been Mrs. Duncan J. Fitzhugh, mind you! But—I picked your *father!*

LAURA (*rising*): Mother, let me clear the table.

AMANDA: No, dear, you go in front and study your typewriter chart. Or practice your shorthand a little. Stay fresh and pretty!—It's almost time for our gentlemen callers to start arriving. (*She flounces girlishly toward the kitchenette.*) How many do you suppose we're going to entertain this afternoon?

(TOM *throws down the paper and jumps up with a groan.*)

LAURA (*alone in the dining room*): I don't believe we're going to receive any, Mother.

AMANDA (*reappearing, airily*): What? No one—not one? You must be joking! (LAURA *nervously echoes her laugh. She slips in a fugitive manner through the half-open portieres and draws them gently behind her. A shaft of very clear light is thrown on her face against the faded tapestry of the curtains.* MUSIC: "THE GLASS MENAGERIE" UNDER FAINTLY. *Lightly.*) Not one gentleman caller? It can't be true! There must be a flood, there must have been a tornado!

LAURA: It isn't a flood, it's not a tornado, Mother. I'm just not popular like you were in Blue Mountain. . . . (TOM *utters another groan.* LAURA *glances at him with a faint, apologetic smile. Her voice catching a little.*) Mother's afraid I'm going to be an old maid.

THE SCENE DIMS OUT WITH "GLASS MENAGERIE" MUSIC.

SCENE II

("*Laura, Haven't You Ever Liked Some Boy?*"

On the dark stage the screen is lighted with the image of blue roses.

Gradually LAURA'S *figure becomes apparent and the screen goes out.*

The music subsides.

LAURA *is seated in the delicate ivory chair at the small clawfoot table.*

She wears a dress of soft violet material for a kimono—her hair tied back from her forehead with a ribbon.

She is washing and polishing her collection of glass.

AMANDA *appears on the fire-escape steps. At the sound of her ascent,* LAURA *catches her breath, thrusts the bowl of ornaments away and seats herself stiffly before the diagram of the typewriter keyboard as though it held her spellbound. Something has happened to* AMANDA. *It is written in her face as she climbs to the landing: a look that is grim and hopeless and a little absurd.*

She has on one of those cheap or imitation velvety-looking cloth coats with imitation fur collar. Her hat is five or six years old, one of those dreadful cloche hats that were worn in the late twenties and she is clasping an enormous black patent-leather pocketbook with nickel clasp and initials. This is her full-dress outfit, the one she usually wears to the D.A.R.

Before entering she looks through the door.

She purses her lips, opens her eyes wide, rolls them upward and shakes her head.

Then she slowly lets herself in the door. Seeing her mother's expression LAURA *touches her lips with a nervous gesture.*)

LAURA: Hello, Mother, I was—(*She makes a nervous gesture toward the chart on the wall.* AMANDA *leans against the shut door and stares at* LAURA *with a martyred look.*)

AMANDA: Deception? Deception? (*She slowly removes her hat and gloves, continuing the swift suffering stare. She lets the hat and gloves fall on the floor—a bit of acting.*)

LAURA (*shakily*): How was the D.A.R. meeting? (AMANDA *slowly opens her purse and removes a dainty white handkerchief which she shakes out delicately and delicately touches to her lips and nostrils.*) Didn't you go to the D.A.R. meeting, Mother?

AMANDA (*faintly, almost inaudibly*): —No.—No. (*Then more forcibly*). I did not have the strength—to go to the D.A.R. In fact, I did not have the courage! I wanted to find a hole in the ground and hide myself in it forever! (*She crosses slowly to the wall and removes the diagram of the typewriter keyboard. She holds it in front of her for a second, staring at it sweetly and sorrowfully—then bites her lips and tears it in two pieces.*)

LAURA (*faintly*): Why did you do that, Mother? (AMANDA *repeats the same procedure with the chart of the Gregg Alphabet.*) Why are you—

AMANDA: Why? Why? How old are you, Laura?

LAURA: Mother, you know my age.

AMANDA: I thought that you were an adult; it seems that I was mistaken. (*She crosses slowly to the sofa and sinks down and stares at* LAURA.)

LAURA: Please don't stare at me, Mother.

(AMANDA *closes her eyes and lowers her head. Count ten.*)

AMANDA: What are we going to do, what is going to become of us, what is the future?

(*Count ten.*)

LAURA: Has something happened, Mother? (AMANDA *draws a long breath and takes out the handkerchief again. Dabbing process.*) Mother, has—something happened?

AMANDA: I'll be all right in a minute. I'm just bewildered—(*Count five.*)—by life. . . .

LAURA: Mother, I wish that you would tell me what's happened!

AMANDA: As you know, I was supposed to be inducted into my office at the D.A.R. this afternoon. (IMAGE: A SWARM OF TYPEWRITERS.) But I stopped off at Rubicam's Business College to speak to your teachers about your having a cold and ask them what progress they thought you were making down there.

LAURA: Oh. . . .

AMANDA: I went to the typing instructor and introduced myself as your mother. She didn't know who you were. Wingfield, she said. We don't have any such student enrolled at the school! I assured her she did, that you had been going to classes since early in January. "I wonder," she said, "if you could be talking about that terribly shy little girl who dropped out of school after only a few days' attendance?" "No," I said, "Laura, my daughter, has been going to school every day for the past six weeks!" "Excuse me," she said. She took the attendance book out and there was your name, unmistakably printed, and all the dates you were absent until they decided that you had dropped out of school. I still said, "No, there must have been some mistake! There must have been some mix-up in the records!" And she said, "No—I remember her perfectly now. Her hands shook so that she couldn't hit the right keys! The first time we gave a speed-test, she broke down completely—was sick at the stomach and almost had to be carried into the wash-room! After that morning she never showed up any more. We phoned the house but never got any answer—while I was working at Famous and Barr, I suppose, demonstrating those—Oh!" I felt so weak I could barely keep on my feet! I had to sit down while they got me a glass of water! Fifty dollars' tuition, all of our plans—my hopes and ambitions for you—just gone up the spout, just gone up the spout like that. (LAURA *draws a long breath and gets awkwardly to her feet. She crosses to the victrola and winds it up.*) What are you doing?

LAURA: Oh! (*She releases the handle and returns to her seat.*)

AMANDA: Laura, where have you been going when you've gone out pretending that you were going to business college?

LAURA: I've just been going out walking.

AMANDA: That's not true.

LAURA: It is. I just went walking.

AMANDA: Walking? Walking? In winter? Deliberately courting pneumonia in that light coat? Where did you walk to, Laura?

LAURA: All sorts of places—mostly in the park.

AMANDA: Even after you'd started catching that cold?

LAURA: It was the lesser of two evils, Mother. (IMAGE: WINTER SCENE IN PARK.) I couldn't go back up. I—threw up—on the floor!

AMANDA: From half past seven till after five every day you mean to tell me you walked around in the park, because you wanted to make me think that you were still going to Rubicam's Business College?

LAURA: It wasn't as bad as it sounds. I went inside places to get warmed up.

AMANDA: Inside where?

LAURA: I went in the art museum and the bird-houses at the Zoo. I visited the penguins every day! Sometimes I did without lunch and went to the movies. Lately I've been spending most of my afternoons in the Jewel-box, that big glass house where they raise the tropical flowers.

AMANDA: You did all this to deceive me, just for the deception? (LAURA *looks down.*) Why?

LAURA: Mother, when you're disappointed, you get that awful suffering look on your face, like the picture of Jesus' mother in the museum!

AMANDA: Hush!

LAURA: I couldn't face it.

(*Pause. A whisper of strings.*)

(LEGEND: "THE CRUST OF HUMILITY.")

AMANDA: (*hopelessly fingering the huge pocketbook*): So what are we going to do the rest of our lives? Stay home and watch the parades go by? Amuse ourselves with the glass menagerie, darling? Eternally play those worn-out phonograph records your father left as a painful reminder of him? We won't have a business career—we've given that up because it gave us nervous indigestion! (*Laughs wearily.*) What is there left but dependency all our lives? I know so well what becomes of unmarried women who aren't prepared to occupy a position. I've seen such pitiful cases in the South—barely tolerated spinsters living upon the grudging patronage of sister's husband or brother's wife!—stuck away in some little mouse-trap of a room—encouraged by one in-law to visit another—little birdlike women without any nest—eating the crust of humility all their life! Is that the future that we've mapped out for ourselves? I swear it's the only alternative I can think of! It isn't a very pleasant alternative, is it? Of course—some girls do marry. (LAURA *twists her hands nervously.*) Haven't you ever liked some boy?

LAURA: Yes. I liked one once. (*Rises.*) I came across his picture a while ago.

AMANDA (*with some interest*): He gave you his picture?

LAURA: No, it's in the yearbook.

AMANDA (*disappointed*): Oh—a high-school boy.

(SCREEN IMAGE: JIM AS HIGH-SCHOOL HERO BEARING A SILVER CUP.)

LAURA: Yes. His name was Jim. (LAURA *lifts the heavy annual from the claw-foot table.*) Here he is in *The Pirates of Penzance.*

AMANDA (*absently*): The what?

LAURA: The operetta the senior class put on. He had a wonderful voice and we sat across the aisle from each other Mondays, Wednesdays and Fridays in the Aud. Here he is with the silver cup for debating! See his grin?

AMANDA (*absently*): He must have had a jolly disposition.

LAURA: He used to call me—Blue Roses.

(IMAGE: BLUE ROSES.)

AMANDA: Why did he call you such a name as that?

LAURA: When I had that attack of pleurosis—he asked me what was the matter when I came back. I said pleurosis—he thought that I said Blue Roses! So that's what he always called me after that. Whenever he saw me, he'd holler, "Hello, Blue Roses!" I didn't care for the girl that he went out with. Emily Meisenbach. Emily was the best-dressed girl at Soldan. She never struck me, though, as being sincere . . . It says in the

Personal Section—they're engaged. That's—six years ago! They must be married by now.

AMANDA: Girls that aren't cut out for business careers usually wind up married to some nice man. (*Gets up with a spark of revival.*) Sister, that's what you'll do!

(LAURA *utters a startled, doubtful laugh. She reaches quickly for a piece of glass.*)

LAURA: But, Mother—

AMANDA: Yes? (*Crossing to photograph.*)

LAURA (*in a tone of frightened apology*): I'm—crippled!

(IMAGE: SCREEN.)

AMANDA: Nonsense! Laura, I've told you never, never to use that word. Why, you're not crippled, you just have a little defect—hardly noticeable, even! When people have some slight disadvantage like that, they cultivate other things to make up for it—develop charm—and vivacity—and—*charm!* That's all you have to do! (*She turns again to the photograph.*) One thing your father had *plenty of*—was charm!

(TOM *motions to the fiddle in the wings.*)

THE SCENE FADES OUT WITH MUSIC

SCENE III

(LEGEND ON SCREEN: "AFTER THE FIASCO—")

(TOM *speaks from the fire-escape landing.*)

TOM: After the fiasco at Rubicam's Business College, the idea of getting a gentleman caller for Laura began to play a more important part in Mother's calculations. It became an obsession. Like some archetype of the universal unconscious, the image of the gentleman caller haunted our small apartment. . . . (IMAGE: YOUNG MAN AT DOOR WITH FLOWERS.) An evening at home rarely passed without some allusion to this image, this spectre, this hope. . . . Even when he wasn't mentioned, his presence hung in Mother's preoccupied look and in my sister's frightened, apologetic manner—hung like a sentence passed upon the Wingfields! Mother was a woman of action as well as words. She began to take logical steps in the planned direction. Late that winter and in the early spring—realizing that extra money would be needed to properly feather the nest and plume the bird—she conduced a vigorous campaign on the telephone, roping in subscribers to one of those magazines for matrons called *The Home-maker's Companion,* the type of journal that features the serialized sublimations of ladies of letters who think in terms of delicate cup-like breasts, slim, tapering waists, rich, creamy thighs, eyes like wood-smoke in autumn, fingers that soothe and caress like strains of music, bodies as powerful as Etruscan sculpture.

(SCREEN IMAGE: GLAMOR MAGAZINE COVER.)

(AMANDA *enters with phone on long extension cord. She is spotted in the dim stage.*)

AMANDA: Ida Scott? This is Amanda Wingfield! We *missed* you at the D.A.R. last Monday! I said to myself: She's probably suffering with that sinus condition! How is that sinus condition? Horrors! Heaven have mercy!—You're a Christian martyr, yes, that's what you are, a Christian martyr! Well, I just now happened to notice that your subscription to the *Companion's* about to expire! Yes, it expires with the next issue, honey!—just when that wonderful new serial by Bessie Mae Hopper is getting off to such an exciting start. Oh, honey, it's something that you can't miss! You remember how *Gone With the Wind* took everybody by storm? You simply couldn't go out if you hadn't read it. All everybody *talked* was Scarlett O'Hara. Well, this is a book that critics already compare to *Gone With the Wind.* It's the *Gone With the Wind* of the post–World War generation!—What?—Burning?—Oh, honey, don't let them burn, go take a look in the oven and I'll hold the wire! Heavens—I think she's hung up!

DIM OUT

(LEGEND ON SCREEN: "YOU THINK I'M IN LOVE WITH CONTINENTAL SHOE-MAKERS?")

(*Before the stage is lighted, the violent voices of* TOM *and* AMANDA *are heard.*)

(*They are quarreling behind the portieres. In front of them stands* LAURA *with clenched hands and panicky expression.*)

(*A clear pool of light on her figure throughout this scene.*)

TOM: What in Christ's name am I—
AMANDA (*shrilly*): Don't you use that—
TOM: Supposed to do!
AMANDA: Expression! Not in my—
TOM: Ohhh!
AMANDA: Presence! Have you gone out of your senses?

TOM: I have, that's true, *driven* out!

AMANDA: What is the matter with you, you—big—big—IDIOT!

TOM: Look—I've got *no thing*, no single thing—

AMANDA: Lower your voice!

TOM: In my life here that I can call my OWN! Everything is—

AMANDA: Stop that shouting!

TOM: Yesterday you confiscated my books! You had the nerve to—

AMANDA: I took that horrible novel back to the library—yes! That hideous book by that insane Mr. Lawrence. (TOM *laughs wildly.*) I cannot control the output of diseased minds or people who cater to them— (TOM *laughs still more wildly.*) BUT I WON'T ALLOW SUCH FILTH BROUGHT INTO MY HOUSE! No, no, no, no, no!

TOM: House, house! Who pays rent on it, who makes a slave of himself to—

AMANDA (*fairly screeching*): Don't you DARE to—

TOM: No, no, *I* mustn't say things! *I've* got to just—

AMANDA: Let me tell you—

TOM: I don't want to hear any more! (*He tears the portieres open. The upstage area is lit with a turgid smoky red glow.*)

(AMANDA'S *hair is in metal curlers and she wears a very old bathrobe, much too large for her slight figure, a relic of the faithless Mr. Wingfield.*)

(*An upright typewriter and a wild disarray of manuscripts is on the drop-leaf table. The quarrel was probably precipitated by* AMANDA'S *interruption of his creative labor. A chair lying overthrown on the floor.*)

(*Their gesticulating shadows are cast on the ceiling by the fiery glow.*)

AMANDA: You *will* hear more, you—

TOM: No, I won't hear more, I'm going out!

AMANDA: You come right back in—

TOM: Out, out out! Because I'm—

AMANDA: Come back here, Tom Wingfield! I'm not through talking to you!

TOM: Oh, go—

LAURA (*desperately*):—Tom!

AMANDA: You're going to listen, and no more insolence from you! I'm at the end of my patience! (*He comes back toward her.*)

TOM: What do you think I'm at! Aren't I supposed to have any patience to reach the end of, Mother? I know, I know. It seems unimportant to you, what I'm *doing*—what I *want* to do—having a little *difference* between them! You don't think that—

AMANDA: I think you've been doing things that you're ashamed of. That's why you act like this. I don't believe that you go every night to the movies. Nobody goes to the movies night after night. Nobody in their right minds goes to the movies as often as you pretend to. People don't go to the movies at nearly midnight, and movies don't let out at two A.M. Come in stumbling. Muttering to yourself like a maniac! You get three hours sleep and then go to work. Oh, I can picture the way you're doing down there. Moping, doping, because you're in no condition.

TOM (*wildly*): No, I'm in no condition!

AMANDA: What right have you got to jeopardize your job? Jeopardize the security of us all? How do you think we'd manage if you were—

TOM: Listen! You think I'm crazy about the *warehouse?* (*He bends fiercely toward her slight figure.*) You think I'm in love with the Continental Shoemakers? You think I want to spend fifty-five *years* down there in that—*celotex interior!* with—*fluorescent—tubes!* Look! I'd rather somebody picked up a crowbar and battered out my brains—than go back mornings! I *go!* Every time you come in yelling that God damn *"Rise and Shine!" "Rise and Shine!"* I say to myself, "How *lucky dead* people are!" But I get up. I *go!* For sixty-five dollars a month I give up all that I dream of doing and being *ever!* And you say self—*self's* all I ever think of. Why, listen, if self is what I thought of, Mother, I'd be where he is—GONE! (*Pointing to father's picture.*) As far as the system of transportation reaches! (*He starts past her. She grabs his arm.*) Don't grab at me, Mother!

AMANDA: Where are you going?

TOM: I'm going to the *movies!*

AMANDA: I don't believe that lie!

TOM (*crouching toward her, overtowering her tiny figure. She backs away, gasping*): I'm going to opium dens! Yes, opium dens, dens of vice and criminals' hang-outs, Mother. I've joined the Hogan gang, I'm a hired assassin, I carry a tommy-gun in a violin case! I run a string of cat-houses in the Valley! They call me Killer, Killer Wingfield, I'm leading a double-life, a simple, honest warehouse worker by day, by night, a dynamic *czar* of the *underworld, Mother.* I go to gambling casinos, I spin away fortunes on the roulette table! I wear a patch over one eye and a false mustache, sometimes I put on green whiskers. On those occasions they call me—*El Diablo!* Oh, I could tell you things to make you sleepless! My enemies plan to dynamite this place. They're going to blow us all sky-high some night! I'll be glad, very happy, and so will you! You'll go up, up on a broomstick, over Blue Mountain with seventeen gentlemen callers! You ugly—babbling old—*witch.* . . . (*He goes through a series of violent, clumsy move-*

ments, seizing his overcoat, lunging to the door, pulling it fiercely open. The women watch him, aghast. His arm catches in the sleeve of the coat as he struggles to pull it on. For a moment he is pinioned by the bulky garment. With an outraged groan he tears the coat off again, splitting the shoulder of it, and hurls it across the room. It strikes against the shelf of LAURA's glass collection, there is a tinkle of shattering glass. LAURA cries out as if wounded.)

(MUSIC LEGEND: "THE GLASS MENAGERIE.")

LAURA (shrilly): My glass!—menagerie. . . . (She covers her face and turns away.)

(But AMANDA is still stunned and stupefied by the "ugly witch" so that she barely notices this occurrence. Now she recovers her speech.)

AMANDA (in an awful voice): I won't speak to you—until you apologize! (She crosses through portieres and draws them together behind her. TOM is left with LAURA. LAURA clings weakly to the mantel with her face averted. TOM stares at her stupidly for a moment. Then he crosses to shelf. Drops awkwardly to his knees to collect the fallen glass, glancing at LAURA as if he would speak but couldn't.)

"The Glass Menagerie" steals in as

THE SCENE DIMS OUT

SCENE IV

(The interior is dark. Faint light in the alley.

A deep-voiced bell in a church is tolling the hour of five as the scene commences.

TOM appears at the top of the alley. After each solemn boom of the bell in the tower, he shakes a little noise-maker or rattle as if to express the tiny spasm of man in contrast to the sustained power and dignity of the Almighty. This and the unsteadiness of his advance make it evident that he has been drinking.

As he climbs the few steps to the fire-escape landing light steals up inside. LAURA appears in night-dress, observing TOM's empty bed in the front room.

TOM fishes in his pockets for the door-key, removing a motley assortment of articles in the search, including a perfect shower of movie-ticket stubs and an empty bottle. At last he finds the key, but just as he is about to insert it, it slips from his fingers. He strikes a match and crouches below the door.)

TOM (*bitterly*): One crack—and it falls through!

(LAURA *opens the door.*)

LAURA: Tom! Tom, what are you doing?

TOM: Looking for a door-key.

LAURA: Where have you been all this time?

TOM: I have been to the movies.

LAURA: All this time at the movies?

TOM: There was a very long program. There was a Garbo picture and a Mickey Mouse and a travelogue and a newsreel and a preview of coming attractions. And there was an organ solo and a collection for the milk-fund—simultaneously—which ended up in a terrible fight between a fat lady and an usher!

LAURA (*innocently*): Did you have to stay through everything?

TOM: Of course! And, oh, I forgot! There was a big stage show! The headliner on this stage show was Malvolio the Magician. He performed wonderful tricks, many of them, such as pouring water back and forth between pitchers. First it turned to wine and then it turned to beer and then it turned to whiskey. I know it was whiskey it finally turned into because he needed somebody to come up out of the audience to help him, and I came up—both shows! It was Kentucky Straight Bourbon. A very generous fellow, he gave souvenirs. (*He pulls from his back pocket a shimmering rainbow-colored scarf.*) He gave me this. This is his magic scarf. You can have it, Laura. You wave it over a canary cage and you get a bowl of gold-fish. You wave it over the gold-fish bowl and they fly away canaries. . . . But the wonderfullest trick of all was the coffin trick. We nailed him into a coffin and he got out of the coffin without removing one nail. (*He has come inside.*) There is a trick that would come in handy for me—get me out of this 2 by 4 situation! (*Flops onto bed and starts removing shoes.*)

LAURA: Tom—Shhh!

TOM: What you shushing me for?

LAURA: You'll wake up Mother.

TOM: Goody, goody! Pay 'er back for all those "Rise an' Shines." (*Lies down, groaning.*) You know it don't take much intelligence to get yourself into a nailed-up coffin, Laura. But who in hell ever got himself out of one without removing one nail?

(*As if in answer, the father's grinning photograph lights up.*)

SCENE DIMS OUT

(*Immediately following: The church bell is heard striking six. At the sixth stroke the alarm clock goes off in* AMANDA'S *room, and after a few*

*moments we hear her calling: "Rise and Shine! Rise and Shine! Laura,
go tell your brother to rise and shine!")*

TOM (*Sitting up slowly*): I'll rise—but I won't shine.

(*The light increases.*)

AMANDA: Laura, tell your brother his coffee is ready.

(LAURA *slips into front room.*)

LAURA: Tom! it's nearly seven. Don't make Mother nervous. (*He stares at
her stupidly. Beseechingly.*) Tom, speak to Mother this morning. Make
up with her, apologize, speak to her!

TOM: She won't to me. It's her that started not speaking.

LAURA: If you just say you're sorry she'll start speaking.

TOM: Her not speaking—is that such a tragedy?

LAURA: Please—please!

AMANDA (*calling from kitchenette*): Laura, are you going to do what I
asked you to do, or do I have to get dressed and go out myself?

LAURA: Going, going—soon as I get on my coat! (*She pulls on a shapeless
felt hat with nervous, jerky movement, pleadingly glancing at* TOM.
Rushes awkwardly for coat. The coat is one of AMANDA'S, *inaccurately
made-over, the sleeves too short for* LAURA.) Butter and what else?

AMANDA (*entering upstage*): Just butter. Tell them to charge it.

LAURA: Mother, they make such faces when I do that.

AMANDA: Stick and stones may break our bones, but the expression on
Mr. Garfinkel's face won't harm us! Tell your brother his coffee is getting cold.

LAURA (*at door*): Do what I asked you, will you, will you, Tom?

(*He looks sullenly away.*)

AMANDA: Laura, go now or just don't go at all!

LAURA (*rushing out*): Going—going! (*A second later she cries out.* TOM
springs up and crosses to the door. AMANDA *rushes anxiously in.* TOM
opens the door.)

TOM: Laura?

LAURA: I'm all right. I slipped, but I'm all right.

AMANDA (*peering anxiously after her*): If anyone breaks a leg on those
fire-escape steps, the landlord ought to be sued for every cent he
possesses! (*She shuts door. Remembers she isn't speaking and returns
to other room.*)

(*As* TOM *enters listlessly for his coffee, she turns her back to him and
stands rigidly facing the window on the gloomy gray vault of the area-
way. Its light on her face with its aged but childish features is cruelly
sharp, satirical as a Daumier print.*)

(MUSIC UNDER: "AVE MARIA.")

(TOM *glances sheepishly but sullenly at her averted figure and slumps at the table. The coffee is scalding hot; he sips it and gasps and spits it back in the cup. At his gasp,* AMANDA *catches her breath and half turns. Then catches herself and turns back to window.*)

(TOM *blows on his coffee, glancing sidewise at his mother. She clears her throat.* TOM *clears his. He starts to rise. Sinks back down again, scratches his head, clears his throat again.* AMANDA *coughs.* TOM *raises his cup in both hands to blow on it, his eyes staring over the rim of it at his mother for several moments. Then he slowly sets the cup down and awkwardly and hesitantly rises from the chair.*)

TOM (*hoarsely*): Mother. I—I apologize. Mother. (AMANDA *draws a quick, shuddering breath. Her face works grotesquely. She breaks into childlike tears.*) I'm sorry for what I said, for everything that I said, I didn't mean it.

AMANDA (*sobbingly*): My devotion has made me a witch and so I make myself hateful to my children!

TOM: *No, you don't.*

AMANDA: I worry so much, don't sleep, it makes me nervous!

TOM (*gently*): I understand that.

AMANDA: I've had to put up a solitary battle all these years. But you're my right-hand bower! Don't fall down, don't fail!

TOM (*gently*): I try, Mother.

AMANDA (*with great enthusiasm*): Try and you will SUCCEED! (*The notion makes her breathless.*) Why, you—you're just *full* of natural endowments! Both of my children—they're *unusual* children! Don't you think I know it? I'm so—*proud!* Happy and—feel I've—so much to be thankful for but—Promise me one thing, son!

TOM: What, Mother?

AMANDA: Promise, son, you'll—never be a drunkard!

TOM (*turns to her grinning*): I will never be a drunkard, Mother.

AMANDA: That's what frightened me so, that you'd be drinking! Eat a bowl of Purina!

TOM: Just coffee, Mother.

AMANDA: Shredded wheat biscuit?

TOM: No, No, Mother, just coffee.

AMANDA: You can't put in a day's work on an empty stomach. You've got ten minutes—don't gulp! Drinking too-hot liquids makes cancer of the stomach. . . . Put cream in.

TOM: No, thank you.

AMANDA: To cool it.

TOM: No! No, thank you, I want it black.

AMANDA: I know, but it's not good for you. We have to do all that we can to build ourselves up. In these trying times we live in, all that we have to cling to is—each other. . . . That's why it's so important to—Tom, I—I sent out your sister so I could discuss something with you. If you hadn't spoken I would have spoken to you. (*Sits down.*)

TOM (*gently*): What is it, Mother, that you want to discuss?

AMANDA: *Laura!*

(TOM *puts his cup down slowly.*)

(LEGEND ON SCREEN: "LAURA.")

(MUSIC: "THE GLASS MENAGERIE.")

TOM:—Oh.—Laura . . .

AMANDA (*touching his sleeve*): You know how Laura is. So quiet but— still water runs deep! She notices things and I think she—broods about them. (TOM *looks up.*) A few days ago I came in and she was crying.

TOM: What about?

AMANDA: You.

TOM: Me?

AMANDA: She has an idea that you're not happy here.

TOM: What gave her that idea?

AMANDA: What gives her any idea? However, you do act strangely. I—I'm not criticizing, understand *that!* I know your ambitions do not lie in the warehouse, that like everybody in the whole wide world—you've had to—make sacrifices, but—Tom—Tom—life's not easy, it calls for— Spartan endurance! There's so many things in my heart that I cannot describe to you! I've never told you but I—*loved your father.* . . .

TOM (*gently*): I know that, Mother.

AMANDA: And you—when I see you taking after his ways! Staying out late—and—well, you *had* been drinking the night you were in that— terrifying condition! Laura says that you hate the apartment and that you go out nights to get away from it! Is that true, Tom?

TOM: No. You say there's so much in your heart that you can't describe to me. That's true of me, too. There's so much in my heart that I can't describe to *you!* So let's respect each other's—

AMANDA: But, why—*why*, Tom—are you always so *restless?* Where do you go to, nights?

TOM: I—go to the movies.

AMANDA: Why do you go to the movies so much, Tom?

TOM: I go to the movies because—I like adventure. Adventure is some- thing I don't have much of at work, so I go to the movies.

AMANDA: But, Tom, you go to the movies *entirely* too *much!*

TOM: I like a lot of adventure.

(AMANDA *looks baffled, then hurt. As the familiar inquisition resumes he becomes hard and impatient again.* AMANDA *slips back into her querulous attitude toward him.*)

(IMAGE ON SCREEN: SAILING VESSEL WITH JOLLY ROGER.)

AMANDA: Most young men find adventure in their careers.

TOM: Then most young men are not employed in a warehouse.

AMANDA: The world is full of young men employed in warehouses and offices and factories.

TOM: Do all of them find adventure in their careers?

AMANDA: They do or they do without it! Not everybody has a craze for adventure.

TOM: Man is by instinct a lover, a hunter, a fighter, and none of those instincts are given much play at the warehouse!

AMANDA: Man is by instinct! Don't quote instinct to me! Instinct is something that people have got away from! It belongs to animals! Christian adults don't want it!

TOM: What do Christian adults want, then, Mother?

AMANDA: Superior things! Things of the mind and the spirit! Only animals have to satisfy instincts! Surely your aims are somewhat higher than theirs! Than monkeys—pigs—

TOM: I reckon they're not.

AMANDA: You're joking. However, that isn't what I wanted to discuss.

TOM (*rising*): I haven't much time.

AMANDA (*pushing his shoulders*): Sit down.

TOM: You want me to punch in red at the warehouse, Mother?

AMANDA: You have five minutes. I want to talk about Laura.

(LEGEND: "PLANS AND PROVISIONS.")

TOM: All right! What about Laura?

AMANDA: We have to be making plans and provisions for her. She's older than you, two years, and nothing has happened. She just drifts along doing nothing. It frightens me terribly how she just drifts along.

TOM: I guess she's the type that people call home girls.

AMANDA: There's no such type, and if there is, it's a pity! That is unless the home is hers, with a husband!

TOM: What?

AMANDA: Oh, I can see the handwriting on the wall as plain as I see the nose in front of my face! It's terrifying! More and more you remind me of your father! He was out all hours without explanation—Then *left!* *Good-bye!* And me with a bag to hold. I saw that letter you got from

the Merchant Marine. I know what you're dreaming of. I'm not standing here blindfolded. Very well, then. Then *do* it! But not till there's
somebody to take your place.

TOM: What do you mean?

AMANDA: I mean that as soon as Laura has got somebody to take care of
her, married, a home of her own, independent—why, then you'll be
free to go wherever you please, on land, on sea, whichever way the
wind blows you! But until that time you've got to look out for your
sister. I don't say me because I'm old and don't matter! I say for your
sister because she's young and dependent. I put her in business college—a dismal failure! Frightened her so it made her sick to her stomach. I took her over to the Young People's League at the church. Another fiasco. She spoke to nobody, nobody spoke to her. Now all she
does is fool with those pieces of glass and play those worn-out records. What kind of a life is that for a girl to lead?

TOM: What can I do about it?

AMANDA: Overcome selfishness! Self, self, self is all that you ever think
of! (TOM *springs up and crosses to get his coat. It is ugly and bulky. He
pulls on a cap with earmuffs.*) Where is your muffler? Put your wool
muffler on! (*He snatches it angrily from the closet and tosses it around
his neck and pulls both ends tight.*) Tom! I haven't said what I had in
mind to ask you.

TOM: I'm too late to—

AMANDA (*catching his arm—very importunately. Then shyly*): Down at
the warehouse, aren't there some—nice young men?

TOM: No!

AMANDA: There *must* be—*some* . . .

TOM: Mother—

(*Gesture.*)

AMANDA: Find out one that's clean-living—doesn't drink and—ask him
out for sister!

TOM: What?

AMANDA: For *sister!* To *meet!* Get *acquainted!*

TOM (*stamping to door*): Oh, my go-osh!

AMANDA: Will you? (*He opens door. Imploringly.*) Will you? (*He starts
down.*) Will you? *Will* you, dear?

TOM (*calling back*): YES!

(AMANDA *closes the door hesitantly and with a troubled but faintly
hopeful expression.*)

(SCREEN IMAGE: GLAMOR MAGAZINE COVER.)

(*Spot* AMANDA *at phone.*)

AMANDA: Ella Cartwright? This is Amanda Wingfield! How are you, honey? How is that kidney condition? (*Count five.*) *Horrors!* (*Count five.*) You're a Christian martyr, yes, honey, that's what you are, a Christian martyr! Well, I just happened to notice in my little red book that your subscription to the *Companion* has just run out! I knew that you wouldn't want to miss out on the wonderful serial starting in this new issue. It's by Bessie Mae Hopper, the first thing she's written since *Honeymoon for Three*. Wasn't that a strange and interesting story? Well, this one is even lovelier, I believe. It has a sophisticated society background. It's all about the horsey set on Long Island!

FADE OUT

SCENE V

(LEGEND ON SCREEN: "ANNUNCIATION." *Fade with music.*)

(*It is early dusk of a spring evening. Supper has just been finished in the Wingfield apartment.* AMANDA *and* LAURA *in light colored dresses are removing dishes from the table, in the upstage area, which is shadowy, their movements formalized almost as a dance or ritual, their moving forms as pale and silent as moths.*

TOM, *in white shirt and trousers, rises from the table and crosses toward the fire-escape.*)

AMANDA (*as he passes her*): Son, will you do me a favor?

TOM: What?

AMANDA: Comb your hair! You look so pretty when your hair is combed! (TOM *slouches on sofa with evening paper. Enormous caption "Franco Triumphs."*) There is only one respect in which I would like you to emulate your father.

TOM: What respect is that?

AMANDA: The care he always took of his appearance. He never allowed himself to look untidy. (*He throws down the paper and crosses to fire-escape.*) Where are you going?

TOM: I'm going out to smoke.

AMANDA: You smoke too much. A pack a day at fifteen cents a pack. How much would that amount to in a month? Thirty times fifteen is how much, Tom? Figure it out and you will be astounded at what you could save. Enough to give you a night-school course in accounting at

Washington U! Just think what a wonderful thing that would be for you, son!

(TOM *is unmoved by the thought.*)

TOM: I'd rather smoke. (*He steps out on landing, letting the screen door slam.*)

AMANDA (*sharply*): I know! That's the tragedy of it. . . . (*Alone, she turns to look at her husband's picture.*)

(DANCE MUSIC: "ALL THE WORLD IS WAITING FOR THE SUNRISE!")

TOM (*to the audience*): Across the alley from us was the Paradise Dance Hall. On evenings in spring the windows and doors were open and the music came outdoors. Sometimes the lights were turned out except for a large glass sphere that hung from the ceiling. It would turn slowly about and filter the dusk with delicate rainbow colors. Then the orchestra played a waltz or a tango, something that had a slow and sensuous rhythm. Couples would come outside, to the relative privacy of the alley. You could see them kissing behind ash-pits and telephone poles. This was the compensation for lives that passed like mine, without any change or adventure. Adventure and change were imminent in this year. They were waiting around the corner for all these kids. Suspended in the mist over Berchtesgaden, caught in the folds of Chamberlain's umbrella—In Spain there was Guernica! But here there was only hot swing music and liquor, dance halls, bars, and movies, and sex that hung in the gloom like a chandelier and flooded the world with brief, deceptive rainbows. . . . All the world was waiting for bombardments!

(AMANDA *turns from the picture and comes outside.*)

AMANDA (*sighing*). A fire-escape landing's a poor excuse for a porch. (*She spreads a newspaper on a step and sits down, gracefully and demurely as if she were settling into a swing on a Mississippi veranda.*) What are you looking at?

TOM: The moon.

AMANDA: Is there a moon this evening?

TOM: It's rising over Garfinkel's Delicatessen.

AMANDA: So it is! A little silver slipper of a moon. Have you made a wish on it yet?

TOM: Um-hum.

AMANDA: What did you wish for?

TOM: That's a secret.

AMANDA: A secret, huh? Well, I won't tell mine either. I will be just as mysterious as you.

TOM: I bet I can guess what yours is.

AMANDA: Is my head so transparent?

TOM: You're not a sphinx.

AMANDA: No, I don't have secrets. I'll tell you what I wished for on the moon. Success and happiness for my precious children! I wish for that whenever there's a moon, and when there isn't a moon, I wish for it, too.

TOM: I thought perhaps you wished for a gentleman caller.

AMANDA: Why do you say that?

TOM: Don't you remember asking me to fetch one?

AMANDA: I remember suggesting that it would be nice for your sister if you brought home some nice young man from the warehouse. I think I've made that suggestion more than once.

TOM: Yes, you have made it repeatedly.

AMANDA: Well?

TOM: We are going to have one.

AMANDA: *What?*

TOM: A gentleman caller!

(THE ANNUNCIATION IS CELEBRATED WITH MUSIC.)

(AMANDA *rises.*)

(IMAGE ON SCREEN: CALLER WITH BOUQUET.)

AMANDA: You mean you have asked some nice young man to come over?

TOM: Yep. I've asked him to dinner.

AMANDA: You really did?

TOM: I did!

AMANDA: You did, and did he—*accept?*

TOM: He did!

AMANDA: Well, well—well, well! That's—lovely!

TOM: I thought that you would be pleased.

AMANDA: It's definite, then?

TOM: Very definite.

AMANDA: Soon?

TOM: Very soon.

AMANDA: For heaven's sake, stop putting on and tell me some things, will you?

TOM: What things do you want me to tell you?

AMANDA: *Naturally* I would like to know when he's *coming!*

TOM: He's coming tomorrow.

AMANDA: *Tomorrow?*

TOM: Yep. Tomorrow.

AMANDA: But, Tom!

TOM: Yes, Mother?

AMANDA: Tomorrow gives me no time!

TOM: Time for what?

AMANDA: Preparations! Why didn't you phone me at once, as soon as you asked him, the minute that he accepted? Then, don't you see, I could have been getting ready!

TOM: You don't have to make any fuss.

AMANDA: Oh, Tom, Tom, Tom, of course I have to make a fuss! I want things nice, not sloppy! Not thrown together. I'll certainly have to do some fast thinking, won't I?

TOM: I don't see why you have to think at all.

AMANDA: You just don't know. We can't have a gentleman caller in a pig-sty! All my wedding silver has to be polished, the monogrammed table linen ought to be laundered! The windows have to be washed and fresh curtains put up. And how about clothes? We have to *wear* something, don't we?

TOM: Mother, this boy is no one to make a fuss over!

AMANDA: Do you realize he's the first young man we've introduced to your sister? It's terrible, dreadful, disgraceful that poor little sister has never received a single gentleman caller! Tom, come inside! (*She opens the screen door.*)

TOM: What for?

AMANDA: I want to ask you some things.

TOM: If you're going to make such a fuss, I'll call it off, I'll tell him not to come.

AMANDA: You certainly won't do anything of the kind. Nothing offends people worse than broken engagements. It simply means I'll have to work like a Turk! We won't be brilliant, but we'll pass inspection. Come on inside. (TOM *follows, groaning.*) Sit down.

TOM: Any particular place you would like me to sit?

AMANDA: Thank heavens I've got that new sofa! I'm also making payments on a floor lamp I'll have sent out! And put the chintz covers on, they'll brighten things up! Of course I'd hoped to have these walls re-papered. . . . What is the young man's name?

TOM: His name is O'Connor.

AMANDA: That, of course, means fish—tomorrow is Friday! I'll have that salmon loaf—with Durkee's dressing! What does he do? He works at the warehouse?

TOM: Of course! How else would I—

AMANDA: Tom, he—doesn't drink?

TOM: Why do you ask me that?

AMANDA: Your father *did!*

TOM: Don't get started on that!

AMANDA: He *does* drink, then?

TOM: Not that I know of!

AMANDA: Make sure, be certain! The last thing I want for my daughter's a boy who drinks!

TOM: Aren't you being a little premature? Mr. O'Connor has not yet appeared on the scene!

AMANDA: But will tomorrow. To meet your sister, and what do I know about his character? Nothing! Old maids are better off than wives of drunkards!

TOM: Oh, my God!

AMANDA: Be still!

TOM (*leaning forward to whisper*): Lots of fellows meet girls whom they don't marry!

AMANDA: Oh, talk sensibly, Tom—and don't be sarcastic! (*She has gotten a hairbrush.*)

TOM: What are you doing?

AMANDA: I'm brushing that cow-lick down! What is this young man's position at the warehouse?

TOM (*submitting grimly to the brush and the interrogation*): This young man's position is that of a shipping clerk, Mother.

AMANDA: Sounds to me like a fairly responsible job, the sort of a job *you* would be in if you just had more *get-up*. What is his salary? Have you got any idea?

TOM: I would judge it to be approximately eighty-five dollars a month.

AMANDA: Well—not princely, but—

TOM: Twenty more than I make.

AMANDA: Yes, how well I know! But for a family man, eighty-five dollars a month is not much more than you can just get by on. . . .

TOM: Yes, but Mr. O'Connor is not a family man.

AMANDA: He might be, mightn't he? Some time in the future?

TOM: I see. Plans and provisions.

AMANDA: You are the only young man that I know of who ignores the fact that the future becomes the present, the present the past, and the past turns into everlasting regret if you don't plan for it!

TOM: I will think that over and see what I can make of it.

AMANDA: Don't be supercilious with your mother! Tell me some more about this—what do you call him?

TOM: James D. O'Connor. The D. is for Delaney.

AMANDA: Irish on *both* sides! *Gracious!* And doesn't drink?

TOM: Shall I call him up and ask him right this minute?

AMANDA: The only way to find out about those things is to make discreet inquiries at the proper moment. When I was a girl in Blue Mountain and it was suspected that a young man drank, the girl whose attentions he had been receiving, if any girl *was,* would sometimes speak to the minister of his church, or rather her father would if her father was living, and sort of feel him out on the young man's character. That is the way such things are discreetly handled to keep a young woman from making a tragic mistake!

TOM: Then how did you happen to make a tragic mistake?

AMANDA: That innocent look of your father's had everyone fooled! He *smiled*—the world was *enchanted!* No girl can do worse than put herself at the mercy of a handsome appearance! I hope that Mr. O'Connor is not too good-looking.

TOM: No, he's not too good-looking. He's covered with freckles and hasn't too much of a nose.

AMANDA: He's not right-down homely, though?

TOM: Not right-down homely. Just medium homely, I'd say.

AMANDA: Character's what to look for in a man.

TOM: That's what I've always said, Mother.

AMANDA: You've never said anything of the kind and I suspect you would never give it a thought.

TOM: Don't be suspicious of me.

AMANDA: At least I hope he's the type that's up and coming.

TOM: I think he really goes in for self-improvement.

AMANDA: What reason have you to think so?

TOM: He goes to night school.

AMANDA (*beaming*): Splendid! What does he do, I mean study?

TOM: Radio engineering and public speaking!

AMANDA: Then he has visions of being advanced in the world! Any young man who studies public speaking is aiming to have an executive job some day! And radio engineering? A thing for the future! Both of these facts are very illuminating. Those are the sort of things that a mother should know concerning any young man who comes to call on her daughter. Seriously or—not.

TOM: One little warning. He doesn't know about Laura. I didn't let on that we had dark ulterior motives. I just said, why don't you come have dinner with us? He said okay and that was the whole conversation.

AMANDA: I bet it was! You're eloquent as an oyster. However, he'll know about Laura when he gets here. When he sees how lovely and sweet and pretty she is, he'll thank his lucky stars he was asked to dinner.

TOM: Mother, you mustn't expect too much of Laura.

AMANDA: What do you mean?

TOM: Laura seems all those things to you and me because she's ours and we love her. We don't even notice she's crippled any more.

AMANDA: Don't say crippled! You know that I never allow that word to be used!

TOM: But face facts, Mother. She is and—that's not all—

AMANDA: What do you mean "not all"?

TOM: Laura is very different from other girls.

AMANDA: I think the difference is all to her advantage.

TOM: Not quite all—in the eyes of others—strangers—she's terribly shy and lives in a world of her own and those things make her seem a little peculiar to people outside the house.

AMANDA: Don't say peculiar.

TOM: Face the facts. She is.

(THE DANCE-HALL MUSIC CHANGES TO A TANGO THAT HAS A MINOR AND SOMEWHAT OMINOUS TONE.)

AMANDA: In what way is she peculiar—may I ask?

TOM: (gently): She lives in a world of her own—a world of—little glass ornaments, Mother. . . . (Gets up. AMANDA remains holding brush, looking at him, troubled.) She plays old phonograph records and— that's about all—(He glances at himself in the mirror and crosses to door.)

AMANDA (sharply): Where are you going?

TOM: I'm going to the movies. (Out screen door.)

AMANDA: Not to the movies, every night to the movies! (Follows quickly to screen door.) I don't believe you always go to the movies! (He is gone. AMANDA looks worriedly after him for a moment. Then vitality and optimism return and she turns from the door. Crossing to portieres.) Laura! Laura! (LAURA answers from kitchenette.)

LAURA: Yes, Mother.

AMANDA: Let those dishes go and come in front! (LAURA appears with dish towel. Gaily.) Laura, come here and make a wish on the moon!

LAURA (entering): Moon—moon?

AMANDA: A little silver slipper of a moon. Look over your left shoulder, Laura, and make a wish! (LAURA looks faintly puzzled as if called out of sleep. AMANDA seizes her shoulders and turns her at an angle by the door.) No! Now, darling, wish!

LAURA: What shall I wish for, Mother?

AMANDA (her voice trembling and her eyes suddenly filling with tears): Happiness! Good Fortune!

(The violin rises and the stage dims out.)

SCENE VI

(IMAGE: HIGH SCHOOL HERO.)

TOM: And so the following evening I brought Jim home to dinner. I had known Jim slightly in high school. In high school Jim was a hero. He had tremendous Irish good nature and vitality with the scrubbed and polished look of white chinaware. He seemed to move in a continual spotlight. He was a star in basketball, captain of the debating club, president of the senior class and the glee club and he sang the male lead in the annual light operas. He was always running or bounding, never just walking. He seemed always at the point of defeating the law of gravity. He was shooting with such velocity through his adolescence that you would logically expect him to arrive at nothing short of the White House by the time he was thirty. But Jim apparently ran into more interference after his graduation from Soldan. His speed had definitely slowed. Six years after he left high school he was holding a job that wasn't much better than mine.

(IMAGE: CLERK.)

He was the only one at the warehouse with whom I was on friendly terms. I was valuable to him as someone who could remember his former glory, who had seen him win basketball games and the silver cup in debating. He knew of my secret practice of retiring to a cabinet of the washroom to work on poems when business was slack in the warehouse. He called me Shakespeare. And while the other boys in the warehouse regarded me with suspicious hostility, Jim took a humorous attitude toward me. Gradually his attitude affected the others, their hostility wore off and they also began to smile at me as people smile at an oddly fashioned dog who trots across their path at some distance.

I knew that Jim and Laura had known each other at Soldan, and I had heard Laura speak admiringly of his voice. I didn't know if Jim remembered her or not. In high school Laura had been as unobtrusive as Jim had been astonishing. If he did remember Laura, it was not as my sister, for when I asked him to dinner, he grinned and said, "You know, Shakespeare, I never thought of you as having folks!"

He was about to discover that I did. . . .

(LIGHT UP STAGE.)

(LEGEND ON SCREEN: "THE ACCENT OF A COMING FOOT.")

(*Friday evening. It is about five o'clock of a late spring evening which comes "scattering poems in the sky."*)

(*A delicate lemony light is in the Wingfield apartment.*)

(AMANDA *has worked like a Turk in preparation for the gentleman caller. The results are astonishing. The new floor lamp with its rose-silk shade is in place, a colored paper lantern conceals the broken light fixture in the ceiling, new billowing white curtains are at the windows, chintz covers are on chairs and sofa, a pair of new sofa pillows make their initial appearance.*)

(*Open boxes and tissue paper are scattered on the floor.*)

(LAURA *stands in the middle with lifted arms while* AMANDA *crouches before her, adjusting the hem of the new dress, devout and ritualistic. The dress is colored and designed by memory. The arrangement of* LAURA'S *hair is changed; it is softer and more becoming. A fragile, unearthly prettiness has come out in* LAURA: *she is like a piece of translucent glass touched by light, given a momentary radiance, not actual, not lasting.*)

AMANDA (*impatiently*): Why are you trembling?
LAURA: Mother, you've made me so nervous!
AMANDA: How have I made you nervous?
LAURA: By all this fuss! You make it seem so important!
AMANDA: I don't understand you, Laura. You couldn't be satisfied with just sitting home, and yet whenever I try to arrange something for you, you seem to resist it. (*She gets up.*) Now take a look at yourself. No, wait! Wait just a moment—I have an idea!
LAURA: What is it now?

(AMANDA *produces two powder puffs which she wraps in handkerchiefs and stuffs in* LAURA'S *bosom.*)

LAURA: Mother, what are you doing?
AMANDA: They call them "Gay Deceivers"!
LAURA: I won't wear them!
AMANDA: You will!
LAURA: Why should I?
AMANDA: Because, to be painfully honest, your chest is flat.
LAURA: You make it seem like we were setting a trap.
AMANDA: All pretty girls are a trap, a pretty trap, and men expect them to be. (LEGEND: "A PRETTY TRAP.") Now look at yourself, young lady. This is the prettiest you will ever be! I've got to fix myself now! You're going to be surprised by your mother's appearance! (*She crosses through portieres, humming gaily.*)

(LAURA *moves slowly to the long mirror and stares solemnly at herself.*)

(*A wind blows the white curtains inward in a slow, graceful motion and with a faint, sorrowful sighing.*)

AMANDA (*off stage*): It isn't dark enough yet. (*She turns slowly before the mirror with a troubled look.*)

(LEGEND ON SCREEN: "THIS IS MY SISTER: CELEBRATE HER WITH STRINGS!" MUSIC.)

AMANDA (*laughing, off*): I'm going to show you something. I'm going to make a spectacular appearance!

LAURA: What is it, Mother?

AMANDA: Possess your soul in patience—you will see! Something I've resurrected from that old trunk! Styles haven't changed so terribly much after all. . . . (*She parts the portieres.*) Now just look at your mother! (*She wears a girlish frock of yellowed voile with a blue silk sash. She carries a bunch of jonquils—the legend of her youth is nearly revived. Feverishly.*) This is the dress in which I led the cotillion. Won the cakewalk twice at Sunset Hill, wore one spring to the Governor's ball in Jackson! See how I sashayed around the ballroom, Laura! (*She raises her skirt and does a mincing step around the room.*) I wore it on Sundays for my gentlemen callers! I had it on the day I met your father—I had malaria fever all that spring. The change of climate from East Tennessee to the Delta—weakened resistance—I had a little temperature all the time—not enough to be serious—just enough to make me restless and giddy! Invitations poured in—parties all over the Delta!—"Stay in bed," said Mother, "you have fever!"—but I just wouldn't.—I took quinine but kept on going, going!—Evenings, dances!—Afternoons, long, long rides! Picnics—lovely!—So lovely, that country in May.—All lacy with dogwood, literally flooded with jonquils!—That was the spring I had the craze for jonquils. Jonquils became an absolute obsession. Mother said, "Honey, there's no more room for jonquils." And still I kept on bringing in more jonquils. Whenever, wherever I saw them, I'd say, "Stop! Stop! I see jonquils!" I made the young men help me gather the jonquils! It was a joke, Amanda and her jonquils! Finally there were no more vases to hold them, every available space was filled with jonquils. No vases to hold them? All right, I'll hold them myself! And then I—(*She stops in front of the picture. MUSIC.*) met your father! Malaria fever and jonquils and then—this—boy. . . . (*She switches on the rose-colored lamp.*) I hope they get here before it starts to rain. (*She crosses upstage and places the jonquils in bowl on table.*) I gave your brother a little extra change so he and Mr. O'Connor could take the service car home.

LAURA (*with altered look*): What did you say his name was?

AMANDA: O'Connor.

LAURA: What is his first name?
AMANDA: I don't remember. Oh, yes, I do. It was—Jim!

(LAURA *sways slightly and catches hold of a chair.*)

(LEGEND ON SCREEN: "NOT JIM!")

LAURA (*faintly*): Not—Jim!
AMANDA: Yes, that was it, it was Jim! I've never known a Jim that wasn't nice!

(MUSIC: OMINOUS.)

LAURA: Are you sure his name is Jim O'Connor?
AMANDA: Yes. Why?
LAURA: Is he the one that Tom used to know in high school?
AMANDA: He didn't say so. I think he just got to know him at the warehouse.
LAURA: There was a Jim O'Connor we both knew in high school—(*Then, with effort.*) If that is the one that Tom is bringing to dinner—you'll have to excuse me, I won't come to the table.
AMANDA: What sort of nonsense is this?
LAURA: You asked me once if I'd ever liked a boy. Don't you remember I showed you this boy's picture?
AMANDA: You mean the boy you showed me in the yearbook?
LAURA: Yes, that boy.
AMANDA: Laura, Laura, were you in love with that boy?
LAURA: I don't know, Mother. All I know is I couldn't sit at the table if it was him!
AMANDA: It won't be him! It isn't the least bit likely. But whether it is or not, you will come to the table. You will not be excused.
LAURA: I'll have to be, Mother.
AMANDA: I don't intend to humor your silliness, Laura. I've had too much from you and your brother, both! So just sit down and compose yourself till they come. Tom has forgotten his key so you'll have to let them in, when they arrive.
LAURA (*panicky*): Oh, Mother—*you* answer the door!
AMANDA (*lightly*): I'll be in the kitchen—busy!
LAURA: Oh, Mother, please answer the door, don't make me do it!
AMANDA (*crossing into kitchenette*): I've got to fix the dressing for the salmon. Fuss, fuss—silliness!—over a gentleman caller!

(*Door swings shut.* LAURA *is left alone.*)

(LEGEND: "TERROR!")

(*She utters a low moan and turns off the lamp—sits stiffly on the edge of the sofa, knotting her fingers together.*)

(LEGEND ON SCREEN: "THE OPENING OF A DOOR!")

(TOM and JIM *appear on the fire-escape steps and climb to landing. Hearing their approach,* LAURA *rises with a panicky gesture. She retreats to the portieres.*)

(*The doorbell.* LAURA *catches her breath and touches her throat. Low drums.*)

AMANDA (*calling*): Laura, sweetheart! The door!

(LAURA *stares at it without moving.*)

JIM: I think we just beat the rain.
TOM: Uh-huh. (*He rings again, nervously.* JIM *whistles and fishes for a cigarette.*)
AMANDA (*very, very gaily*): Laura, that is your brother and Mr. O'Connor! Will you let them in, darling?

(LAURA *crosses toward kitchenette door.*)

LAURA (*breathlessly*): Mother—you go to the door!

(AMANDA *steps out of kitchenette and stares furiously at* LAURA. *She points imperiously at the door.*)

LAURA: Please, please!
AMANDA (*in a fierce whisper*): What is the matter with you, you silly thing?
LAURA (*desperately*): Please, you answer it, *please!*
AMANDA: I told you I wasn't going to humor you, Laura. Why have you chosen this moment to lose your mind?
LAURA: Please, please, please, you go!
AMANDA: You'll have to go to the door because I can't!
LAURA (*despairingly*): I can't either!
AMANDA: *Why?*
LAURA: I'm *sick!*
AMANDA: I'm sick, too—of your nonsense! Why can't you and your brother be normal people? Fantastic whims and behavior! (TOM *gives a long ring.*) Preposterous goings on! Can you give me one reason —(*Calls out lyrically.*) COMING? JUST ONE SECOND!—why should you be afraid to open a door? Now you answer it, Laura!
LAURA: Oh, oh, oh . . . (*She returns through the portieres. Darts to the victrola and winds it frantically and turns it on.*)

AMANDA: Laura Wingfield, you march right to that door!

LAURA: Yes—yes, Mother!

(*A faraway, scratchy rendition of "Dardanella" softens the air and gives her strength to move through it. She slips to the door and draws it cautiously open.*)

(TOM *enters with the caller,* JIM O'CONNOR.)

TOM: Laura, this is Jim. Jim, this is my sister, Laura.

JIM (*stepping inside*): I didn't know that Shakespeare had a sister!

LAURA (*retreating stiff and trembling from the door*): How—how do you do?

JIM (*heartily extending his hand*): Okay!

(LAURA *touches it hesitantly with hers.*)

JIM: Your hand's *cold,* Laura!

LAURA: Yes, well—I've been playing the victrola. . . .

JIM: Must have been playing classical music on it! You ought to play a little hot swing music to warm you up!

LAURA: Excuse me—I haven't finished playing the victrola. . . .

(*She turns awkwardly and hurries into the front room. She pauses a second by the victrola. Then catches her breath and darts through the portieres like a frightened deer.*)

JIM (*grinning*): What was the matter?

TOM: Oh—with Laura? Laura is—terribly shy.

JIM: Shy, huh? It's unusual to meet a shy girl nowadays. I don't believe you ever mentioned you had a sister.

TOM: Well, now you know. I have one. Here is the *Post Dispatch.* You want a piece of it?

JIM: Uh-huh.

TOM: What piece? The comics?

JIM: Sports! (*Glances at it.*) Ole Dizzy Dean is on his bad behavior.

TOM (*disinterest*): Yeah? (*Lights cigarette and crosses back to fire-escape door.*)

JIM: Where are *you* going?

TOM: I'm going out on the terrace.

JIM (*goes after him*): You know, Shakespeare—I'm going to sell you a bill of goods!

TOM: What goods?

JIM: A course I'm taking.

TOM: Huh?

JIM: In public speaking! You and me, we're not the warehouse type.

TOM: Thanks—that's good news. But what has public speaking got to do with it?

JIM: It fits you for—executive positions!

TOM: Awww.

JIM: I tell you it's done a helluva lot for me.

(IMAGE: EXECUTIVE AT DESK.)

TOM: In what respect?

JIM: In every! Ask yourself what is the difference between you an' me and men in the office down front? Brains?—No!—Ability?—No! Then what? Just one little thing—

TOM: What is that one little thing?

JIM: Primarily it amounts to—social poise! Being able to square up to people and hold your own on any social level!

AMANDA (*off stage*): Tom?

TOM: Yes, Mother?

AMANDA: Is that you and Mr. O'Connor?

TOM: Yes, Mother.

AMANDA: Well, you just make yourselves comfortable in there.

TOM: Yes, Mother.

AMANDA: Ask Mr. O'Connor if he would like to wash his hands.

JIM: Aw, no—no—thank you—I took care of that at the warehouse. Tom—

TOM: Yes?

JIM: Mr. Mendoza was speaking to me about you.

TOM: Favorably?

JIM: What do you think?

TOM: Well—

JIM: You're going to be out of a job if you don't wake up.

TOM: I am waking up—

JIM: You show no signs.

TOM: The signs are interior.

(IMAGE ON SCREEN: THE SAILING VESSEL WITH JOLLY ROGER AGAIN.)

TOM: I'm planning to change. (*He leans over the rail speaking with quiet exhilaration. The incandescent marquees and signs of the first-run movie houses light his face from across the alley. He looks like a voyager.*) I'm right at the point of committing myself to a future that doesn't include the warehouse and Mr. Mendoza or even a night-school course in public speaking.

JIM: What are you gassing about?

TOM: I'm tired of the movies.

JIM: Movies!

TOM: Yes, movies! Look at them—(*A wave toward the marvels of Grand Avenue.*) All of those glamorous people—having adventures—hogging it all, gobbling the whole thing up! You know what happens? People go to the *movies* instead of *moving!* Hollywood characters are supposed to have all the adventures for everybody in America, while everybody in America sits in a dark room and watches them have them! Yes, until there's a war. That's when adventure becomes available to the masses! *Everyone's* dish, not only Gable's! Then the people in the dark room come out of the dark room to have some adventures themselves—Goody, goody!—It's our turn now, to go to the South Sea Island—to make a safari—to be exotic, far-off!—But I'm not patient. I don't want to wait till then. I'm tired of the *movies* and I am *about* to move!

JIM (*incredulously*): Move?

TOM: Yes.

JIM: When?

TOM: Soon!

JIM: Where? Where?

(THEME THREE MUSIC *seems to answer the question, while* TOM *thinks it over. He searches among his pockets.*)

TOM: I'm starting to boil inside. I know I seem dreamy, but inside—well, I'm boiling! Whenever I pick up a shoe, I shudder a little thinking how short life is and what I am doing!—Whatever that means. I know it doesn't mean shoes—except as something to wear on a traveler's feet! (*Finds paper.*) Look—

JIM: What?

TOM: I'm a member.

JIM (*reading*): The Union of Merchant Seamen.

TOM: I paid my dues this month, instead of the light bill.

JIM: You will regret it when they turn the lights off.

TOM: I won't be here.

JIM: How about your mother?

TOM: I'm like my father. The bastard son of a bastard! See how he grins? And he's been absent going on sixteen years!

JIM: You're just talking, you drip. How does your mother feel about it?

TOM: Shhh!—Here comes Mother! Mother is not acquainted with my plans!

AMANDA (*enters portieres*): Where are you all?

TOM: On the terrace, Mother.

(*They start inside. She advances to them.* TOM *is distinctly shocked at her appearance. Even* JIM *blinks a little. He is making his first contact with girlish Southern vivacity and in spite of the night-school course in public speaking is somewhat thrown off the beam by the unexpected outlay of social charm.*)

(*Certain responses are attempted by* JIM *but are swept aside by* AMANDA's *gay laughter and chatter.* TOM *is embarrassed but after the first shock* JIM *reacts very warmly. Grins and chuckles, is altogether won over.*)

(IMAGE: AMANDA AS A GIRL.)

AMANDA (*coyly smiling, shaking her girlish ringlets*): Well, well, well, so this is Mr. O'Connor. Introductions entirely unnecessary. I've heard so much about you from my boy. I finally said to him, Tom—good gracious!—why don't you bring this paragon to supper? I'd like to meet this nice young man at the warehouse!—Instead of just hearing him sing your praises so much! I don't know why my son is so standoffish—that's not Southern behavior! Let's sit down and—I think we could stand a little more air in here! Tom, leave the door open. I felt a nice fresh breeze a moment ago. Where has it gone to? Mmm, so warm already! And not quite summer, even. We're going to burn up when summer really gets started. However, we're having—we're having a very light supper. I think light things are better fo' this time of year. The same as light clothes are. Light clothes an' light food are what warm weather calls fo'. You know our blood gets so thick during th' winter—it takes a while fo' us to *adjust* ou'selves!—when the season changes . . . It's come so quick this year. I wasn't prepared. All of a sudden—heavens! Already summer!—I ran to the trunk an' pulled out this light dress—Terribly old! Historical almost! But feels so good—so good an' co-ol, y'know. . . .

TOM: Mother—

AMANDA: Yes, honey?

TOM: How about—supper?

AMANDA: Honey, you go ask Sister if supper is ready! You know that Sister is in full charge of supper! Tell her you hungry boys are waiting for it. (*To* JIM.) Have you met Laura?

JIM: She—

AMANDA: Let you in? Oh, good, you've met already! It's rare for a girl as sweet an' pretty as Laura to be domestic! But Laura is, thank heavens, not only pretty but also very domestic. I'm not at all. I never was a bit. I never could make a thing but angel-food cake. Well, in the South we had so many servants. Gone, gone, gone. All vestige of gracious living! Gone completely! I wasn't prepared for what the future brought me. All of my gentlemen callers were sons of planters and so of course I assumed that I would be married to one and raise my family on a large piece of land with plenty of servants. But man proposes—and woman accepts the proposal!—To vary that old, old saying a little bit—I married no planter! I married a man who worked for the telephone company!—That gallantly smiling gentleman over there! (*Points to the picture.*) A telephone man who—fell in love with long-distance!—Now he travels and I don't even know where!—But what am I going on for about my—tribulations? Tell me yours—I hope you don't have any! Tom?

TOM (*returning*): Yes, Mother?

AMANDA: Is supper nearly ready?

TOM: It looks to me like supper is on the table.

AMANDA: Let me look—(*She rises prettily and looks through portieres.*) Oh, lovely!—But where is Sister?

TOM: Laura is not feeling well and she says that she thinks she'd better not come to the table.

AMANDA: What?—Nonsense!—Laura? Oh, Laura!

LAURA (*Off stage, faintly*): Yes, Mother.

AMANDA: You really must come to the table. We won't be seated until you come to the table! Come in, Mr. O'Connor. You sit over there, and I'll—Laura? Laura Wingfield! You're keeping us waiting, honey! We can't say grace until you come to the table!

(*The back door is pushed weakly open and* LAURA *comes in. She is obviously quite faint, her lips trembling, her eyes wide and staring. She moves unsteadily toward the table.*)

(LEGEND: "TERROR!")

(*Outside a summer storm is coming abruptly. The white curtains billow inward at the windows and there is a sorrowful murmur and deep blue dusk.*)

(LAURA *suddenly stumbles—she catches at a chair with a faint moan.*)

TOM: Laura!

AMANDA: Laura! (*There is a clap of thunder.*) (LEGEND: "AH!") (*Despairingly.*) Why, Laura, you *are* sick, darling! Tom, help your sister into the living room, dear! Sit in the living room, Laura—rest on the sofa. Well! (*To the gentleman caller.*) Standing over the hot stove made her ill!—I told her that it was just too warm this evening, but—(TOM *comes back in.* LAURA *is on the sofa.*) Is Laura all right now?

TOM: Yes.

AMANDA: What *is* that? Rain? A nice cool rain has come up! (*She gives the gentleman caller a frightened look.*) I think we may—have grace—now . . . (TOM *looks at her stupidly.*) Tom, honey—you say grace!

TOM: Oh . . . "For these and all thy mercies—" (*They bow their heads,* AMANDA *stealing a nervous glance at* JIM. *In the living room* LAURA, *stretched on the sofa, clenches her hand to her lips, to hold back a shuddering sob.*) God's Holy Name be praised—

THE SCENE DIMS OUT

SCENE VII

(*A Souvenir.*)

(*Half an hour later. Dinner is just being finished in the upstage area which is concealed by the drawn portieres.*

As the curtain rises LAURA *is still huddled upon the sofa, her feet drawn under her, her head resting on a pale blue pillow, her eyes wide and mysteriously watchful. The new floor lamp with its shade of rose-colored silk gives a soft, becoming light to her face, bringing out the fragile, unearthly prettiness which usually escapes attention. There is a steady murmur of rain, but it is slackening and stops soon after the scene begins; the air outside becomes pale and luminous as the moon breaks out.*

A moment after the curtain rises, the lights in both rooms flicker and go out.)

JIM: Hey, there, Mr. Light Bulb!

(AMANDA *laughs nervously.*)

(LEGEND: "SUSPENSION OF A PUBLIC SERVICE.")

AMANDA: Where was Moses when the lights went out? Ha-ha. Do you know the answer to that one, Mr. O'Connor?
JIM: No, Ma'am, what's the answer?
AMANDA: In the dark! (JIM *laughs appreciably.*) Everybody sit still. I'll light the candles. Isn't it lucky we have them on the table? Where's a match? Which of you gentlemen can provide a match?
JIM: Here.
AMANDA: Thank you, sir.
JIM: Not at all, Ma'am!
AMANDA: I guess the fuse has burnt out. Mr. O'Connor, can you tell a burnt-out fuse? I know I can't and Tom is a total loss when it comes to mechanics. (SOUND: GETTING UP: VOICES RECEDE A LITTLE TO KITCHEN-ETTE.) Oh, be careful you don't bump into something. We don't want

our gentleman caller to break his neck. Now wouldn't that be a fine howdy-do?

JIM: Ha-ha! Where is the fuse-box?

AMANDA: Right here next to the stove. Can you see anything?

JIM: Just a minute.

AMANDA: Isn't electricity a mysterious thing? Wasn't it Benjamin Franklin who tied a key to a kite? We live in such a mysterious universe, don't we? Some people say that science clears up all the mysteries for us. In my opinion it only creates more! Have you found it yet?

JIM: No, Ma'am. All these fuses look okay to me.

AMANDA: Tom!

TOM: Yes, Mother?

AMANDA: That light bill I gave you several days ago. The one I told you we got the notices about?

TOM: Oh.—Yeah.

(LEGEND: "HA!")

AMANDA: You didn't neglect to pay it by any chance?

TOM: Why, I—

AMANDA: Didn't! I might have known it!

JIM: Shakespeare probably wrote a poem on that light bill, Mrs. Wingfield.

AMANDA: I might have know better than to trust him with it! There's such a high price for negligence in this world!

JIM: Maybe the poem will win a ten-dollar prize.

AMANDA: We'll just have to spend the remainder of the evening in the nineteenth century, before Mr. Edison made the Mazda lamp!

JIM: Candlelight is my favorite kind of light.

AMANDA: That shows you're romantic! But that's no excuse for Tom. Well, we got through dinner. Very considerate of them to let us get through dinner before they plunged us into everlasting darkness, wasn't it, Mr. O'Connor?

JIM: Ha-ha!

AMANDA: Tom, as a penalty for your carelessness you can help me with the dishes.

JIM: Let me give you a hand.

AMANDA: Indeed you will not!

JIM: I ought to be good for something.

AMANDA: Good for something? (*Her tone is rhapsodic.*) *You?* Why, Mr. O'Connor, nobody, *nobody's* given me this much entertainment in years—as you have!

JIM: Aw, now, Mrs. Wingfield!

AMANDA: I'm not exaggerating, not one bit! But Sister is all by her lonesome. You go keep her company in the parlor! I'll give you this lovely old candelabrum that used to be on the altar at the church of the Heavenly Rest. It was melted a little out of shape when the church burnt down. Lightning struck it one spring. Gypsy Jones was holding a revival at the time and he intimated that the church was destroyed because the Episcopalians gave card parties.

JIM: Ha-ha.

AMANDA: And how about coaxing Sister to drink a little wine? I think it would be good for her! Can you carry both at once?

JIM: Sure. I'm Superman!

AMANDA: Now, Thomas, get into this apron!

(*The door of kitchenette swings closed on* AMANDA'S *gay laughter; the flickering light approaches the portieres.*)

(LAURA *sits up nervously as he enters. Her speech at first is low and breathless from the almost intolerable strain of being alone with a stranger.*)

(THE LEGEND. "I DON'T SUPPOSE YOU REMEMBER ME AT ALL!")

(*In her first speeches in this scene, before* JIM'S *warmth overcomes her paralyzing shyness,* LAURA'S *voice is thin and breathless as though she has just run up a steep flight of stairs.*)

(JIM'S *attitude is gently humorous. In playing this scene it should be stressed that while the incident is apparently unimportant, it is to* LAURA *the climax of her secret life.*)

JIM: Hello, there, Laura.

LAURA (*faintly*): Hello. (*She clears her throat.*)

JIM: How are you feeling now? Better?

LAURA: Yes. Yes, thank you.

JIM: This is for you. A little dandelion wine. (*He extends it toward her with extravagant gallantry.*)

LAURA: Thank you.

JIM: Drink it—but don't get drunk! (*He laughs heartily.* LAURA *takes the glass uncertainly; laughs shyly.*) Where shall I set the candles?

LAURA: Oh—oh, anywhere . . .

JIM: How about here on the floor? Any objections?

LAURA: No.

JIM: I'll spread a newspaper under to catch the drippings. I like to sit on the floor. Mind if I do?

LAURA: Oh, no.

JIM: Give me a pillow?

LAURA: What?

JIM: A pillow!

LAURA: Oh . . . (*Hands him one quickly.*)

JIM: How about you? Don't you like to sit on the floor?

LAURA: Oh—yes.

JIM: Why don't you, then?

LAURA: I—will.

JIM: Take a pillow! (LAURA *does. Sits on the other side of the candelabrum.* JIM *crosses his legs and smiles engagingly at her.*) I can't hardly see you sitting way over there.

LAURA: I can—see you.

JIM: I know, but that's not fair, I'm in the limelight. (LAURA *moves her pillow closer.*) Good! Now I can see you! Comfortable?

LAURA: Yes.

JIM: So am I. Comfortable as a cow. Will you have some gum?

LAURA: No, thank you.

JIM: I think that I will indulge, with your permission. (*Musingly unwraps it and holds it up.*) Think of the fortune made by the guy that invented the first piece of chewing gum. Amazing, huh? The Wrigley Building is one of the sights of Chicago.—I saw it summer before last when I went up to the Century of Progress. Did you take in the Century of Progress?

LAURA: No, I didn't.

JIM: Well, it was quite a wonderful exposition. What impressed me most was the Hall of Science. Gives you an idea of what the future will be in America, even more wonderful than the present time is! (*Pause. Smiling at her.*) Your brother tells me you're shy. Is that right, Laura?

LAURA: I—don't know.

JIM: I judge you to be an old-fashioned type of girl. Well, I think that's a pretty good type to be. Hope you don't think I'm being too personal—do you?

LAURA (*hastily, out of embarrassment*): I believe I *will* take a piece of gum, if you—don't mind. (*Clearing her throat.*) Mr. O'Connor, have you—kept up with your singing?

JIM: Singing? Me?

LAURA: Yes. I remember what a beautiful voice you had.

JIM: When did you hear me sing?

(VOICE OFF STAGE IN THE PAUSE.)

VOICE (*off stage*):

> O blow, ye winds, heigh-ho,
> A-roving I will go!
>   I'm off to my love
>   With a boxing glove—
> Ten thousand miles away!

JIM: You say you've heard me sing?

LAURA: Oh, yes! Yes, very often . . . I—don't suppose you remember me—at all?

JIM (*smiling doubtfully*): You know I have an idea I've seen you before. I had that idea soon as you opened the door. It seemed almost like I was about to remember your name. But the name that I started to call you—wasn't a name! And so I stopped myself before I said it.

LAURA: Wasn't it—Blue Roses?

JIM (*springs up. Grinning*): Blue Roses! My gosh, yes—Blue Roses! That's what I had on my tongue when you opened the door! Isn't it funny what tricks your memory plays? I didn't connect you with the high school somehow or other. But that's where it was; it was high school. I didn't even know you were Shakespeare's sister! Gosh, I'm sorry.

LAURA: I didn't expect you to. You—barely knew me!

JIM: But we did have a speaking acquaintance, huh?

LAURA: Yes, we—spoke to each other.

JIM: When did you recognize me?

LAURA: Oh, right away!

JIM: Soon as I came in the door?

LAURA: When I heard your name I thought it was probably you. I knew that Tom used to know you a little in high school. So when you came in the door—Well, then I was—sure.

JIM: Why didn't you *say* something, then?

LAURA (*breathlessly*): I didn't know what to say, I was—too surprised!

JIM: For goodness' sakes! You know, this sure is funny!

LAURA: Yes! Yes, isn't it, though . . .

JIM: Didn't we have a class in something together?

LAURA: Yes, we did.

JIM: What class was that?

LAURA: It was—singing—Chorus!

JIM: Aw!

LAURA: I sat across the aisle from you in the Aud.

JIM: Aw.

LAURA: Mondays, Wednesdays and Fridays.

JIM: Now I remember—you always came in late.

LAURA: Yes, it was so hard for me, getting upstairs. I had that brace on my leg—it clumped so loud!

JIM: I never heard any clumping.

LAURA (*wincing at the recollection*): To me it sounded like—thunder!

JIM: Well, well, well, I never even noticed.

LAURA: And everybody was seated before I came in. I had to walk in front of all those people. My seat was in the back row. I had to go clumping all the way up the aisle with everyone watching!

JIM: You shouldn't have been self-conscious.

LAURA: I know, but I was. It was always such a relief when the singing started.

JIM: Aw, yes, I've placed you now! I used to call you Blue Roses. How was it that I got started calling you that?

LAURA: I was out of school a little while with pleurosis. When I came back you asked me what was the matter. I said I had pleurosis—you thought I said Blue Roses. That's what you always called me after that!

JIM: I hope you didn't mind.

LAURA: Oh, no—I liked it. You see, I wasn't acquainted with many—people. . . .

JIM: As I remember you sort of stuck by yourself.

LAURA: I—I—never had much luck at—making friends.

JIM: I don't see why you wouldn't.

LAURA: Well, I—started out badly.

JIM: You mean being—

LAURA: Yes, it sort of—stood between me—

JIM: You shouldn't have let it!

LAURA: I know, but it did, and—

JIM: You were shy with people!

LAURA: I tried not to be but never could—

JIM: Overcome it?

LAURA: No, I—I never could!

JIM: I guess being shy is something you have to work out of kind of gradually.

LAURA: (*sorrowfully*): Yes—I guess it—

JIM: Takes time!

LAURA: Yes—

JIM: People are not so dreadful when you know them. That's what you have to remember! And everybody has problems, not just you, but practically everybody has got some problems. You think of yourself as having the only problems, as being the only one who is disappointed. But just look around you and you will see lots of people as disappointed as you are. For instance, I hoped when I was going to high school that I would be further along at this time, six years later, than I am now—You remember that wonderful write-up I had in *The Torch?*

LAURA: Yes! (*She rises and crosses to table.*)

JIM: It said I was bound to succeed in anything I went into! (LAURA *returns with the annual.*) Holy Jeez! *The Torch!* (*He accepts it reverently. They smile across it with mutual wonder.* LAURA *crouches beside him and they begin to turn through it.* LAURA's *shyness is dissolving in his warmth.*)

LAURA: Here you are in *Pirates of Penzance!*

JIM (*wistfully*): I sang the baritone lead in that operetta.

LAURA (*rapidly*): So—*beautifully!*

JIM (*protesting*): Aw—

LAURA: Yes, yes—beautifully—beautifully!

JIM: You heard me?

LAURA: All three times!

JIM: No!

LAURA: Yes!

JIM: All three performances?

LAURA (*Looking down*): Yes.

JIM: Why?

LAURA: I—wanted to ask you to—autograph my program.

JIM: Why didn't you ask me to?

LAURA: You were always surrounded by your own friends so much that I never had a chance to.

JIM: You should have just—

LAURA: Well, I—thought you might think I was—

JIM: Thought I might think you was—what?

LAURA: Oh—

JIM (*with reflective relish*): I was beleaguered by females in those days.

LAURA: You were terribly popular!

JIM: Yeah—

LAURA: You had such a—friendly way—

JIM: I was spoiled in high school.

LAURA: Everybody—liked you!

JIM: Including you?

LAURA: I—yes, I—I did, too—(*She gently closes the book in her lap.*)

JIM: Well, well, well!—Give me that program, Laura. (*She hands it to him. He signs it with a flourish.*) There you are—better late than never!

LAURA: Oh, I—what a—surprise!

JIM: My signature isn't worth very much right now. But some day—maybe—it will increase in value! Being disappointed is one thing and being discouraged is something else. I am disappointed but I am not discouraged. I'm twenty-three years old. How old are you?

LAURA: I'll be twenty-four in June.

JIM: That's not old age!

LAURA: No, but—

JIM: You finished high school?

LAURA (*with difficulty*): I didn't go back.

JIM: You mean you dropped out?

LAURA: I made bad grades in my final examinations. (*She rises and replaces the book and the program. Her voice strained.*) How is—Emily Meisenbach getting along?

JIM: Oh, that kraut-head!

LAURA: Why do you call her that?

JIM: That's what she was.

LAURA: You're not still—going with her?

JIM: I never see her.

LAURA: It said in the Personal Section that you were—engaged!

JIM: I know, but I wasn't impressed by that—propaganda!

LAURA: It wasn't—the truth?

JIM: Only in Emily's optimistic opinion!

LAURA: Oh—

(LEGEND: "WHAT HAVE YOU DONE SINCE HIGH SCHOOL?")

(JIM *lights a cigarette and leans indolently back on his elbows smiling at* LAURA *with a warmth and charm which lights her inwardly with altar candles. She remains by the table and turns in her hands a piece of glass to cover her tumult.*)

JIM (*after several reflective puffs on a cigarette*): What have you done since high school? (*She seems not to hear him.*) Huh? (LAURA *looks up.*) I said what have you done since high school, Laura?

LAURA: Nothing much.

JIM: You must have been doing something these six long years.

LAURA: Yes.

JIM: Well, then, such as what?

LAURA: I took a business course at business college—

JIM: How did that work out?

LAURA: Well, not very—well—I had to drop out, it gave me—indigestion—

(JIM *laughs gently.*)

JIM: What are you doing now?

LAURA: I don't do anything—much. Oh, please don't think I sit around doing nothing! My glass collection takes up a good deal of my time. Glass is something you have to take good care of.

JIM: What did you say—about glass?

LAURA: Collection I said—I have one—(*She clears her throat and turns away again, acutely shy.*)

JIM: (*abruptly*): You know what I judge to be the trouble with you? Inferiority complex! Know what that is? That's what they call it when someone low-rates himself! I understand it because I had it, too. Although my case was not so aggravated as yours seems to be. I had it until I took up public speaking, developed my voice, and learned that I had an aptitude for science. Before that time I never thought of myself as being outstanding in any way whatsoever! Now I've never made a regular study of it, but I have a friend who says I can analyze people better than doctors that make a profession of it. I don't claim that to be necessarily true, but I can sure guess a person's psychology, Laura! (*Takes out his gum.*) Excuse me, Laura. I always take it out when the flavor is gone. I'll use this scrap of paper to wrap it in. I know how it is to get it stuck on a shoe. Yep—that's what I judge to be your principal trouble. A lack of confidence in yourself as a person. You don't have the proper amount of faith in yourself. I'm basing that fact on a number of your remarks and also on certain observations I've made. For instance that clumping you thought was so awful in high school. You say that you even dreaded to walk into class. You see what you did? You dropped out of school, you gave up an education because of a clump, which as far as I know was practically non-existent! A little physical defect is what you have. Hardly noticeable even! Magnified thousands of times by imagination! You know what my strong advice to you is? Think of yourself as *superior* in some way!

LAURA: In what way would I think?

JIM: Why, man alive, Laura! Just look about you a little. What do you see? A world full of common people! All of 'em born and all of 'em going to die! Which of them has one-tenth of your good points! Or mine! Or anyone else's, as far as that goes—Gosh! Everybody excels in some one thing. Some in many! (*Unconsciously glances at himself in the mirror.*) All you've got to do is discover in *what*! Take me, for instance. (*He adjusts his tie at the mirror.*) My interest happens to lie in electro-dynamics. I'm taking a course in radio engineering at night school, Laura, on top of a fairly responsible job at the warehouse. I'm taking that course and studying public speaking.

LAURA: Ohhhh.

JIM: Because I believe in the future of television! (*Turning back to her.*) I wish to be ready to go up right along with it. Therefore I'm planning to get in on the ground floor. In fact, I've already made the right connections and all that remains is for the industry itself to get under way! Full steam—(*His eyes are starry.*) Knowledge—Zzzzzp! Money—Zzzzzp!—Power! That's the cycle democracy is built on! (*His attitude is convincingly dynamic.* LAURA *stares at him, even her shyness eclipsed in her absolute wonder. He suddenly grins.*) I guess you think I think a lot of myself!

LAURA: No—o-o-o, I—

JIM: Now how about you? Isn't there something you take more interest in than anything else?

LAURA: Well, I do—as I said—have my—glass collection—

(*A peal of girlish laughter from the kitchen.*)

JIM: I'm not right sure I know what you're talking about. What kind of glass is it?

LAURA: Little articles of it, they're ornaments mostly! Most of them are little animals made out of glass, the tiniest little animals in the world. Mother calls them a glass menagerie! Here's an example of one, if you'd like to see it! This one is one of the oldest. It's nearly thirteen. (*He stretches out his hand.*) (MUSIC: "THE GLASS MENAGERIE.") Oh, be careful—if you breathe, it breaks!

JIM: I'd better not take it. I'm pretty clumsy with things.

LAURA: Go on, I trust you with him! (*Places it in his palm.*) There now—you're holding him gently! Hold him over the light, he loves the light! You see how the light shines through him?

JIM: It sure does shine!

LAURA: I shouldn't be partial, but he is my favorite one.

JIM: What kind of a thing is this one supposed to be?

LAURA: Haven't you noticed the single horn on his forehead?

JIM: A unicorn, huh?

LAURA: Mmm-hmmm!

JIM: Unicorns, aren't they extinct in the modern world?

LAURA: I know!

JIM: Poor little fellow, he must feel sort of lonesome.

LAURA (*smiling*): Well, if he does he doesn't complain about it. He stays on a shelf with some horses that don't have horns and all of them seem to get along nicely together.

JIM: How do you know?

LAURA (*lightly*): I haven't heard any arguments among them!

JIM (*grinning*): No arguments, huh? Well, that's a pretty good sign! Where shall I set him?

LAURA: Put him on the table. They all like a change of scenery once in a while!

JIM (*stretching*): Well, well, well, well—Look how big my shadow is when I stretch!

LAURA: Oh, oh, yes—it stretches across the ceiling!

JIM (*crossing to door*): I think it's stopped raining. (*Opens fire-escape door.*) Where does the music come from?

LAURA: From the Paradise Dance Hall across the alley.

JIM: How about cutting the rug a little, Miss Wingfield?

LAURA: Oh, I—

JIM: Or is your program filled up? Let me have a look at it. (*Grasps imaginary card.*) Why, every dance is taken! I'll just have to scratch some out. (WALTZ MUSIC: "LA GOLONDRINA.") Ahhh, a waltz! (*He executes some sweeping turns by himself then holds his arms toward* LAURA.)

LAURA (*breathlessly*): I—can't dance!

JIM: There you go, that inferiority stuff!

LAURA: I've never danced in my life!

JIM: Come on, try!

LAURA: Oh, but I'd step on you!

JIM: I'm not made out of glass.

LAURA: How—how—how do we start?

JIM: Just leave it to me. You hold your arms out a little.

LAURA: Like this?

JIM: A little bit higher. Right. Now don't tighten up, that's the main thing about it—relax.

LAURA (*laughing breathlessly*): It's hard not to.

JIM: Okay.

LAURA: I'm afraid you can't budge me.

JIM: What do you bet I can't? (*He swings her into motion.*)

LAURA: Goodness, yes, you can!

JIM: Let yourself go, now, Laura, just let yourself go.

LAURA: I'm—

JIM: Come on!

LAURA: Trying!

JIM: Not so stiff—Easy does it!

LAURA: I know but I'm—

JIM: Loosen th' backbone! There now, that's a lot better.

LAURA: Am I?

JIM: Lots, lots better! (*He moves her about the room in a clumsy waltz.*)

LAURA: Oh, my!

JIM: Ha-ha!

LAURA: Oh, my goodness!

JIM: Ha-ha-ha! (*They suddenly bump into the table.* JIM *stops.*) What did we hit on?

LAURA: Table.

JIM: Did something fall off it? I think—

LAURA: Yes.

JIM: I hope that it wasn't the little glass horse with the horn!

LAURA: Yes.

JIM: Aw, aw, aw. Is it broken?

LAURA: Now it is just like all the other horses.

JIM: It's lost its—

LAURA: Horn! It doesn't matter. Maybe it's a blessing in disguise.

JIM: You'll never forgive me. I bet that that was your favorite piece of glass.

LAURA: I don't have favorites much. It's no tragedy, Freckles. Glass breaks so easily. No matter how careful you are. The traffic jars the shelves and things fall off them.

JIM: Still I'm awfully sorry that I was the cause.

LAURA (*smiling*): I'll just imagine he had an operation. The horn was removed to make him feel less—freakish! (*They both laugh.*) Now he will feel more at home with the other horses, the ones that don't have horns . . .

JIM: Ha-ha, that's very funny! (*Suddenly serious.*) I'm glad to see that you have a sense of humor. You know—you're—well—very different! Surprisingly different from anyone else I know! (*His voice becomes soft and hesitant with a genuine feeling.*) Do you mind me telling you that? (LAURA *is abashed beyond speech.*) I mean it in a nice way . . . (LAURA *nods shyly, looking away.*) You make me feel sort of—I don't know how to put it! I'm usually pretty good at expressing things, but—This is something that I don't know how to say! (LAURA *touches her throat and clears it—turns the broken unicorn in her hands.*) (*Even softer.*) Has anyone ever told you that you were pretty? (PAUSE: MUSIC.) (LAURA *looks up slowly, with wonder, and shakes her head.*) Well, you are! In a very different way from anyone else. And all the nicer because of the difference, too. (*His voice becomes low and husky.* LAURA *turns away, nearly faint with the novelty of her emotions.*) I wish that you were my sister. I'd teach you to have some confidence in yourself. The different people are not like other people, but being different is nothing to be ashamed of. Because other people are not such wonderful people. They're one hundred times one thousand. You're one times one! They walk all over the earth. You just stay here. They're common as—weeds, but—you—well, you're—*Blue Roses!*

(IMAGE ON SCREEN: BLUE ROSES.)

(MUSIC CHANGES.)

LAURA: But blue is wrong for—roses . . .

JIM: It's right for you—You're—pretty!

LAURA: In what respect am I pretty?

JIM: In all respects—believe me! Your eyes—your hair—are pretty! Your hands are pretty! (*He catches hold of her hand.*) You think I'm making this up because I'm invited to dinner and have to be nice. Oh, I could do that! I could put on an act for you, Laura, and say lots of things without being very sincere. But this time I am. I'm talking to you sincerely. I happened to notice you had this inferiority complex that keeps you from feeling comfortable with people. Somebody needs to build your confidence up and make you proud instead of shy and turning away and—blushing—Somebody ought to—Ought to—*kiss* you, Laura! (*His hand slips slowly up her arm to her shoulder.*) (MUSIC SWELLS TUMULTUOUSLY.) (*He suddenly turns her about and kisses her on the lips. When he releases her* LAURA *sinks on the sofa with a bright, dazed look.* JIM *backs away and fishes in his pocket for a cigarette.*) (LEGEND ON SCREEN: "SOUVENIR.") Stumble-john! (*He lights the ciga-rette, avoiding her look. There is a peal of girlish laughter from* AMANDA *in the kitchen.* LAURA *slowly raises and opens her hand. It still contains the little broken glass animal. She looks at it with a tender, bewildered expression.*) Stumble-john! I shouldn't have done that— That was way off the beam. You don't smoke, do you? (*She looks up, smiling, not hearing the question. He sits beside her a little gingerly. She looks at him speechlessly—waiting. He coughs decorously and moves a little farther aside as he considers the situation and senses her feelings, dimly, with perturbation. Gently.*) Would you—care for a—mint? (*She doesn't seem to hear him but her look grows brighter even.*) Peppermint—Life Saver? My pocket's a regular drug store— wherever I go . . . (*He pops a mint in his mouth. Then gulps and de-cides to make a clean breast of it. He speaks slowly and gingerly.*) Laura, you know, if I had a sister like you, I'd do the same thing as Tom. I'd bring out fellows and—introduce her to them. The right type of boys of a type to—appreciate her. Only—well—he made a mistake about me. Maybe I've got no call to be saying this. That may not have been the idea in having me over. But what if it was? There's nothing wrong about that. The only trouble is that in my case—I'm not in a situation to—do the right thing. I can't take down your number and say I'll phone. I can't call up next week and—ask for a date. I thought I had better explain the situation in case you misunderstood it and— hurt your feelings. . . . (*Pause. Slowly, very slowly,* LAURA'S *look changes, her eyes returning slowly from his to the ornament in her palm.*)

(AMANDA *utters another gay laugh in the kitchen.*)

LAURA (*faintly*): You—won't—call again?

JIM: No, Laura, I can't. (*He rises from the sofa.*) As I was just explaining, I've—got strings on me, Laura, I've—been going steady! I go out all the time with a girl named Betty. She's a home-girl like you, and Catholic, and Irish, and in a great many ways we—get along fine. I met her last summer on a moonlight boat trip up the river to Alton, on the *Majes-tic.* Well—right away from the start it was—love! (LEGEND: LOVE!) (LAURA *sways slightly forward and grips the arm of the sofa. He fails to notice, now enrapt in his own comfortable being.*) Being in love has made a new man of me! (*Leaning stiffly forward, clutching the arm of the sofa,* LAURA *struggles visibly with her storm. But* JIM *is oblivious, she is a long way off.*) The power of love is really pretty tremendous! Love is something that—changes the whole world, Laura! (*The storm abates a little and* LAURA *leans back. He notices her again.*) It hap-pened that Betty's aunt took sick, she got a wire and had to go to

Centralia. So Tom—when he asked me to dinner—I naturally just accepted the invitation, not knowing that you—that he—that I—(*He stops awkwardly.*) Huh—I'm a stumble-john! (*He flops back on the sofa. The holy candles in the altar of* LAURA'S *face have been snuffed out. There is a look of almost infinite desolation.* JIM *glances at her uneasily.*) I wish that you would—say something. (*She bites her lip which was trembling and then bravely smiles. She opens her hand again on the broken glass ornament. Then she gently takes his hand and raises it level with her own. She carefully places the unicorn in the palm of his hand, then pushes his fingers closed upon it.*) What are you—doing that for? You want me to have him?—Laura? (*She nods.*) What for?

LAURA: A—souvenir . . .

(*She rises unsteadily and crouches beside the victrola to wind it up.*)

(LEGEND ON SCREEN: "THINGS HAVE A WAY OF TURNING OUT SO BADLY!")

(OR IMAGE: "GENTLEMAN CALLER WAVING GOOD-BYE!—GAILY.")

(*At this moment* AMANDA *rushes brightly back in the front room. She bears a pitcher of fruit punch in an old-fashioned cut-glass pitcher and a plate of macaroons. The plate has a gold border and poppies painted on it.*)

AMANDA: Well, well, well! Isn't the air delightful after the shower? I've made you children a little liquid refreshment. (*Turns gaily to the gentleman caller.*) Jim, do you know that song about lemonade?
  "Lemonade, lemonade
    Made in the shade and stirred with a spade—
    Good enough for any old maid!"

JIM (*uneasily*): Ha-ha! No—I never heard it.

AMANDA: Why, Laura! You look so serious!

JIM: We were having a serious conversation.

AMANDA: Good! Now you're better acquainted!

JIM (*uncertainly*): Ha-ha! Yes.

AMANDA: You modern young people are much more serious-minded than my generation. I was so gay as a girl!

JIM: You haven't changed, Mrs. Wingfield.

AMANDA: Tonight I'm rejuvenated! The gaiety of the occasion, Mr. O'Connor! (*She tosses her head with a peal of laughter. Spills lemonade.*) Oooo! I'm baptizing myself!

JIM: Here—let me—

AMANDA (*setting the pitcher down*): There now. I discovered we had some maraschino cherries. I dumped them in, juice and all!

JIM: You shouldn't have gone to that trouble, Mrs. Wingfield.

AMANDA: Trouble, trouble? Why it was loads of fun! Didn't you hear me cutting up in the kitchen? I bet your ears were burning! I told Tom how outdone with him I was for keeping you to himself so long a time! He should have brought you over much, much sooner! Well, now that you've found your way, I want you to be a very frequent caller! Not just occasional but all the time. Oh, we're going to have a lot of gay times together! I see them coming! Mmm, just breathe that air! So fresh, and the moon's so pretty! I'll skip back out—I know where my place is when young folks are having a—serious conversation!

JIM: Oh, don't go out, Mrs. Wingfield. The fact of the matter is I've got to be going.

AMANDA: Going, now? You're joking! Why, it's only the shank of the evening, Mr. O'Connor!

JIM: Well, you know how it is.

AMANDA: You mean you're a young workingman and have to keep workingmen's hours. We'll let you off early tonight. But only on the condition that next time you stay later. What's the best night for you? Isn't Saturday night the best night for you workingmen?

JIM: I have a couple of time-clocks to punch, Mrs. Wingfield. One at morning, another one at night!

AMANDA: My, but you *are* ambitious! You work at night, too?

JIM: No, Ma'am, not work but—Betty! (*He crosses deliberately to pick up his hat. The band at the Paradise Dance Hall goes into a tender waltz.*)

AMANDA: Betty? Betty? Who's—Betty! (*There is an ominous cracking sound in the sky.*)

JIM: Oh, just a girl. The girl I go steady with! (*He smiles charmingly. The sky falls.*)

(LEGEND: "THE SKY FALLS.")

AMANDA (*a long-drawn exhalation*): Ohhhh . . . Is it a serious romance, Mr. O'Connor?

JIM: We're going to be married the second Sunday in June.

AMANDA: Ohhhh—how nice! Tom didn't mention that you were engaged to be married.

JIM: The cat's not out of the bag at the warehouse yet. You know how they are. They call you Romeo and stuff like that. (*He stops at the oval mirror to put on his hat. He carefully shapes the brim and the crown to give a discreetly dashing effect.*) It's been a wonderful evening, Mrs. Wingfield. I guess this is what they mean by Southern hospitality.

AMANDA: It really wasn't anything at all.

JIM: I hope it don't seem like I'm rushing off. But I promised Betty I'd pick her up at the Wabash depot, an' by the time I get my jalopy down there her train'll be in. Some women are pretty upset if you keep 'em waiting.

AMANDA: Yes, I know—The tyranny of women! (*Extends her hand.*) Good-bye, Mr. O'Connor. I wish you luck—and happiness—and success! All three of them, and so does Laura!—Don't you, Laura?

LAURA: Yes!

JIM (*taking her hand*): Good-bye, Laura. I'm certainly going to treasure that souvenir. And don't you forget the good advice I gave you. (*Rises his voice to a cheery shout.*) So long, Shakespeare! Thanks again, ladies—Good night!

(*He grins and ducks jauntily out.*)

(*Still bravely grimacing,* AMANDA *closes the door on the gentleman caller. Then she turns back to the room with a puzzled expression. She and* LAURA *don't dare to face each other.* LAURA *crouches beside the victrola to wind it.*)

AMANDA (*faintly*): Things have a way of turning out so badly. I don't believe that I would play the victrola. Well, well—well—Our gentleman caller was engaged to be married! Tom!

TOM (*from back*): Yes, Mother?

AMANDA: Come in here a minute. I want to tell you something awfully funny.

TOM (*enters with macaroon and a glass of the lemonade*): Has the gentleman caller gotten away already?

AMANDA: The gentleman caller has made an early departure. What a wonderful joke you played on us!

TOM: How do you mean?

AMANDA: You didn't mention that he was engaged to be married.

TOM: Jim? Engaged?

AMANDA: That's what he just informed us.

TOM: I'll be jiggered! I didn't know about that.

AMANDA: That seems very peculiar.

TOM: What's peculiar about it?

AMANDA: Didn't you call him your best friend down at the warehouse?

TOM: He is, but how did I know?

AMANDA: It seems extremely peculiar that you wouldn't know your best friend was going to be married!

TOM: The warehouse is where I work, not where I know things about people!

AMANDA: You don't know things anywhere! You live in a dream; you manufacture illusions! (*He crosses to door.*) Where are you going?

TOM: I'm going to the movies.

AMANDA: That's right, now that you've had us make such fools of ourselves. The effort, the preparations, all the expense! The new floor lamp, the rug, the clothes for Laura! All for what? To entertain some other girl's fiancé! Go to the movies, go! Don't think about us, a mother deserted, an unmarried sister who's crippled and has no job! Don't let anything interfere with your selfish pleasure! Just go, go, go—to the movies!

TOM: All right, I will! The more you shout about my selfishness to me the quicker I'll go, and I won't go to the movies!

AMANDA: Go, then! Then go to the moon—you selfish dreamer!

(TOM *smashes his glass on the floor. He plunges out on the fire-escape, slamming the door.* LAURA *screams—cut by door.*)

(*Dance-hall music up.* TOM *goes to the rail and grips it desperately, lifting his face in the chill white moonlight penetrating the narrow abyss of the alley.*)

(LEGEND ON SCREEN: "AND SO GOOD-BYE . . .")

(TOM'S *closing speech is timed with the interior pantomine. The interior scene is played as though viewed through soundproof glass.* AMANDA *appears to be making a comforting speech to* LAURA *who is huddled upon the sofa. Now that we cannot hear the mother's speech, her silliness is gone and she has dignity and tragic beauty.* LAURA'S *dark hair hides her face until at the end of the speech she lifts it to smile at her mother.* AMANDA'S *gestures are slow and graceful, almost dancelike, as she comforts the daughter. At the end of her speech she glances a moment at the father's picture—then withdraws through the portieres. At close of* TOM'S *speech,* LAURA *blows out the candles, ending the play.*)

TOM: I didn't go to the moon, I went much further—for time is the longest distance between two places—Not long after that I was fired for writing a poem on the lid of a shoe-box. I left Saint Louis. I descended the steps of this fire-escape for a last time and followed, from then on, in my father's footsteps, attempting to find in motion what was lost in space—I traveled around a great deal. The cities swept about me like dead leaves, leaves that were brightly colored but torn away from the branches. I would have stopped, but I was pursued by something. It always came upon me unawares, taking me altogether by surprise. Perhaps it was a familiar bit of music. Perhaps it was only a piece of transparent glass—Perhaps I am walking along a street at night, in some strange city, before I have found companions. I pass the lighted window of a shop where perfume is sold. The window is filled with pieces of colored glass, tiny transparent bottles in delicate colors, like bits of a shattered rainbow. Then all at once my sister touches my shoulder. I turn around and look into her eyes . . . Oh, Laura, Laura, I tried to leave you behind me, but I am more faithful than I intended to be! I reach for a cigarette, I cross the street, I run into the movies or a bar, I buy a drink, I speak to the nearest stranger—anything that can blow your candles out! (LAURA *bends over the candles.*)—for nowadays the world is lit by lightning! Blow out your candles, Laura—and so good-bye. . . .

(*She blows the candles out.*)

THE SCENE DISSOLVES

Production Notes

Being a "memory play," *The Glass Menagerie* can be presented with unusual freedom of convention. Because of its considerably delicate or tenuous material, atmospheric touches and subtleties of direction play a particularly important part. Expressionism and all other unconventional techniques in drama have only one valid aim, and that is a closer approach to truth. When a play employs unconventional techniques, it is not, or certainly shouldn't be, trying to escape its responsibility of dealing with reality, or interpreting experience, but is actually or should be attempting to find a closer approach, a more penetrating and vivid expression of things as they are. The straight realistic play with its genuine frigidaire and authentic ice-cubes, its characters that speak exactly as its audience speaks, corresponds to the academic landscape and has the same virtue of a photographic likeness. Everyone should know nowadays the unimportance of the photographic in art: that truth, life, or reality is an organic thing which the poetic imagination can represent or suggest, in essence, only through transformation, through changing into other forms than those which were merely present in appearance.

These remarks are not meant as comments only on this particular play. They have to do with a conception of a new, plastic theater which must take the place of the exhausted theater of realistic conventions if the theater is to resume vitality as a part of our culture.

THE SCREEN DEVICE

There is *only one important difference between the original and acting version of the play* and that is the *omission* in the latter of the device which I tentatively included in my *original* script. This device was the use of a screen on which were projected magic-lantern slides bearing images or titles. I do not regret the omission of this device from the . . . Broadway production. The extraordinary power of Miss Taylor's performance made it suitable to have the utmost simplicity in the physical production. But I think it may be interesting to some readers to see how this device was conceived. So I am putting it into the published manuscript. These images and legends, projected from behind, were cast on a section of wall between the front-room and dining-room areas, which should be indistinguishable from the rest when not in use.

The purpose of this will probably be apparent. It is to give accent to certain values in each scene. Each scene contains a particular point (or several) which is structurally the most important. In an episodic play, such as this, the basic structure or narrative line may be obscured from the audience; the effect may seem fragmentary rather than architectural. This may not be the fault of the play so much as a lack of attention in the audience. The legend or image upon the screen will strengthen the effect of what is merely allusion in the writing and allow the primary point to be made more simply and lightly than if the entire responsibility were on the spoken lines. Aside from this structural value, I think the screen will have a definite emotional appeal, less definable but just as important. An imaginative producer or director may invent many other uses for this device than those indicated in the present script. In fact the possibilities of the device seem much larger to me than the instance of this play can possibly utilize.

THE MUSIC

Another extra-literary accent in this play is provided by the use of music. A single recurring tune, "The Glass Menagerie," is used to give emotional emphasis to suitable passages. This tune is like circus music, not when you are on the grounds or in the immediate vicinity of the parade, but when you are at some distance and very likely thinking of something else. It seems under those circumstances to continue almost interminably and it weaves in and out of your preoccupied consciousness; then it is the lightest, most delicate music in the world and perhaps the saddest. It expresses the surface vivacity of life with the underlying strain of immutable and inexpressible sorrow. When you look at a piece of delicately spun glass you think of two things: how beautiful it is and how easily it can be broken. Both of those ideas should be woven into the recurring tune, which dips in and out of the play as if it were carried on a wind that changes. It serves as a thread of connection and allusion between the narrator with his separate point in time and space and the subject of his story. Between each episode it returns as reference to the emotion, nostalgia, which is the first condition of the play. It is primarily Laura's music and therefore comes out most clearly when the play focuses upon her and the lovely fragility of glass which is her image.

THE LIGHTING

The lighting in the play is not realistic. In keeping with the atmosphere of memory, the stage is dim. Shafts of light are focused on selected areas or actors, sometimes in contradistinction to what is the apparent center. For instance, in the quarrel scene between Tom and Amanda, in which Laura has no active part, the clearest pool of light is on her figure. This is also true of the supper scene, when her silent figure on the sofa should remain the visual center. The light upon Laura should be distinct from the others, having a peculiar pristine clarity such as light used in early religious portraits of female saints or madonnas. A certain correspondence to light in religious paintings, such as El Greco's, where the figures are radiant in atmosphere that is relatively dusky, could be effectively used throughout the play. (It will also permit a more effective use of the screen.) A free, imaginative use of light can be of enormous value in giving a mobile, plastic quality to plays of a more or less static nature.

T.W.

In retrospect one sees that the appearance of *The Glass Menagerie* in 1945 marked the beginning (at any rate, the public beginning) of one of the most exciting dramatic careers in postwar America. Williams's later plays, all dealing with love's failure in a world brutalized and perverse to the extent to which it betrays love, have not fulfilled the promise of quiet loveliness that *The Glass Menagerie* gave, but his imaginative use of the stage and the poetry of his realistic dialogue have hardly diminished in power. He argues no themes, is not a master of suspense, but he makes of the theater significant space for living characters. A dimension of meaning—wistfulness, tragi-comedy—is (to take an example) added to the bittersweet drama of the Wingfields by the smiling face of the footloose father, the happy doughboy, that presides over the heart-breaks of his deserted family. The aliveness is harder to analyze. The effect of Amanda's speech, "Sticks and stones may break our bones, but the expression on Mr. Garfinkel's face won't harm us!" has something to do with the way the associations of the first half clash with the prosaism of rhythm and reference of the second. The child's jingle of studied unconcern at being spiritually hurt becomes a brittle defense against poverty and humiliation and does not quite cover the cruelty that poverty and humiliation entail: Laura's having to face Mr. Garfinkel. The speech is a sad, soft woman's effort to be gay and hard. Williams's plays are full of such speeches. They ring true; people seem to talk like that. The very idiosyncrasies of image, diction, and cadence amount to lifelikeness.

Williams's success as the realist of frustration and despair may at first seem to contradict the artistic theory he propounds in the "Production Notes" to *The Glass Menagerie*. Actually, the theory explains the success. "Everyone" (he says in the notes) "should know nowadays the unimportance of the photographic in art: that truth, life, or reality is an organic thing which the poetic imagination can represent or suggest, in essence, only through transformation, through changing into other forms than those which were merely present in appearance." The crucial words here are "in essence." Williams's characters get their faintly fantastic inner glow from being "essences." They are convincingly real *because* they are more than lifelike prototypes. They are defined, assume shape and three dimensions, in terms of their obsessions, their mannerisms, their associations with certain objects. Amanda is fluttering gentility, forlorn Southern belle of vivacious humor long frayed by wear, puzzled and panicked because of her daughter's failure to attract a single specimen of the breed of males by which, in Amanda's set of values, a woman's success and happiness are measured. Laura is defined by her glass menagerie. The animals both symbolize her fragility and her quaint beauty and represent the world of lovely imagination into which she escapes from typing charts and speed tests. Tom writes poems on the lids of shoe boxes, and his emblems are the movies and the pirate ship, escapist symbols of glamorous adventure. Jim O'Connor chews gum and believes in Dale Carnegie and the future of television. These are portraits not in depth but in sharp focus. The method may represent

Williams's limitation; he is neither a profound nor a versatile writer. But it makes his plays.

Williams's vignettes of the frustrations of ordinary people suggest Chekhov in their reliance on mood and atmosphere and in their near-plotlessness. No one who reads Chekhov right will find anything paradoxical in the fact that Williams also scorns dramatic photography. His attitude, of course, is quite orthodox among contemporary playwrights, who all have read their Strindberg and Pirandello. But in *The Glass Menagerie* Williams is not just following fashion; the break with realism can be justified on the intrinsic grounds that the play is a "memory play." Its premise is the subjectivity of modern relativism: reality, it implies, is not what happened but how you feel about what happened. Clearly, the solidities of naturalistic staging would have crushed Tom's delicate memories of mother and sister. The transparent apartment, the easy transitions from one point of time to another, the use of light and music to throw characters, objects, and events into relief—all this is a kind of poetry of the theater and psychologically true to the play's status as a record of inner experience. At the same time, the inner experience has been objectified by the theater medium. When Tom gulps his coffee and quarrels with his mother he is simply another character, though the stage is his own mind. His double function in the play insures esthetic distance. The play is enclosed by the narrator-director-character's memory, the Shakespeare of the shipping room.

But the memory device has not made the play rigid nor us uncomfortable. Only the literal-minded would object to Tom's staging a scene at which he was not himself present—the climactic one between Laura and Jim. By the strict logic of Tom's being the rememberer, the scene is construction by inference or, possibly, by report by either one or both of the two principals. But merely to begin speculating and explaining along these lines shows up the irrelevance of the whole issue. The play works by a higher logic than mere consistency of decorum, just as it is also too subtle to need the projection of theme-focusing "legends" and "images" on a screen wall that Williams had planned originally. It makes its meaning without such obvious and heavy-handed new stagecraft devices.

In keeping with the memory-play premise the plot is slight. Much of the play is little more than a tenuously coherent sequence of scenes of people getting on each other's nerves when their dreams and longings clash and wound. What story there is begins late: Tom, giving in to his mother's nagging, provides a gentleman caller for his sister, and for a few moments there is a promise of happy ending as the princess almost comes out of the spell that shyness and lameness have cast upon her. But the prince of the magic kiss turns out to be very much engaged, and the music from the old victrola again takes over from the Paradise Dance Hall band. In these elusive, fleeting, pastel reminiscences of moods, the only element of intrigue—the coincidence that Tom's friend turns out to be Laura's secret high-school ideal—seems almost to belong to another, more mechanical, kind of playwriting.

Whose play is *The Glass Menagerie*? Not Tom's; he is not himself the main character of his memories. And Jim is even more than Tom primarily a means to an end: a nice young man caught in an awkward situation, decent enough to sense its pathos, half-educated enough to try to remedy it with newspaper column psychology, and socially deft enough to get out without too much embarrassment. The end both he and Tom serve is one they share with most of Tennessee Williams's male characters: to reveal female lovelornness and broken illusions. The play is Laura's and Amanda's, mother's and daughter's both, not the one's more than the other's, although Amanda mainly exists in terms of Laura's situation. Laura's unfitness for social life—her scene with Jim is almost a tender parody of a home date—is her distinction. She is exquisite because she is different and rare—blue roses among red, unique as a unicorn. Like her unicorn, she is fragile. She would be less precious were she more robust. The unicorn loses its horn during the dance, and Laura—dancing, kissed—becomes for a moment like other girls. But as her mother's laughter tinkles in the kitchen the gentleman caller announces his unavailability, and her and her mother's dream shatters—not on human cruelty, for Jim is not cruel, but on the blind, casual cruelty of life itself: "Things have a way of turning out so badly." There is hardly the stuff of tragedy in middle-aged girlishness and pathetic shyness due to a physical defect, in frustration by coincidence. The play is squarely in the modern democratic tradition that assumes that serious drama can be made of the sufferings of small people and which proceeds to write such plays, foregoing claims to traditional tragic magnitude of destiny and language. But *The Glass Menagerie* is something more as well. In Tom's final memory image Amanda passes from exasperating silliness to a kind of tragic dignity as the eternal mother sorrowing for her sorrowing child. The child becomes the girl of candles in a world "lit by lightning."

The Glass Menagerie fittingly introduces the sequence of Williams's plays, for it anticipates important themes and motifs and images of his later, more violent critiques of the spiritual desolation of the modern world. The notion that the weakest, the most vulnerable, are the best because their weakness and vulnerability signify sensitivity and imagination has become almost a hallmark with Williams. Fragile objects have continued to be important symbols in his plays. And the moon rising over Garfinkel's delicatessen suggests the blend of romantic daydream and sordidness, of sentimentality and comic realism, that defines his dramatic world.

Appendix

Biographical Notes and Suggested References

SOPHOCLES (?496–406 B.C.) was born in Colonus, then a suburb of Athens. This town is the setting for *Oedipus at Colonus,* the last of the nearly 120 plays he is said to have written. Only seven are extant today, and only three of these can be dated with any certainty: *Antigone,* 442 B.C.; *Philoctetes,* 409; and *Oedipus at Colonus,* close to 406. Of the others, *Ajax* is thought to be an early play, *Oedipus Rex* is usually dated 430–425, *Electra* is probably later than *Oedipus Rex,* and for *Trachiniae* there is no agreement on date. In the annual competition among playwrights writing for the Dionysiac festival, Sophocles won the prize eighteen times. His trilogies, unlike Aeschylus's, consisted of plays unrelated in subject matter. He was the first tragic writer to put three characters (in addition to the chorus) on stage at the same time.

Chronologically, Sophocles is the second of the three great Athenian tragedians—some thirty years younger than Aeschylus, some fifteen years older than Euripides. His manhood roughly coincides with the flowering of Athenian civilization between the defeat of the Persians in 480 B.C. and the surrender to Sparta at the end of the Peloponnesian War in 404. He was active in political and military affairs. His fame as playwright may have earned him his public employments. Sophocles himself reports that his friend Pericles said that he was a better poet than general. By all accounts, Sophocles was handsome, charming, popular, and well-to-do. Aristophanes, the writer of comedies and Sophocles' younger contemporary, summed up the tenor of his life in calling him "contented among the living, contented among the dead"—a curious but provocative judgment in view of the fact that it concerns one of the greatest of tragic poets.

Suggested Reading

Adams, Sinclair M. Sophocles the Playwright. *Toronto: University of Toronto Press, 1957.*

Bieber, Margarete. The History of the Greek and Roman Theater. *2nd rev. ed. Princeton, N.J.: Princeton University Press, 1960.*

Bowra, C. M. Sophoclean Tragedy. *Oxford: Clarendon Press, 1944.*

Butcher, S. H. Aristotle's Theory of Poetry and Fine Arts. *New York: Dover Publications, 1951.*

Fergusson, Francis. "Oedipus Rex: *The Tragic Rhythm of Action." In* The Idea of a Theater. *Princeton, N.J.: Princeton University Press, 1949.*

Kirkwood, Gordon M. A Study of Sophoclean Drama. *Ithaca, N.Y.: Cornell University Press, 1958.*

Kitto, H. D. F. Greek Tragedy: A Literary Study. *Garden City, N.Y.: Doubleday (Anchor), 1954.*

Knox, Bernard M. W. The Heroic Temper. *Berkeley: University of California Press, 1964.*

Waldock, A. J. A. Sophocles the Dramatist. *Cambridge, Eng.: Cambridge University Press, 1951.*

Whitman, Cedric H. Sophocles: A Study in Heroic Humanism. *Cambridge, Mass.: Harvard University Press, 1951.*

Woodward, Thomas, ed. Sophocles: A Collection of Critical Essays. *Englewood Cliffs, N.J.: Prentice-Hall, 1966.*

ANTIGONE

Records

Members of Columbia University (*in Greek*). Folkway Records 9912 (1 record, mono)

McGill University students. Folkway Records 9861 (1 record, mono)

Tutin, Adrian, Brett. Caedmon TRS-320 (2 records, stereo). CDL 5320 (cassette tape)

Film

Greek, 1962. Directed by George Tzavellas, with Irene Papas. (88 min., 16mm, sound, black-and-white, subtitles). Audio Film Center, 406 Clement Street, San Francisco, Calif. 94118. (Rental)

WILLIAM SHAKESPEARE (1564–1616). Enough is known about Shakespeare, both as citizen and as man of the theater, to refute all speculation that he was not the author of the plays ascribed to him. His life is better documented than those of most of his literary contemporaries. The evidence consists of church and court records and of references, both friendly and unfriendly, to his professional life. The late seventeenth and early eighteenth centuries knew a number of colorful legends about his early life, but these have not been verified by modern scholarship.

He was the son of a substantial tradesman in Stratford-on-Avon. Presumably he received a good grammar-school education (including training in Latin) till he was about sixteen. At eighteen he married Anne Hathaway, who was eight years older than he and with whom he had three children. In the early 1590's he turns up in London as a rising young poet and actor-playwright, a member of the company of the Chamberlain's Men, later (1603) known as the King's Men. When the company built the Globe Theater in 1599, Shakespeare was listed as the second of nine shareholders. In or shortly before 1612 he retired to Stratford, apparently a prosperous man. Friends and colleagues (including Ben Jonson) speak affectionately of him as a witty and cheerful companion.

The First Folio edition of Shakespeare's plays in 1623 established the conventional division of the canon into comedies, histories, and tragedies. (The First Folio includes thirty-six plays, but modern scholars count thirty-seven plays as wholly or almost wholly his.) It is a convenient division, particularly because it is traditional, but it takes no note of Shakespeare's development as a dramatist or of the generic variety within some single plays, and it obscures the range of plays within the same category. *Romeo and Juliet,* from about 1595, is a different kind of tragedy from *King Lear* and *Coriolanus,* from about 1606 and 1608, respectively. A history play like *Richard II* could qualify as tragedy and major parts of *Henry IV,* Part 1 as comedy. And "comedy" is not a very accurate collective term for plays as different as *The Comedy of Errors, A Midsummer Night's Dream, The Merry Wives of Windsor, The Merchant of Venice, Twelfth Night, Measure for Measure,* and *The Tempest.*

The exact chronology of Shakespeare's plays remains uncertain, but there is general agreement that most of the histories were written early; that *Hamlet* is the earliest of the major tragedies and only a little later than such "high" romantic comedies as *As You Like It* and *Twelfth Night;* that the period of "dark" or "problem" comedies of moral ambiguity, like *Troilus and Cressida* and *Measure for Measure,* partly coincides with the period of the mature tragedies; and that the allegorical romances on the themes of forgiveness and reconciliation, like *The Winter's Tale* and *The Tempest,* reflect a post-tragic view of life and are among Shakespeare's last plays.

Suggested Reading

Bentley, Gerald E. Shakespeare: A Biographical Handbook. *New Haven, Conn.: Yale University Press, 1961.*

Bradley, A. C. Shakespearean Tragedy. *New York: Meridian Books, 1955* (*first publ. 1904*).

Campbell, Oscar J., and Edward G. Quinn. The Reader's Encyclopedia of Shakespeare. *New York: Thomas Y. Crowell, 1966.*

Chute, Marchette. Shakespeare of London. *New York: E. P. Dutton, 1949.*

Dean, Leonard F., ed. Shakespeare: Modern Essays in Criticism. *New York: Oxford University Press, 1957.*

———, ed., A Casebook on Othello. *New York: Thomas Y. Crowell Co., 1961.*

Granville-Barker, H. Prefaces to Shakespeare. *Princeton, N.J.: Princeton University Press, 1946.*

———, and G. B. Harrison. A Companion to Shakespeare Studies. *Garden City, N.Y.: Doubleday (Anchor), 1960.*

Halliday, F. B., Shakespeare: A Pictorial Biography. *New York: Thomas Y. Crowell Co., 1956.*

Harbage, Alfred, ed. Shakespeare: The Tragedies: A Collection of Critical Essays. *Englewood Cliffs, N.J.: Prentice-Hall, 1964.*

Harrison, G. B., Introducing Shakespeare. *3rd ed., rev. and expanded. London: Penguin Books, 1966.*

Heilman, Robert B., Magic in the Web: Action and Language in Othello. *Lexington: University of Kentucky Press, 1956.*

Knight, G. Wilson. The Wheel of Fire. *London: Methuen, 1949.*

Nagler, A. M. Shakespeare's Stage. *New Haven, Conn.: Yale University Press, 1964.*

Ridley, M. R., ed., Othello (*Arden edition*). *London: Methuen and Co., 1958.*

Rosenberg, Marvin, The Masks of Othello. *Berkeley: University of California Press, 1961.*

Van Doren, Mark, Shakespeare. *Garden City, N.Y.: Doubleday & Company (Anchor Book), 1939.*

Webster, Margaret. Shakespeare without Tears. *Rev. ed. Cleveland: World Publishing Company, 1955.*

OTHELLO

Records

Robeson, Ferrer. Columbia Special Products CSL-153 (*3 records, mono*)

Cambridge University Marlowe Society. Argo 121/4 (*4 records, mono*)

Dublin Gate Theatre. Spoken Arts 783 (*1 record, mono*)

Marshall, Robinson, Claire, Donegan. Folkway Records 9618 (*1 record, mono*)

Olivier. RCA VDS-100 (*4 records, stereo*)

Silvera, Massey, Johnson. Caedmon SRS-S-225 (*3 records, stereo*)

Films

German, 1922. Directed by Dimitru Buchowetski, with Emil Jannings,
Werner Krauss (100 min., 16mm, silent, black-and-white). Audio
Film Center, 406 Clement Street, San Francisco, Calif. 94118. (Rental)

Russian, 1955. Directed by Sergei Youtkevich (108 min., 16mm, sound,
color, dubbed). Brandon Films, 221 W. 57th Street, New York, N.Y.
10019. (Rental)

American (United Artists), 1955. Directed by Orson Welles, with
Orson Welles (92 min., 16mm, sound, black-and-white). Contem-
porary Films. McGraw-Hill Book Co., 330 W. 42nd Street, New York,
N.Y. 10036. (Rental)

British, 1965. Directed by Stuart Burge, with Sir Laurence Olivier,
Maggie Smith (166 min., 16mm, sound, color). Warner Brother 17
Arts, Non-Theatrical Division, 200 Park Ave., New York, N.Y. 10017.
(Rental)

JEAN BAPTISTE POQUELIN (MOLIÈRE) (1622–1673) was the son of a well-
to-do upholsterer attached to the royal court. Both upholstering and
law studies proved abortive, and in 1643 young Poquelin co-founded a
theatrical company and took the name Molière (its significance is unknown) as a stage name. Unsuccessful in Paris, the company toured the
provinces between 1645 and 1658. These were Molière's years of ap-
prenticeship. In 1659 he experienced his first success as a playwright
with the brief satire *The Affected Ladies*. In 1661 the company, enjoying
royal patronage, established itself in its own theater, the Palais-Royal,
in Paris. Until his death, Molière continued to write plays for his company, mainly comedies, and to act, mainly in comic parts. Many of his
plays enraged the pious and the learned, and Louis XIV's favor proved
fickle. As a result, the fortunes of the company remained insecure, despite Molière's popularity with the enlightened part of his audience. His
marriage to a much younger woman appears to have been unhappy, and
his children died in infancy. Grim irony attended his death: he suffered
a hemorrhage while performing the title role of his own comedy *The
Hypochondriac* and died a few hours afterwards.

Like Shakespeare's, the best of Molière's plays belong to world literature. Their farcical plots are vehicles for intimate studies of self-duped
eccentrics whose single-minded psychological biases (or "humors") reduce them to stiff human grotesques, unable and unwilling to accommodate themselves to the norms of joyous and healthy social relationships. In Molière's comedies, as in the tragedies of his contemporary
Racine, character is destiny. Besides *The Misanthrope*, the best known

among them are *School for Wives* (1662), *Tartuffe* (1664, 1669), *The Miser* (1668), *The Gentleman Burgher* (1670), and *the Learned Ladies* (1672).

Suggested Reading

Fernandez, Ramon. *Molière: The Man Seen through His Plays.* *Translated by Wilson Follet.* New York: Hill and Wang *(Dramabook), 1958.*
Gossman, Lionel. *Men and Masks: A Study of Molière.* *Baltimore: Johns Hopkins Press, 1963.*
Guicharnaud, Jacques, ed. *Molière: A Collection of Critical Essays.* *Englewood Cliffs, N.J.: Prentice-Hall, 1964.*
Hubert, Judd D. *Molière and the Comedy of Intellect.* *Berkeley: University of California Press, 1962.*
Lewis, D. Wyndham. *Molière, the Comic Mask.* *London: Eyre and Spottiswoode, 1959.*
Moore, Will. *Molière, a New Criticism.* *Oxford: Clarendon Press, 1962.*

THE MISANTHROPE

Records
Comédie Française (in French). Period Records 1504 *(1 record, mono)*
APA Repertory Company. Caedmon TRS-337 *(3 records, stereo)*

HENRIK IBSEN (1828–1906) was born in Skien, a small town in southern Norway. His father, a merchant of some social standing in the town, went bankrupt when the boy was eight, and the family thereafter lived in reduced circumstances. At sixteen Ibsen was apprenticed to a druggist in another small town. Two years later a servant-girl in the household gave birth to his illegitimate child. There is good reason to believe that these early experiences of financial hardship and social disgrace conditioned the shrewd sense of business, the reticence, and the excessive outer propriety that characterized Ibsen in later life, and both financial ruin and bastardy are recurrent motifs in his plays. He wrote his first play in 1848, under the influence of the liberalism of the February revolution in France of that year. Having soon abandoned a plan to study medicine, he was a free-lance journalist for a few years and flirted briefly with political radicalism. In the 1850's and early 1860's he held positions as salaried playwright and director at theaters in Bergen and Christiania (Oslo). Norway's failure to help Denmark in her war against Prussia in 1864 disillusioned him deeply (though he did not himself volunteer for service), and he and his wife and son left Norway for twenty-seven years of self-imposed exile in Italy and Germany. By the time he returned in 1891 he was a world figure. He died in Christiania after several years' illness.

Ibsen's iconoclasm, compact dramaturgy, and use of realistic symbols have earned him his reputation as "the father of modern drama." His canon, however, includes other kinds of plays than those on which, until fairly recently, his reputation was almost exclusively based. Most of his early plays were works of national romanticism, dealing with saga and peasant subject matter. His first popular success was the philosophical dramatic poem *Brand* (1866), which was followed by the complementary, antithetical *Peer Gynt* (1867). Together, these two verse dramas provide a clue to much that has been found obscure in the realistic plays that followed. Ibsen himself considered *Emperor and Galilean* (1873), a ten-act "world-historical drama" about the conflict between paganism and Christianity in the fourth-century Roman emperor Julian the Apostate, his most important work—a judgment no one else has shared. In the late 1870's and 1880's he wrote the social problem plays in prose by which he first attained international fame. The most important of these are *A Doll's House* (1879), *Ghosts* (1881), *An Enemy of the People* (1882), *The Wild Duck* (1884), *Rosmersholm* (1886), and *Hedda Gabler* (1890). Actually, the last three of these subordinate social problematics to individual psychology, and they mark, in some ways, a transition to Ibsen's final phase, in which he continued to anatomize the marriage relationship in heavily symbolic plays of little external action and of some autobiographical import. The most important of his last four plays are *The Master Builder* (1892) and *When We Dead Awaken* (1899).

Suggested Reading

Bradbook, Muriel. Ibsen the Norwegian. *New ed. London: Chatto & Windus, 1966 (first publ. 1948).*

Downs, Brian W. Ibsen: the Intellectual Background. *Cambridge, Eng.: Cambridge University Press, 1946.*

————. A Study of Six Plays by Ibsen. *Cambridge, Eng.: Cambridge University Press, 1950.*

Fjelde, Rolf, ed. Ibsen: A Collection of Critical Essays. *Englewood Cliffs, N.J.: Prentice-Hall, 1965.*

Lucas, Frank L. The Drama of Ibsen and Strindberg. *London: Cassell, 1962.*

McFarlane, James W., ed. Discussions of Henrik Ibsen. *Boston: D. C. Heath, 1962.*

————, tr. and ed. Ibsen [*the collected works in English*]. *London, New York: Oxford University Press, 1960.*

————. Ibsen and the Temper of Norwegian Literature. *London: Oxford University Press, 1960.*

Meyer, Michael. Ibsen: A Biography. *Garden City, N.Y.: Doubleday, 1971.*

Northam, John. Ibsen's Dramatic Method. *London: Faber and Faber,*
1953.

Sprinchorn, Evert, ed. Ibsen: Letters and Speeches. *New York: Hill and
Wang (Dramabook), 1964.*

Tennant, P. F. D. Ibsen's Dramatic Technique. *Cambridge, Eng.: Bowes
& Bowes, 1948.*

Weigand, Hermann. The Modern Ibsen. *New York: E. P. Dutton, 1960
(first publ. 1925).*

HEDDA GABLER

Record
*Plowright, Quayle, Nesbitt, Magee. Caedmon TRS-322 (3 records,
stereo)*

ANTON PAVLOVICH CHEKHOV (1860–1904) was born in Taganrog on the Sea
of Azov in southern Russia, the grandson of a serf and the son of a
grocer. A harsh boyhood was followed by medical studies in Moscow.
He received his degree in 1884, but he never practiced medicine very
regularly and in his last years not at all. In order to pay for his studies
and support his family, he began to write and sell small, comical narrative sketches. In 1886, a successful collection of short stories, somewhat
in the manner of de Maupassant, brought him acceptance in leading
literary circles. His early one-act plays, most of them comedies, were
quite successful, his first full-length play, *Ivanov* (1887), somewhat less
so, and his next serious dramas failed. In 1890, tired with literary life, he
traveled to the penal colony on the island of Sakhalin in the Sea of
Okhotsk, off the east coast of Siberia. He returned home by way of
Singapore and Ceylon. In 1898, *The Seagull,* which had been a humiliat-
ing fiasco in St. Petersburg two years earlier, was a brilliant success in
the newly opened Moscow Art Theater, under the direction of Konstantin Stanislavsky. *The Seagull* established not only Chekhov's reputation as a major playwright but also the success of the Stanislavsky
"method" of realistic, inner-motivated acting and the finances of the
new theater. Stanislavsky and Chekhov, however, did not always agree
on the interpretation of his plays. In 1901 Chekhov married one of the
leading actresses in the Moscow Art Theater, but his bad health—he had
contracted tuberculosis in his early twenties—forced them to live apart
for long periods. While she acted in Moscow, he spent the cold months
of the year in Yalta on the Crimea. He wrote three additional plays for
the Moscow Art Theater: *Uncle Vanya* (1899, a revision of *The Wood
Demon,* which he had written ten years earlier), *The Three Sisters* (1901),

and, his greatest success, *The Cherry Orchard* (1904). He died at a sanatorium in southern Germany.

Chekhov's major plays continue both to succeed in the theater and to elude final criticism. The social conditions they reflect are no longer actual, if they ever were. In disjointed dialogue and understated plots they chronicle small and stagnant lives and have no apparent theses. Rather than photographs and stenograms of reality or social problem plays, they are images that reduce to ironic order the unchanneled flow of banality by which most of human life happens.

Suggested Reading

Jackson, Robert L. Chekhov: A Collection of Critical Essays. *Englewood Cliffs, N.J.: Prentice-Hall, 1967.*

Magarshack, David. Chekhov the Dramatist. *New York: Hill and Wang (Dramabook), 1960.*

Simmons, Ernest J. Chekhov. *Boston: Little, Brown, 1962.*

Toumanova, Princess Nina Andronikova. Anton Chekhov: The Voice of Twilight Russia. *New York: Columbia University Press, 1960.*

Valency, Maurice J. The Breaking String: The Plays of Anton Chekhov. *New York: Oxford University Press, 1966.*

THE CHERRY ORCHARD

Record
Minneapolis Theater Co., with Jessica Tandy. Caedmon TRS-314 (3 records, stereo)
Film
American, 1967. Directed by John Barnes, with Maureen Stapleton, Donald Moffat (43 min., 16mm, sound, color and black-and-white, 2 parts). Encyclopaedia Britannica Education Corporation, 425 N. Michigan Ave., Chicago, Ill. 60611. (For sale. Also available for general rental in commercial film libraries, public library film collections, and college audio-visual centers.)

TENNESSEE WILLIAMS (b. 1914) was born in Columbus, Ohio. Of his family he has said that "there was a combination of Puritan and Cavalier strains in my blood which may be accountable for the conflicting impulses I often represent in the people I write about." The family's move to St. Louis in 1926 brought the boy a sense of loss of social class; it is the "feel" of his own home milieu (though not its particulars) that he sketches in *The Glass Menagerie*. His college career during the depression was interrupted by a job as clerk in the shoe company for which his father was a salesman. He received his B.A. degree from Iowa in 1938.

After a succession of odd jobs (including Hollywood scriptwriting) he won recognition as playwright with *The Glass Menagerie* in 1945. Early in his career he substituted "Tennessee" (in honor of the state of his pioneer forefathers) for his given name, Thomas Lanier. His early works include poetry and fiction. He has written one novel, *The Roman Spring of Mrs. Stone* (1950).

Noteworthy in a long series of plays are *A Streetcar Named Desire* (1947, awarded the Pulitzer Prize), *Summer and Smoke* (1948), *The Rose Tattoo* (1951), the expressionistic *Camino Real* (1953), *Cat on a Hot Tin Roof* (1955, awarded the Pulitzer Prize), *Sweet Bird of Youth* (1959), *The Night of the Iguana* (1961). Several of his plays have been made into successful motion pictures, most of them representative of Hollywood's new trend in the treatment of sex. Among them are *Twenty-Seven Wagons Full of Cotton* (1946, filmed as *Baby Doll*) and *Suddenly Last Summer* (1957). Many critics have found his recent plays "decadent" denials of all human values. In an autobiographical sketch some years ago he called his "politics" "humanitarian."

Suggested Reading

Downer, Alan S. *Fifty Years of American Drama. Chicago: Henry Regnery, 1951.*

Jones, Robert E. *"Tennessee Williams' Early Heroines,"* Modern Drama 2 *(1959): 211–219.*

Lumley, Frederick. *Trends in Twentieth Century Drama. London: Rockliff, 1956.*

Nelson, Benjamin. *Tennessee Williams. New York: Ivan Obelensky, 1961.*

Popkin, Henry. *"The Plays of Tennessee Williams,"* Tulane Drama Review 4 *(Spring, 1960): 45–64.*

Tischler, Nancy M. *Tennessee Williams. New York: The Citadel Press, 1961.*

Vowles, Richard B. *"Tennessee Williams: The World of His Imagery,"* Tulane Drama Review 3 *(December, 1958): 51–56.*

THE GLASS MENAGERIE

Record
Cliff, Harris, Tandy, D. Wayne. Caedmon TRS-301 (2 records, stereo)

Suggested General References

Theory

Abel, Lionel. *Metatheatre. New York: Hill and Wang (Dramabook), 1963.*

Artaud, Antonin. The Theater and Its Double. *Translated by Mary Caroline Richards. New York: Grove Press, 1958.*

Barnet, Sylvan, Morton Berman, and William Burto, eds. Aspects of the Drama: A Handbook. *Boston: Little, Brown, 1962.*

Bentley, Eric. The Life of the Drama. *New York: Atheneum, 1964.*

Brereton, Geoffrey. Principles of Tragedy. *Coral Gables, Fla.: University of Miami Press, 1968.*

Brook, Peter. The Empty Space. *London and New York: Atheneum, 1968.*

Brooks, Cleanth, and Robert B. Heilman. Understanding Drama: Twelve Plays. *New York: Henry Holt, 1948.*

Butcher, S. H. Aristotle's Theory of Poetry and Fine Art. *New York: Dover Publications, 1951.*

Calderwood, James L., and Harold E. Toliver, eds. Perspectives on Drama. *New York: Oxford University Press, 1968.*

Clark, Barrett H., ed. European Theories of Drama, with a Supplement on the American Drama. *New York: Crown Publishers, 1947.*

Cole, Toby, ed. Playwrights on Playwriting: The Meaning and Making of Modern Drama from Ibsen to Ionesco. *New York: Hill and Wang (Dramabook), 1960.*

Cook, Albert. The Dark Voyage and the Golden Mean. *New York: W. W. Norton, 1966.*

Corrigan, Robert W., ed. Comedy: Meaning and Form. *San Francisco: Chandler, 1965.*

_____, ed. Tragedy: Vision and Form. *San Francisco: Chandler, 1965.*

Corrigan, Robert W., and James L. Rosenberg, eds. the Context and Craft of Drama. *San Francisco: Chandler, 1964.*

Downer, Alan S. The Art of the Play: An Anthology of Nine Plays. *New York: Henry Holt, 1955.*

Drew, Elizabeth. Discovering Drama. *New York: W. W. Norton, 1937.*

Eliot, T. S. Poetry and Drama. *Cambridge, Mass.: Harvard University Press, 1951.*

Ellis-Fermor, Una. The Frontiers of Drama. *2nd ed. London: Methuen, 1964.*

Ellmann, Richard, and Charles Feidelson, Jr., eds. The Modern Tradition: Backgrounds of Modern Literature. *New York: Oxford University Press, 1965.*

Enck, John J., Elizabeth T. Forter, and Alvin Whitley, eds. The Comic in Theory and Practice. *New York: Appleton-Century-Crofts, 1960.*

Felheim, Marvin, ed. Comedy: Plays, Theory, and Criticism. *New York: Harcourt, Brace & World, 1962.*

Fergusson, Francis. The Human Image in Dramatic Literature. *Garden City, N.Y.: Doubleday (Anchor), 1957.*

_____. The Idea of a Theater. *Garden City, N.Y.: Doubleday (Anchor), 1949.*

Frye, Northrop. Anatomy of Criticism. *Princeton, N.J.: Princeton University Press, 1957.*

Guthke, Carl Siegfried. Modern Tragicomedy. *New York: Random House, 1966.*

Heilman, Robert B. Tragedy and Melodrama: Versions of Experience. *Seattle: University of Washington Press, 1968.*

Henn, Thomas R. The Harvest of Tragedy. *New York: Barnes and Noble, 1966.*

Kerr, Walter. Tragedy and Comedy. *New York: Simon and Schuster, 1967.*

Krook, Dorothea. Elements of Tragedy. *New Haven and London: Yale University Press, 1969.*

Lauter, Paul, ed. Theories of Comedy. *Garden City, N.Y.: Doubleday (Anchor), 1964.*

Levin, Richard, ed. Tragedy: Plays, Theory, and Criticism. *New York: Harcourt, Brace & World, 1960.*

Mandel, Oscar. A Definition of Tragedy. *New York: New York University Press, 1961.*

Nicoll, Allardyce. The Theatre and Dramatic Theory. *New York: Barnes and Noble, 1962.*

———. The Theory of Drama. *London: G. G. Harrap, 1937.*

Nietzsche, Friedrich. The Birth of Tragedy *and* The Genealogy of Morals. *Translated by Francis Golffing. Garden City, N.Y.: Doubleday (Anchor), 1956.*

Olson, Elder. Tragedy and the Theory of Drama. *Detroit: Wayne State University Press, 1966.*

Peacock, Ronald. The Art of Drama. *London: Routledge & Kegan Paul, 1957.*

Raphael, D. D. The Paradox of Tragedy. *Bloomington, Ind.: Indiana University Press, 1960.*

Sewall, Richard B. The Vision of Tragedy. *New Haven, Conn.: Yale University Press, 1959.*

———, and Lawrence Michel, eds. Tragedy: Modern Essays in Criticism. *Englewood Cliffs, N.J.: Prentice-Hall, 1963.*

Styan, J. L. The Dark Comedy. *Cambridge, Eng.: Cambridge University Press, 1962.*

———. The Elements of Drama. *Cambridge, Eng.: Cambridge University Press, 1960.*

Thompson, Alan R. The Anatomy of Drama. *2nd ed. Berkeley: University of California Press, 1946.*

Van Laan, Thomas F. The Idiom of Drama. *Ithaca and London: Cornell University Press, 1970.*

Williams, Raymond. Modern Tragedy. *Stanford, Cal.: Stanford University Press, 1966.*

History and Criticism

Bentley, Eric. In Search of Theater. *New York: Alfred A. Knopf, 1953.*
————. The Playwright as Thinker. *New York: Meridian Books, 1957.*
Bogard, Travis, and William I. Oliver, eds. Modern Drama: Essays in
  Criticism. *New York: Oxford University Press, 1965.*
Brustein, Robert. The Theatre of Revolt. *Boston: Atlantic-Little, Brown,
  1962.*
Clark, Barrett H., and George Freedley, eds. A History of Modern
  Drama. *New York: D. Appleton-Century, 1947.*
Corrigan, Robert W., ed. Theatre in the Twentieth Century. *New York:
  Grove Press, 1963.*
Dickinson, Hugh. Myth on the Modern Stage. *Urbana, Ill.: University
  of Illinois Press, 1969.*
Downer, Alan S. Fifty Years of American Drama. *Chicago: Henry Reg-
  nery, 1951.*
Esslin, Martin. The Theatre of the Absurd. *Garden City, N.Y.: Double-
  day (Anchor), 1961.*
Freedman, Morris, ed. Essays in the Modern Drama. *Boston: D. C.
  Heath, 1964.*
————. The Moral Impulse: Modern Drama from Ibsen to the Present.
  Carbondale, Ill.: Southern Illinois University Press, 1967.
Gassner, John. Form and Idea in Modern Theatre. *New York: Dryden
  Press, 1956.*
————. Masters of the Drama. *3rd rev. ed. New York: Dover Publica-
  tions, 1954.*
————. The Theatre in Our Times. *New York: Crown Publishers, 1954.*
Grossvogel, David I. The Blasphemers (*original title:* Four Playwrights
  and a Postscript: Brecht, Ionesco, Beckett, Genet). *Ithaca, N.Y.:
  Cornell University Press, 1962.*
————. The Self-Conscious Stage in Modern French Drama. *New York:
  Columbia University Press, 1958.*
Knight, G. Wilson. The Golden Labyrinth. *New York: W. W. Norton,
  1962.*
Krutch, Joseph Wood, "Modernism" in Modern Drama. *Ithaca, N.Y.:
  Cornell University Press, 1953.*
Lucas, Frank L. The Drama of Chekhov, Synge, Yeats, and Pirandello.
  London: Cassell, 1963.
Lumley, Frederick. Trends in Twentieth Century Drama. *New York:
  Oxford University Press (Essential Books), 1960.*
Nicoll, Allardyce. World Drama from Aeschylus to Anouilh. *London:
  G. G. Harrap, 1949.*
Porter, Thomas E. Myth and Modern American Drama. *Detroit: Wayne
  State University Press, 1969.*

Steiner, George. The Death of Tragedy. *New York: Alfred A. Knopf,*
1961.

Valency, Maurice. The Flower and the Castle: An Introduction to Modern Drama. *New York: Macmillan, 1963.*

Wellwarth, George E. The Theater of Protest and Paradox. *New York:*
New York University Press, 1964.

Williams, Raymond. Drama from Ibsen to Brecht. *New York: Oxford*
University Press, 1969.

Theater Arts

Cole, Toby, and Helen Krich Chinoy, eds. Actors on Acting. *New York:*
Crown Publishers, 1949.

Goodman, Randolph. Drama on Stage. *New York: Holt, Rinehart and*
Winston, 1961.

Gorelik, Mordecai. New Theatres for Old. *New York: S. French, 1940.*

Macgowan, Kenneth, and William Melnitz. The Living Stage: A History
of the World Theater. *Englewood Cliffs, N.J.: Prentice-Hall, 1955. (A*
shorter version is The Golden Ages of the Theater, *1959.*)

Nicoll, Allardyce. The Development of the Theatre. *5th rev. ed. New*
York: Harcourt, Brace & World, 1966.

Stanislavsky, Constantin. An Actor Prepares. *Translated by Elizabeth*
Reynolds Hapgood. New York: Theatre Arts Books, 1936.

Reference

Anderson, Michael, Jacques Guicharnaud, and others, eds. Crowell's
Handbook of Contemporary Drama. *New York: Thomas Y. Crowell,*
1971.

Bowman, Walter P., and Robert Hamilton Ball. Theatre Language: A
Dictionary of Terms in English of the Drama and Stage from Medieval to Modern Times. *New York: Theatre Arts Books, 1936.*

Gassner, John, and Edward Quinn. The Reader's Encyclopedia of
World Drama. *New York: Thomas Y. Crowell, 1969.*

Hartnoll, Phyllis, ed. The Oxford Companion to the Theatre. *3rd ed.*
London: Oxford University Press, 1967.

Matlaw, Myron, ed. Modern World Drama: An Encyclopedia. *New*
York: E. P. Dutton, 1972.

Some Useful Collections of Plays

Bentley, Eric, ed. The Play: A Critical Anthology. *Englewood Cliffs, N.J.:*
Prentice-Hall, 1951.

————, ed. The Modern Theatre, I–VI. Garden City, N.Y.: Doubleday (Anchor), 1955–1960.

————, ed. The Great Playwrights, I–II. Garden City, N.Y.: Doubleday, 1970.

Block, Haskell and Robert Shedd, eds. Masters of Modern Drama. New York: Random House, 1961.

Clayes, Stanley, David Spencer, E. Bradlee Watson, and Benfield Pressey, eds. Contemporary Drama Series [five collections]. New York: Charles Scribner's Sons, 1941–1962.

Corrigan, Robert W., ed. The Modern Theatre. New York: Macmillan, 1964.

Downer, Alan S., ed. The Art of the Play. New York: Henry Holt, 1955.

Gassner, John, ed. Treasury of the Theatre, I–II. 3rd ed. New York: Simon and Schuster, 1967.

Grene, David, and Richmond Lattimore, eds. The Complete Greek Tragedies, I–IV. Chicago: University of Chicago Press, 1959.

Alvin Kernan, ed. Character and Conflict: An Introduction to Drama. 2nd ed. New York: Harcourt, Brace & World, 1969.

————, ed. Classics of the Modern Theater. New York: Harcourt, Brace & World, 1965.

Films

See Feature Films on 8 and 16. A Directory of Feature Films Available for Rental, Lease, and Sale in the U.S. 2nd ed. Compiled and edited by James L. Limbacher. New Haven, Conn.: Readers Press, 1968. For educational films see, Index to 16mm Educational Films, National Information Center for Educational Media. New York: University of Southern California, Los Angeles, and McGraw-Hill Book Co., 1967.